PERSONAL COMPUTERS AND INTELLIGENT SYSTEMS
Information Processing 92

VOLUME III

IFIP Transactions A: Computer Science and Technology

International Federation for Information Processing

Technical Committees:

SOFTWARE: THEORY AND PRACTICE (TC2)
EDUCATION (TC3)
SYSTEM MODELLING AND OPTIMIZATION (TC7)
INFORMATION SYSTEMS (TC8)
RELATIONSHIP BETWEEN COMPUTERS AND SOCIETY (TC9)
COMPUTER SYSTEMS TECHNOLOGY (TC10)
SECURITY AND PROTECTION IN INFORMATION PROCESSING SYSTEMS (TC11)
ARTIFICIAL INTELLIGENCE (TC12)
HUMAN-COMPUTER INTERACTION (TC13)
FOUNDATIONS OF COMPUTER SCIENCE (SG14)

IFIP Transactions Abstracted/Indexed in:
INSPEC Information Services

A-14

PERSONAL COMPUTERS AND INTELLIGENT SYSTEMS
Information Processing 92

Proceedings of the IFIP 12th World Computer Congress
Madrid, Spain, 7-11 September 1992

VOLUME III

Edited by

FRIEDRICH H. VOGT
University of Hamburg
Hamburg, Germany

1992

NORTH-HOLLAND
AMSTERDAM • LONDON • NEW YORK • TOKYO

ELSEVIER SCIENCE PUBLISHERS B.V.
Sara Burgerhartstraat 25
P.O. Box 211, 1000 AE Amsterdam, The Netherlands

ISBN: 0 444 89749 6
ISBN Set: 0 444 89750 X
ISSN: 0926-5473

This book is printed on acid-free paper.

Printed in The Netherlands

IFIP PRESIDENT'S INTRODUCTION

The latest of the twelve IFIP Congresses coincides with the 500th anniversary of one of the discoveries of the New World. Hardly by chance the venue of the Congress is charming Madrid, where many celebrations will commemorate an event that leads us back half a millenium in history.

This Congress is a turning point in IFIP's tradition of organizing its Congresses on a three-yearly basis. All future Congresses will be held every two years: the 13th is scheduled for 1994 in Hamburg, Germany and the 14th in Canberra, Australia.

In the last three years, our world has undergone sweeping changes. This period, falling between the 11th and the 12th IFIP Computer Congress, will have a very special place in mankind's history, not only for its political developments, but also for the enormous progress in data-processing which is to be demonstrated in Madrid.

The significant influence of the IFIP Technical Committees and Working Groups on the structure and contents of Congress' 92 made it possible for hundreds of IFIP specialists, both academics and practitioners, to consider this Congress as their own creation. At the Congress there will be many other who will come in touch with IFIP for the first time. Naturally, our hope is that they will be able identify IFIP as their own international professional organization.

At a time when many human activities rely on the use of computers, the organization of a World Computer Congress is not an ordinary endeavor. Thanks to the outstanding professionalism and rich experience of the Congress' International Program Committee, participants will have a variety of choices to explore the many tracks and trends in the domain of data-processing.

Finally, I would like to wish the Congress participants a most fruitful and enjoyable stay in Spain. I am convinced that at this most important IFIP event you will meet old friends and make many new ones.

Academician Blagovest Sendov
President, International Federation for Information Processing

EDITOR'S FOREWORD

This volume of the Proceedings presents contributions on the two subconference topics:

– Expanding the Power of the Personal Computer, and
– Enhancing Intelligence in Informational Systems.

It is introduced by a general keynote adress about

– Complex Adaptive Systems

as well as those on:

– Cooperative Research Programs, and
– Encouraging Academic/Practitioner Collaboration

For the first time in IFIP's history, special attention is being given to the field of of Personal Computer (PCs). For more than a hundred million people internationally, these machines represent a gateway to the world of computer-aided work. The enormous breadth of impact of personal computing on society has made this area a focus of attention for the computer industry as a whole. Not surprisingly, the tremendous expansion in the ways in which personal computers are applied poses many new and interesting technical challenges.

The second subconference topic deals with enhancing intelligence in informational systems. This subject has become all the more important as an area of research given the broader community of users made possible by PCs. The problems of incorporating human knowledge and decision-making skills into intelligent information systems are among the most interesting and difficult of those facing the designers of such systems.

This volume concludes with a discussion of various ways to conduct cooperative research programs in line with IFIP's role as a facilitator of collaboration between academia and industry.

I would like to thank Richard Schwartz for encouraging W. Brauer and myself to introduce the exciting area of PC technology to IFIP. He has also been instrumental in helping to attract leading technologists from the PC industry to present their views to the world informatics community.

Friedrich H. Vogt
University of Hamburg

TABLE OF CONTENTS

Office Automation

Multimedia and Networking

---

* Paper not submitted

PROGRAM COMMITTEE CHAIRMAN'S FOREWORD

Innovation cycles in computer technology are extremely short, and the research results of today will be used tomorrow in products of daily practice. It is not only the single breakthrough result which may have such an immediate effect but it is more and more also the incremental innovation, based on many research and development findings in many different areas of computer technology, communications, and electronics - contributed by people from many different countries - that drives the rapid growth of the computer industry. Communication and collaboration of people from different fields and different countries is therefore a growing need.

IFIP's World Computer Congresses are ideal platforms to meet researchers and practitioners, educators and users, leading professionals and young innovators, to discuss ideas, experiences, problems in a wide forum of people from all parts of the world and all parts of computer science and technology.

IFIP Congress 92 starts a new congress line. Congresses now take place more often, i.e. every even year: 1992 in Madrid, Spain, 1994 in Hamburg, Germany, 1996 in Canberra, Australia. The Congress structure was changed: we have 4 parallel streams for the core areas of software, hardware, theory, and education; from the many possible other areas only a few were selected for the 1992 Congress - the next Congresses will make another selection. These additional topics are presented in one (full-length) stream, two 3-day subconferences and 4 symposia. In addition to the traditional presentation of invited and submitted papers, the presentation of posters is encouraged to give more people the opportunity to participate actively in the Congress.

The program committee's composition and structure is also new. I wanted to give the people from the country in which the Congress is organized a much greater influence and I wanted a modular structure and distributed operation of the committee. This resulted in having 7 subcommittees consisting of people from several countries, but with a representative from Spain in each of them; these committees had their own way of inviting speakers and selecting the papers submitted to their respective subcommittee chairmen. The kernel program committee consisting of the subcommittee chairman and the Spanish representative plus a (varying) small number of other subcommittee members met only 3 times (in Madrid, Munich, Madrid). The subcommittees also had their additional ways and means of announcing the call for papers.

The number of submitted papers was much higher than expected on the basis of previous IFIP Congress experiences: For the streams and subconferences we received in total almost 500 submitted papers whose authors come from almost 50 countries. Several of these submissions were carefully solicited. From all the submissions 171 were accepted for presentation and publication - in addition to the 34 invited talks in the streams and subconferences plus 32 invited talks in the 4 symposia and the two keynote speeches contributed by the program committee to the opening and closing sessions. Most of these papers as well as many statements of the speakers in the 19 panel discussions are printed in the 3 proceedings volumes.

That the proceedings are published in three distinct volumes, each with another emphasis and each targeting at different groups of readers is also an innovation of this IFIP Congress. I would like to thank in particular the traditional IFIP Congress proceedings publisher, Elsevier

(North-Holland), and its excellent IFIP liaison, Mrs. Stephanie Smit for making this possible as well as for the flexibility in the cooperation with the program committee and the editors. My sincere thanks go also to the three proceedings editors who also have been very active program committee members.

I was very happy that so many prominent people have been willing to devote quite a lot of their scarce time to work intensively within the program committee. It was a great pleasure for me to work with them. In particular I would like to express my great appreciation and sincere thanks to the very efficient and reliable vice chairman Carlos Delgado Kloos as well as to the subcommittee chairmen, who had more or less to work as the chairmen of full-size conferences, and to the poster and tutorial organizer. The symposia organizers Brian Oakley, Bernard Glasson, Bernd Page and Joseph Traub managed quite independently to set up very attractive programs which on the one hand are emphasizing IFIP's concern on university - industry collaboration and on the other hand present newly developing working groups. It was very easy for me to work with them and I thank them particularly.

Special thanks are also due to the two prominent keynote speakers our committee was able to find:

Philip Kahn, Chairman of C.E.O. and President of Borland International speaks on "Software Craftsmanships in the 90's".

Pamela Mc Corduck, a world famous writer on computing and its relationship to culture and civilization, speaks on art and artificial intelligence - and her speech is also documented in these proceedings (cordial thanks for that!).

Not only the Congress program, also the Congress site will be very influential for attracting the participants from around the world. The Spanish organising committee under the chairmanship of Mrs. Rosa Alonso and with the help of the Spanish representative to the IFIP General Assembly, Angel Alvarez, did an enormous job in preparing this large Congress - many thanks and good luck to them.

Munich, May 1992

Wilfried Brauer
Program Committee Chairman

ORGANIZING COMMITTEE CHAIRWOMAN'S FOREWORD

First of all, it is an honour for me to be able to state that the support conferred by Spain to this 12th World Computer Congress has been wholly emphasized by the personal attention given to this celebration by His Majesty and by His attendance at the Opening Ceremony.

This is the first time that this biennial broad-based Congress has been held in Spain, hosted by FESI (Federacion Espanola de Asociaciones de Informatica), the Spanish member organization of IFIP (International Federation for Information Processing). FESI is a federation of Spanish professional Associations, foundations concerned with information technology, computer science schools and national research institutions.

This 12th IFIP Congress '92 will cover the main areas of information technology applicable to both academic and industrial fields.

Under the theme, "From Research to Practice", the Congress will demonstrate the relevant role that advanced computer technology and its application play in long-term corporate benefits and show how, daily, actions are taken to increase that role.

To comply with the Congress' aims, an extensive program has been implemented. Firstly, a technical programme has been scheduled, including five parallel streams, two subconferences and four symposia. Six one-day pre-congress tutorials have been organized, an exhibition of products, scientific books and publications, and a wide range of technical visits. An excellent – and typical – social program has also been carefully prepared, full of attractive events, such as the reception and the Congress banquet.

An additional attraction to the Congress could be the celebration of EXPO '92 (Seville) and the nomination of Madrid Cultural '92 and other no less important events in the country, such as the Olympic Games in Barcelona.

It is unnecessary to say that the accomplishment and success of an event like a World Congress is the result of a group of persons working together as a team, trying to solve all the problems – big and small – in order to provide the international attendance and speakers with the best possible scenario for all the technical and social events. To face up to this challenge, there have been people working hard for a long period of time, always in pursuit of an international contribution to the progress of science and even – and why not? – looking for improvements in the quality of life of all human beings.

For all these reasons, and many others, I would like to express my most sincere thanks to all those persons without whose contribution it would not have been possible to come to a happy end.

Thanks to Mr. Brauer, Program Committee Chair, to all the members of the Committee, to the Committee of Honour, to the Spanish Authorities, to all Patrons, Institutions and, finally and most warmly, to all my colleagues and friends on the Organizing Committee as well as the FESI President, Spanish IFIP representative and to the Alcatel and Fundesco teams, whom I had the opportunity of chairing during so many hard working but wonderful days.

Rosa Alonso

IFIP CONGRESS '92 COMMITTEES

International Program Committee

Chair: Wilfried Brauer, Technical University of Munich, Germany
Vice Chair: Carlos Delgado Kloos, Technical University of Madrid, Spain
Past Chair: Hervé Gallaire, GSI, France
OC Chair: Rosa Alonso, Alcatel N.V.

Subcommittees

Stream 1: Software Development and Maintenance

Chair: A. Nico Habermann, National Science Foundation, USA
Members: P. Botella, Technical Univ. of Catalonia, Barcelona, Spain
L.M. Koroleff, Moscow State Univ., Russia
R. Kurki-Suonio, Tampere Univ. of Technology, Finland
A. Yonezawa, Univ. of Tokyo, Japan

Stream 2: Algorithms and Efficient Computation

Chair: Jan van Leeuwen, University of Utrecht, The Netherlands
Members: J. Diaz, Technical Univ. of Catalonia, Barcelona, Spain
S. Even, The Technion, Haifa, Israel
R.M. Karp, Univ. of California at Berkeley, USA

Stream 3: From Architectures to Chips

Chair: Gerald Reijns, Delft University of Technology, The Netherlands
Members: C. Delgado Kloos, Technical University of Madrid, Spain
E. Hörbst, Siemens A.G., Munich, Germany
Y. Tohma, Tokyo Institute of Technology, Tokyo, Japan

Stream 4: Informatics and Education

Chair: Peter Bollerslev, Ministry of Education, Copenhagen, Denmark
Members: R. Aiken, Temple Univ., Philadelphia, PA, USA
A. Balasubrahmanian, Indira Gandhi National Open Univ., Delhi, India
I. Stanchev, Research Center for Education in Informatics, Sofia, Bulgaria
A. Vaquero, Complutense Univ., Madrid, Spain

Stream 5: The Vulnerability of the Information Society: Social, Legal, and Security Aspects

Chair: Klaus Brunnstein, University of Hamburg, Germany
Members: W. Caelli, Queensland Univ. of Technology, Brisbane, Australia
R. Moeller, Sears & Roebuck, Chicago, USA
J.A. Pino, Univ. of Chile, Santiago, Chile
F. Sáez-Vacas, Technical Univ. of Madrid, Spain

Subconference 1: Expanding the Power of the Personal Computer

Chair: Friedrich H. Vogt, University of Hamburg, Germany
Members: I. Agamirzian, FORTHINFO, St. Petersburg, Russia
C.P. Lucena, Catholic Univ., Rio de Janeiro, Brazil
R. Puigjaner, Univ. of the Balearic Islands, Palma de Mallorca, Spain
B. Robinet, IBM France, Paris, France
R. Schwartz, Borland European Technology Center, Paris, France

Subconference 2: Enhancing the Intelligence in Information Systems

Chair: Gordon Davis, University of Minnesoty, USA
Members: R. Benjamin, Rochester, New York, USA
J.P. Laurent, Univ. de Savoie, Chambery, France
M. Lundeberg, Stockholm School of Economics, Sweden
J. Motiwalla, National Univ. of Singapore, Singapore
A. Olivé, Techn. Univ. of Catalonia, Barcelona, Spain

Symposium Organizers:

Symposium 1: Cooperative Research Programs
Brian Oakley, Logica Cambridge Ltd., U.K.

Symposium 2: Informatics for Environmental Protection
Bernd Page, University of Hamburg, Germany

Symposium 3: Encouraging Academic / Practitioner Collaboration
Bernard Glasson, Curtin Univ. Perth, Australia

Symposium 4: Continuous Algorithms and Complexity
Joseph Traub, Columbia Univ., New York, NY, USA

Spain's Organizing Committee

Chair: Rosa Alonso, Alcatel N.V.
Members: Jose Ignacio Boixo, ALI
Miguel Angel Eced, AEIA
Jaume Argila, ATI
Nuria Castell, Technical Univ. of Catalonia
Francisco Fernández-Campón, Alcatel Standard Electrica S.A.
Manuel Gamella, FUNDESCO
Javier Leach, Complutense University of Madrid
Luis Maté, Technical Univ. of Madrid
Roberto Molero, ERITEL
Luis A. Petit, CITEMA
Ramón Puigjaner, Univ. of the Balearic Islands
Antonio San Martin, FYCSA - Alcatel

Personal Computers and Intelligent Systems / F.H. Vogt (Editor)
Information Processing 92, Volume III
Elsevier Science Publishers B.V. (North-Holland)

Kissin´ cousins: New science and new art

Pamela McCorduck

P. O. Box 7032, Princeton, New Jersey

Abstract

In the last decade, a new approach to the scientific study of certain dynamic processes has emerged. It embodies a point of view, a host of questions, a set of techniques, and some tentative definitions, all encompassed by the term "complex adaptive systems." It crosses traditional disciplinary boundaries, aiming to explain in scientific terms phenomena that appear in both the natural and the social worlds, phenomena that, up to now, could neither be modeled nor understood by traditional scientific approaches. Perhaps not surprisingly, a few artists have sensed this new science in the air, and have begun to produce art in the same spirit. This paper describes briefly what complex adaptive systems entail, and then discusses more thoroughly two examples of the new art arising in this spirit.

1. INTRODUCTION

The arts and sciences have often been "kissin´ cousins," to borrow a term from the southern United States. Kissin´ cousins are not related by blood; not officially nor even technically family; but kissin´ cousins are on intimate terms with each other, attending birthdays, weddings, holiday dinners, and even funerals together; and at these occasions bestowing and receiving kisses, of course: hence the phrase. From Albrecht Dürer to John Constable, from Georges Seurat to Pablo Picasso, painters have had their antennae up and scanning, ready to appropriate whatever the scientists were doing, sometimes even anticipating them. In literature, an entire literary genre called science fiction exists. But so-called mainstream writers, poets as well as novelists, have also been known to take a serious interest in science and technology. The 19th-century novelist George Meredith, for example, was simultaneously a fan and a critic of the scientific method, while James Joyce and and

Virginia Woolf (who personally despised each other´s work), nevertheless had ears wide open to whatever music was wafting out of the scientific spheres of the early 20th century. Very occasionally, a single individual has embodied both the kissin´ cousins of art and science: Leonardo, for instance, or Goethe.

So it goes. Yet we must concede that there´s sometimes interference in the air. In the late 1980s, I attended a discussion led by the curator of a major art exhibition which featured the work of many fashionable American and European postmodern painters. Our group mixed artists with scientists, prompting the curator to remark in a friendly and innocent way that as he was preparing the exhibition, he was struck to find in nearly every studio he visited a copy of a then-popular book that blended physics and Eastern mysticism.

The scientists in the group were appalled. Science as kitsch! Their worst fears about the vulgarization of science confirmed. And why, a biochemist in the group wanted to know, were painters in the late 1980s so enthralled with the best ideas of the 1920s? If they must borrow from science, hadn´t they heard that science had moved on?

A fair question. Without deprecating the best scientific ideas of the 1920s, or fashionable art of the 1980s, some profound ideas have emerged from science in the last few years. Let me call your attention to one such set of scientific ideas, and then speak of some new art that has arisen in the same spirit.

2. COMPLEX ADAPTIVE SYSTEMS

The new science I have in mind is called, rather awkwardly, the study of *complex adaptive systems.* With renaissance zest, this approach cuts across a host of traditional disciplines, aiming to understand what the evolution of life on earth and the behavior of an economy have in common; what characteristics are shared by the behavior of the human nervous system and the behavior of its immune system; and any one of these open to comparison with, say, an ecosystem, or the development of human languages.

Some of the salient features of complex adaptive systems can be found in Fig. 1. This isn´t all to be said about such systems, and some of those statements might be a little mysterious to you, but I wish to concentrate here on art, not science.

Very briefly, complex adaptive systems are dynamic systems that arise spontaneously from simple elements or processes, and organize themselves into more complex entities. You can´t tell how such a system

---

Fig. 1

CHARACTERISTICS OF COMPLEX ADAPTIVE SYSTEMS

Complex adaptive systems are networks of elements, processes, and systems that arise spontaneously from simpler systems and organize themselves into more complex aggregate systems.

Their dynamic behavior cannot be successfully predicted merely by studying the component parts, but can only be seen when the entire system is at work (*emergent behavior*).

Information exchange takes place not only among levels of such systems, but also with the environment in which a complex adaptive system is embedded.

The information exchange between the complex adaptive system and its environment not only changes the system itself (as it adapts to changes in the environment) but sometimes even changes the environment (*co-evolution*).

A complex adaptive system codes its knowledge in highly compressed models, schema, or theories.

In novel situations, a complex adaptive system *unfolds* these models, schema, or theories to make predictions, govern behavior, or both.

Complex adaptive systems appear everywhere in the natural and human social worlds. For example:

- biological evolution
- the behavior of the mammalian immune system
- individual learning and thinking in animals, including humans
- human cultural evolution
- the evolution of human languages
- the behavior of the global economy

will behave by studying or analyzing its component parts. Instead, you must observe the *entire system in action*--and that, of course, is the opposite from past science, where analysis of component parts was the most successful way to discover how things worked.

Complex adaptive systems are entities that rely on passing around information, *feedback* in a word, to tell them what's happening, and what they should do next with themselves. Information flows not only around the system itself, reshaping the various sub-systems, telling them what to do next, but information also flows in from the environment in which the complex adaptive system is embedded. The environment itself is also dynamic, of course, sometimes changing rapidly. As a complex adaptive system takes information in from the environment, it tries to adapt to this information by changing its behavior.

But often as these systems adapt to outside changes, they simultaneously feed information back into that environment, where a reciprocal change might take place. Thus even as the system is adapting to the changing environment, the environment adapts to the changing system; and this is known as *co-evolution*., the scientific equivalent of Dr. Doolittle's wonderful beast called the Pushmepullyou.

As the examples suggest, complex adaptive sysems have always existed, but until the advent of the computer, there was no way to study them with scientific rigor. And while science as an enterprise has been very successful at decomposing a large part of the world, and studying those parts piece by piece to understand the whole, other phenomena simply will not yield to that kind of analysis. These, then, are the problems that might finally yield to large-scale study of the whole instead of the parts, the complex adaptive systems approach.

Some laboratories and research sites where work is underway in complex adaptive systems include the Santa Fe Institute, devoted entirely to these studies; Los Alamos National Laboratories; California Institute of Technology; the University of Michigan; Stanford University; Princeton University; and Vienna University. With that brief introduction to complex adaptive systems, let me to turn to literature and art in the same spirit.

3. NEW LITERATURE AND ART IN THE SPIRIT OF A NEW SCIENCE

I have already suggested that most fashionable American visual art of the late 1980s was suffused with scientific ideas of the 1920s. I can now add the melancholy news that fashionable American literature of the 1980s (and so far, much of the 1990s) might lead you to believe that nothing besides the telephone, the internal combustion engine, and TV had been invented in this century. All around us, evidence accumulates that a new human sensibility is being created worldwide by information technology--these two themselves fine examples of adaptive, co-evolving systems, by the way--but most literature remains mute about this momentous, truly epochal change. When the engine of all this change, the computer, occasionally makes a cameo appearance in serious art and literature, that appearance is almost always disappointingly banal.

But some artists and writers have begun to pay attention: they are assimilating, appropriating these ideas into their art. Or in some cases, they have arrived at the frontier independently, following their own very good instincts.

3.1 Literature in the spirit of complex adaptive systems

When one of the Sages of Paris, Roland Barthes, famously declared the "death of the author" in 1968, he had no idea that he´d been anticipated by Theodor Holm (Ted) Nelson, who conceived a way of killing off the single author in 1962, and announced it in 1965 as hypertext. Hypertext, as most here know, is pieces of text--single words, sentences, phrases, poems, paragraphs, even entire documents by several authors--connected to other pieces of text in a dynamic network, so that an individual reader can read his or her way through that network in any way that suits the moment, or the reader´s inclinations. Along that path may be other paths to follow, and so the reader explores a personally chosen web, not merely the path laid out by the author, the authority.

Now, overthrowing the tyranny of the linear text has been a project of European literature since Laurence Sterne gave us *Tristram Shandy* in the 18th century. A colleague argues that the multiple annotations that characterize medieval scholasticism had the same goals--I´ll take his word for it since I won´t be investigating the medieval scholastics at this late date. In any case, many, perhaps most, of the strategies of fiction as we know it are designed to circumvent that linearity, whether flashbacks, or changing point of view, or pretending it´s all a dream, or leaving it ambiguous as to whether an event "really" happened, and so on.

Hypertext, it can be argued, is in some sense the automating--or even the long-awaited full realization, the *literalization*--of the struggle scholars and novelists have always undertaken against linearity, by tracing associations and footnoting ideas; by adding parenthetical remarks, marginalia, and bibliographies; by exploding some points, or events, and collapsing others; by representing a series of points of view, some of them conflicting, etc. Moreover, nothing has ever stopped a reader from jumping around in a book's text, flipping backward as a reminder of when a character first came on stage, or flipping forward to the last page to find out whodunit.

We are speaking of degrees here, true; but we are also speaking of a quantitative change so great that it makes a qualitative difference, the order-of-magnitude effect. The speed and thoroughness and flexibility of doing all this in a computer environment makes it a whole new game. Linearity is no longer a tyrant to be overthrown; linearity isn't even an issue.

Though hypertext is a useful pedagogical tool, my point here is its use as a tool for writers and readers of fiction who--as Ted Nelson and Roland Barthes both foresaw--are becoming if not interchangeable, if not quite full co-authors of the text, then something different from the traditional stance of despot author and subordinate reader.

Let me illustrate this with a specific novella called *afternoon* by a midwest American novelist, Michael Joyce **(1)**. *Afternoon* comes not in a codex, a bound book, but on a Macintosh disk. You enter the web at a certain point, and where you go from there is up to you.

I have read *afternoon* six or seven times. Each has been a new experience, because whenever I've entered *afternoon*, I've taken a new path, in fact, many new paths--through the very rich web the author provides. Those accustomed to computer games with much text, such as the early versions of "Adventure" will understand this experience of finding yourself moving from space to space, and sometimes arriving back where you formerly were, but with new knowledge; so that you are, however slightly, a changed person, and you therefore move on with different goals this time, in different directions. In other words, you and the text are slowly beginning to change each other, in the spirit of complex adaptive systems as I described earlier.

One of the differences between *afternoon* and "Adventure" is that though the novella is certainly entertaining, it also makes serious literary claims upon its reader, raising questions about our lives and their meanings today, in this world of computers and satellite networks and expert systems and knowledge engineering--in short, the here and now. It is serious fiction written by a gifted novelist who began by writing conventional linear texts, but knew the moment he sat down at his word-processor that there in front of him was an instrument to break the linear tyranny of the codex book once and for all.

Inside the web of *afternoon* you discover that the author has indeed laid down certain paths and forbidden others: at times you pass through a portal and may not return where you came from: certain decisions foreclose other possibilities forever. Sometimes you can do the electronic equivalent of keeping a thumb on one page and riffling through the other pages with your index finger, but sometimes you can't.

Meanwhile, you aren't necessarily confined--if that's the word--to what the author of *afternoon* has proposed as text, no matter how rich, surprising, and sometimes contradictory it is. You can add your own pieces of text, or, to give them their proper name, writing spaces. Seated at your Macintosh, you can, if you wish, become co-author of *afternoon* with Michael Joyce--knowing very well that somebody else, coming along behind you, or coming up beside you, might in his or her turn, rewrite the text yet again. Hypertext is not only a very complex web of connected reading spaces, but of writing spaces too. You and the complex novella *afternoon* begin to adapt to each other, two systems co-evolving as it were. Hypertext permits this literally. (My own work in the last few months has been in hypertext, and I find it very different from writing in the style I've used all my life as a professional writer.)

Many of the literary works we treasure most are exactly those that have tried valiantly to overthrow, or at least subvert, the tyranny of linear text, and it remains to be seen whether these classics will in the future be regarded as no more than quaint experiments, like cupping to cure fevers or arsenic to cure syphillis, and superseded by a technology that actually does what the various strategies of linear text have attempted--simulated--so cleverly, bravely, all these centuries. Or perhaps we'll go to the printed codex book for a different experience, just as we go to view oil portraits even though these days photographs are the most common images of remembrance; just as we go to the theatre, even though movies and television exist.

3.2. Art in the spirit of complex adaptive systems

In art, we come closer yet to the new science of complex adaptive systems. The robot artist called Aaron is a large, complex computer program that has been making drawings for the past 20 years, continuously learning new techniques from its teacher, then going off to work on its own, never once repeating itself on paper(**2**). And like every good student, it has taught its teacher much too.

Each stage you see in Aaron's work, from abstraction to figuration, represents additional knowledge that Aaron has learned and embodied in its drawings--and its knowledge has become wider, deeper, and more sophisticated over time.

In my view, the program Aaron is a work of art in its own right, the creation of a human painter, Harold Cohen, on the faculty of visual arts at the University of California in San Diego. Cohen was a much-honored abstract artist with an international reputation in the mid-1960s, when, for fun, he learned how to program a computer. He began to sense that if the machine wasn't exactly thinking, it was making decisions in ways that reminded him of how he decided what to put on a canvas next.

Like most artists, and certainly all critics, Cohen had theories about art-making. But there was no way to test such theories: one was about as arguable as another. Suppose, however, you transformed those theories into executable computer code? Valid theories would cause the computer to produce art.

And that was the beginning of a quarter-century quest for answers to many questions. As the questions grew more complicated, the answers more elaborate, so did the computer program and the drawings it made, until now, Aaron is deep in the spirit of complex adaptive systems.

What makes Aaron lay claim to being a complex adaptive system? Aaron undertakes a drawing using only general rules: do a drawing with some people and some trees; do a drawing with some people where one of them holds a potted plant. Aaron decides, pretty much randomly, how many "some" people is; Aaron decides, again randomly, what the plant will look like; Aaron decides, randomly, the disposition and postures of those figures on the picture plane, even their appearance. Aaron also knows very general rules about drawing techniques in the Western tradition, some rules of representation, and it knows something about the real world. All these are its *schema*, its *models*, which it unfolds as general rules by which to make many different specific drawings.

Aaron begins at random on the picture plane, and improvises as it goes along, constantly checking itself, feeding back to itself where it is, how it's doing, according to these general rules. If, in the course of a drawing, Aaron discovers that it can't fit the number of figures on the picture plane it originally planned, the program leaves well enough alone, and quits. In that sense, it is completely adaptive.

From all this, then, it follows that Aaron makes its drawings autonomously--no hands-on. Once a drawing is begun, there is no way for a human to interfere, to change it in mid-drawing. No drawing is ever identical to one that has come before. This is *not* because Aaron remembers its past work; it's because the decision-tree Aaron follows is so rich and complex that among the literally millions of decisions it makes, it will never take exactly the same path twice. Each more or less random major decision leads to many minor decisions that take the drawing down a different--often very different--pathway. Each more or less random major decision forecloses other possibilities.

As Aaron draws, it exhibits many of the major features of complex adaptive systems: a set of general *schema* that unfold only when needed; a large degree of *randomness*; constant *feedback* to itself;

followed by *adaptation* to that feedback. No central feature of the program is in charge while a drawing is underway: instead, an ensemble of routines and subroutines trigger each other as needed, out of which emerges a drawing: the drawing is the *emergent property* of the program called Aaron.

But Aaron itself is not yet a fully functioning adaptive system. It can´t yet learn something altogether new without the hand of Harold Cohen adding another line of code to express whatever new thing it is Aaron will know. Aaron doesn´t frequent the galleries and listen to what critics and the viewing public have to say, and change its drawings accordingly. In the words of physicist Murray Gell-Mann, one of the founders of complex adaptive system studies, Aaron lacks "learning from the genome"; it lacks learning from the individual organism; and unless you regard Harold Cohen the painter as Aaron´s cultural environment, it lacks cultural learning. If, however, you change Cohen´s stance from being Aaron´s "environment" and include the human artist as simply another part of the art-making loop (a knotty philosophical question, I grant you) then no question that Aaron, Cohen, and the drawings are all themselves a complex adaptive system, and at the same, time, part of an even larger complex adaptive system called the History of Western Art.

CONCLUSIONS

Neither of these artistic examples, not the hypertext novella, nor the drawings of Aaron, is a stand-alone, authentic-in-every-detail, complex adaptive system in the sense meant by scientists, although I hope you´re persuaded that they are very much in the spirit of such inquiries, that they´re all kissin´ cousins.

Once we include a human being in the loop--Aaron and Harold Cohen; the novella *afternoon* and its reader, or potential co-author--we shade out of the spirit and comfortably into the letter of that frontier of science called complex adaptive systems. *Each* system, artificial and biological, is changing, adapting to new information, and causing reciprocal changes in the system with which it co-evolves.

Where is this leading us? Scientists who study complex adaptive systems have sometimes confided to me that they believe they´re laying out the agenda for all significant scientific research for the next few decades. If they are correct, then the artists I speak of here are laying out comparable agendas for art and literature. What does this mean? A world of autonomous art robots, making art faster than humans can look at it? Stories that tell themselves? Images and stories that adapt themselves for a given audience--but thereby transform what that audience desires? Art and literature that goes on evolving after the biological artist or writer is dead? Art and literature that fuses the sensibility or aesthetics or knowledge or concerns of several, even many, artists and writers?

For as we´ve seen, this is well underway in text. The solitary author bravely faces death before the hypertext firing squad, and frankly, it´s only cold comfort to know that our execution transforms the baffling questions of postmodern literary theory into what mathematicians would call the trivially obvious.

I don´t expect the complete demise of the printed codex book in my lifetime, though even I begin to get more information electronically (from a networked computer screen, from CNN). Books will remain long after some serious transitional problems with computers are solved (portability, resolution, repair). When most of us get our imaginative experiences from a combination of virtual reality, hypertext, and technology-not-yet-thought-of, some antiquarians will still crave books.

If the end is in sight for the codex book, a domination lasting about 500 years, that is not to say the end is in sight for text. Jay David Bolter makes a very strong, and to me, persuasive, case in his book,*Writing Space,* that if we´re at the end of what he calls the "Late Age of Print", we´re on the threshold of a golden age of text(**3**). The Early Bronze-Age version of how our text might appear to us in the future is the Sony Data Diskman, which weighs just over a pound, can store 100,000 pages of text on an optical disk, and uses six standard search-and-retrieval methods.

A simple message emerges again and again in the study of complex adaptive systems: *adapt or die.* As biological entities, of course we´ll die. But if we want our memes to carry on, those cultural equivalents of our genetic endowment, and a far faster agent of change than biological agents, then we must adapt to that world out there we live in, changing it willfully even as it changes us.

REFERENCES

1 Joyce, Michael. *afternoon.* Cambridge, Mass.: Eastgate Systems, Inc., 1988.

2 McCorduck, Pamela. *Aaron´s Code: Art, Artificial Intelligence, and the Work of Harold Cohen.* New York: W. H. Freeman & Co., 1991.

3 Bolter, Jay David. *Writing Space: The Computer, Hypertext, and the History of Writing.* Hillsdale, New Jersey: Lawrence Erlbaum Asociates, 1990. Includes hypertext disk.

SUBCONFERENCE: EXPANDING THE POWER OF THE PERSONAL COMPUTER

Programme Committee and List of Referees:

Chair: F. H. Vogt
Univ. of Hamburg, Hamburg, Germany

I. Agamirzian
St. Petersburg Institute for Informatics, St. Petersburg, Russia

C. P. Lucena
Pontificia Universidade Católica, Rio de Janeiro, Brazil

R. Puigjaner
Universitat de les Illes Balears, Palma, Spain

B. Robinet
Univ. of Paris VI, Paris, France

R. Schwartz
Borland European Technology Center, Paris, France

Personal Computers and Intelligent Systems / F.H. Vogt (Editor)
Information Processing 92, Volume III
Elsevier Science Publishers B.V. (North-Holland)

THE ELECTRONIC FRONTIER: WHERE PERSONAL COMPUTING GOES FROM HERE

Esther Dyson

EDventure Holdings, 375 Park Avenue, New York, New York 10152, USA;
0005113763@mcimail.com

Keywords: software, personal computing, computers and society

This article focuses on the business and social implications of technological developments in personal computing, including global networking, object-oriented programming, pen computing and groupware.

1. THE ELECTRONIC FRONTIER

The electronic frontier is our industry's new business environment. We are creating it, and we will operate within it. When we as an industry started, we were a fringe group -- hot stocks, exotic technology, weird science. But now we're so big that we matter. Like it or not, other people take this industry seriously, obliging us to take ourselves seriously too. Adulthood gives you freedom -- and also responsibility.

In that sense, **Mitch Kapor**, founder of Lotus Development, is one of this industry's leading grown-ups. Rather than relive his exciting childhood with another start-up, he has taken on a bigger challenge by founding the Electronic Frontier Foundation. Right now the frontier is still the last bastion of freedom, but with so many settlers, it needs a set of policies to govern its growth. The electronic frontier exists not just in Silicon Valley, but everywhere that telephone lines, cable tv, wireless phones, satellites and other media reach. The idea isn't (at least in our minds) that it should be centrally controlled or even financed, but that there should be clear policies by which local control operates and local nodes can *inter*operate.

"In order to have local control," says Kapor, "we have to do something now. There are lots of forces already in motion; we have to wake up to them." Overcoming his natural aversion to large institutional concentrations of power, he has been spending a lot of time in Washington recently, reverse-engineering the public-policy process with intellectual curiosity and a certain interest in the outcome.

Setting policies for the Frontier

Kapor now delivers "scouting reports" from the frontier and from Washington, outlining the need for a widespread, user-to-user communication platform -- both communication standards and a public network accessible to everyone. A model familiar to us all is the Apple II and the PC, which together created a vigorous, flourishing personal computer industry. The difference is the need for public funding to create a similar widely available platform for personal communication and wide-area networking -- the platform that will support much of the technology to be covered in the three days of the Forum.

Encouraging such developments is the basic task of the Electronic Frontier Foundation. We're personally uncomfortable with the notion of government funding for anything; however, since the government does have an industrial policy, it might as well favor the electronic frontier rather than the industrial backwaters it currently succors.

What does the industry need to do? (Aside from joining the EFF, of course.) It has to pay attention to debates among the RBOCs and cable tv interests and newspapers, funding decisions in Congress, and other seemingly far-off events. An industry that grew up on self-reliance is now about to come under the sway of external forces. We can't control them but we can influence them. We are no longer in the truck-building business, so to speak, but in the transportation business; government decisions about highways, airport funding and freight prices affect us. We are part of the country we live in.

In addition to funding, it's important to have standards for the loose collection of linked networks that comprises the global network, underlying a diversity of services. Just as personal computer standards fostered a variety of applications, so will network standards foster interconnection and network applications: e-mail and information access and shop-by-mail, wide-area applications built with **XcelleNet**, support groups run on **CompuServe**, online newspapers and other services from **The Washington Post** and **America Online**, vendor-sponsored information access from **Prodigy Services**, information markets such as **American Information Exchange**, telecommuting, political action (for and against whatever you're for). Configuration services such as that potentially run by **Trilogy Development**, travel agencies, and others will all operate over the network, allowing customers direct contact with vendors or efficient third-party packaging of services.

Like the physical frontier of the last century, the electronic frontier right now is a wild, confusing place -- not because the people in it are bad, but because there are no clear laws, no visible boundaries, no clear routes of travel. Everything from the rules of ownership of intellectual property to the obligations of public utilities and the definitions of new kinds of services have not yet been determined. Like other early settlers, we have to get together and define the government and laws we want. Otherwise some other government will do it for us.

Setting policies for the Frontier

Allan Weis of **Advanced Network & Services** runs the Internet in particular. (Read and listen carefully; it's confusing!) The Internet grew out of ARPANET, a Defense Department-funded research project started in the Sixties. Ostensibly limited to educational and research uses and provided "free," the Internet now supports about 4 million users. Most of those don't connect to the Internet directly, but get to it through regional networks or commercial carriers such as MCI. One of the major segments of the Internet in the US is the National Science Foundation backbone service, which connects the research and education sites sponsored by the agency. The current NSFNET backbone service is managed by ANS as part of ANS' network. ANS is a not-for-profit company formed by IBM and MCI with donations of about $5 million each plus equipment, and by Merit, a consortium of Michigan universities. ANS also sells its network attachments to commercial customers -- thus opening up the Internet to commercial traffic amidst some controversy. The Commercial Internet Exchange, a group of Internet-connected independent services, is also bringing in commercial customers. This competition is a little awkward, given that ANS has both for-profit and not-for-profit arms, while CIX members are basically commercial. In order to make things punctiliously correct, NSF has announced plans to solicit bids on a new contract for network services when the current contract with ANS expires in the fall of 1992.

Clearly, keeping the commercial and noncommercial parts of the Internet separate is a messy proposition. Indeed, we think it would make more sense to make the whole venture for-profit, and simply to subsidize the Internet by subsidizing its users. That of course would mean that only the favored people at a university, instead of random students, would have access to the Internet once it was explicitly charged for. How to resolve this? One way, in the long run, is to make it so cheap to everyone (through widespread installation and usage) that this is no longer an issue.

These new media and infrastructures raise perplexing questions. Is the electronic infrastructure the equivalent of the highway system, something that should be built by the government for the good of the country? Or are there ways for the government to *fund* it while allowing private enterprise to build it? Or is that taxing the many for the good of the networked few?

What's the role of the RBOCs, the government, private enterprise? How can we get people to use it -- assuming that we should? What does it mean to this industry -- as medium, customer base, competition? Who's responsible for the content? What happens to the press? What about privacy and data ownership?

The Internet is going commercial: more and more non-research, non-education types are joining in. But what is commercial: Two researchers arguing about a project that may one day become a product? An MIT research assistant discussing a job with a Sun Microsystems team leader? Two commercial product developers discussing the finer points of e-mail? Or two salesmen discussing the finer points of e-mail pricing? What about Juan and Alice, both students, trading sweet nothings? Or a Soviet scientist-entrepreneur seeking conference invitations in the West? (Note that the global net still doesn't usually reach to where most people are much of the time: walking or riding around, sitting in meetings, in other people's offices.)

Whither the establishment?

In this world of filtered, mediated communications, what's the role of press and government? If everyone can communicate with everyone, what's left for the press and the government to do in an increasingly flat world? Two things happen. People form their own communities, and the press and the government (the good ones, anyway) try to set a broader agenda, drawing people's attention beyond their own interests and self-interest.

Communities are natural. The idea of the global village was misguided; people can't operate on such a large scale. Instead, they form new villages, unconstrained by space, but clustered on some common interest (or self-interest): user groups, health issues, professional societies, etc. People have a persistent tendency to form tribes -- which can be either healthy or self-destructive. People with common interests can get human satisfaction from sharing them and can work together effectively; on the other hand, they can also shut out the outside world and disregard the claims of outside society (a tendency that manifests itself in warfare, protectionism and other geopolitical misbehavior).

Online services will cater to this tendency by allowing users to form tightly linked communities and markets. Aside from the "small-i internet," which is a self-organizing, fluid community without a clear commercial structure yet, and e-mail services such as MCI, the current leaders are **CompuServe**, **Prodigy** and **America Online** (as opposed to information services which deliver information but not access to other people). Each has a different business model. With about 1.4 million individual users (750,000 households), Prodigy's business model is akin to an interactive version of cable tv, delivering targeted information to targeted consumers with some interactivity and transaction capabilities added. CompuServe and America Online are targeted more at people who use their computers to manipulate information as well as receive it.

While Prodigy does pay some outside services, CompuServe and America Online have more of a cottage-industry approach -- with America Online addressing people at home while CompuServe addresses them at work (although that distinction is fuzzy). Also, CompuServe encourages a sort of information market, where private entrepreneurs (or software vendors wanting to offer on-line support) can apply to run forums. CompuServe actually pays them a percentage of the traffic they generate -- usually around 5 to 10 percent. Altogether, CompuServe has 225 hardware and software support forums and 120 non-computer forums. CompuServe Information Services revenues in 1991 were about $100 million, from 925,000 users.

Prodigy has borne the brunt of controversy recently: Is Prodigy an editorial product subject to control by the publisher, or is it a common carrier that should allow anything to be transmitted and in turn be absolved of any liability? (Note that only governments and monopolies can censor; in a competitive market, when publishers refuse to publish something, the source can find other outlets.) Perry argues that Prodigy and similar services are both -- but should two such distinct entities be mingled?

Content on the network

A side from the political issues, how will the global network change how we receive information and live our lives? The stunning success of **Dell Computer** is due not only to its machines and distribution strategy, but also to how the company uses e-mail and groupware internally. For instance, when we recently bought a laptop from Dell, word filtered back to Michael Dell. (We didn't get a discount, but at least our purchase was appreciated in high places!) This raises interesting questions: How much garbage does Michael get in his daily load of e-mail? Is e-mail simply a new avenue for tomorrow's corporate climbers? Will we all be drowned in a sea of horizontal, non-hierarchical communication? (Nor is Dell alone: **Richard Schwartz** at **Borland**, for example, keeps in touch with Scotts Valley mostly by MCI mail -- as do many Borland employees throughout the US.)

While technologists are excited about multimedia, text filtering and other developments, who's going to create the content? While most of the traditional press is afraid of high-tech, and the American Newspaper Publishers Association is waging war against cable tv companies and RBOCs, the traditional press actually has a real edge in these new markets if it could only get over its fears. After all, technology could leverage the scarce resource they control -- informed reporters and editors capable of sound judgment.

Yes, technology will raise the relative power of free-lancers to find both short-term employers and readers -- bypassing the formal media entirely. But the press does have brand-name power -- increasingly important in a world of cacophonous, overwhelming information. Just as newly free people in the East are bewildered at the proliferation of new media and don't know what to believe, so will we too (from a broader base) find the array of information sources difficult to sort out. The press, if it does its job well, will be able to leverage its credibility. Its role is not just to create (or find out information), but to assess it and digest it for the ultimate readers. Who gave it that right? No one, which is why we don't believe in a government-controlled press. But a variety of media companies have earned leading positions by providing credible information over the years (or titillating entertainment, in other cases).

The Washington Post Company is an excellent case in point. The company is already the owner of Legi-Slate, an online database of current legislative proceedings. **Ralph Terkowitz**, vp information technology, is looking for software that could make Legi-Slate more useful and more broadly available. Currently the service has its own unique interface; to use it, you have to work with Legi-Slate's proprietary indexing scheme and query syntax. Something like the Wide-Area Information Server standard could help solve the problem if it were widely enough implemented. Terkowitz is also working on providing the content and format for a CD ROM project that would use some of the superfluous information that currently stuffs the archives, floors and disk drives of the Post's key properties, the Washington Post newspaper itself and Newsweek magazine. In the course of reporting stories, its journalists routinely gather far more information, photographs and other material than they can or want to use in existing formats. One result is Newsweek Focus, in which Newsweek offers its readers additional editorial content in their specific field of interest (you pay extra for extra pages). The Post is now looking at higher-tech ways of offering "tell-me-more" service -- for example, on CD-ROM. While extra material can't just be put wholesale onto a CD-ROM, some of it could, with a little amount of editing, provide useful background for the daily news.

Thomas Malone of **MIT's Center for Coordination Science** addresses the electronic frontier from a more macroeconomic perspective. As communications among firms improve, there's no longer as great a need for large firms. Outsourcing is one sign of this; so, perhaps, are some of the alliances and decentralizations in the industry. Communications makes firms more flexible; customers needn't be tied to a single supplier; employees can more easily find work. As technology makes it easier for separate modules to fit together on one level, the communications infrastructure makes it easier to find and assemble those modules on another. Theoretically this will lead to a more efficient world, but what about those old virtues of loyalty, team spirit and personal leadership?

2. OBJECTS IN BUSINESS AND TECHNOLOGY

Object orientation allows us to use 1s and 0s to model reality, making software easier to use and modify. Overall, it allows us to build software out of fungible components, instead of creating software monoliths that are difficult to change. **David Liddle**, formerly at Xerox PARC and now starting up **Interval Research**, has devoted the last few years to fostering the development of supporting architectures and component libraries.

Liddle will discuss the business implications of such fundamental changes in architecture: Hardware, system software and applications used to be three separate, nicely defined layers. Now, many functions that were once applications are now being generalized and are being offered as part of an operating environment, such as **Transarc's Encina** and **Tivoli's WizDOM.** But that operating environment isn't an operating *system*; it's really a fluid layer of interchangeable modules that sit on top of a small operating system kernel. Thus we now have four layers -- or actually, a collection of objects sitting on top of or around the operating system, which is itself really just a thin layer around the hardware.

This modularity is changing business dynamics for suppliers of these components. Application vendors are getting involved in setting standards for some of these modules, most recently mail. Lotus, Novell, Borland, IBM and Apple now all support the Vendor-Independent Messaging interface spec -- a development spurred by Lotus's Open Mail Interface. This API will run on a variety of platforms, as opposed to Microsoft's Mail API, which is specific to Windows (for now). In the long run, operating system vendors will lose some of their power -- but not so much to individual application vendors as to users. It will be harder for any single vendor to gain (or retain) a stranglehold over the industry. Object-orientation allows customers to acquire mostly coherent, cohesive systems from a fragmented supplier community.

But that doesn't mean that everything is in place already. First, we'll need system integrators, using technology like that shown by **Trilogy Development** to assemble systems. Some will be mere distribution channels; others will build and customize systems out of components. One big issue is how those components will be charged for, especially as they get reused, incorporated into other components and otherwise lose their identity in users' systems. Some big vendors such as DEC are looking at getting into the information utility business, where they will build systems themselves and charge users for transactions. How will they compensate the creators of the components they use? What distribution channels and payment mechanisms will we use? What does this mean for definition and protection of intellectual property?

Meanwhile, what about all these alliances and downsizings? **IBM** is devolving into a larger number of smaller units, some of them operating quite autonomously. One thing we hope to hear from **Jim Cannavino** is exactly how autonomous he feels, and how he now operates under the IBM corporate umbrella. Simultaneously, what does he owe to IBM's many partners? Can an alliance work without direct financial links to focus a company's efforts? Conversely, how many alliances can you have at the same time? How can a small company such as NeXT or GO have a serious impact on a company like IBM in the first place? What management objectives you are measured by?

Microsoft is taking a different approach: It needs few alliances because of its marketplace power. Third parties support its products without direct encouragement. **Bill Gates** has hired Jim Allchin from Banyan and Paul Leach from Apollo/HP. They are working (among other things) on Cairo, Microsoft's next-generation system, which will be fully distributed and secure, with its own object-oriented file system. This is the kind of robust underpinning that we'll need to realize all the object-oriented fantasies -- including information at your fingertips.

Sun's Bill Joy has now started Aspen Smallworks, a research center for technologies that may or may not appear as Sun products. He's concerned that vendors (Sun/HP included) focus too much on features and functions at the expense of elegance and simplicity. In short, you can't *add* elegance to existing systems; you have to start with it, since elegance belongs to an architecture as a whole.

Alliances and value

There are two kinds of alliances: Those focused on complementary offerings that fit together (like objects), and those where competing companies band together. (Guess which works better and lasts longer.) One has to do with open APIs that allow vendors' products to work together; the other with enforced APIs, usually so that the have-nots can compete with a single more successful vendor whose APIs needn't be *enforced*; they've already been *selected* by market forces. (Let the free market attract value-added instead of relying on alliances and contracts.) OSF was one such competing partners alliance; so is the Vendor-Independent Messaging interface steering group. Some survive; others, such as ACE, may founder. How much can such alliances change history, and how much are they simply artifacts of market forces?

The softwareless software company...? Who will own the value in the future? Except for the OS vendors themselves, everyone would prefer to see the operating system become a commodity. And it will, starting on the client side first. The value will lie in the tools, class libraries and installable components -- including object-oriented databases that will take over the role of file systems and naming services. Most OS functions will be managed by modules that sit on top of a vanishingly small kernel.

Standards are just temporary rigidities in a continuously evolving marketplace. There's a short magic moment where one vendor "owns" the standard and no one else does, which is when people make their money. But eventually a standard either falls into disuse or is effectively cloned, depending on the owner's attitudes to intellectual property. (Ashton-Tate, for example, clung tightly to dBASE, while IBM gave the PC away.) Then the market moves on to another layer such as operating environments, or another platform such as pentops, and new players emerge. The new players of the future, we believe, will be those who control class libraries (not programming languages, communications protocols or architectures), network facilities and communication networks, and who can charge for services and transactions.

Object-oriented technology: Can we get there from here?

Reusing code is often listed as one of the benefits of object-oriented computing. However, object-orientation alone doesn't make code worth reusing. Like most magic, it works only if you follow some additional rules. The trick is to reuse the right modules, and to modify them appropriately. Rather than explore the wonderfulness of objects, accordingly, we'll discuss how to make the transition.

There are lots of ways to be object-oriented without writing in Smalltalk or C++ -- and lots of ways current products can move towards object-orientation. Vendors focused on object-oriented technology need help from the application vendors, who must start making their apps more open, with clean interfaces, so that these tools and environments can exploit their capabilities. While these vendors can impart leverage to an object's functions, it's the application vendors who provide the actual functions to be leveraged.

For starters, an object-oriented database can hold all kinds of useful data -- what Borland calls "user-familiar objects" -- such as spreadsheets, diagrams, voice annotations and the related components of a compound document, along with routing rules, integrity constraints and other methods. What makes an object-oriented database such as **Ontos** different from a database that holds objects is the OODB's ability to manage the richness of objects itself, rather than merely to supply data to an application that supplies that richness at runtime. Thus an object-oriented database can manage objects according to their individual behavior and structure without the presence of any application at all. (Another way to state this is that at least part of the application is maintained with the data *in* the database, as methods.) What's the practical implication? In many cases, very little, but when you start dealing with complex objects and integrity requirements, an object-oriented database models the abstractions more closely, performs better, and is easier to work with. You don't have to model the constructs with relational joins and application code; you can simply put them with the data.

A script for success

Another way to leverage existing applications and treat them as "objects" is to write scripts with them (regardless of how they're stored). Basically, scripting is a way of reusing application code, forming it into meta-applications that use and sequence discrete functions of the underlying applications. Thus the commands of the underlying applications become the user's programming language, manipulated in the syntax of the scripting tool. With familiar applications, even a fairly naive end-user can exercise a surprising amount of power. Alternatively, a scripter can create applications for other users. **UserLand's Dave Winer**, who developed the Frontier scripting tool, urges application vendors to make their applications scriptable: "We already have applications out there designed to serve users' needs, but they need to be wired right [with open APIs or AppleEvents] so that they can be automated, customized, simplified and integrated."

Objects will also create a need for network operating systems that know how to find and handle objects, find their parents and methods, synchronize their activities and so forth. **Darrell Miller** of **Novell** is trying to assemble the requisite technology -- internally and from third parties -- to make that happen on top of NetWare. (Implementations of the OMG's Object Request Broker will also provide many such services but not the OS itself.)

3. PENS AND GROUPWARE

Over the last year, skepticism about pen computing turned to enthusiasm. Now, it's meeting with impatience: Where are the machines? Although there are pen machines out there -- most notably products from long-time supplier GRiD and from newcomer Momenta -- the flow of pencentric machines predicted last year hasn't yet materialized. This may be a good thing, since the operating systems are late too. Application vendors such as **Slate** are champing at the bit, waiting for the machines and OSes to start shipping this spring. It took more than 20 months to ship Excel after the Mac came out, 16 months after the PC for 1-2-3, says veteran **Vern Raburn**, now chairman of **Slate**. He confidently predicts 12 vendors shipping pen computers by year-end, supporting at least 50 applications. Call it PENt-up supply.

Are pen machines worth waiting for? For all that **GO** stresses PenPoint's scalability, it now requires a high-end, 386-based computer to run acceptably, as does Microsoft's Windows for Pen Computing (known to friends as Pen-Windows). Of course, by the time the installed base amounts to much, more powerful hardware will abound, and 2-pound 486-based pen computers will probably sell for about $2000.

Meanwhile, **GeoWorks** has announced Pen/GEOS (for Graphical Environment Operating System), targeted at even smaller machines for under $500. **Brian Dough-**

erty of GeoWorks and **Jeff Hawkins** of **Palm Computing** are working together, along with hardware vendors such as GRiD and Poqet, and components suppliers such as Chips & Technologies. Hawkins is enthusiastic about GeoWorks, but he's also enthusiastic about $400 palm computers in general: "If Apple has one," he says, "we'll support it too. We want to be the Slate of mass-market palmtops." (How quickly role models are risen!) Palm Computing shares ownership of a low-resource handwriting technology with GRiD, which Hawkins started developing during a two-year leave from GRiD when he was working on neurobiology at Berkeley. (Yes, the two technologies are related.) Dougherty, meanwhile, should find the pen computing market refreshingly open after selling a respectable 400,000 copies of the PC/GEOS desktop operating system. That will look like peanuts if this consumer market takes off.

One year after most of the excitement, we're still fervent believers in pen computing. But we place more emphasis on the physical form factor -- having carried a few of them around. Only when the physical machine passes muster can the software play its role: supporting developers, enabling the system to hold a lot of data compactly (as objects), managing intermittent communications smoothly, and understanding the user's intentions with a minimum of effort by the user.

The bandwidth between the user and the machine and between the machine and the rest of the world should be minimal, while the ability to interpret information at either end should be maximized. Pen gestures are just one way -- but an important way -- of low-bandwidth, high-content communication between person and machine. Does this mean a whole new operating system? We believe it does, but there will be a lot of trial and error before the ultimate system is achieved.

Groupware: Three visions

Aside from Notes, **NCR's Cooperation** is one of the few large-scale groupware tools/environments out in the market, with customers such as Hartford Insurance & Citibank. It's a potentially significant means of differentiating NCR now that the company is vigorously promoting open systems. Already, says NCR's **Gil Williamson**, customers have benefited not just from the software itself, but from the process they go through as they install it. Frequently, they end up redesigning their processes, gaining efficiency not just from automation but from better *business* design.

While NCR works from a platform, supporting third-party applications with its integrating environment, **Borland** and **Lotus** both work from their own application suites out. They have overall similar views of the future capabilities of software/groupware, but the implementation details affect the flavor of their systems. Both companies agree that most business processes are concerned not just with data sharing, but with stating, negotiating and fulfilling commitments. Without perhaps using such language, both companies will give users the tools to set up and monitor the completion of tasks. For example, setting up a meeting isn't simply a matter of sharing data. It requires a proposal and a confirmation -- or agreement on a new date.

Notes: Adding sending to sharing

Lotus Notes is built around a logically central database, even though it's physically replicated and distributed. The system offers a shared repository of knowledge that's available in different formats and subsets to all its users (subject to security authorizations).

Notes was developed independently of Lotus and indeed wasn't really understood by the company until recently. (Now that **John Landry** has arrived, the company is undergoing a dramatic shift in its orientation -- and its visible self-esteem.) Now, Notes is being extended and redefined, to be more open to other environments (partly through the DDE and OLE facilities of Windows) and to integrate with e-mail, especially Lotus's own cc:Mail, although the company was also the catalyst behind the VIM interface, over which it has sensibly ceded control to a steering group. Lotus is also incorporating some workflow capabilities into Notes, using technology from Action Technologies. (A small piece of this will be demoed at the Forum: The system will notify users via SkyTel message receivers when they have mail, and will monitor whether messages are answered.) Says Lotus's Terry Rogers: "We've been sharing; now we have to start sending as well."

Borland: Starting with the familiar

By contrast, Borland starts from its own desktop applications out -- what it calls "User-Familiar Objects." Basically, it is extending its Borland Object Component Architecture (BOCA), moving beyond data-sharing and user-object sharing (forms, reports and queries) through a database to workgroup support through messaging over transports such as those supporting VIM. A traditional database approach lets users share subsets of data, with the database jealously maintaining the integrity of the data.

Workgroup computing however, includes some abstraction of the users as well; they don't just share data, but work with discrete objects that may cross application and database boundaries. Users deal with *each other*, not just with the database. The individuals can exchange messages and commitments. The database moves from being a central manager of the data to being a repository for data managed by the individual UFOs and individual users (even though underneath it all, Interbase maintains data integrity, versions and other database niceties). Interbase is a relational database with the ability to handle BLOBs (or basic large objects); Borland got it along with dBASE in the Ashton-Tate acquisition.

All this extends an approach first visible in SideKick 2, where individual users manage their own data, but it is mingled and reconciled (carefully) with others' calendars and contact lists. SideKick 2 includes facilities for reconciling a personal contact list with the corporate list, or the calendar a user keeps on a laptop with the one he keeps at work. Such reconciliation isn't traditional database management, but requires application-specific techniques or transactions that reflect the particular content and functions relevant to the data of a particular application (call them the UFO's methods). In the future, this approach will encompass the entire Borland application suite, and complying applications from other vendors as well. Data will be able to be shared and reconciled across applications such as spreadsheets (cf. Lotus's Chronicle), databases, appointment books, documents, etc.

The InterBase foundation will also manage workflow transactions (although they won't look like database transactions, but rather like messages that are simply recorded by the database). While Lotus wants a single logical database, Borland is comfortable with the notion of multiple different sites, with data shared only as necessary. "The world isn't always completely in synch, and people share point-to-point, not just through a database," says Borland's **Richard Schwartz**. "So why not reflect this in your software?"

Personal Computers and Intelligent Systems / F.H. Vogt (Editor)
Information Processing 92, Volume III
Elsevier Science Publishers B.V. (North-Holland)

MICROSOFT WINDOWS FOR PEN COMPUTING

by Pradeep Singh, Group Product Manager and Lisa Weil, Product Manager

ABSTRACT

The following pages discuss Microsoft's vision of pen computing focusing on the Windows for Pen Computing operating system. The features of the operating system will be described to show how Windows for Pens extends the Windows environment to pen computing to meet the market needs.

Keyword Codes: D.4.0; K.8.0
Keywords: Operating Systems, General; Personal Computing, General

A VISION FOR PENS

Computing changed dramatically during the 1980s. Computer technology moved to the desktop, becoming widely available and essential for everyday decision making. In the 1990s, Microsoft believes, continuing advances will make computers more personal, making them indispensable, something you reach for naturally whenever and wherever you need to retrieve, record or analyze information. Pens will play a very significant role in making this happen.

Pens offer unique advantages. They are one of the most familiar, natural input devices we know. We learn to use them at a very early age. Pens also adapt well to small form factors and can be used standing up or sitting down. Unlike keyboards or mice, they do not require a flat stable surface. Unlike keyboards, they do not need to accommodate two hands working side-by-side. Consider the many ways and places we use pens today. We use them with notepads, address books, calendars to-do lists, and shopping lists. The pen is also the ultimate 'graphical' instrument. You can print characters *or* draw freeform images and symbols (diagrams, maps, pictures, etc.).

Combine the pen with a powerful graphical user interface, the increased miniaturization of technology, increased capabilities in computing power and capacity, advances in handwriting recognition technology and data compression and you have a powerful foundation for the highly portable, highly intuitive "personal" systems that will drive computing in the 90's. Pens will enable the creation of new software applications that explore new metaphors and expand and enhance the range of functions available to users. Pens will also bring computing to new users including highly mobile users who do not use computers today. Pen technology will be a major ingredient in a compelling, exciting new form of computing that allows users to explore information, rather than struggle with it.

For the past three years, Microsoft has been working on integrating support for pens in the Microsoft® Windows™ graphical environment. Microsoft® Windows™ for Pen Computing extends the Windows environment to pen computing. Customers can leverage the familiarity and portability offered by pens while also leveraging the availability of Windows applications, development tools, and connectivity solutions. Customers can use the pen with the general purpose operating system that enjoys the most overwhelming support in our industry today *and* promises customers continued innovation through offerings that range from object-oriented technology to exciting multimedia capabilities.

THE MARKET FOR PEN COMPUTERS

Visualize any of the following scenarios:

- **Nurses and Doctors** track and record patient histories as they make their rounds. They use clipboard-like computers and pens to look-up and enter patient information drawn via a wireless network from servers through-out the hospital. Because the information is captured in real-time, patient trends as well as costs incurred across the hospital can be tracked and summarized accurately and efficiently.

- **Insurance Claims Adjusters** assess automobile damages on-site, looking up relevant part and cost information with the tap of the pen. The availability of accurate cost information specific to the make and model of the car enables the adjuster to print the estimate and write a check to the repair shop at the end of the visit. The insurer saves money through more accurate estimates and the elimination of rekeyed data.

- **Consumer Goods Sales Representatives** track inventory and the effect of promotional campaigns in retail stores. The data is captured on-site using pen and pen computer. At the end of the day, the information is transmitted via phone line back to headquarters. The next day the product manager accesses this same information, analyzing the results using her favorite spreadsheet product. Conclusions are drawn and the next steps to be taken are incorporated in a memo to manufacturing and mail to the field.

- **Financial Analysts** crunch numbers all day at their desks. Presenting the results to management or customers, an analyst performs "what if" analyses right there in the meeting using a pen to change a number or drag a line on a chart. The screen of the analyst's laptop converts easily to a slanted writing surface supporting the pen, enabling the analyst to work easily and naturally even under pressure.

- **Project Managers** managing complex projects worry about the effective synchronization of people, resources and time. In a meeting of key players, the cost of one component sky rockets while another slips by 3 weeks. On a white board that displays the schedule for all to see, the project manager uses the pen to change the component's cost and then drags a scrolling time line out 3 weeks. Everyone sees the effect. The trade-offs are clear and negotiations begin. Decisions are made and the project continues without delay.

More generally, imagine everyday business people maintaining their calendars on always-accessible computers that feel more like notepads and calendars than the computers we know today. People will jot down notes in meetings and conduct interactive presentations using these new computers. Automated whiteboards will be used to facilitate group brainstorming sessions. Individual proposals scratched on notepads will be transmitted via wireless connection to a whiteboard for group review. On the desktop, pens will be used to edit and annotate documents through simple gestures or handwritten comments.

Just as pens today are seamlessly woven into our everyday lives, they will be woven into this computerized world of tomorrow, enabling us to work as naturally as we do today -- and also do much more. The challenge is in how we make this happen -- transitioning from the tools we use today to those of tomorrow. Microsoft expects pen computing will begin with the following markets:

• **Mobile service providers** (field sales and service representatives, field engineers, route managers, insurance adjusters) These users will require a mix of custom and general purpose solutions and new pen computers, probably in the form of electronic clipboards. These clipboard computers may only offer the keyboard as an option. Users will look-up information on-site, or capture it in machine-readable format. The information will then be instantly available for further processing. Useful trends, warnings or summary data will be available not only for the professional in the field but will also be communicated to other users via cellular communications or other network solutions.

• **Mobile professionals** will use a mix of new applications as well as existing applications on new, pen computers. These users are today's laptop and notebook users. In fact, they comprise the fastest growing segment of the computer hardware market. The next generation of notebook PCs will most likely be "convertible," allowing the user to detach the display from the keyboard and base of the PC for pen-exclusive uses. At the same time, users will have the option to re-combine these components for applications that benefit from a keyboard or mouse. These pen-inclusive computers offer excellent added value as data entry devices. They will also have tremendous future potential as they begin leveraging ever-smaller, less-expensive compact disk storage and applications that offer easy data retrieval and output.

• **Deskbound professionals** who travel occasionally, and have a continuing need for desktop systems can control the pace -- and cost -- of their migration to pen computing by adding pen devices to their existing hardware as a first step. Overtime, desktop solutions will most likely be more modular, consisting of a base station with network connections, keyboard, extra memory, and a detachable small notebook or electronic clipboard which serves as a subset and can be taken to meetings.

INTRODUCING WINDOWS FOR PENS

Windows for Pens is an OEM (Original Equipment Manufacturer) product which will be licensed and sold to OEMs offering a variety of exciting new pen computers. The modular design of the Windows operating system enables the integration of pen extensions into the base Windows 3.1 product.

Our strategy in designing Windows for Pens was to ensure Microsoft's ability to deliver on the promise of pen computing while also ensuring customers' ability to leverage investments made in Windows-based applications, ISVs' ability to leverage the rich base of Windows application code and development tools, and OEMs' ability to sell solutions to viable markets.

In designing Windows for Pens, we focused on two key criteria:

- **customer ability to leverage the familiarity and portability offered by pens**
- **customer ability to leverage the Windows environment**

The following pages highlight the ways in which Windows for Pens extends the Windows environment to pen computing and meets these key criteria.

LEVERAGING THE PEN

The Natural Feel of the Pen

Windows for Pens enables customers to use the pen in ways that actually mimic pen and paper, supporting the natural feel of the pen. This is possible through Windows for Pens support for:

- **INK**

Windows for Pens enables applications to work with ink in a variety of ways. At the most basic level, users expect to see ink flow from their pen when they drag it across the 'page'. Using the pen, users can print, scribble a quick note, draw a diagram, or simply doodle. Depending on the application, ink can be saved as it appears on the page, it can translated to typed text (i.e. recognized), or it can be translated as a special symbol (i.e. a gesture) to indicate an action to be taken. Ink can also be saved as is and, at a later point in time, translated to another format. Pen and ink together enable an exciting array of new application functions such as note-taking, signature capture, diagram generation and the natural annotation of documents.

- **GESTURES**

Gestures are special handwritten symbols that are similar to proofreading symbols. Gestures enable users to ***select*** and ***act*** upon something in a ***single***, ***simple*** motion. For example, a user might scratch out a word to make it disappear. Windows for Pens supports three types of gestures:

13 Standard System-Wide Gestures
These gestures enable basic commands like edit, cut, copy and paste. These gestures are available across all Windows for Pens applications. Examples of our basic gestures include:

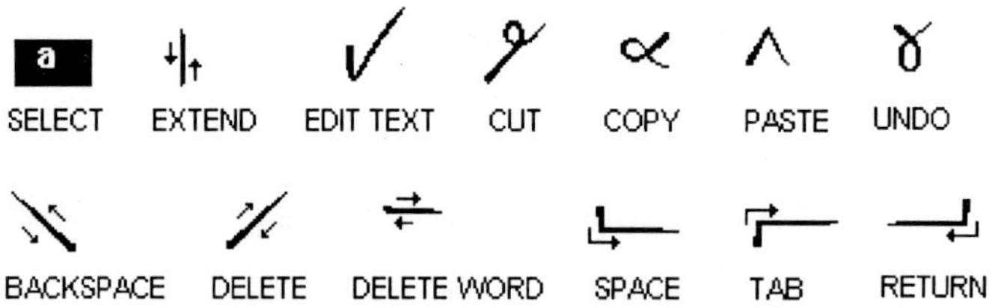

Custom Application Gestures
Application developers have the option to leverage the Windows for Pens gesture set or add new gestures using circled character gestures or special gesture recognizers.

User Assignable Gestures

Users can assign specially designated symbols (circled characters from the alphabet) to standard application commands and use them across one or more applications. For example, a "b" with a circle around it can be used to bold text whether it is in a word processor, spreadsheet, or notetaker. An "a" with a circle around it can be used to insert standard addressing information in a document or memo.

- **RECOGNITION**

Developing good handwriting recognition that adapts completely to users' needs as opposed to forcing users to adapt to the recognition system is difficult. Recognition engines must anticipate a broad, incredibly varied spectrum of users and writing styles which include left and right-handed users, foreign and U.S. trained users, and users who mix printing and cursive characters in unpredictable ways. Dramatic variation is possible even with a single individual printing under different circumstances and pressures.

Microsoft Windows for Pen Computing offers a recognition strategy that ensures customers and developers maximum flexibility in matching handwriting technology with their specific needs. Windows for Pens supports an **open, modular recognition strategy** enabling customers to replace or *supplement* the Windows for Pens recognizer with other third party recognizers. Microsoft developers chose this approach to:

- Stimulate the development of third-party English-language recognizers
- Encourage the development of other, application-specific recognizers (e.g., shapes, shorthand, mathematical and other special symbols and functions)
- Allow for the use of non-English recognizers (e.g., Kanji, Cyrillic, etc.)
- Offer customers the choice of the recognizer that suits their needs (e.g. a neural network recognizer that can be extensively trained)

The Microsoft Recognizer

Microsoft's handwriting recognition engine incorporates four steps:

- **Feature extraction or data compression**, during which the recognizer separates useful data from "noise" or unnecessary information
- **Segmentation**, during which the recognizer resolves the input into separate characters
- **Shape recognition** to match the input character against the most likely prototype character stored in the engine
- **Dictionary recognition** to fit the recognized character into the context of other characters around its position. This step may cause the handwriting recognition engine to revise its original best-guess answers.

With Windows for Pens, recognizers can run in the background, processing text in real time, or can be turned off for processing at a later time. The first release of Microsoft Windows for Pen Computing will process handwriting recognition at the real-time rate of two to three characters per second and will recognize upper- and lower-case handwriting, numbers and selected punctuation marks. While the function offered by the Microsoft recognition engine is highly sophisticated, the overhead incurred is impressively small. The total size of the recognition engine *and* the database of handwriting samples is approximately 300 KB.

Training Your Handwriting

The Microsoft Recognizer includes the capability to do initial training or on-the-fly training. While the Microsoft Recognizer includes a database of country-specific handwriting samples and training should not be necessary, persistent problems with individual characters or gestures can be corrected. For example, users entering information in a form may find a persistent problem recognizing a character. The user can call upon the trainer, reference the problem character, indicate the appropriate translation using an on-screen keyboard and then return to complete the form. Additionally, while cursive recognition is not yet possible, stubborn habits of stringing characters such as "th" together can also be addressed. Contiguous stroke combinations (similar to cursive writing) can be trained as character strings (up to three characters) to help produce the desired translation.

Support for Innovative Pen Applications

Windows for Pens offers applications the ability to combine the simplicity of the pen with the simple visual appeal of the Windows graphical environment. Users can use the pen to tap on icons, buttons, and pull-down menus to explore information and options. The Windows environment supports OLE, Object Linking and Embedding, encouraging developers to move toward a more "data-centric" rather than purely "application-centric" view of computing. OLE enables users to work with compound documents that include ink, text, graphics, images, even animation and sound. Users invoke the appropriate function as they create or edit objects within a document. The end result is a more intuitive metaphor that reflects the way people really think and work.

Windows for Pens builds on the basic foundation of the Windows operating system offering applications:

- **CUSTOM COMMANDS**

Custom gestures enable developers and users to leverage the pen in ways that are meaningful to particular applications or uses. Custom gestures can be as simple (and powerful) as the flick of the pen to turn a page. Slate Corporation's PenBook for Windows for Pens incorporates the "flick" gesture. A flick to the left is the equivalent of moving one page forward in a document. A flick to the right moves the user one page back. Hansen's Field Geographic Information System for utilities customers enables field service repair people to enter the exact time a job is completed simply by writing a "T" with a circle around it.

- **INKING SUPPORT**

Windows for Pens provides special custom controls to enable developers to create special fields or areas in applications that capture ink or recognize input. Ink can be saved as is, stored and recalled for later use. To support ink, Windows for Pens utilizes special data compression capabilities with compression rates that average 4:1. Ink can also be recognized and translated automatically (by default) or ink can be translated upon the user's request at a later point in time.

- **Recognition Support**

To support and enhance recognition, Windows for Pens offers applications the ability to pass information to the recognizer, providing contextual hints. Applications can specify parameters indicating for instance if only numeric information is expected, or if a valid entry for a field can be only 1 of 20 possibilities. A zip code field may only expect numeric data. A form with fields requesting "City" and "State" information may only expect cities and states located on the East coast. The recognizer returns probabilistic information back to the application, enabling the application to make intelligent trade-offs. Applications can also add custom dictionaries to aid the recognizer limiting the range of possible entries or expanding the possibilities to include specialized acronyms and industry-specific jargon.

- **Scalability**

Windows for Pens applications will run on pen computers that vary in size and scale. Windows for Pens provides information to enable the application to make intelligent trade-off decisions to determine appropriate scaling strategies. Many of these decisions can only be made by the application. For instance, consider a pen computer that offers 3"x5" display. It may be most appropriate for a simple forms application to scale all its fonts to a smaller proportion. Automatically wrapping the information on the form could make it unreadable. On the other hand, it might be far more sensible for a word processor or communications package to wrap information to fit the small display. Scaling the information proportionately might make large amounts of text completely unreadable.

Support for exciting new pen computers

Many innovations in the base Windows product are expressly suited to pen computing where the computer itself is a smaller, more mobile form factor such as the NCR 3125 Notepad. Windows Advanced Power Management features and support for Flash EPROM (silicon storage which can take the place of a more fragile hard disk) offer excellent support for smaller, more mobile pen computers. Windows extensible design enables Windows for Pens to scale down to a total system size of 2MB. Most of this 2MB system can be run in ROM, freeing memory and storage for applications and data. Windows for Pens builds further upon these Windows innovations, offering the ability to scale to a variety of form factors and display information either in portrait or landscape mode.

Leveraging Windows

Leveraging Windows Development Tools and Applications

Using Windows for Pens, customers can use the pen with well-behaved, unmodified Windows 3.0 applications to:

- Point and tap as they would with a mouse
- Issue commands using the standard set of 13 system-wide gestures
- Print characters in any text field. Handwritten entries are translated and displayed as typed text.

These capabilities are also possible with the Windows 3.0 environment development tools. This is especially important in the pen market where many customers are interested in implementing customized pen solutions for new users (i.e.: truck drivers, inventory clerks, sales people, etc.). These customers can leverage existing development tools for Windows like the Visual Basic™ Programming System for Windows or Toolbook® from Asymetrix. The ability to leverage the broad array of both Windows-based applications and development tools means that customers can deploy custom or general purpose solutions quickly --and cost effectively. Customers can also implement applications that are compatible at the file *and* application level. Application compatibility is no longer a trivial issue. Rich file and application formats that incorporate complex features like outlining, embedded objects, and graphical formats can pose difficult and costly challenges for customers interested in implementing true enterprise-wide solutions.

Connectivity solutions

In addition to being able to leverage Windows-based applications and development tools, customers also benefit by being able to leverage the broad array of proven connectivity solutions with Windows. These include traditional networking solutions as well as wireless connectivity solutions. Both are equally important in supporting the implementation of pen applications that need to be integrated into the enterprise.

A General Purpose OS With Broad Industry Support Today and Tomorrow

Windows for Pens offers customers a general purpose operating system that enjoys broad industry support from OEMs, ISVs, and customers. Windows for Pens provides optimum support for the pen while also providing continued support for other input devices. While pens offer exciting opportunities, there are still instances where other input devices offer superior performance. Keyboards continue to offer greater utility in those instances where medium or high volume data entry is required. Voice may someday succeed the keyboard in this capacity. However, even voice can benefit from the assistance of a simple pointing device. (How do you effectively say, 'Delete the fourth word on the 10th line of the 3rd paragraph'?) As computing solutions become an integral part of our lives, they must adapt, offering the right mix of tools to a mix of users who, despite varying skills must all work together. In this context, proprietary or special niche solutions offer limited economy or utility.

For customers interested in implementing enterprise-wide solutions, a general purpose OS like Windows for Pens offers numerous advantages. To realize the true benefits of pen computing, information that is captured in the field must typically be *communicated* and *integrated* back into a company's existing systems for further processing. While the user in the field may use a pen, the next user in the chain -- whether in a field office or company headquarters -- is most likely going to process that information using the same or similar application either with a pen -- or keyboard or mouse.

Windows for Pens is fundamentally based on Windows and continues to benefit from the evolution and innovations of Windows that include Truetype®, OLE, 32-bit addressability, pre-emptive multi-tasking, multimedia extensions and more.

WINDOWS FOR PENS OEM AND ISV SUPPORTERS

ISVs

More than 120 ISVs have announced their support for Windows for Pens. This list includes major Windows environment supporters such as Borland, Microsoft, Software Publishing, Micrografx, and Corel. This list also includes exciting pen software start-ups such as Slate, Pensoft, Ink, and Quill as well as a number of Vertical ISVs such as ADP, Sales Technologies and Logica. Recognition firms supporting Windows for Pens include CIC, Nestor, and OCR Systems.

OEMs

The following OEMs have publicly announced their intention to build Windows for Pens machines: Toshiba, NCR, Samsung, Grid, Epson, NEC, Hitachi, Wang, Momenta, Calcomp, Kyocera, Canon, Sharp, Oki, Eden Group, Mitsubishi, Sanyo, Summagraphics, Fujitsu, Scenario, Telegroup, Dell, Zenith, AST Research, Olivetti, Tusk, Inc., Microslate, Superscript, and Wacom, Inc. Customers can expect to see pen hardware available on the market beginning in Q1 and Q2 '92.

Microsoft Corporation (NASDAQ "MSFT") develops, markets and supports a wide range of software for business and professional use, including operating systems, network products, languages and applications, as well as books, hardware and CD-ROM products for the microcomputer marketplace.

#########

#########

The information contained in this document represents the current view of Microsoft Corporation on the issues discussed as the date of publication. Because Microsoft must respond to changing market conditions, it should not be interpreted to be a commitment on the part of Microsoft, and Microsoft cannot guarantee the accuracy of any information presented after the date of publication.

Personal Computers and Intelligent Systems / F.H. Vogt (Editor)
Information Processing 92, Volume III
Elsevier Science Publishers B.V. (North-Holland)

An open model for developing knowledge-based user interfaces

Xie Li, Du Xing and Sun Zhongxiu

Computer Science Department, Nanjing University, Nanjing, 210008 P.R.CHINA
Fax: (86)(25)300710

Abstract

This paper proposes an open model for developing user interfaces. The layered structure of the open model encourages the interface design to be open, and using knowledge to represent the interfaces bridges the gap between the interface designer and the user.

Keyword Codes: H.5.2; I.2.4
Keywords: User Interfaces; Knowledge Representation

1. INTRODUCTION

With the wide utilization of interactive information systems, human-computer interaction (HCI) is becoming a dominant factor that determines the success or failure of software system. Dividing the interactive system into two components: computational part and dialogue part is now widely accepted among interface researchers [1]. Dialogue part is becoming so complex that the design of it must be guided by special guidelines, and made by special designers.

This paper proposes an open model for user interfaces. It divides interactive systems into six layers: I/O Media, Concept, Semantic/Syntax, Domain, Mode/Style, and Computation, and uses the knowledge to represent the functions of each layer. The rationale of the open model is:
-- *Open*: Much evidence has shown that the software industry requires urgently the software to be open. The open model of interfaces is our attempt to allow the interface open, and to make the interface have a consistent structure.
-- *Knowledge*: Using knowledge to represent the functions of interfaces narrows the distance between the interface designer and the user, makes the interface design more natural, and encourages repetitive refinement.

In Section 2, we firstly analyze how the user expresses his interaction intention and propose a User Presentation Model (UPM) to describe it. Based on UPM, in Section 3, we propose the open model of interfaces. Section 4 outlines the experimental interface KZ3/KJM. Some interesting issues such as integration of multi dialogue styles are discussed in the fifth section. Concluding remarks are also given in this section.

2. USER PRESENTATION MODEL

There are mainly three knowledge that the user owes in order to communicate with the computer:

task, how to express, how to do. The underlying purpose of the user interacting with the computer is to allow it to perform certain operations to complete a task. *Task knowledge* is the representation of those tasks. Based on the tasks, the user forms the dialogue intention. Usually, his intention is expressed through a sequence of user's actions that can be felt by the computers. *How to express knowledge* helps the user to select proper actions to express his intention, and how to perform the actions is described by *how to do knowledge*.

Understanding thoroughly *how to express knowledge* of the user is the basis for understanding his dialogue intention. User Presentation Model (UPM) is the framework proposed by us to represent *how to express knowledge*. It consists of five components: intention, decomposition, method, rule and action. *Intention* is the representation of the user's intention to perform one task. *Decomposition* describes how the user decomposes the intention into a sequence of concepts. *Method* depicts how to express certain concepts through an action sequence. *Rule* defines the conditions under which certain method can be applied. *Action* represents how to perform the basic physical actions. The inherent hierarchy underlying the process for the user to express his intention is illustrated from the above description (Figure 1).

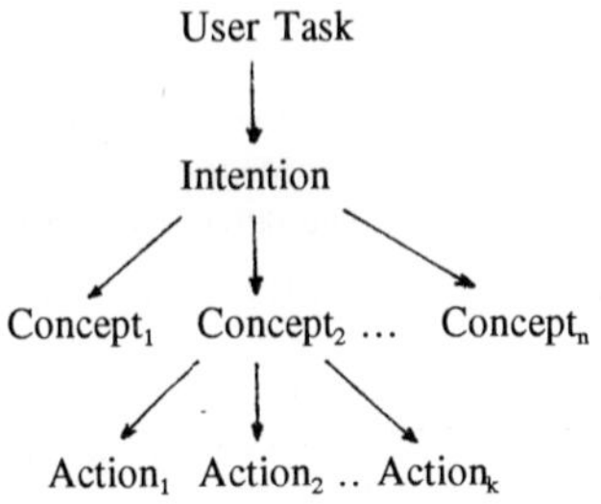

Figure 1. Hierarchy of the user to express his intention

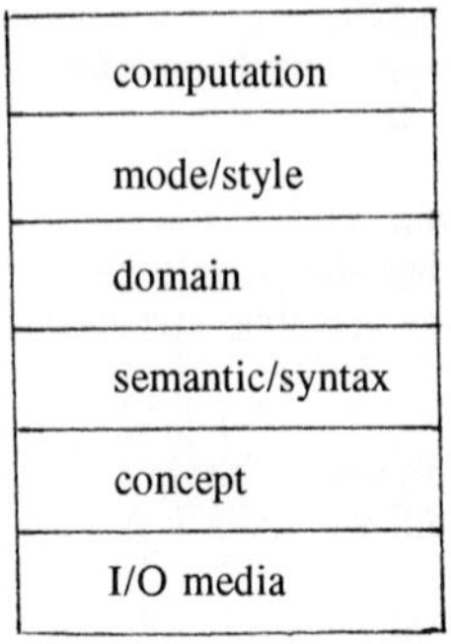

Figure 2. Open model structure

3. PHILOSOPHY OF OPEN MODEL

Based on UPM and our previous work [2], we propose the open model to study the inherent nature of interfaces, and build up a widely-applicable model to guide the design of human factor aspects of software.

3.1 Layered structure

According to the open model, an interactive system is divided into six layers (Figure 2).

I/O Media Layer This layer is responsible for the management of various input/output (I/O) devices, and realizing the mapping from the user's actions to the actions' internal forms.

Concept Layer Concept Layer analyzes which concepts an action or an action sequence refers to. The layer tries to know the underlying concepts of users' actions.

Semantic/Syntax Layer Extracting the meanings from concept sequences and representing the meanings in an internal language are the primary job of this layer.

Domain Layer It is usually not sufficient to merely have linguistic and world knowledge to understand the user's concepts. Domain Layer utilizes the domain knowledge to refine the semantic meanings extracted by Semantic/Syntax Layer and obtains the precise understanding.

Mode/Style Layer Applying application's interface specification knowledge, this layer converts the user's meanings into the operation sequence acceptable to the application.

Computation Layer Computation Layer is the application's functional parts. It executes the operation sequences to meet the user's requests.

3.2 Knowledge as its function specification

Knowledge is the core of the open model. Each layer is represented by its knowledge. The reasoning engine applies the knowledge to realize functions of each layer. Knowledge is used for developing and maintaining the interface. Any modification of knowledge would lead to the change of the interface.

I/O Media Knowledge concerns more closely with the hardware. It covers not only the devices drive knowledge but also how to represent actions and give primitive feedbacks. The former is usually provided by operating systems and represented procedurally. The latter is represented by rules which have the form:

action ==> notation:primitive feedbacks.

Following is one example of those rules:

click mouse middle button at (x y) ==> Mouse_Click_M(x y):Beep().

Concept Knowledge describes the relationship between the user's action sequences and concept sequences they refer to. Some context knowledge of the actions is also required. Consequently, the concept knowledge is represented by:

<action sequence> and <context conditions>
==> <concept sequence>:composite feedbacks.

For a dragging action, one of its concept knowledge is:

<MS_Drag_M(x1 y1)(x2 y2)> and
IN_BOUND((x1 y1) Icon(File)) ^ IN_BOUND((x2 y2) Icon(Trash))
==> <Delete File>:Highlight(Trash).

Semantic/Syntax Knowledge consists of two parts: semantic knowledge which defines the meanings of concepts, and syntax knowledge which describes the syntactic requirements about the user's inputs. Frame structures are adopted as the representing means. They describe precisely and concisely what the concept means and what the variables appeared in the description are. Following is part of the description about the concept Show:

```
(E_Frame  Concept_Name Show
     Variable_Set (Object Place)
     Constraints  IS_FILE_NAME(Object) ^ IS_POSITION(Place)
     Pre          EXIST(Object,Cp1) ^ -CAN_BE_SEEN(Cp1)
     Post         EXIST(Object,Place) ^ CAN_BE_SEEN(Place)
```

....).

The syntax knowledge presents the grammar of the user's requests. In order to allow different kinds of dialogue styles coexisted, we adopt the technique that is only concerned with what are the valid elements of the request rather than the order of them to represent the syntactic knowledge. This technique combines closely the semantic and syntax knowledge, and works well when processing simple requests.

Domain knowledge is expressed in predicates. For the Unix domain, the domain knowledge may include the following predicates:

CAN_BE_SEEN(Screen), IS_POSITION(Screen)

which indicate the facts that materials on Screen can be seen. Screen is position of Unix. But for Vi, it may have the predicate:

INTEGER(x) ^ INTEGER(y) ^ GREATER(x 0) ^ GREATER(y 0) ^
BELOW(x 1024) ^ BELOW(y 782) --> IS_POSITION((x y))

to define one position in Vi.

Mode/Style Knowledge describes applications interface knowledge. It reflects what the valid inputs of applications are. For a command line interface such as Unix, the knowledge about the command Cat looks like this:

```
(E_Frame C7   Comm_Name (Cat var)
              Constraints IS_FILE_NAME(var)
              Pre   EXIST(var,Disk)
              Post  EXIST(var,Screen)
              ....).
```

3.3 Layer specification

The messages passed between the layers of the open model are represented by layer specifications. There are five specifications available among the adjacent layers of the open model:

(1) Action Representation Notation (ARN) is a notation symbol set used to represent the user's actions. For example, if the user firstly moves the mouse from (20,30) to (70,80), types the letters A, this sequence of actions is represented by ARN:

MS_Move(20,30)(70,80) A.

Using this notation, we specify precisely the user's actions.

(2) Concept Specification (CS) is defined theoretically by two parts: a standard glossary of concept terminology, and a grammar through which concepts are grouped. Here the grammar may be very loose. Syntactic problems are to be solved by Semantic/Syntax Layer. So CS is simplified into a standard and extendable concept glossary.

(3) Any predicates pair which is composed of the system known predicates and constants with the first predicates describing the preconditions of the user's request and the second presenting the postconditions of the request is considered as the form of Meaning Specification. If there are variables appearing in the predicates, it is called Rough-Meaning Specification (RMS). In contrary, it is termed Precise-Meaning Specification (PMS).

(4) Application Interface Specification (AIS) presents what forms of inputs satisfy with the

application interface requirements and are the valid inputs of the application. For example, if the application is Unix, AIS is Unix command specification and the specification for the command "list filename" -- ls is:
ls [-aAcCdfFgilLqrRstu] filename.

4. EXPERIMENTAL SYSTEM KZ3/KJM

4.1 Overview of KZ3/KJM

Based on the open model, an experimental interface KZ3/KJM has been developed for Unix, and has the following distinctive functions:
-- *support multi media and styles input*. The user may use different input devices with different dialogue styles such as direct manipulation, menu, command and natural language to interact with Unix;
-- *user customization*. The interface may be modified and updated by the user through the change of each layer's knowledge;
-- *application customization*. Unix is not the only interface that can be supported by KZ3/KJM. By changing the domain knowledge, the user may use KZ3/KJM as other applications' interfaces.

KZ3/KJM is implemented in Common Lisp and C on Sun 4/260 workstation. It consists of
(1) 9 modules: Input Media Controller, Concept Extracting, Idea Understanding, Domain Refinement, Mode, Screen Layout, Interface Update, System-State Evaluator, and Knowledge Base Management ;
(2) 2 databases: System-State Description, Screen Description;
(3) 5 knowledge bases: each for one layer.
Messages passed among the modules are based on the layer specifications. (Figure 3)

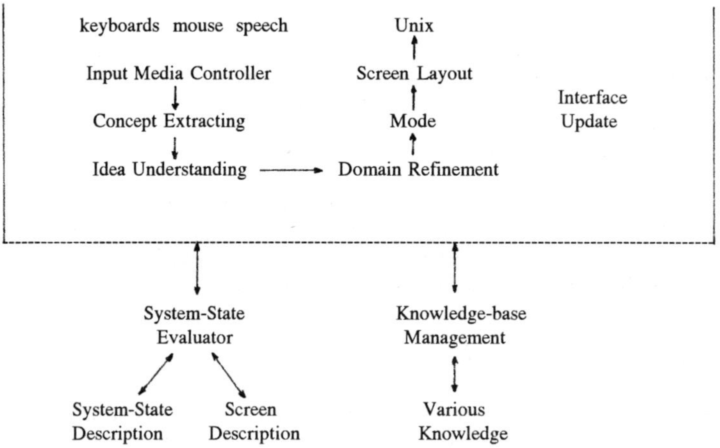

Figure 3. KZ3/KJM architecture

4.2 Case study

In this subsection, we illustrate how the open model and KZ3/KJM work by an example dialogue.
Example:

Purpose of user: see the content of the file ABC.

Actions of user: move the mouse to the icon EYE, click the middle button of the mouse, type in A B C through the keyboard, press ENTER key.

I/O Media Layer controls the operations of input devices, specifies those actions in ASN: <MS_Move(n/a n/a)(32 43) MS_Click_M(32 43) A B C Enter>.
Concept Layer finds that the action sequence of the following piece of knowledge:

Rule3: <MS_Move(n/a n/a)(x y) MS_Click_M(x y)>
and IN_BOUND((x y) ICON(Show))
==> <Show>:Display("show")

matches with <MS_Move(n/a n/a)(32 43) MS_Click_M(32 43)> and the context conditions are satisfied with the interpretation of the variable pair (X Y) with (32 43). Concept Layer obtains that the concept "Show" is what the user refers to by the mouse actions. Actions A B and C are converted into "ABC". The Enter means Req_Over. Consequently, the result of this layer is:

Show ABC Req_Over.

Semantic/Syntax Layer analyzes if the above CS meets the syntactic requirements about the user's input, then uses the semantic meanings of the concept "Show" which is described partly by pre and post conditions of this concept:

Pre: EXIST(Object, Cp1) ^ -CAN_BE_SEEN(Cp1)
Post: EXIST(Object,Cp2) ^ CAN_BE_SEEN(Cp2)

to achieve the rough understanding (RMS) of the user's request by substituting ABC for Object:

Pre: EXIST(ABC, Cp1) ^ -CAN_BE_SEEN(Cp1)
Post: EXIST(ABC,Cp2) ^ CAN_BE_SEEN(Cp2).

Within Domain Layer, there are some facts represented by predicates about the concepts in the domain (Unix):

CAN_BE_SEEN(Screen), CAN_BE_SEEN(Printer),
-CAN_BE_SEEN(Disk), -CAN_BE_SEEN(Tape).

According to those predicates, Domain Layer interprets Cp1 and Cp2 in RMS and gets the precise meanings expressed by PMS:

(1) Pre EXIST(ABC,Tape) (2) Pre EXIST(ABC,Disk)
Post EXIST(ABC,Screen) Post EXIST(ABC,Screen)
(3) Pre EXIST(ABC,Tape) (4) Pre EXIST(ABC, Disk)
Post EXIST(ABC,Printer) Post EXIST(ABC,Printer).

The ambiguity of the user's request results in the four possible PMSs (1), (2), (3) and (4).

Mode/Style Layer employs the Unix (SunOS) application interface knowledge to process (1), (2), (3) and (4) respectively and converts them into Unix commands or command sequences if required. For (2) and (4), Mode/Style Layer uses the knowledge about the command Cat and Lp:

(E_Frame C2 (E_Frame C8
Comm_Name (Cat var) Comm_Name (Lp var)
Pre EXIST(var,Disk) Pre EXIST(var,Disk)
Post EXIST(var,Screen)) Post EXIST(var,Printer))

to directly get the corresponding commands: Cat ABC and Lp ABC. But for (1) and (3), command sequences are needed. Mode/Style Layer utilizes goal-oriented deduction [3] to form the command sequences. For (1), using C2 and C13:

(E_Frame C13
Comm_Name (Tar xvf /dev/rst0 var)

Pre EXIST(var,Tape)
Post EXIST(var,Disk))
Mode/Style Layer infers the command sequence: <Tar xvf /dev/rst0 ABC; Cat ABC>, and for (3): <Tar xvf /dev/rst0 ABC; Lp ABC>. Finally, those commands are executed by Computation Layer.

5. DISCUSSION AND CONCLUDING REMARKS

5.1 Discussion

Multi-interaction styles such as natural language, command line and direct-manipulation can be used simultaneously. These styles are transparent to semantic and above layers because the concept layer realizes the mapping from actions to concepts. It not only allows the mixed use of several dialogue styles between user's requests but also permits its use among one request.

According to the open model, the interface is divided into layers and each layer is represented by its knowledge source. Domain Layer and Model/Style Layer are closely connected with the application the interface serves for. Changing those two layers' knowledge means the same as changing the application it can serves. So the open model interface has a high portability (domain independence).

Nielsen [4] proposed a layered description of HCI from a linguistic perspective. It has some limitation on describing wider range of interaction. Tayler [5] presented "layered protocols" to provide a descriptive framework to the design of interfaces in a principled way, which came from the concepts that HCI can be designed on level of abstraction.

5.2 Concluding remarks

This paper proposes an open model for HCI which provides a layered framework for interface design. It makes the interface design more efficient and natural. Designers may use modular approach to constructing interfaces. The natural integration of different dialogue styles makes the interface more powerful, and the declarative knowledge representation enables the interface adaptable and encourages repetitive refinement. The experimental interface KZ3/KJM has shown the bright future of the open model.

REFERENCES

1 Ehrich, R.W., and Hartson, H.R. DMS -- An environment for dialogue management. Proceedings of COMPCON 81. IEEE, NewYork, (1981) P. 121.

2 Xie, L. and Du, X. An Approach to General Intelligent Interface for HCI. Proceedings of the 3rd International Conference on Human-Computer Interaction, (1989) 853-860.

3 Wos, L., Overbeek, B., Lusk, E. & Boyle, J. Automated Reasoning: Introduction and Applications. Englewood Cliggs, N.J. (1984).

4 Nielsen, J. A virtual protocol model for computer-human interaction. International Journal of Man-Machine Studies, 24, (1986) 301-312.

5 Tayler, M. M. Layered protocols for computer-human dialogue. International Journal of Man-Machine Studies, 28, (1988) 175-257.

Personal Computers and Intelligent Systems / F.H. Vogt (Editor)
Information Processing 92, Volume III
Elsevier Science Publishers B.V. (North-Holland)

Modelling Interaction of Blind People Using Graphical User Interfaces

Gerhard Weber

Institut für Informatik, Universität Stuttgart and F.H. Papenmeier GmbH, Breitwiesenstr. 20-22, D-7000 Stuttgart 80, F.R. Germany

Abstract

Blind users have access to standard application programs with text-based user interfaces either by a speech synthesizer or by a braille display. But graphical user interfaces are inaccessible to blind users due to pixel-based coloured output.

Our approach for including non-visual media into a user interface is to define a language for modelling (existing) user interfaces. Such a language consists of several types of graphical screen objects, their dynamic properties and access methods to additional output devices. An event-based language is studied to identify its properties for modelling interaction through multiple input devices.

A pilot study has been implemented that allows combined speech and braille feedback for mouse movements while simultaneous keyboard interaction is still possible. For the first time pixel-based text has been made accessible to blind users in an interactive manner. Testing this implementation with blind users can give insight into possible adaptations of complex graphical user interfaces.

Keyword Codes: I.5.4; K.8.0
Keywords: Blind Users; Pattern Recognition, Application; Personal Computing

1. INTRODUCTION

Among the people with special needs are blind people a small user group. Nonetheless blind people have pioneered in recent years use of natural speech output and tactile displays in their professional work. While sighted users more and more are accepting talking clocks and talking calculators tens of thousands of work places for blind people have been equipped either with speech synthesizers capable of an unlimiterd vocabulary or displays showing braille. Thereby blind users become able to work with standard application software.

The concepts of adding to existing user interfaces designed for sighted users non-visual output devices are not appropiate for every type of user interface. Especially graphical user interfaces as found in workstations and increasingly in PCs are inaccessible to blind users (see Vanderheiden89 and Stephanidis91).

While blind users are unable to operate a CAD program due to its graphical nature, blind users are also unable to create text with a WYSIWYG text editor, and similarily they are unable to complete forms in a database retrieval software if these applications are running under a graphical user interface. Especially reading and simultaneously pointing are not possible for blind users listening to speech or reading a line-based braille display (see Weber89).

Closing this gap is not only possible by using better features of acoustic or tactile output devices but by adapting the dialogue in a flexible way through modelling the interaction between user and computer. This requires to develop a conceptual solution for the design of future multimedia user interfaces already including mechanisms not only to generate non-visual output but also to integrate visual output with non-visual output in a more refined way compared to what is possible with current multimedia user interfaces.

2. ADDING A BRAILLE DISPLAY

Originally, braille was created to directly substitute every french character by a pattern of touchable raised bulbs. This 6-dot braille is a notation with at most 64 characters. When taking into account foreign alphabets language specific notations become necessary. Additionally several braille characters are corresponding to more than one ink print character (see Fig. 1a and for 8-dot braille Fig. 1b).

Figure 1: Examples of a) 6-dot and b) 8-dot braille

6-dot braille is used by blind people when writing on paper. Paperless braille ("soft") displays as installed frequently in Europe and in Canada are 8-dot Braille displays showing one line of text. Every character displayed on the screen is directly translated into its tactile counterpart.

The state of art in braille displays is either a hardware-based or a software-based mechnism to periodically copy the contents of one line of the screen to the braille display (actually the copy mechanism looks at the part of the memory that stores the characters shown on the screen). It is up to the user to decide wether he wants to read the information shown on a braille display or wether he wants to continue typing on the keyboard.

Figure 2 shows as an example the screen contents created by the editing program WORD. Among the screen objects shown on the screen are the cursor and text with attributes (colour combinations, especially *inverted*). The counterpart of the cursor is a braille character with all dots raised. Colour and other attributes of text cannot be combined with braille characters. This information is thus hidden from the user while text is read.

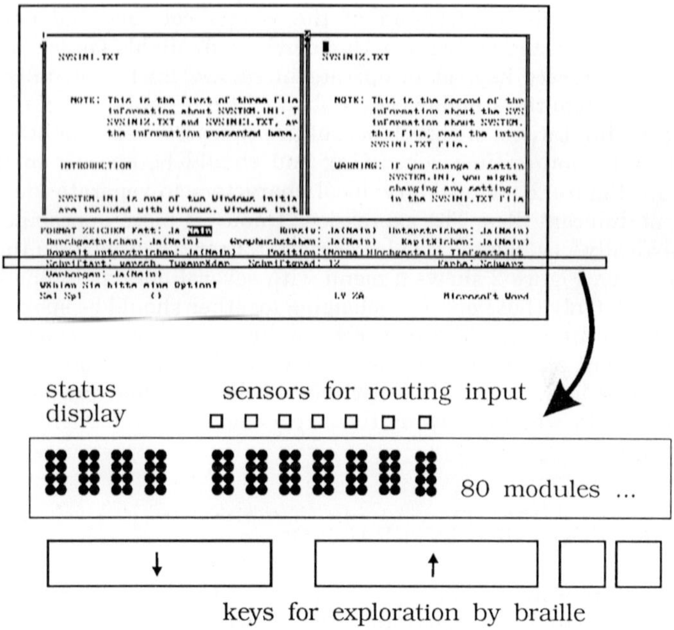

Figure 2: Braille displays show one line of text

Modern braille displays have additionally to the standard keyboard a set of keys to allow the user to explore the screen contents line by line independently of the application program (see also Figure 2). Thus they have their own seperate user interface and require the user to spend time for interacting with it. Part of this functionality is for example to allow to extract just the attributes of each character instead of the character itself.

3. ADDING A SPEECH SYNTHESIZER

Synthetic speech is an acoustic output medium. When adding a speech synthesizer to a standard application program time for listening to the presentation is added to that time spent for interaction with the computer. Any spoken information has to be carefully selected not to overload this acoustic channel and not to slow down the user.

A screen review program is extending the operating system to accomplish this task. Similarily to a braille display the user interacts solely with this program in a *review mode* for exploration of the screen contents independently of the application program. Only a few commercially available speech review programs require a seperate keypad to operate in review mode - usually the review is handled through the standard keyboard.

One of the limitations of speech output are characters of graphical nature since a verbal desription is time consuming and should be specific to the application program. Figure 2 includes graphical characters to separate views of the same file or of different files. The expression "frame" is more appropiate than "double line vertically", or "double line lower right corner" to pronounce these characters. Additionally, Figure 2 shows a menu with several options in one line which can be selected. Only those options belonging together should be spoken.

To add to this text editor a speech synthesizer a screen review program needs to know about screen objects like windows and menus in order to identify those portions of a line the user is expecting to belong to this view or to this option of the menu both when reviewing the screen contents and when working with the editor.

4. CHARACTERIZING INTERACTION

The design of input and ouput devices is a technological issue. Working with an application program is an interaction between the user and the computer. The dialogue can be initiated by the computer (eg. in pop-up menus) or by the user (eg. in command languages). Each style of interaction needs to be adapted for a blind user.

Dialogue focus is the place on the screen that needs to be perceived to continue in interacting with the computer. It might be not at all necessary to look resp. touch the display to continue, so there is no dialogue focus defined. Consequently the display needs not to be updated and no word needs to be spoken. In a dialogue controlled by the computer the dialogue focus is determined by the application program. In a dialogue controlled by the user the dialogue focus is determined by the user's input.

Tracking is a functionalitiy of the adaptation of a user interface for blind users to determine, follow and display the dialogue focus[1]. Usually the dialogue focus is an area including the area where feedback for the next input operation will be given (the next dialogue focus). But for example a review mode allows to leave the orignal spot on the screen where the dialogue focus was considered to be. This new dialogue focus is possibly disjunct from the previous dialogue focus.

---

[1] This is also applicapable to screen enlargement devices for people with low vision

Routing is an interaction method that produces input for the application to map the application's dialogue focus with the dialogue focus as specified by the user when being in review mode. Routing is considered as an interaction method for sighted users when eye-tracking is possible (see Jacob90).

Cursor tracking refers to tracking the cursor. The size of the dialogue focus varies from one character, one word, to the total number of the braille modules. A screen review program either spells each character individualy, or speaks a word completely.

Some applications use the cursor as built into the hardware of the display unit. This cursor is commonly called the hardware cursor and can be determined very accurately. It is possible that there are more cursors defined in an application and the size of the cursor may vary. A soft cursor is then described by the changes the user has achieved.

Cursor routing refers to routing of the cursor. It is possible that the cursor cannot be routed to every place on the screen. Even in full-screen text editors it is for example not possible to place the cursor on a line containing status information. Routing is usually performed by artificially generating keystrokes for cursor movements.

Mouse tracking refers to tracking the mouse pointer. Additionally special care has to be taken to give feedback for a change of the mouse pointer's shape, that is if the dialogue focus is the mouse pointer itself. A change of the pointer's shape indicates the new functionality of the mouse. For this change an appropiate feedback has to be generated.

Mouse routing refers to routing the mouse pointer. This term is currently only applicapable in a textual environment. The mouse pointer corresponds in a textual environment always to one character and not to a single pixel. Routing of the mouse pointer is usually possible to any place on the screen. Routing is performed by changing the functionality of the mouse interface or if possible using the features of the mouse interface. Mouse routing introduces no additional functionalitiy of the mouse. Klicking of mouse buttons is still necessary[2].

5. ADAPTING GRAPHICAL USER INTERFACES

As introduced in the beginning there is a need to adapt graphical user interfaces for blind users. Even in a textual environment are interaction methods on the basis of windows, scroll bars and buttons possible. Adapting graphical user interfaces implies a refined model of screen objects compared to the simple model on the basis of lines containing characters and words. A language is necessary to describe when non-visual output is produced for which operation of the application program resp. which kind of input of the user.

Modelling the user interface has been studied already in the light of finding formal methods for the construction, description and evaluation of user interfaces

---

[2] Mouse routing is still under investigation by most manufacturers of braille displays

(see Farooq88 for an overview). A formal rule-based model described by a Event Reponse Language (ERL) has been implemented by Hill (see Hill86) for a drawing program. We use this language in the following sections.

Each production in ERL consists on the left side of a rule of an event (or explicitly *no event* (denoted by ---) and a (possibly empty) list of *states*. The antecedent of a rule can assign *values* to components of states, *set* a state or send *output events*.

Evaluation of rules is done in the following way: a rule is applicable if its event has been originated and all states are set. Only then the antecedent is interpreted which in turn can set states. Rules are examined in parallel whether they are applicable. If the conditional part of a rule has been accepted its states are reset.

One of the advantages of ERL is that simultaneous input of mouse and keyboard can be expressed. In a procedural language mouse input can be incorpated only by defining all those screen objects in advance at which the mouse pointer could arrive in order to call the appriate procedure when it actually reaches a screen object's position (see e.g. Jacob86)

6. GRABRA - A PILOT STUDY

Braille and speech for output combined with all above described input devices (keyboard, mouse, keys for exploration, and routing input) can improve accessabilty to user interfaces for blind users. A study has been undertaken at the University of Stuttgart in close cooperation with the company Papenmeier to evaluate together with blind users such an approach.

As an application has been choosen WORD 5.0 for DOS. WORD is tought for example in the local school for the blind. WORD is assisting mouse input, preview of the text layout, and a graphics mode to show fonts with different typefaces.

A blind user can use WORD since all word processing features are accessible by keyboard-based interaction. Nevertheless, it marks a change in the design of user interfaces towards graphical user interfaces (see Stephanidis91). Blind people do not have access to the graphical features of WORD - although they were built into the product to improve efficency of the dialogue with WORD.

GRABRA is addressing the graphics mode of WORD, implements cursor tracking, mouse tracking and mouse routing. The configuration of our setup consists of a speech synthesizer, a braille display, a pixel-based screen and at the same time a text-based screen. This two-monitor approach is important for graphical user interfaces as a sighted co-worker needs to know what the blind user "sees" at any time.

To recognize graphical characters a pattern matcher compares the result of an ideal scan on the pixel-based screen with a set of pretrained fonts. This training includes several optimization steps. Thereby the pattern matcher becomes fast enough to allow normal speed of typing on a fast PC.

GRABRA performs cursor tracking on the braille display by updating the position of the cursor or by updating the dialogue focus. Mouse tracking, is performed on the braille display in the same way but simultaneousely each new word is spoken the mouse points to. If the movement of the mouse is too fast to speak each word completely there are two possibilities:

- prevent the speech synthesizer from completing the current word and start with the new word, or
- let the speech synthesizer complete the current word and suppress the new word.

The second approach has been implemented in GRABRA, additionally while the user listens to the verbal output a non-verbal sound is generated through the built-in speaker. We use ERL for partial documentation of cursor and mouse tracking by identifying the events, the data structures describing the screen contents and by ERL productions. The following events are used:
INT16 - WORD has polled the keyboard
KEY_RELEASE - the user has releases a key
INDEX - a spoken utterance has been completed
LINE and ROUTING - review or routing keys of the braille display were typed
The following screen objects are used: The screen is described by lines and frames for text, menu, and preview area. Frames are configured in a configuration file. We are referring to this data structure with line numbers to translate a pixel-based screen to a line of text. One of the three frames is referred to by the variable *actual_frame*. The following are some of the rules implemented in GRABRA:

```
INITIALLY →         Keyboard↑
INT16  Keyboard →   Keyboard_Tick ↑
                    Mouse_Tick ↑
                    Keyboard ↑
KEY_RELEASE  →  Keyboard ↑
--- Keyboard_Tick  → determine cursor_y, cursor_x and actual_frame
                    translate line at cursor_y from graphics to text
                    set cursor attribute at cursor_x, cursor_y
INDEX Mouse_Tick →    last_spoken_index = INDEX.value
                          Mouse_Tick↑
--- Mouse_Tick  →  determine mouse position (mouse_x, mouse_y)
                    translate line at mouse_y from graphics to text
                    determine word around screen[mouse_x, mouse_y]
                    if (word_index > last_spoken_index) then { generate sound}
                    else {  inc(word_index)
                              send word_index and word to speech synthesizer }
```

Using this approach it is possible to explore a preview of the final text layout generated by the editor with the mouse and simultaneously to type on the keyboard while the dialogue focus is adjusted according to the above rules.

7. CONCLUSION

Both braille displays and multi-lingual speech synthesizers with an unlimited vocabulary are used by blind people to get access to application programs with a textual user interface. An event driven interpretation of a computable model of the screen objects and of their dynamic behaviour allows to monitor the activities of the original user interface even if two-handed input from keyboard and mouse has to be accepted. With GRABRA an implemenation of an adaptation of a graphical user interface can be evaluated with blind users.

8. ACKNOWLEDGEMENTS

Prof. Gunzenhäuser and Mr. Bornschein made this pilot study possible. Mr. Kochanek and Mr. Recker programmed different versions of the pattern matcher.

9. REFERENCES

Farooq, Mohammad; Dominick, W.D.: A survey of formal tools and models for developing user interfaces, Int. Journal of Man - Machine Studies, No. 29, (1988) 479-496.

Hill, Ralph D.: Supporting Concurrency, Communication and Synchronization in Human - Computer Interaction - The Sassafras UIMS, ACM Transactions on Graphics, Vol. 5, No. 3 (1986) 179 - 210.

Jacob, Robert J.K.: What you look at is what you get: eye movement-based interaction techniques, Proceedings CHI 90, ACM (1990) 11-18.

Jacob, Robert J.K.: A specification language for direct-manipulation user interfaces, ACM Transactions on Graphics, Vol. 5, No. 4 (1986) 283-317.

Schwerdtfeger, Richard S.: Making the GUI talk, BYTE, Dec 1991, 118-128

Stephanidis, C; Weber, G., et. al.: Access to Graphical User Interfaces by Blind people, Royal National Institute for the Blind: London, 1991.

Vanderheiden, Gregg C.: Non-visual alternative display techniques for output from graphics-based computers, Journal of Visual Impairment & Blindness, No. 83 (1989) 383-390.

Weber, G.: Reading and pointing - modes of interaction for blind users, in G.X.Ritter (ed.) Information Processing '89, Elsevier Science Publishers: Amsterdam (1989) 535-540.

Personal Computers and Intelligent Systems / F.H. Vogt (Editor)
Information Processing 92, Volume III
Elsevier Science Publishers B.V. (North-Holland)

N/JOY - An Object Oriented System of Office Workbenches: Tools instead of Menus

G. Haring and M. Tscheligi

Vienna User Interface Group, Department of Applied Computer Science, Institute of Statistics and Computer Science, University of Vienna, Lenaugasse 2/8, 1080 Wien, Email.: A4424daf@awiuni11.bitnet

Abstract

Office environments can be seen as a network of configurable office workbenches, where each workbench is adapted according to the task requirements and the user prerequisites by parameterizable tools. The paper describes the design philosophy of a software system with a high quality second generation user interface and its realization (N/JOY), supporting these characteristics. Instead of menus, which do not exist at all in the system, the functionality of the system is represented to the user by interacting tool objects, which can be configured according to the task to be performed and which were designed using a real life look metaphor, guaranteeing, that the user immediately recognizes them when the user sees them and additionally understands their meaning. The concept of interconnected office workbenches is the basis for a fully cooperative work environment for highly interrelated office tasks in a physically distributed system.

Keyword Codes: H.1.2; H.5.2
Keywords: User/Machine Systems; User Interfaces

1. INTRODUCTION

Office activities in any business organization can be seen as a network of interacting and communicating office workbenches. Each workbench can be dedicated to specific tasks performed by members of the organization according to their capabilities and skills, using task adequate tools. These tools can be seen as functionality most appropriately casted into a specific form. Examples of such office tools are pencils, sheets of paper, copy machines, etc. Some of the tools are general ones, which can be applied in the execution of many different tasks, other tools are specialized ones for a single tasks. Of course the efficient usage of a tool requires a certain knowledge of it, its behaviour and interaction with the user. Therefore each tool on an office workbench should be adapted to the task to be performed and if possible to the knowledge level of its user (tool parameterization and configuration).

According to this characterization each software system which is designed to realize office functionality has to respect in its user interface the following aspects. *Connectivity* of office workbenches is supported. The user interface should enable the user to profit from existing workbench interconnections. Especially the user has the possibility to move between different workbenches in a flexible manner. In addition the user can transfer tools from one workbench to another. *Tools* exist in an explicit way on each workbench. The use of menus distracts the user unnecessarily from task performance as our experience from the observation of user behaviour has shown. An alternative approach is the total renunciation of menus and the realization of functionality by a collection of interacting objects. *Creation* and *adaptation* of tools and workbenches is supported by the user interface. According to the specific task and user requirements the whole environment can be flexibly realized in different instances and with adjusted behaviour parameters. *Real life look* is the metaphor to be used to represent all parts of the environment. This should guarantee that the user immediately recognizes the tools when the user sees them and additionally the user understands their meaning, their manipulation and their effects.

An existing example of a system with a high quality user interface is N/JOY, the world of objects, which was developed to realize the coexistence of word processing, graphics, database and spreadsheet functionality in a uniform and consistent interaction style. In the following sections the product specific accomplishment of the above mentioned office workbench requirements is described. Section 2 introduces the concept of rooms and doors. Section 3 gives insight into existing tools for the office workbench. Section 4 describes the parameterization of the environment. In section 5 the systematic usage of the real life as the leading metaphor for the development is discussed. The final section 6 is dedicated to an outlook to future research and its transfer to upcoming product versions.

2. WORKBENCH CONNECTIVITY

N/JOY extends the well known office metaphor (with objects on and around the desktop) to an office building metaphor and beyond that to all objects of real life. The office building acts as the framework of all tools and so as the container of all installed workbenches.

The presentation of an office building immediately gives the user the intended user model: the tasks are carried out in the usual work environment. The user has to enter the building containing the office by opening the main door. Thereby an identification password may be asked corresponding to the key of the door. Behind the entrance the user may find a corridor with some further doors. One is the exit leading out of the office building. The others may be entries to different workbenches. There is nothing uncommon in this corridor; it is just a room in the building as every further room behind any of the presented doors. The doors act as an explicit visualization of the connectivity mechanism between different workbenches (Figure 1). In technical terms the user changes to his working directory, knowing nothing about directories, subdirectories, commands to change a directory or established links. The doors may be locked with different keys to install access rights. The door label can be altered in a direct manipulative style by simply clicking on it and typing.

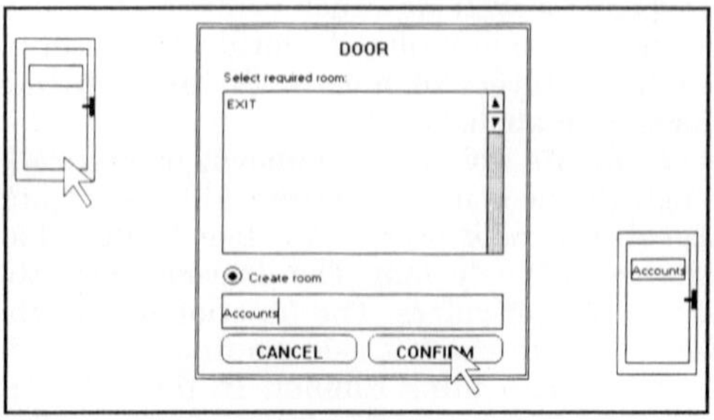

Figure 1. Doors

In this system the user is enabled to build rooms and doors, connecting rooms as desired. A door always connects two rooms. If a new door from one room to a target room is built, this certainly results also in a door from the target room to the starting room. Rooms are the framework of all workbench tools and can be equiped according to the special requirements and tasks of the user by the simple placement of necessary tools in the particular room. So a special room for calculation tasks can be installed or a room only acts as archive. The generation of rooms with restricted tool availability is no problem. If the system is used by more than one user each staff member gets one or more rooms.

The user also has the possibility to transfer tools from one workbench to another workbench by simply dragging the tool in question to the door representing the target workbench. So a special tool adjustment can also has its influence in other workbenches. Beside the transfer of the original instance of an tool it is a matter of course to transfer copies of that tool.

The concept of office building, rooms and doors can be used for a networked environment with no additional learning effort for the user already familiar with the system. The primary navigation style of this system can also be extended to the outside of the office building, where other buildings could stand for the fulfillment of other tasks.

3. TOOLS

All functionality in N/JOY is packaged in tools represented as autonomous and manipulable objects lying on the screen. This results in an explicitly represented model world, where the user manipulates mentally as well as physically well defined objects with intuitive understandable manipulation primitives. All functions are integrated into the model world and presented to the user as objects having equal rights. The user does not make a distinction between a manipulated world and a manipulator world. The manipulator world is usually a menu bar which is used in all comparable systems.

We completely omit global menu bars as well as other common forms of menus. Menus are a feature external to a manipulated world. The user is liberated from searching through multiple layers of menus. So in particular troublesome imperative commands have been abolished.

A typical working situation (room) with its inventory is shown in Figure 2. The user has entered the room through the door in the upper right corner and can also leave the working room through this door. Below the door lies the tool catalog which contains all tools available in the system. The drawer below the catalog may contain various tools like pencils or rulers. The functionality of the printer, copier and trash can is self-evident. On the left side we find some pads with the stationery needed, some pencils, and a filing cabinet. In the center of the room the user manipulates a document which remained open from the last working session. In the document a bar of the bar chart is manipulated directly.

In the following the semantic of these and some other tools are described in little more detail. The central tool of N/JOY is the document. The document consists of pages. On these pages text, matrix and graphic frames can be established. To visualize the creation possibility of documents, pads are used. Activating the pad a new document is coming into existence. The frames in the document are presented by small slips of paper. These paper slips can be recognized by an image on the pad. To distinguish the slip pads from other pads this image is used and slip pads have a different size (Figure 3). Folder and cabinets are used to put aside documents unused at the moment. As another possibility for the placement of tools a drawer can be used.

The delete function is presented by a trash can. The trash can in this system does not only delete text but also works for every available tool. As already mentioned a copy machine is used for the duplication of tools and a printer for printing documents. As special feedback a sheet of paper is shown on top of the printer if the printer is active. Another machine is used for the production of pads: the printing machine. With the printing machine the user is able to create pads out of documents, the user wishes to use as a form.

Another special object of this system is the pencil. A pencil acts as representative for the bundling of specific text attributes (see Figure 4 for document with an active pencil - shown slanted in the system - and one other pencil) . The attributes are selected by means of a dialogbox and are shown within the pencil representation. The color of the pencil corresponds to the color of the text the pencil is going to write. To use different text styles the necessary pencils are lying around the document. So often used pencils are immediately available. To change the text style a click on the pencil needed will work. As an important characteristic of the usage of pencils the user is able to work with a selected text style as long as the user holds the same pencil in his hand. This improves the mode of interaction used by common text processors, where the system always continues to write with the attributes of the character before the next text insertion position.

To represent the search function we decided to use a special trained dog, a retriever (Figure 3). The dog can be adjusted to specific search strings. Several dogs with several search strings searching for different search strings are possible as we see later. Import and export features are not necessary in the manual fulfillment of tasks, but they are an integral part of almost all office oriented software systems.

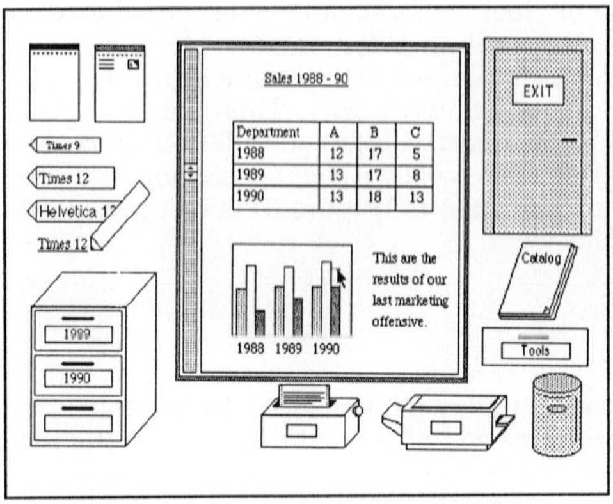

Figure 2. A typical working room

Figure 3 . Some tools

Help is offered to the user by a special help tool. The user gets general help by activating the help object. If another tool is marked before, tool specific help is shown. The help tool can be adjusted to show various levels of help. An error tool contains the last error which occurred in the system and which is of interest to the user. A signal lamp (Figure 3) visualizes the occurrence of an error. If the user knows what is going wrong, the user does not has to take care of this situation. If the user is interested in the error condition the error tool can be opened and so the user gets a corresponding message. The behaviour of this and other tools is designed not to burden the user with obtrusive system messages.

4. CREATION AND ADAPTION

The source for new objects in N/JOY is the catalog. The catalog contains all objects available in the system. With this tool the user can "order" tools in any number from the system according to requirements and preferences. With the tools selected from the catalog the general user (a user without locked access to a catalog) can arrange the office workbench according to personal requirements. If additional tools are introduced by later enhancements of the product they can simply be integrated into the old catalog or another new catalog is available to explicitly visualize the existence of new product features. Catalogues may also be adjusted to different user classes.

New tool instances are dragged out of the catalog. Multiple instances of the same tool type can exist simultaneously and can be parameterized by means of the dialogbox primitive with special value settings. So the above mentioned set of pencils can be installed or there are more than one printer representing several physical print devices. The principle of parameterization [1] holds for all available tools in the system. With this feature, which enables the user to prepare the tools in advance, the user will not be distracted during task performance by permanent cycles of tool adjustment. The possibility of parameterization is the prerequisite to work without menus. All functional features of traditional menu styles are accomplished with parameterizable tools.

Tools can be colored by the user in an arbitrary way. This feature is very important for tools of the same type to distinguish between different instances. With the color an easy distinction between the tools without special labels can be established. To accomplish this task a color palette (Figure 3) is integrated into the system.

5. REAL LIFE LOOK

The daily real life acts as a special and well known system realization (metaphor) to support the user in the formation of a mental model for the new system. The whole functionality is offered by objects the user knows from the usual activity. The real life is the metaphor used to map the functionality of the system to visible objects, attributes of objects and relations among objects. The real life metaphor can be regarded as generalization of the well known desktop metaphor, whereby the used associations are extended to the whole office environment and further to all objects of daily life. So for example the internal view of a folder is designed according an often used substructure: using interleafs (Figure 5).

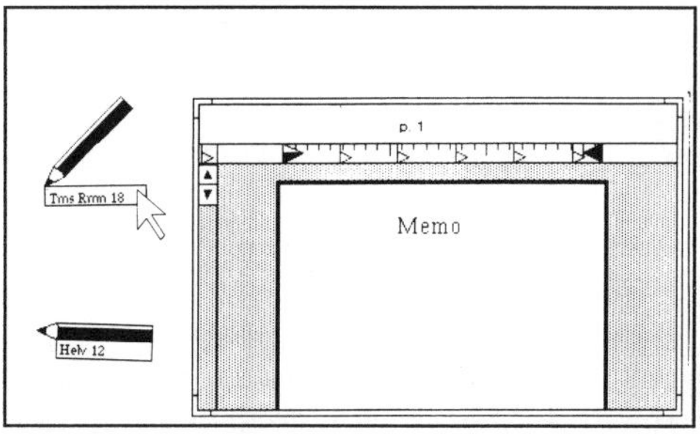

Figure 4. Pencils

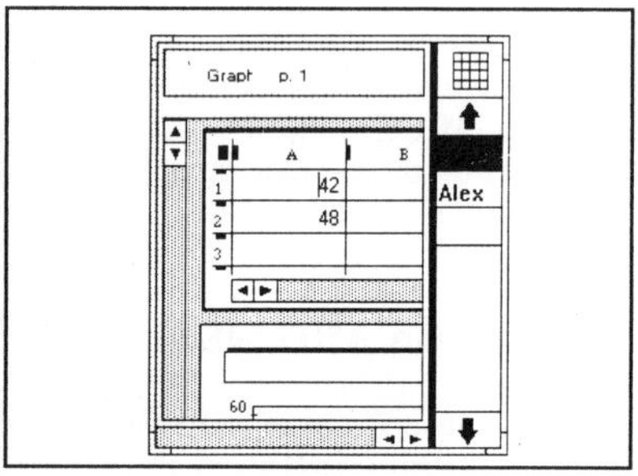

Figure 5 . Open folder

Some authors tried to integrate characteristics of daily life into their systems. The Alternate Reality Kit [2, 3] simulates real physical processes. Card and

Henderson introduced the room model [4], where doors are used to change between different workspaces in the context of a window system. In all these systems only some system functions are transfered to the user by associations to real life, but they do not proclaim a general user interface philosophy.

6. CONCLUSION AND FUTURE RESEARCH

The power of PC-based systems depends on the degree of adaptability of the software tools to task requirements and user profiles. The paper presented the design philosophy of the user interface of an existing software system (N/JOY) and its realization as an available product, which fulfills these requirements. The basic idea was to represent the total office environment as a set of interconnected office workbenches.

Each office workbench can be configured with task specific tools. The functionality is represented by interacting tool objects, completely replacing a menu oriented use of the system. All parts of the environment are represented using the real life look metaphor, guaranteeing their immediate recognition by the user. The concept of interconnected office workbenches, realized by the room principle in N/JOY, makes the easy extendibility of the product into a fully cooperative work environment possible, where - according to the concept of interpersonal computing - different users in a physically distributed office environment can work on logically related workbenches in an interacting way. Ongoing research activity concerns the user interface problems in a fully interpersonal computing environment, e. g. concurrent access control and view definitions to the same document, consistency and coherence problems [5].

7. References

1 Penz, F., Manhartsberger, M., Tscheligi, M., Haring, G.: The power of parameterizable objects in modern user interfaces. In: Diaper, D. et al (Eds.) Human-computer-interaction- INTERACT´90, pp. 469-472. North-Holland, Amsterdam, 1990.

2 Smith, R. B.: The Alternate Reality Kit: An Animated Environment for Creating Interactive Simulations. In: Proceedings of the 1986 IEEE Workshop on Visual Languages, pp. 99-106. IEEE Computer Society Press, Los Alamitos, 1986.

3 Smith, R. B.:Experiences With The Alternate Reality Kit: An Example of the Tension between Literalism and Magic. In: Proceedings of the CHI+GI´87 Conference on Human Factors in Computing Systems and Graphics Interface, pp. 61-67. ACM, New York, 1987.

4 Card, S. K., Henderson, A., Jr.: A Multiple, Virtual-Workspace Interface to Support User Task Switching. In: Proceedings of the CHI+GI´87 Conference on Human Factors in Computing Systems and Graphics Interface, pp. 53-59. ACM, New York, 1987.

5 Ellis, C. A., Gibbs, S. J., Rein, G. L.: Groupware: Some Issues and Experiences. Communications of the ACM 34, 1, pp. 38-58 (1991).

Personal Computers and Intelligent Systems / F.H. Vogt (Editor)
Information Processing 92, Volume III
Elsevier Science Publishers B.V. (North-Holland)

Programming Environments for End-Users†

D. D. Cowan[a], R. Ierusalimschy[b] and T. M. Stepien[c]

[a,c]Computer Science Department and Computer Systems Group, University of Waterloo, Waterloo, Ontario, Canada, N2L 3G1

[b]Departamento de Informática, Pontifícia Universidade Católica, Gávea, 22453-Rio de Janeiro-RJ, Brazil

Abstract

Technological developments in programming languages and reusable software components have reached a stage where end-users may be able to build their own custom software systems. This paper describes the type of systems which end-users might construct and then presents requirements for language and system features for an end-user programming environment.

Keyword Codes: D.2.2; D.2.6
Keywords: Software Engineering, Tools and Techniques; Programming Environments

1. INTRODUCTION

As we move more closely to a symbolic economy, knowledge workers will require computer systems with access to databases and various analysis, simulation, modelling and visualization tools. Because of time requirements these knowledge workers will require access to "instant" software; they will not be able to wait for the lengthy software design and implementation cycle. Thus, knowledge workers as end-users should have access to a large repository of reusable application and user interface components, which can be "glued" or bound together into new configurations.

Smalltalk [2] was one of the first attempts to provide such a software technology and has made contributions to some of the programming concepts described in this paper. Other technologies for reusing software are usually based on a programming language and range from the shell languages prevalent on Unix systems to many of the new micro-based "object-oriented" systems such as HyperCard [3], Toolbook [4], Visual Basic [5], or Rexx [6]. Future systems may use more visual programming [7] or the approach used in NeXTstep [8] or in the work on demonstrational interfaces [9].

†A longer version of this paper is in [1].

We expect the technologies for reusing software will be based on the programming language paradigm for the foreseeable future as we make progress toward a more friendly method of combining software components. In this paper we examine the character of end-user programming (EUP) and the supporting language structures and environments.

2. CHARACTERISTICS OF END-USER PROGRAMMING (EUP)

The main distinguishing feature of EUP is the fact that the programmer and the user of a piece of software are usually the same person. Thus, the programmer can create a succession of experimental prototypes, since there should be minimal impact on other users.

End-users often use existing applications, features of the operating system and a glue language (also called a *command* or *script* language) to develop task-specific software. The end-user writes a program in the glue language to pass data among applications and send them commands. Many of these applications, are reusable components and have a well-defined programming interface or port, and/or their own scripting language. Thus, an application can often be fully operated both through the normal user interface and also with a set of language-based commands. Unfortunately, each application often has its own version of a script language thus making the end-user's programming task more difficult.

Many software applications also have a record function which allows the application to "memorize" the set of commands to perform a specific task. Creative use of this facility might allow many of these command sequences to be produced using a form of demonstrational programming.

A different approach which has met with considerable success is in the area of user interfaces. Although programming user interfaces is complex, the task can often be simplified immensely and transformed into a form of visual programming. Simplification occurs for two reasons; first, user interfaces are composed of a small number of different objects, and second, user interfaces are primarily visual in nature. Thus, EUP can be partially visual and yet still use the more traditional programming model where unavoidable. It is the authors' expectation that the traditional programming model will always be part of EUP, but its use will diminish as we discover how to modify the programming paradigm for various components of EUP tasks. Examples of systems which use this approach are HyperCard, Toolbook, and Visual Basic.

End-user programs can act as data-type transformers between two or more software systems. For example, consider a program which selects data from an SQL database to produce a graph or chart. The commands to the database will be in SQL and the results in a table, while the commands to the plotting package could be in the form of drawing commands with the data as a sequence of strings. Currently, an end-user program might copy the data from the database, transform the data into its new format, and then pass the data to the plotting program. Such an approach could impact performance in both space and time, since at some point three copies of the data exist, and the data has been transformed twice. In order to minimize copying, the interface to the plotting package should contain functions which would allow specification of the range and domain of the plot and would pass the package the y-coordinate for a given x-coordinate. The end-user program would transform these functions into equivalent database retrieval commands. This mechanism, outlined in Figure 1, requires that the function invocations in the end-user program be dynamically linked to the function bodies in the reusable components. One implementation of this concept is in the Dynamic Link Library (DLL) of Windows 3.0 [10].

```
select x,y from datatable where x < maximum
select count(x) from datatable
select max(y) from datatable
plot.range(maximum)
plot.domain(max(y))
i := 0
while i < count(x)
   select x,y from database
   plot.point(x,y)
   move to next x,y in database
endwhile
```

Figure 1. A Simple Transformer for the End-user Program

End-user programs also need dynamic or late binding. Consider a database containing a map stored as a large graph. Operations on the map are defined by a graph package with a graphical user interface. The graph package is independent of the access mechanism for the graphs, all the package requires are nodes, arcs and cost functions associated with the arcs. The graph package will display a portion of a map and allow operations such as selecting two points in order to compute the shortest path. This example introduces further complications. First, the graph package uses a portion of the graph for display purposes and a different portion of the graph to compute the shortest path; in both cases the entire map may not be necessary. Second, the entire application is operated from the user interface of the graph package rather than from the end-user program.

In this example, functions would be a better way to pass portions of the graph, since they can be requested on demand. Thus, the graph package should have a functional interface which allows requests for nodes, arcs and cost functions. The end-user program will contain transformation functions to change the request for nodes and arcs into suitable database requests. Since the end-user program and the graph package will be connected after the graph package is compiled and linked, there must be a method of dynamic binding which will connect the transformation functions to the function interface of the graph package. Figure 2 outlines the code for this example.

3. CHARACTERISTICS OF AN END-USER PROGRAMMING LANGUAGE

Years of experience and observation strongly support the contention that the requirements for end-user programming languages substantially differ from languages designed for other programming tasks. Most programs produced by end-users will be short initially, although they may grow to several hundred lines. End-users will be "amateur" programmers; we can not expect end-users to use a formal design cycle or programming concepts, such as encapsulation or inheritance, since their exposure to substantive training in programming may be minimal. Hence, we should protect end-users from many common programming mistakes. This "protection" can be built into the language and the programming environment.

```
-- Initialization
   bind graph.origin to origin
   bind graph.destination to destination
   bind graph.arcs to arcs
   bind graph.cost to cost

-- Transformer Functions
   function origin (x : arc)
      select x from arc_table
     y := arc_origin(x)
     return (y : node)
   endfunction
   function destination (x : arc)
     select x from arc_table
     y := arc_destination(x)
     return (y : node)
   endfunction
   function arcs (x : node)
     select x from node_table
     for all arcs
       append arc to arc_list
     return (y : arc_list)
   endfunction
   function cost (x : arc)
     select x from arc_table
     return (arc_cost : integer)
   endfunction
```

Figure 2. A Transformer Using Dynamic Binding

The procedural model is one which has evolved through the experience and seems to be natural to most users. Thus, we can expect end-users to choose an end-user programming language (EUPL) which is primarily procedural rather than functional.

3.1. Control Constructs

An EUPL should contain standard control constructs such as sequence, loop and choice. An EUPL should also support an event-driven model, since end-user programs will be activated by external programs such as those in a user interface or a device driver. The language should also contain some form of procedure.

Since programs written in an EUPL glue together reusable components, the programs must be able to communicate with these components using both synchronous and asynchronous communication. The ability to handle asynchronous events can be extended to any type of communication not just user interface input events.

Some function invocations in reusable components are related to function code in the end-user program. Thus, the language and its environment must be able to support some form of dynamic binding.

3.2. Types

The types of variables are often redundantly specified in declaration statements to assist with compile-time verification or static type-checking, and performance improvement. Since end-users are present during program operation to correct errors, the need to find errors at compile-time is significantly reduced. Also the end-user program is usually not in control during most of a computation and hence performance should not be an issue. Since introducing this redundancy adds complexity to the programming process with little or no gain in either compile-time or run-time performance, explicit declaration of types should be avoided in an EUPL.

Many programming languages use the concept of primitive types and then use them in different ways to create more complex type structures. The primitive types must be chosen carefully to be highly readable to the end-user. Moreover they must be completely abstracted from the underlying implementation. For example, an integer type which allows the manipulation of its constituent bits or overflows without warning, is not an appropriate representation. In the same vein the user should not be concerned with mundane issues such as memory allocation.

More complex notions such as abstract data types, classes and inheritance do not need to be accessible to the programmer. The concepts of inheritance and data encapsulation are motivated by software engineering arguments which are beyond the experience of most end-users. Motivating these concepts seems to be difficult, although a rationale may be discovered which can present these concepts in familiar terms.

3.3. Safety

The EUPL should be safe. It should be impossible to combine types and produce a nonsense result. Some form of either compile-time or run-time type checking should be part of the implementation. It also should not be possible for the program to leave the thread of control. For example, creating an undefined pointer should not be allowed. Of course we are assuming here that the reusable components are "correct" and do not create undefined pointer problems.

4. THE END-USER PROGRAMMING ENVIRONMENT

End-users will not in general create large programs; they are programming to make the environment in which they perform their current set of tasks more productive. In some sense the end-users will want to automate their access to computer tools they already use. Also from a programming point of view, the user and the programmer are identical, and so the distinction between compile-time and run-time becomes blurred. Both a compile-time and a run-time error are really forms of output, unlike a production system, where a run-time error is unacceptable.

4.1. Compile-time and Run-time Environment

Amateurs are more likely to make errors and wish to experiment with various programming constructs, in effect they are almost always in a learning and debugging mode. Timely feedback is important and the programming environment should support a fast edit-compile-run cycle for ease of experimentation.

Clear error diagnostics at both compile and run-time are obviously essential characteristics; the error should be described in a normal language and its location should determined as accurately as possible.

Run-time errors should only be generated by the end-user's code, not by reusable components. Errors in reusable components can not be traced by end-users since they had no control over the construction of such a component. Error conditions of this type are discussed more in Section 4.3.

4.2. Reusable Components and Object Libraries

Most of the code in an end-user program will be concerned with connecting together various software tools, user interface components and device drivers, since the end-user will want to automate access to computer tools already being used. Extensive libraries of tools and objects will have to be available with well defined interfaces and command languages. Each component in a library will have extensive help files accessible by the end-user. This help text will describe how the object can be activated or used. Access to some components will be through some set of tools which will use a paradigm such as visual programming.

Reusable components will have to be encapsulated so that they have an interface which can be operated through function calls. Some of these functions will be bound to the end-user program at compile or run-time. In general, reusable components should support dynamic binding.

4.3. Communication and Communication Safety

Access to software tools, user interface objects and device drivers through the EUPL, implies that the EUPL and the underlying environment must support two-way communication with other software systems. Such communication with other software systems should be safe, since lack of response is often a difficult error to trace. At least three possible conditions have to be considered to ensure safe delivery: Was the message delivered? Was the message correct? Was the message executed? The reusable software component or the underlying system should send a response indicating the outcome of the communication.

The underlying system must also provide support for synchronous and asynchronous communication. However, any timing critical problems should be handled by the reusable components rather than the end-user program.

5. CONCLUSION

End-user programming will require some knowledge of procedural programming for the foreseeable future, but the use of procedural programming will diminish as more and more end-user tasks can be "automated". We currently have the knowledge and tools to create fairly hospitable end-user programming environments on certain classes of computer systems. Broadly practiced end-user programming is very close to reality.

6. REFERENCES

1 D. D. Cowan, R. Ierusalimschy, and T. M. Stepien. Programming Environments for End-Users, Technical Report CS-92-09. Computer Science, University of Waterloo, Waterloo, Ontario, 1992.

2 Adele Goldberg and David Robson. *Smalltalk-80, the Language and its Implementation*. Addison-Wesley, Palo Alto, CA, January 1983.

3 Danny Goodman. *The Complete HyperCard 2.0 Handbook.* Bantam Books, 3rd edition, August 1990.

4 Asymetrix Corporation, Bellevue, WA. *Using Toolbook, a Guide to Building and Working with Books*, 1989.

5 Microsoft Corporation. *Microsoft Visual Basic Programmer's Guide.* Microsoft Corporation, 1991.

6 William S. Hawes. *ARexx User's Reference Manual, The REXX Language for the Amiga*. Commodore-Amiga, Inc., Maynard, MA, 1987.

7 Shi-Kuo Chang, editor. *Principles of Visual Programming Systems.* Prentice-Hall, 1990.

8 NeXT Computer, Inc. *The NeXTstep Advantage, Application Development with NeXTstep*, 1991.

9 Brad A. Myers. Demonstrational Interfaces: A Step Beyond Direct Manipulation. In *People and Computers VI*, pages 11--30. Cambridge University Press, 1991.

10 Charles Petzold. *Programming Windows*. Microsoft Press, 2nd edition, 1990.

Personal Computers and Intelligent Systems / F.H. Vogt (Editor)
Information Processing 92, Volume III
Elsevier Science Publishers B.V. (North-Holland)

Distributed Intelligent Agents

Stanley J. Rosenschein

Teleos Research, 576 Middlefield Road, Palo Alto, California 94301, USA

Keyword Codes: H.4.1; H.5.3; I.2.11
Keywords: Office Automation, Group and Organization Interfaces, Distributed Artificial Intelligence

Extended Abstract

Agents as a metaphor for complex computer systems

The protean nature of software presents unique opportunities and challenges to software designers. The opportunities lie in being able to craft systems of almost unlimited variety. The challenge lies not only in inventing new forms of software, but in creating models and metaphors that will allow desigers and users alike to control these systems and to organize their understanding of the systems' abilities and behavior in particular instances.

In the case of algorithmic input-output programs, like calculating greatest common divisors, computing statistics on a set of data, or compiling a Pascal program, the functionality of the program is modeled by relating properties or aspects of the input to those of the output. In modern interactive systems, graphical user interfaces typically provide visual objects from everyday life to which many intuitions about interpretation and use adhere. In more open-ended domains which exhibit ongoing behavior, however, such as operating systems, network management systems, or factory control systems, modeling the system's behavior comprehensibly becomes correspondingly more difficult. The notion of an "agent" is often useful in these circumstances because it abstracts away from the particulars of how information is encoded or what specific actions are produced and focuses instead on the *content* of the information to be encoded and the *goals* to be achieved by the system.

Modeling agents, singly and in collections

We are familiar with intelligent agents from everyday life because our common-sense accounts of the behaviors of other humans are linguistically couched in terms of this model. Roughly speaking, our everyday account of human activity is centered on the collection of information from the world through the external senses and its use for attaining goals. The information collected is used by people to update and maintain a set of *beliefs* that encode what they know (or think they know) about the world, and these beliefs are identified by their propositional content or by sentences expressing that propositional content, e.g., the belief that *it is raining*. Similarly, desires are identified by their content, as are intentions, e.g., the desire *to play football* or the intentiont *to go to the store*. These beliefs, desires, and intentions are time-varying collections of elements, and certain invariant rationality conditions are typically satisfied, along with certain conditions relating the states of these components to sensory inputs and action outputs.

Researchers in philosophy (see, for example, [Hintikka, Bratman]), and more recently Artificial Intelligence and Computer Science (for example [Cohen, Halpern]) have developed formal models of these ideas based on logical formulations of the mental attitudes of belief, desire, and intention.

Efficient implementations

Much of the work on multi-agent coordination in AI is also based on the attribution to agents of complex mental states, especially states of mutual belief and joint commitment. The content of these states is often described symbolically using the tools of mathematical logic, and their computational realization is either assumed to involve automated inference or is left entirely unspecified. Recent work on the synthesis of reactive agents has resulted in tools for compiling symbolic descriptions into provably real-time systems (for example, [Kaelbling]). This work involves the use of offline inference to compute circuit realizations of machines satisfying certain logical specifications. In the full paper we describe a natural generalization of these techniques to the synthesis of efficient multi-agent systems embodying mutual belief and joint commitment.

The key idea involves techniques for synthesizing update circuitry and action-selection circuitry in state machines. In the single-agent case, update circuitry can be derived from logical descriptions of state transitions in the environment by having a compiler attempt to prove the strongest knowledge postcondition that can be derived from the fact that the agent knew that P held at time t and that input I was received. The update circuitry is extracted from the proof. Similar techniques can be used for generating action-selection circuitry, except that goal-reduction rules are used instead of rules describing transitions of the environment.

To generalize these techniques to the multi-agent case, the compiler must manipulate a language of common knowledge states and mutual commitment to extract circuits for the individual agents that maintain the appropriate common knowledge conditions and select individual actions that are consistent with the joint goals being pursued by the group. The full version of this paper describes preliminary work on such techniques.

Future research directions

Models of agents to date, including the more abstract logical models, have been somewhat brittle in their treatment of certain important phenomena. For instance, belief updating in the presence of uncertainty is a difficult conceptual area for which no broadly accepted stylized engineering approach has been developed but one which is clearly necessary in practical systems. Similarly, graded preferences (rather than all-or-nothing desires) have proved difficult to model. Clearly, when preferences can be expressed using classical tools such as objective functions in linear programming, precise algorithmic solutions exist. However, to provide a broader software engineering approach to usable intelligent agents, much research on this topic will be needed. The language in which information about beliefs, desires, and intentions is communicated between human and artificial agents will also be the subject of further research.

Finally, for distributed agents to be of practical use in a software environment where they interact with humans in a flexible way, much work will be needed on the particular conventions and protocols that humans and agents might share in actually carrying out common tasks, such as task delegation, meeting scheduling, and information handling. For an example of early work along these lines, see Winograd, [Winograd]. This is a rich area where insights from anthropology, cognitive science, and computer science can be combined in a creative and mutually illuminating way.

References

J. Hintikka. *Knowledge and Belief.* Cornell University Press, Ithaca, NY, 1962.

M. Bratman. *Intention, plans and practical reason.* Cambridge, MA: Harvard University Press, 1987.

Philip R. Cohen and Hector J. Levesque. Persistence, Intention, and Commitment. *Intentions in Communication.* Ed. Philip R. Cohen, Jerry Morgan, and Martha E. Pollack, The MIT Press, 1990.

J. Y. Halpern and Y. Moses. Knowledge and common knowledge in a distributed environment. *Journal of the ACM*, 37(3):549–587, 1990. A preliminary version appeared in *Proceedings of the 3rd ACM Symposium on Principles of Distributed Computing*, 1984.

Leslie Pack Kaelbling and Stanley J. Rosenschein. Action and Planning in Embedded Agents. *Robotics and Autonomous Systems*, 6(1):35–48, 1990. Also published in *Designing Autonomous Agents: Theory and Practice from Biology to Engineering and Back.* Ed. Pattie Maes, The MIT Press/Elsevier, 1991.

T. Winograd. *A Language/Action Perspective on the Design of Cooperative Work.* Human Computer Interaction, 3(1):3–30, 1988.

Personal Computers and Intelligent Systems / F.H. Vogt (Editor)
Information Processing 92, Volume III
Elsevier Science Publishers B.V. (North-Holland)

Trends in PC Database Technology

Robert E. Shostak

Borland International
1800 Green Hills Road, Scotts Valley, CA 95006

Keyword Codes: H.2.1, H.2.3, H.2.4
Keywords: Database Management, Logical Design; Languages; Systems

Abstract

In the last ten years we have seen the emergence and maturation of practical, general-purpose, relational database management systems on the personal computer. The first of these, like the machines they ran on, were little more than toys when compared to their mainframe cousins. The latest generation of PC database managers, however, embody state-of-the-art relational technology, and feature sophisticated query optimization systems, GUI interfaces, connectivity to PC and mainframe-based servers, and interoperability with other PC applications. Indeed, it is fair to say that intense growth and competition in the PC software arena in the last several years has pushed the state of the art in PC DBMS technology beyond its mainframe counterpart.

Given the general thrust toward object-orientation in all aspects of software engineering, it is fair to ask whether the next generation of DBMS to grace the desktop of the typical corporate PC user will in fact be object-oriented (OODB). To begin to answer this question, we examine what object-orientation actually means in the database context, and to what extent it is appropriate for mainstream business applications.

The object-oriented model for program construction is predicated on the fairly simple idea that software organized as a system of modular, self-contained "objects" is more easily maintainable, extensible, and "reusable" than software that is not. At first blush, this may seem a simple reiteration of what software methodologists have been touting for years - the benefits of structured, hierarchical design. But we need to be careful - object orientation implies much more than just hierarchical design. The point is that instead of concentrating on what *functions* need to be provided (as defined by a procedure hierarchy), object-orientation focuses on the *entities* that the functions operate upon (the object hierarchy). The design process thus centers on formulating a collection of encapsulated, abstract data types. The design language centers on means for defining these types, and on extensibility mechanisms for creating new types as variations of old ones. Because the basic objects in any application tend to change less frequently than the functions the application are required to support, modularization based on objects rather than actions permits an application to evolve in a more graceful manner. The use of the extensibility mechanisms (derivation and polymorphism) of object-oriented languages, moreover, results in an economy of conceptual and implementational effort needed to create an application.

It would seem clear that the arguments in favor of object orientation in program development should apply *a fortiori* to database development. And indeed, a number of object-oriented database systems, often the result of academic research and development efforts, have relatively recently sprung onto the commercial scene. These include, to name just a few, Vbase [Andrews87], ONTOS [Andrews91], GemStone [Purdy87], ODE [Agrawal89], SIM [Jagannathan88], and ORION [Banerjee87]. Most of these systems run primarily on Unix-based workstations, although some, such as GemStone, run on networks with a file (or object) server and one or more satellite IBM PC or Smalltalk-80 workstations. Many were intended to support an integrated programming environment; VLSI CAD and CASE tools are typical applications, as are network management and geographical information systems.

One can think of these systems either as databases that have been given object-oriented data manipulation languages, or as object-oriented programming languages that have been given persistent objects. In some cases, such as Vbase, separate languages are provided for type definition (TDL) and data manipulation (COP). In others, such as GemStone, a unified language (SmallTalk-based OPAL) is used. Some newer systems, such as ONTOS, are based on extensions to C++ that add persistency.

None of these systems, of course, was intended to address the typical corporate and small business applications that the mainstay PC database systems, such as Borland's Paradox and DBase, are currently used for. And in at least one respect, they represent a step backward by comparison to relational systems. Because object-oriented systems are primarily programming environments, the means they provide for accessing data is *procedural* in nature. By contrast, the most important developments in PC-based DBMS products have centered on providing *declarative* mechanisms for data access that can be used by nonprogrammers. The user thus concentrates on specifying *what* it is he is looking for, and is completely freed from worrying about *how* it is to be done. The QBE (Query-by-Example) paradigm [Zloof77] pioneered on personal computers by the Paradox DBMS is such a mechanism, and has become the *de facto* standard for ad hoc query formulation. While some OODB systems have been retrofitted with query languages based on relational calculus (Object SQL, for example) even these languages are generally considered to be too low-level for the average corporate user.

In the short run, we can expect to see features of object-oriented languages integrated to increasing degrees within the data manipulation languages of PC database products. The Object PAL application language of Paradox for Windows is an example. Looking toward the future, we may expect to find PC database systems that fully embrace the key tenets of object-oriented programming while retaining their emphasis on declarative mechanisms. A certain class of object-oriented databases based on *semantic models* may well be the precursors of such systems. The principle idea of semantic models is that certain aspects of the relationships among the different entities that comprise a database are described declaratively and enforced automatically by the DBMS. Database schemas specified using semantic models resemble conventional entity-relationship diagrams in which entities are modelled as object types, and attributes as mappings from one object to another. Thus, for example, the **PhoneNo** attribute of an **Employee** record might map to a domain of complex **PhoneNum** objects as opposed to the usual domain of alphanumeric strings. Semantic integrity constraints can be specified as an integral part of the schema. For example, the attribute mappings may be specified as single-valued or multiple-valued. Moreover, a given object type may be defined as a *subtype* of one or more other types. Going a step farther, database managers based on semantic models may allow *predicate-defined* subtypes, i.e., subtypes whose instances are derived from instances of the supertype by computation as opposed to explicit enumeration. Ultimately, we are likely to see PC database systems based on semantic models in which user-friendly query tools, such as QBE, become the means of declarative definition of predicate-defined subtypes.

References

[Agrawal89] R. Agrawal and N.H. Gehani. ODE (Object Database and Environment): The Language and the Data Model. *Proceedings of ACM-SIGMOD 1989 International Conference on Management of Data.* ACM, 1989.

[Andrews87] T. Andrews and C. Harris, Combining language and database advances in an object-oriented development environment. *Proceedings of the Conference on Object-Oriented Programming Systems, Languages, and Applications*, pp. 430-440, Orlando, FL. ACM, October 1987.

[Andrews91] T. Andrews, C. Harris, and Kiril Sinkel. ONTOS: A Persistent Database for C++. *Object-Oriented Databases with Applications to CASE, Networks, and VLSI CAD.*
Rajiv Gupta and Ellis Horowitz, ed. Prentice Hall, Englewood Cliffs, NJ, 1991.

[Banerjee87] J. Banerjee, W. Kim, H.J. Kim, and H.F.Korth. Semantics and implementation of schema evolution in object-oriented databases. *Proceedings of the ACM SIGMOD International Conference on Management of Data,* pp. 311-322. ACM SIGMOD, May 1987.

[Jagannathan88] D. Jagannathan, R.L. Fritchman, B.L. Guck, J.P. Thompson, and D.M. Tolbert. SIM: A database system based on the semantic data model. *Proceedings of the ACM SIGMOD International Conference on Management of Data*, pp. 46-55, ACM SIGMOD, June 1988.

[Purdy87] A. Purdy, B. Schuchardt, and D. Maier. Integrating an object server with other worlds. *ACM Transcations on Office Information Systems*, 5(1), pp. 27-47, January 1987.

[Zloof77] M.M. Zloof. Query-By-Example: A Database Language. *IBM Systems Journal* 16:4, pp. 324-343, 1977.

Personal Computers and Intelligent Systems / F.H. Vogt (Editor)
Information Processing 92, Volume III
Elsevier Science Publishers B.V. (North-Holland)

Activity-based Information Retrieval: Technology in Support of Personal Memory

Michael G. Lamming and William M. Newman

Rank Xerox EuroPARC, 61 Regent Street, Cambridge CB2 1AB, England
lamming.europarc@rx.xerox.com, newman.europarc@rx.xerox.com

Abstract

Much information is hard to retrieve because the need to do so was not foreseen at the time the information was stored. This problem appears hard to solve with the aid of computers. However, research in the area of autobiographical memory suggests the use of retrieval cues relating to the kinds of activities in which the user was engaged at the time of storage. These are highly correlated with the time at which the event took place, and thus can be used for indexing, taking advantage of the accurate time-stamps that computers usually apply automatically when information is stored. In the proposed activity-based retrieval system, data on the user's activity are gathered automatically to support retrieval by, for example, browsing through an 'autobiography' of work episodes. The paper discusses some of the difficulties with this approach, and presents the results of three experiments in which autobiographical episodes were reconstructed by means of automatically collected activity data. It concludes with some comments on the technical feasibility and social acceptability of such an approach to information retrieval.

Keyword Codes: H.3.0; H.4.1; H.5.1
Keywords: Information Systems Applications; Multimedia Information Systems; Office Automation

1. INTRODUCTION

The advent of the networked personal computer has greatly increased the user's ability to manipulate information of all kinds. Tools now readily available support text preparation, illustration, spreadsheet manipulation, electronic mail, data analysis and, with the advent of systems like the Multimedia PC, audio/video playback and editing. However, the tools for storing and retrieving this information remain primitive, largely unchanged from the tools available on the time-shared systems of the 1960s and 1970s. There have been major innovations since then, such as the desktop filing system [Smith] and efficient methods for free-text search [IBM], but these go only a little way towards enabling users to deal with the explosion of information around them.

The research programme described here has a goal of improving the user's ability to retrieve information and recall events in the workplace. It aims to help in the very wide variety of everyday situations where the user cannot locate information unaided, nor can standard computer-based tools help. For example, the user may wish to locate an electronic note written after a meeting held several months ago, but may remember neither the file-name of the note nor the date of the meeting. Another example, common in these days of widespread videotaping, is to recall an important remark made at a seminar, about which only a brief note was made: what exactly did the speaker say, and where is it on the videotape? As these examples illustrate, retrieval problems are often the result of lack of foresight or simply lack of opportunity to store and index the information at the appropriate time. As our information world expands, this happens increasingly often.

We describe here an approach to the design of information retrieval systems. The approach exploits advances in understanding of human recall and retrieval, and in so-called Ubiquitous Computing technologies [Weiser]. It envisages computer-based systems that explicitly supplement human memory. It envisages personal devices, such as the one in the artist's impression of Figure 1, that support browsing through autobiographical data to find episodes corresponding, say, to the two examples of note-taking above. In this paper, we describe an overall technical strategy based on automatic sensing of time-stamped activity data. We itemise some of the serious difficulties--technical, psychological and social--to be overcome in implementing this strategy. The paper then describes briefly three projects we have undertaken, in which we have built and tested prototype systems. A final section summarises our progress to date towards overcoming the difficulties, and discusses the prospects for an activity-based solution to human memory problems.

2. RECONSTRUCTING EPISODES FROM TIME-STAMPED DATA

One of the characteristics of electronic information, which we employ in our approach to retrieval, is its frequent inclusion of accurate time-stamps indicating time of activity. Files, for example, store the time of creation, access or modification along with the data; videotaped material can include timecode; electronic messages state the time of sending, and fax machines print the time of receipt on incoming pages. These time-stamps can be useful in locating the information. In most instances, however, relying on time-stamps is only of limited use for retrieval, since people are notoriously poor at remembering purely temporal information [Michon].

Research in the area of autobiographical memory offers a solution to this problem, for it suggests that people often use retrieval cues relating to the kinds of activities in which they were engaged at the time of the event [Reiser]. Such activities are of course highly correlated with the time at which the event took place. Thus the human activities of Figure 3 correlate with the electronic processes

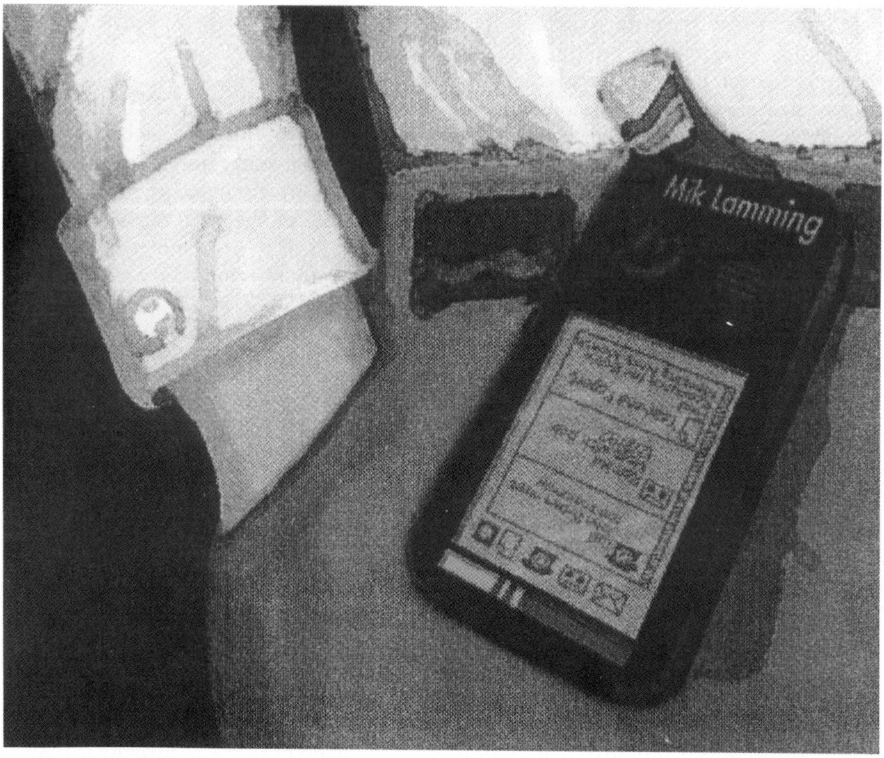

Figure 1: A Portable Memory Aid

of Figure 2. We believe that it should be possible to generate records of such activities with no effort on the part of the user. Our approach is to use these records as a basis for locating electronic activities and their related information.

Our method thus involves monitoring human activity and linking it to electronic activity. We have explored a number of methods of capturing the human activities of the workplace: changes in location, telephoning, use of workstations. These activity data do not correspond particularly closely to users' recollections of events. We have therefore developed episode recognisers that transform the raw activity data into episode descriptions that resemble users' recollections quite closely. For example, from location data we can identify meetings with others and periods spent alone.

Activity-based retrieval has been inspired in part by recent work by Tulving, Baddeley and others on models of episodic and autobiographical memory [Tulving, Brewer, Baddeley86]. Linton, for example, has proposed a hierarchical model of

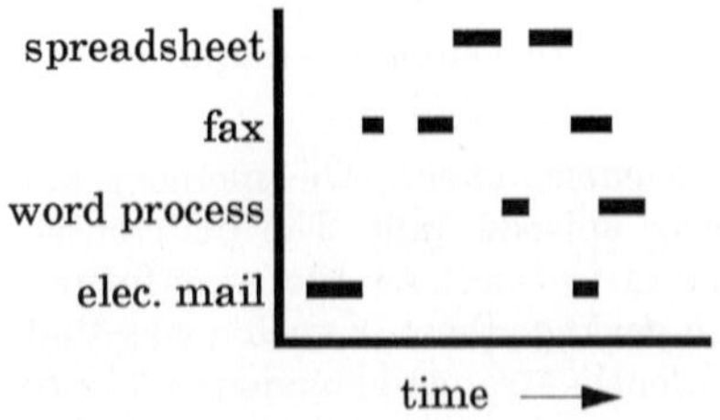

Figure 2: Electronic Information Activities.

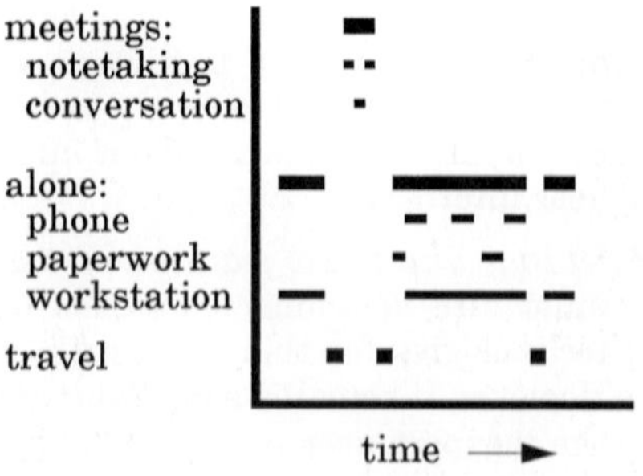

Figure 3: Human activities corresponding to Figure 2.

memory in which events and episodes are formed from smaller units, which she calls elements and details [Linton]. The work of Bjork and his colleagues, on limits to retrieval capacity and on the value of contextual clues, has provided valuable pointers [Bjork78, Bjork88]. Both Linton and Baddeley have described long-term effects, helping us to identify problems to which activity-based retrieval might be applied [Linton, Baddeley77, Pinto]. We have also been encouraged by the work of Schank and others on various systems that exploit aspects of human autobiographical memory [Schank, Wilson, Lansdale].

3. THE CHALLENGES OF THE ACTIVITY-BASED APPROACH

The design and construction of an activity-based retrieval aid presents a number of challenging problems, which include:

- *Understanding the user's needs for retrieval tools.* There is little or no published data on human retrieval problems in the workplace. They are undoubtedly frequent, but it is hard to assess the value of building tools to solve them.
- *Automatic sensing of activity.* The activity-based approach depends on sensing activity data automatically, in a manner that does not require intervention by the user, and indeed that the user can be unaware of. The technology for this is largely unavailable, because there has been very little need for it.
- *Reconstruction of episodes from activity data.* Technologies that sense activity collect large amounts of very fine-grain data, far too detailed to be of use in retrieval. The user needs to be able to browse through a reconstruction of episodes that match his or her recollections; these episodes often have durations of minutes (e.g., telephone calls), hours (e.g., meetings) or longer. A major problem, therefore, is to develop algorithms for converting fine-grain activity data into records of recognisable episodes.

- *Building powerful portable or hand-held terminals.* A memory aid is unlikely to be useful unless it is always accessible. The terminal for browsing must therefore be small enough to be carried with the user, and yet capable of displaying useful amounts of information; it must also support an appropriate user interface.
- *Hiding unwanted features of the distributed environment.* The memory aid must also be connected to the user's store of episode data. The distributed technologies for this are mostly available or in prospect for the near future. However, it remains a challenging problem to package them in such a way that the inexpert user is unaffected by their frequently strange behaviour and can confidently rely on them for day-to-day memory support.
- *Designing and building usable retrieval tools.* The construction of such tools is not just a long-term goal: to support experiments, prototype tools must be built and tested at stages along the way. A particular problem in testing these tools is that they must support real retrieval tasks, caused by real memory lapses. Therefore they must be designed and implemented to a high enough standard to be used in earnest during the experimental period.
- *Safeguarding the user's privacy.* This problem, although last in the list, is often first in the mind of participants. The activity-based approach involves collecting and analysing data about the user's personal activities; most users regard this as an infringement of their privacy. Any networked system of this kind will inevitably arouse serious concerns over possible misuse, e.g., by management, and over the general ethics of using technology in this fashion.

Our approach to these problems has been to mount a number of experiments, each one addressing several of the problems from a particular angle. Three of these are described in the sections that follow.

4. PEPYS: AN AUTOMATIC DIARY GENERATOR

We have developed a program, called Pepys, that generates diaries automatically. It uses activity data gathered from active badges: these use infra-red coded signals, picked up by wall-mounted sensors, to inform a central server of badge-wearers' locations [Want]. It incorporates a recogniser that looks for episodes of three basic types in the raw badge data: gatherings of two or more users (e.g., meetings), periods spent alone by users, and travel by users between locations in the building. The diaries are prepared and distributed daily to users via electronic mail; a typical diary is shown in Figure 4. A more detailed description of the system and its use may be found in [Newman91b].

We have conducted preliminary studies of the accuracy and usefulness of Pepys. These two aspects are of course closely linked: errors in Pepys' reconstructions reduce users' interest in it as a retrieval aid. Some errors are difficult to eradicate because they reside in the raw data. For example, users forget to wear their badges, or wear them at waist level where they sometimes are not sensed by the

Diary for Tuesday, October 30, 1991

14:14 In office [50 mins]
15:04 In and out of event in Nathan's office; with W. Nathan, R. Hatton [45 mins]
15:50 In office [10 mins]
16:00 In Conference room [4 mins]
16:05 Attended part of event in Commons; with B. Andrews, M. Morton, R. Hatton [7 mins]
16:13 Mostly in office [44 mins]
16:57 Attended event in Wright's office; with P. Wright [7 mins]
17:04 Looked in on event in Morton's office; with I. David, M. Morton [1 min]
17:05 Mostly in office [2 hr 3m]
    17:05 In office [5 mins]
    17:11 In event in office; with P. Wright, I. David [1h 2mins]
    18:13 In office [36 mins]
    18:50 Meeting in office; with W. Nathan [13 mins]
    19:03 In office [5 mins]
19:09 In 2nd floor rear area [2 mins]
19:11 Last seen

Figure 4: An example of a diary generated by Pepys.

system. The result is that other users receive diaries listing periods 'alone' when in fact others were present. Discounting errors caused by faulty data collection, the accuracy of Pepys' episode recognition is high, at least 90 percent. This has been enough to encourage a number of interesting uses of diaries, for example to remind the user of commitments made yesterday that imply follow-up work today. Visitors to EuroPARC have found Pepys useful in writing trip reports -- an application that we find gratifying since we identified this possible use at the outset.

5. VIDEO DIARIES: TESTING THE USE OF VIDEO RECORDINGS TO ENHANCE RECALL

Reliance solely on location-based episodes, as in Pepys, limits the utility of the memory aid. For example, during long periods spent alone in one's office there is insufficient detail to support recall; when several meetings involve the same people it is difficult to distinguish one meeting from another. One way of solving this problem is to provide video recordings of these episodes. There are some severe technical problems with this approach, but we were interested in investigating its usefulness so that we could judge whether the problems were worth solving. We therefore built and tested a Video Diary System, based around the capture and browsing of low-quality time-lapsed video [Lamming92].

Our goal was to create a system capable of storing many days' or weeks' worth of video images and of supporting rapid random-access to these images. We based the system around an in-house video network which provides a camera and monitor in each office and open space, with a central crossbar video switch accessible to workstations in the building. With this system it is possible to switch cameras so as to keep an individual almost continuously within view, and to route the video signal to a single recording station. Automatic switching, without the user's intervention, is achieved by means of the active badge system mentioned above. The badge server is linked to a client application, Tracker, which it notifies of each new location of the user; Tracker then transmits a suitable request to the video switch. Video output is fed to a workstation where a frame grabber digitises each frame and displays it on the screen. In order to store several weeks of data, we use exchangeable magneto-optic disks, storing quarter-size (one-sixteenth area) frames at the rate of 6 to 12 per minute, and using colour dithering to reduce the data further, to about 25K bytes per frame. With this relatively unsophisticated compression scheme we can normally fit at least two weeks' worth of data onto a single 650M byte disk.

We tested the ability of the Video Diary to assist recall. Subjects were asked to remember the activities of a particular day under three conditions: unaided, with the help of Pepys diaries, and with both Pepys and the Video Diary. Each subject was asked, on different occasions, to recall the activities of a previous day of recording; these recalls occurred after 1 day, 1 week, 2.5 weeks and 4 weeks. The average results from three subjects are shown in Figure 5. There was a clear

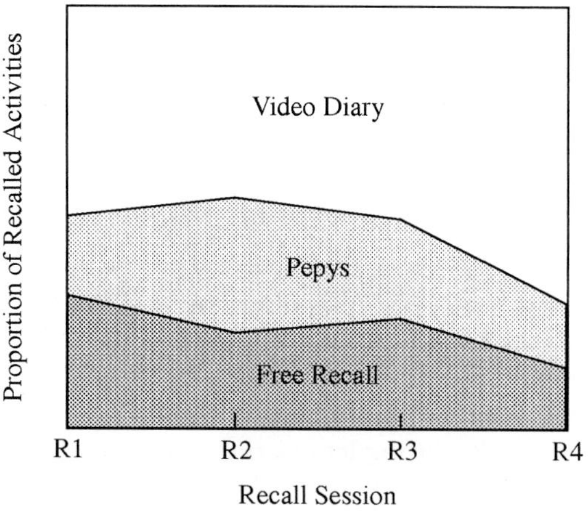

Figure 5: The number of basic activities recalled for each of the three conditions over the four recall sessions. The plot shows the number of basic activities recalled for each condition summed over the previous conditions. Thus the plots for Pepys and Video Diary conditions show the increase in the number of activities using these memory aids.

indication that the Video Diary helped users remember their activities, particularly over longer periods of recall. It was also clear that the presence of people or objects acts as an important cue in recall, reaffirming our original research hypothesis. Although the Video Diary often helped, it also occasionally confused the user by presenting a video image that could not be related to a recalled event.

6. EXPERIMENTS IN TRACKING PAPER DOCUMENTS

The location-based episodes of Pepys are often too coarse in grain, and need supplementing with other forms of activity to provide the necessary detail. An episode description such as "11:23 In office [1h 26m]" is both too uninformative and too long in duration to be useful for some retrieval tasks. Taken in combination, however, several types of activity can provide adequate precision. We envision the possibility of a multi-activity record including a wide variety of entries such as "11:30 Reading letter from J Smith [2 mins]".

We have built a prototype system, called Marcel, to recognise episodes concerned with paperwork [Newman91a]. As with Pepys, our aim is automatically to produce episode descriptions that match users' recollections. Marcel uses a video camera mounted over the user's desk to identify the documents on the desk surface. Images from the camera are fed to a frame store where they are digitised and thresholded. The resulting binary image is processed to extract features of the document that can be used to construct a unique descriptor; an activity database stores descriptors together with the time and location of identification. The primary features used for descriptor generation are the positions of the ends of the lines of text on the page. The descriptor includes an encoding of each line's left-hand end relative to the left margin, and of the line's length, as shown in Figure 6.

Marcel's database stores the text content of each page, indexed by its descriptors. Documents may be entered into the database either via a desktop scanner and optical character recognition, or directly from an electronic master, such as might be sent to a laser printer. We have been able to achieve reliable recognition of documents in the database, even under relatively poor lighting conditions and with interference from other objects on the desk, such as the user's hands. Rotated documents are recognisable up to a tilt angle of approximately 15 degrees. Recognition time, using a Sun SparcStation/2, is about 8 seconds. These performance figures appear adequate to support experiments in using document-related episodes for retrieval.

7. CONCLUSION: RESULTS FROM EXPERIMENTS

These three experiments have provided some initial indications of solution strategies for the problems listed at the start of this paper. They have been augmented by other experiments, but space does not permit reports of these in this

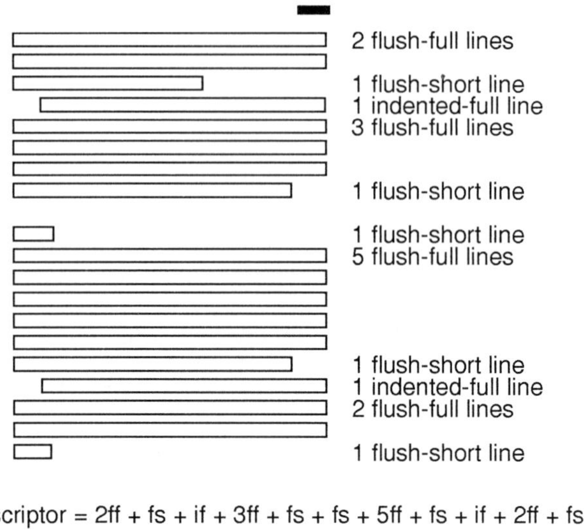

Figure 6: Generating a descriptor from line end positions.

paper; they include construction of a portable note-taker which keys the user's notes to points in a video or audio recording [Lamming91], and recent work on the analysis of workstation activity [Flynn].

7.1 Understanding the user's needs for retrieval tools

In order to estimate the need for memory aids, we have conducted some preliminary studies of workplace activity. These suggest that the recall of workplace activities is largely reliant on episodes of four types: meetings with other people, phone conversations, workstation-based tasks and paperwork. Further studies, aimed at categorising the types of memory problems encountered, are in progress at the time of writing.

7.2 Automatic sensing of activity

We have learned that the accuracy and comprehensiveness of available sensing technologies leave a lot to be desired. Active badges frequently 'lose' people, and sometimes receive spurious signals off reflective surfaces; video cameras have limited fields of view. We have also learned that so-called 'unobtrusive' technologies are often much more distracting to users than one would anticipate. This is an area where more work is needed.

7.3 Reconstruction of episodes from activity data

We have found episode reconstruction to be one of the more difficult aspects of activity-based retrieval. The development of a recogniser to support the generation of Pepys diaries, for example, involved several months of design effort; results to date on analysis of workstation activity suggest that this may pose an even harder problem. Given the inaccuracies and other flaws in the data we collect, and our limited understanding of how to apply meaning to activity, we expect this to be a continuing research challenge.

7.4 Building powerful portable or hand-held terminals

Progress towards building networked hand-held terminals has been described in [Weiser]. It is now feasible to build a device measuring 65 x 80 mm incorporating a display, control buttons, a pen interface, and an infra-red link for communication (Figure 7). We anticipate that our research will ultimately rely to a large extent on such devices.

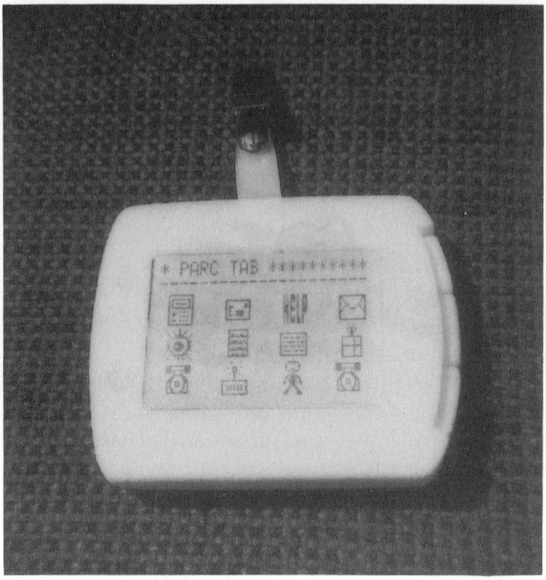

Figure 7: Model of a Hand-held Terminal.

7.5 Hiding unwanted features of the distributed environment

While it may ultimately be possible to build some of the necessary sensing technology into a portable memory aid, there will always need to be a link to the ubiquitous environment that surrounds the user. We see increasingly clearly, however, that the memory aid must present itself as a personal device to the user, and hide the complexity of the distributed infrastructure. Another major issue will be the provision of safeguards to privacy so that, for example, two users' wireless devices can exchange information securely in the presence of a third user.

7.6 Designing and building usable retrieval tools

By focusing on specific areas of application we have been able to attain an adequate level of usability in several of our prototypes. The Pepys diary system has been particularly successful, maintaining a small community of 'converts' a year after its introduction, i.e., well after its novelty must have worn off. We have come to appreciate that systems which aim to support human memory retrieval may require special attention to the user interface; otherwise the cognitive load imposed by interaction can outweigh the reduction in load on the user's memory. There is a need for low-intensity user interfaces that demand little or no attention from the user [Newman90].

In building prototypes of relatively narrow functionality, we have had to give considerable thought to how to ensure that the tools would actually be used during the experimental period. In the case of Pepys, users were encouraged to wear their badges by providing other badge applications, such as a program that automatically unlocks the main entrance to the laboratory when the user clicks a button on the badge. Marcel has been extended to permit limited forms of interaction with the document as it lies on the desk surface, and has been shown useful for tasks such as machine translation of foreign words [Newman92]. Until we can build full-scale retrieval aids we anticipate that our prototypes will need to include such add-on benefits for the user.

7.7 Safeguarding the user's privacy

The design of a device to record episodes of activity data must address privacy issues head-on. Our programme therefore maintains two threads of research: one is aimed at understanding the nature of privacy issues and of other social issues raised by the programme; the other investigates ways of designing the technology to protect the user against loss of privacy. Our studies of the social issues have focused on the active badges and on the boundary between what is public and private, a boundary that is many ways tacit but whose infringement can cause considerable distress[Harper]. The studies help us, therefore, to see this boundary as something we can affect by our designs, and that we should only affect in ways that are acceptable to the user. They have also made clear to us the user's need for control over the entry of technology into his or her work environment.

In designing the technology to support activity-based retrieval, therefore, we have built in safeguards against unnecessary access to data, and have provided users with controls and with the ability to opt out. The data gathered from badges for use by Pepys has, from the start, been encoded so as to make it extremely difficult for unauthorised programs to use. More recently we have introduced higher-level controls that allow individual users to identify other users who may have access to information about their location, past or present.

Some of these safeguards are, we hope, temporary precautions necessitated by the highly distributed architecture we are forced to use in the absence of a more personal device. However even a completely personal device will not solve all problems of privacy. Any such device would be capable of sensing activity that the owner does not see (e.g., if it is left in the office when the user takes the day off), and would remember details for ever that the owner would soon, perhaps thankfully, forget. However we believe a personal memory device will, in the long run, offer its users benefits that far outweigh any drawbacks, and that go some of the way towards enabling them to manage the information that surrounds them in the workplace.

8. ACKNOWLEDGEMENTS

We acknowledge the major contributions to this research made by Marge Eldridge, Richard Harper, Phil Barnard, Debra Bekerian and Mike Flynn. We are also grateful for the many helpful suggestions and contributions from our colleagues at EuroPARC and at Xerox PARC. We would also like to thank the project's external reviewer, Dr Jerry Elkind.

9. REFERENCES

[Baddeley77] Baddeley, A. and Hitch, G.J. *"Recency re-examined."* In Dornic, S., ed. *Attention and Performance VI*. Hillsdale: Erlbaum. 1977

[Baddeley86] Baddeley, A., *Working Memory.* Oxford: Clarendon Press. 1986.

[Bjork78] Bjork, R. A. *"The Updating of Human Memory." The Psychology of Learning and Motivation. Vol 12.* pp. 235-259. 1978

[Bjork88] Bjork, E. L. and Bjork, R. A, *"On the adaptive aspects of retrieval failure in autobiographical memory."* In Gruneberg, P. E., Morris, P. E., and Sykes, R.N. (eds) *Practical Aspects of Memory: Current Research and Issues. Vol. 1 Memory in Everyday Life.* Chichester: John Wiley & Son. 1988.

[Brewer] Brewer, W. F, "What is autobiographical memory?" In David C. Rubin (Ed) *Autobiographical Memory* (pp 25-49) Cambridge University Press.

[Buxton] Buxton, W., and Moran, T. P., "EuroPARC's Integrated Interactive Intermedia Facility (IIIF): Early Experiences." Proc. IFIP WG8.4 Conference on Multi-user Interfaces and Applications, Heraklion, Crete, September 1990.

[Flynn] Flynn, M., and Newman, W. M. *"Monitoring Workstation Activity."* EuroPARC internal report. In preparation.

[Harper] Harper, R. H. R. *"The Locator: an analysis of active badge applications."* EuroPARC internal report 92-3. 1992.

[IBM] IBM World Trade Corp., *Storage and Information Retrieval System (STAIRS) - General Information Manual, Second Edition*, IBM Germany, Stuttgart, April 1972.

[Lamming91] Lamming, M. G. *"NoTime - A Tool for Notetakers."* EuroPARC internal report 91-135. 1991.

[Lamming92] Lamming, M. G., Eldridge, M. A., and Flynn, M. *"Would a Prosthetic Memory be Better with Pictures?"* Submitted for publication. Also available as EuroPARC internal report 92-1

[Lansdale] Lansdale, M., and Edmonds, E. "Using memory for events in the design of personal filing systems." University of Loughborough, Dept. of Human Sciences, 1989.

[Linton] Linton, M. *"Ways of searching the contents of memory."* In Rubin, D.C., ed. *Autobiographical Memory.* Cambridge: Cambridge Univ. Press. 1986.

[Michon] Michon, J. A. *"Processing of temporal information and the cognitive theory of time experience."* In Fraser, J.T., Haber, F.C., and Mueller, G.H., eds. *The Study of Time*. Heidelberg: Springer Verlag. 1972

[Newman90] Newman, W. M., *"Interacting with Ubiquitous Systems."* Invited presentation, Eurographics 90, Montreux, Switzerland. 1990.

[Newman91a] Newman, W. M., *"Interacting with Paper Documents."* Proc. Nord-Data '91, Den Norske Dataforening, Oslo. 1991.

[Newman91b] Newman, W. M., Eldridge, M. and Lamming, M. G. *"Pepys: Generating Autobiographies by Automatic Tracking."* Proc. E-CSCW 91, Amsterdam. Kluwer, 1991.

[Newman92] Newman, W. M. and Wellner, P. *"A desk supporting interaction with paper documents."* To appear, Proc CHI '92.

[Pinto] Pinto, A. da C., and Baddeley, A. *"Where did you park your car? Analysis of a naturalistic long-term recency effect."* European J. of Cogn. Psych., 3, 297-313, 1991.

[Reiser] Reiser, B.J., Black, J.B., and Kalamarides, P. *"Strategic memory search processes."* In Rubin, D.C., ed. *Autobiographical Memory.* Cambridge: Cambridge Univ. Press. 1986.

[Schank] Schank, R. C., and Abelson, R. P. *Scripts, Plans, Goals, and Understanding.* Hillsdale: Erlbaum. 1977.

[Smith] Smith, D. C., Irby, C., Kimball, R and Harslem, E., *"The STAR User Interface: An Overview."* Proceedings of the AFIPS 1982 National Computer Conference, 50 , pp 515-528. 1982.

[Tulving] Tulving, E., *Elements of Episodic Memory.* Oxford: Oxford Univ. Press. 1983

[Want] Want, R. *"The Active Badge Location System."* Olivetti Research Laboratories, The Old Addenbrooks Site, 24a Trumpington St., Cambridge, England CB2 1QN, 1990.

[Weiser] Weiser, M. The Computer for the 21st Century. Scientific American Vol. 265. No. 3. September 1991.

[Wilson] Wilson, P. *"Towards the electronic pocket diary."* Design Studies. Vol 5, no. 2. pp. 98-105. 1984.

Personal Computers and Intelligent Systems / F.H. Vogt (Editor)
Information Processing 92, Volume III
Elsevier Science Publishers B.V. (North-Holland)

Documental languages to improve PC database interoperability

Jose M. Perez-Rosado

Department of Telematic Engineering, Technical University of Madrid, C/ Sangenjo, 4, 28034 Madrid, Spain

Abstract

Database interoperability is a key research issue today. Interoperability is even more necessary in PC due to the fact that, on one hand, they are usually connected to large networks with thousands of users and a large number of private and corporate databases and, on the other hand, they access regularly to Videotext and retrieval information databases. Today there are available tools for providing connectivity: OSI protocols, SQL database query language, de facto standard PC operating systems, etc. However tools for coping with the semantic description of remote data have not being proposed yet. In this paper we explore some possibilities given by documental languages used for years in libraries. Particularly, the Universal Decimal Classification (UDC) is studied. Its use as PC database metadata language is proposed.

Keyword Codes: H.2.5; H.3.3; K.8.0
Keywords: Heterogeneous Databases; Information Search and Retrieval; Personal Computing, General

1. INTRODUCTION

Interoperability is one of the key issues today. Based on the OSI Reference Model (ISO 7498) on one hand and on de-facto standards like IBM's SNA architecture or TCP/IP protocol on the other, large networks have been built: EURONET, TELENET, TYMNET, TRANSPAC, IBERPAC, etc. Now those networks are being interconnected by routers and gateways, in such a way that a PC connected to a LAN in, lets say, Madrid can access a database located in one host or PC in, lets say, Singapore. This could also be done before, but now there is an important difference: a PC owner can reach information sources with no specific relation with him or her at all. That is, before, a PC was connected to a specific network and was supposed to access only certain databases located on nodes of that network. That *closed world assumption* is no valid any more. Today, PC's connected to networks can access a wide variety of different *open* databases belonging to different owners and with no special relation to them. Networks like Internet are reported to have several million users[1]. This is at the same time a cause and an effect of the trend towards open systems pursued by customers and followed by manufacturers.

All this is paving the way to have real connectivity, but, what about interoperability? When a user access a remote PC, and assuming that the suitable security rights are granted, how can he or she understand the information stored in it?

2. INTEROPERABILITY: STATE OF THE ART

In the enterprise world partial solutions (mainly involving connectivity) have been given. First, a user can connect remotely to the host and use the specific query language of its DBMS. This is called *remote access*. One proposal by ISO (Remote Database Access Service and Protocol) is on the way of becoming an international standard. One disadvantage appears when the user needs to access several databases, because he or she has to know well the schema and DML of each database. Besides, the integration of different results has to be done manually. For solving those problems, databases belonging to one organization can form a *federation* [ShLa90]. In that case, one user can access several databases at one time. Federated databases can have a global schema (MULTIBASE, ADDS, Calida, Mermaid, INGRES/STAR), or not (MRDSM, Sybase) (cf [Pere91] for a broader description). Both systems have the advantage of providing a global answer to a query involving more than one database. In the first case, the user has to know only the global schema or a specific view and the global DML. In the second case, the global schema is replaced by a multidatabase language. The user has to know it and the schemas of the involved databases too. On the other hand, the global schema approach has the burden of having to build (and maintain!) it. This, what is a problem in an enterprise environment, can be even unfeasible in a real open environment [LiMR90].

In public access database environments there is a similar situation, the user has to follow a sequence of simple menus (like in Videotext databases like Teletel, Ibertex, etc.) or use a specific query language for each system (like in information retrieval databases like Dialog/Dialog[2], ESA/Quest, Echo/CCL, Blaise/Elhill, Télésystèmes/Questel, etc. [Amat88]). In this case, there are several disadvantages: first, the user needs to know several retrieval languages and access to the thesaurus of each database to know how it is structured. Then, to obtain a global answer the user has to identify information sources in a global directory, query each of them and obtain the result composing different answers.

In both worlds there is a need for greater connectivity and, as a first step, common query languages are becoming standards: in the enterprise environment, the relational model and SQL are the de facto standards. Actually, that standardization process is slower in the public database environment, with each system or network providing its common language, even though organizations like the Commission of the European

---

[1] 3,5 million users estimated for Internet (Communications Week, Nov. 25, 1991)

[2] Database names and retrieval languages are separated by '/'

Community are sponsoring global retrieval languages like CCL. Second, global directories exist in both environments and federations can be created. Besides, the Directory Service (CCITT Recommendation X.500) is being widely discussed by CCITT and ISO. Third, multidatabase languages capable of coping with differences in schema structure, attribute names, data units and values have been proposed (MSQL [Lit.87], Pegasus [LiMR90]).

But there are some more steps to take towards interoperability. Mainly, tools for understanding remote information are needed. We need to understand both the syntax and semantic of remote information. Referred to syntax, ISO has proposed and standardized a general notation for describing the syntax of any data, the Abstract Syntax Notation ASN.1 (ISO 8824). We still need tools for describing remote semantics. In that direction, concepts like metadata information has been proposed in the literature [MaRo86]. In this paper we propose a contribution to meet that ambitious goal.

3. A WELL-KNOWN EXAMPLE

In the rest of the paper we use a set of well-known databases, first introduced by W. Litwin in his work about multidatabase interoperability [LiAb87]. The example consists of three databases which model applications existing on the French public videotext system Teletel. Their schemas appear in Table 1.

Table 1
Example Database Schemas

DB Michelin:	R (r#, rname, street, type, stars, avprice, tel)
	C (c#, cname)
	M (r#, c#, price)
DB Kleber:	REST (rest#, name, street, type, forks, t#, owner, meanprice)
	C (c#, cname, ncal)
	MENU (rest#, c#, price)
DB Gault_M:	R (r#, rname, street, qual, tel, type, avprice)
	C (c#, cname, ncal)
	M (r#, c#, price)

It can be a good exercise to try to understand the meaning of those databases only by using those schemas. Based on relation and attribute names we can figure out what those databases are modelling (certain restaurant guides) and what aspects of that universe are being modeled (restaurants appearing in each guide and courses served by each restaurant) and what properties of them (address, type, average price and quality rates of restaurants and price of courses). Of course, to make those assumptions we have used an implicit knowledge, what is called *common sense*. Unfortunately, common sense is difficult to acquire and to represent in machine-readable form.

Once we have figured out what those databases are about, and assuming we are interested on them, the usual process is to browse each database to see what information it contains. A sample of the content of those databases as implemented in the Database Laboratory of the Department of Telematic Engineering (DIT) is shown in Table 2.

Table 2
Sample data of Kleber and Michelin Databases

DB Kleber

Select * from C;

c#	cname	ncal
00	cocido	01300
01	gazpacho	00500
02	rabo de toro	00800
03	paella	01100
...		

Select * from MENU

rest#	c#	price
00	01	01400
00	03	02500
01	01	00900
01	02	03000
...		

Select * from REST;

rest#	name	street	type	forks	t#	owner	meanprice
00	zambra	velázquez	flamenco	!!!	4355264	perez	03500
01	maravillas	gran vía	castellano	!!!!	4335331		07000
02	tao tao	fuencarral	chino	!!	4612655	huan	01500
...							

DB Michelin

Select * from R;

r#	rname	street	type	stars	avprice	tel
00	florida park	retiro	lujo	****	08500	5737804
01	corral del moro	morería	arabe	**	02500	2658446
02	tao tao	fuencarral	chino	*	01500	4612655
...						

However, seeing the content of every database can only assure us that we are in fact browsing the right databases. To know more in detail what is the meaning of each field we could match the fields in the databases to those in our own database, which are our perception of the reality. This is even more necessary if we want to extract information from more than one database through *interdatabase queries* [LiAb87] provided by a multidatabase query language like MRDSM or MSQL. One possible matching is shown in Table 3 (we have intentionally used Spanish field names in our database, *My_Rest*).

In this case there is a one-to-one correspondence among fields. This is the general case covered by heterogeneous databases in literature, even though more complex cases have been studied recently (cf [DeMi89]). Once we have matched database fields, we can solve heterogeneities in schema structure, relation name or attribute name, type and value among different databases using existing techniques (cf [DaHw82], [DeAT87b]).

Table 3
Correspondence among fields of example databases

Michelin	Kleber	Gault_M	My_Rest
R	REST	R	REST
C	C	C	PLATO
M	MENU	M	MENU
r#	rest#	r#	nrest
rname	name	rname	nombre
street	street	street	calle
type	type	type	tipo
stars	forks	qual	calificac
avprice	meanprice	avprice	precio
tel	t#	tel	tfno
---	owner	---	---
c#	c#	c#	nplato
cname	cname	cname	nombre
price	price	price	precio
---	ncal	ncal	ncal

What information is needed to do that correspondence without browsing data?. We are thinking about two classes of information. First, a *high level* information. It is used to know the exact domain of the database. Here it can be useful to have a *formal definition* of the relations that compose the database. Definition of relations in the sense used in *terminological databases* [Fal.91] can be useful. Then, we need a *low level* information. That information tells us the meaning of each field, its content, some examples, the range, etc. We can use the information generated during the analysis and design phase of the database. In Table 4 we show both levels of information. In this case relation definitions have been borrowed from one *authority source*, the Oxford Dictionary [Oxfo74] for greater standardization.

But, even though *high* and *low level* information be available within the remote database and a general mechanism be developed to access it (querying the local database information repository) and we all eventually agree on high and low level information sources and language, we still need one more thing. That information is not easily processed by computers, we should agree in one more easily processable syntax than informal English. We could use numbers, for example. Under a certain convention, data in our information repository could look like Table 5. That should be much easier to process and communicate. The question now is, where do we find the meaning of that sequence of numbers? That problem has been solved many years ago by librarians. Those numbers can be obtained using the UDC classification. The UDC classification is introduced in the Annexe at the end of the paper.

Table 4
Informal relation and field definition

My_Rest	Definition
REST	Place where meals can be bought and eaten
PLATO	one of the several parts of a meal
MENU	list of courses at a meal or of dishes available at a restaurant
nrest	integer number uniquely identifying the restaurants in my list
nombre	Official name of the restaurant
calle	Address of the restaurant; reduced to street. All restaurants are supossed to be in Madrid.
tipo	Type of the restaurant. A broad classification is used
calificac	A subjective qualification of the restaurant
precio	The price of a typical meal in the restaurant w/o special wines
tfno	Telephone; all the numbers are supossed to be local to Madrid
(owner)	Person who owns the restaurant
nplato	Integer number uniquely identifying the courses in my list
nombre	Widely accepted name of the course
precio	Price of the course, w/o taxes
ncal	calory number of the course

Table 5
Relation and field definition according to UDC

My_Rest	UDC Code	UDC Index
REST	64.024.3(083.85)	Restaurants (Guide)
PLATO	641.8(083)	Main and secondary courses (List)
MENU	64.09	Menus
nrest	64.024.3(083.73)	Restaurants(Keys)
nombre	64.024.3::801.313	Restaurants: Proper noun
calle	64.024.3::625.712(464.115-2)	Restaurant: Streets (in Madrid, the capital)
tipo	64.024.3.001.33	Restaurants. Classification
calificac	64.024.3.001.36	Restaurants. Comparison
precio	642.1::658.8.03::311.14	Main Meals: Selling price: Average
tfno	64.023.3::621.395.6::511.1 (464.115-2)	Restaurant: Telephone set: Number (in Madrid, the capital)
(owner)	64.024.3::347.712::801.313	Restaurants: Shopkeeper: Proper noun
nplato	641.8(083.73)	Main and secondary courses (Keys)
nombre	641.8::801.313	Main and secondary courses: Proper noun
precio	641.8::658.8.03	Main and secondary courses: Selling price
ncal	641.8::536.061	Main and secondary courses: Thermal units

4. SUITABILITY OF UDC AS A DATABASE METADATA LANGUAGE

UDC is what is called a *documental language*. A documental language is an artificial language which is used for describing documents in a unique way so that they can be easily retrieved. From that point of view it acts as a communication mean between people and documents. We can say that both speak the same language. Documental languages belong to different classes (see Table 6). They can be *precoordinated* or *postcoordinated*. The former has the concepts defined before analyzing and classifying the documents and offer a fixed schema, while the latter allows to combine different concepts after the analysis. Besides, documental languages can be *hierarchical* or *associative*. Hierarchical languages have a generalization hierarchy in which one concept is included inside one more general forming a tree. Associative languages can associate one document with more than a concept, allowing a richer description, but they tend to create different classes for the same concept, making document retrieval more difficult.

Table 6
Documental languages classification (adapted from [Amat88])

Hierarchical
- Enciclopedic classifications
  - UDC; Library of the Congress; Dewey Classification
  - Patents International Classification
- Special classifications
  - Excerpta Medica; Chemical Substances Index Number
- Facets classifications
  - ↑ *Precoordinated* (shallow analysis)

  - ↓ *Postcoordinated* (deep analysis)
- Thesaurus
  - Engineering Index Thesaurus; ERIC Thesaurus

Associative
- Documental Lexicons
  - Subject Headings; Uniterms; Peek-a-Book; KWIC Indexes; KWOC Indexes; Citation Index

---

From the documental languages presented in Table 6, thesaurus have been widely used in retrieval databases as well as in corporate databases. The reason being the flexibility that thesaurus offer and, at the same time, its hierarchical organization, because they share features from hierarchical and associative languages. But from the point of view of distributed databases, thesaurus lack the universality owned by hierarchical languages. That aspect that is not very important in specialized databases in which users are supposed to access the thesaurus to retrieve information, is critical in a distributed and autonomous environment composed by hundreds or thousands of databases residing in PC's connected to a network. So, a precoordinated, hierarchical documental language like UDC should be better used for database metadata description.

Other aspects that make UDC little suitable for retrieval databases are its rigidity that requires to classify a document as belonging to one specific and preexisting category, and the fact that many new concepts are described with many digits, which makes it difficult to manage. However, rigidity makes more precise the placement and later retrieval of a concept, and in our case, we are not classifying books or complex documents, but relations and attributes which allow a more specific classification. The number of digits is of little importance if a PC is the information manager.

Of course, there are some disadvantages in using UDC, but they are the same than in using any other classification: the process of assigning codes to our concepts must be made by a documentation specialist, to avoid wrong classifications. Besides, UDC is not completely univoque. Some concepts appear in more than one place in the tables. An effort must be made to assign the code more precisely describing the attribute or relation. For example, Restaurants (see Table 5) have the number 64.024.3, classified under Domestic Economy (Code 64), but has the number 725.71 if classified as a building under Architecture (code 72). Finally, UDC is more suitable to describe concepts that are not very complex nor very simple. For example, specific concepts like restaurant's owner name or telephone number are not included by themselves (at least in the generally available abridged edition we have used [UDC75]). So we have joined elemental concepts like *Telephone set* (classified under Electrical Engineering) and *Number* (classified under Mathematics) to form the specific concept. As might be expected, UDC admits that operation.

In summary, UDC allows us to describe information about databases: on one hand, high level information like restaurants guides or lawyers directories can be well described by UDC; on the other hand, low level information, corresponding to attributes like name, key, address, etc. are difficult to express directly and we have to use auxiliary numbers or join very different concepts. In any case we think that it is more useful to have the attributes described in a normalized way, than in natural language (compare Table 5 and Table 4).

5. USE OF UDC LIKE A DATABASE METADATA LANGUAGE IN PC

A multidatabase prototype based on MRDSM [LiAb87] has been developed in the Department of Telematic Engineering of Madrid Technical University. This prototype has been developed on SUN-3/50 and SUN-3/60 workstations using Ingres 6.3 running under UNIX and RTI's Dynamic Open SQL embedded in C. This prototype has served for studying problems involved in knowing the information contained in remote and accessible databases that have been presented in this paper. Now, we plan to move the multidatabase language to a standard PC platform with a CCITT V21, V22, V22bis and V23 modem for network access. At the same time, we plan to develop a tool to represent the UDC codes besides the database schema and data contained in the PC to allow a remote query to obtain a general description of the content of our database in UDC codes. For data exchange we foresee to use ISO ASN.1 syntax. Finally, even though we have used UDC up to now, we do not discard using another precoordinated documental language that could solve the problems cited above.

6. ACKNOWLEDGMENTS

I would like to acknowledge Jesus Villamor and Jose Manuel Ramos for their work in developing the prototype DIT multidatabase language, and Dra. Carmen Costilla for allowing us to use the Database Laboratory premises and equipment.

7. CONCLUSIONS

Today there is a trend to access more and more databases from PCs. Corporate, private, videotext and information retrieval databases are more available than ever for PC users. Efforts in standardization made by organizations like ISO or CCITT are promising connectivity in a near future. However tools for assuring real interoperability still lack. Among them, a tool for describing remote database semantics is needed. In this paper we have introduced documental languages for that purpose and, particularly, Universal Decimal Classification. Finally, plans to develop a PC metadata management tool have been exposed.

8. REFERENCES

[Amat88] Amat, N., "Documentación Científica y Nuevas Tecnologías de la Información", 2ª Ed., Ed. Pirámide, Madrid, 1988, 527 pp.

[DaHw82] Dayal, U. y Hwang, H.-Y., "View definition and generalization for database integration in MULTIBASE: a system for heterogeneous distributed databases", Sixth Berkeley Conf. on Distributed Data Management and Computer Networks, 1982

[DeAT87b] Deen, S.M., Amin, R.R. and Taylor, M.C., "Data Integration in Distributed Databases", IEEE TOSE, Vol. SE-13, No. 7, July 1987, pp. 860-864

[DeMi89] DeMichiel, L.G., "Resolving database incompatibility: an approach to performing relational operations over mismatched domain", IEEE TOKDE, Vol. 1, n 1, December 1989, pp. 485-493

[Fal.91] Falquet, B. et al, "F2Concept, un modèle intégrant la description de la compréhension et l'extension des classes d'objets", VIIèmes Journées Bases de Données Avancées (Lyon, 25-27 Septembre 1991), INRIA-ROCQUENCOURT, Le Chesnay, 1991, pp. 327-344

[FIDa] FID, "FID Publications Catalogue", 7 Hofweg, The Hague, Netherlands

[FIDb] FID, "Extensions and Corrections to the CDU" (yearly)

[LiAb87] Litwin, W. y Abdellatif, A., "An Overview of the Multi-Database Manipulation Language MDSL", Proc. of the IEEE, vol. 75, n 5, May 1987, pp. 621-632

[LiMR90] Litwin, W., Mark, L. and Roussopoulos, N., "Interoperability of multiple autonomous databases", ACM Computing Surveys, Vol. 22, No. 3, September 1990, pp. 267-293

[Lit.87] Litwin, W., Abdellatif, A., Zeroual, A., Nicolas, B. and Vigier, P., "MSQL: a multidatabase language", INRIA Res. Rep. 695.

[MaRo86] Mark, L. y Roussopoulos, N., "Metadata management", IEEE Computer, Vol. 19, No. 12, Dec. 1986, pp. 19-25

[Mill63] Mills, J., "Guide to the Universal Decimal Classification (UDC)", London, British Standard Institution, 1963, 128 pp.

[Oxfo74] Hornby, A.S., "Oxford Advanced Learner's Dictionary of Current English", Oxford University Press, 1974

[Pere91] Perez-Rosado, J.M. "Heterogeneous Distributed Databases: a comparison and classification", Guest Conference, VIIèmes Journées Bases de Données Avancées (Lyon, 25-27 Septembre 1991), INRIA-ROCQUENCOURT, Le Chesnay, 1991, pp. 177-203

[ShLa90] Sheth, A.P. and Larson, J.A., "Federated database systems for managing distributed, heterogeneous, and autonomous databases", ACM Computing Surveys, Vol. 22, No. 3, September 1990, pp. 183-236

[UDC75] Instituto Nacional de Racionalización y Normalización (IRANOR), "Clasificación Decimal Universal. Edición abreviada española", 3ª Ed., FID Nº 517, UNE 50 001, CSIC, Madrid, 1975, 319 pp.

ANNEXE. UDC CLASSIFICATION

The Universal Decimal Classification is a numeric classification widely used in libraries. It makes a classification of all subjects in a decimal and hierarchical fashion. In Table 7 we can see the first level of the classification.

Table 7
First level of UDC

Class	Subject
0	Generalities
1	Philosophy
2	Religion. Theology
3	Social Sciences. Statistics. Politics. Economy. Law. Administration. Social Assistance. Insurances. Education. Trade. Ethnography
4	Not used
5	Physical Sciences. Mathematics. Natural Sciences
6	Applied Sciences. Medicine, Technology
7	Fine Arts. Industrials Arts. Photography. Music. Games. Sports
8	Linguistics. Philology. Literature. Literary Critic
9	Geography. Biography. History

Any topic can be coded using UDC by assigning to it the sequence of digits corresponding to the category in which that topic is placed. It is called the *main number*. For example, *telephone sets* are classified as '621.395.6' (see hierarchy of concepts in Table 8).

UDC is based on the classification created by the american librarian Melvil Dewey in 1876 which incorporated 932 concepts. In 1905 a first complete edition with about 33,000 entries was produced by the Bibliographic International Institute. Several editions have been published since then in different languages. Currently they are updated and published by the International Documentation Federation, an international, non-governmental organization, with members belonging to more than 90 countries. The current complete edition contains more than 150.000 concepts. Usually, abridged editions with 30% or 10% of the complete edition entries are used [UDC75].

UDC consists of a main table, in which concepts are classified in a hierarchical manner (see Table 8) and a set of auxiliary tables which include the so called *auxiliary numbers*. They correspond to a set of concepts that can be in relation to many others; for example the concepts of idiom, form, place, race, country, time and point of view. They can be added to the main numbers to more precisely determine a concept. Besides an alphabetical index is included. It allows us to easily determine the category associated with a certain concept.

Main numbers are divided by dots '.' for easier reading. Besides, other special symbols are used. In this paper we have used the following: *'(...)'* common auxiliary number for *places*; *'(0...)'* common auxiliary number for *form*; *'.00...'* common auxiliary number for *point of view*; *'.0...' special auxiliary number*; *'::'* connection between main numbers to describe a new concept. More details about UDC can be found in [Mill63] and the publications by FID [FIDa] [FIDb].

Table 8
Place of *Telephone set* in the hierarchy of UDC

6 Applied Sciences. Medicine. Technology
- 61 Medicine
- *62* Engineering. Technology
  - 620 Materials. Energy
  - *621* Technology. Mechanical Engineering. Nuclear Engineering. Electrical Engineering
    - *621.3* Electrical Engineering
      - *621.39* Telecommunicatios
        - *621.395* Telephony
        - *621.395.6 Telephone sets*
- 63 Agriculture ...

Personal Computers and Intelligent Systems / F.H. Vogt (Editor)
Information Processing 92, Volume III
Elsevier Science Publishers B.V. (North-Holland)

GLOBAL SYSTEMS INTEGRATION WITH HYPERMEDIA

Peter Maier
SONY Europa GmbH - European Headquarter of Sony Corporation
Hugo-Eckener-Straße 20, 5000 Köln 30, Germany

Keywords: Strategic Information Systems, Marketing Information Systems, Global System Integration, Hypermedia, Executive Support Systems

The requirements for the future are to get rid of today's most important restrictions concerning time, location and organization.

Whereas this characterizes a manifold wider range of benefits than could ever be sufficiently adressed by an "empowered PC", two global aspects can bring us forward: harmonization and orchestration

Historically, the request for power on a per-medium-basis evolved to connectivity requirements, and the birth of the multimedia quality makes it clear that 'systems integration' cannot be any longer a term that is occupied by the IS-industry. Today, we are confronted with the task to harmonize integrated systems with the wide world of multimedia.

In the past, many companies failed in creating Executive Support Systems (see Fig. 1) - they suffered either from the inability to integrate their systems or from the lack of capabilities to attractively compose and 'market' this on-top-system. To overcome the former reason might be a matter of time, whereas the latter one requires to have a new look at the audience (formerly called: users) and the media they are dealing with: HYPER-Tech, not only HI-Tech.

It is a wide-spread fault to incorporate multimedia by "somehow-bring-things-together" procedures, adressing only technical matters and data connectivity of machines. We also need the sophistication of a film director to synchronize media at a high level of perfection - known from the film/video industry and/or recording studios. They incorporate long history of experience in organizing everything an audience expects together and "cook a new record or a new film". The cooks live from their ideas and their affinity to the brain and feelings of human beings.

We use the term 'hypermedia' to adress the orchestration of multimedia and integrated systems into an instrument that will even be accepted and played on by executives - the top-of-the-audience.

In the near future we will meet a systems world that is coming affine to human brain

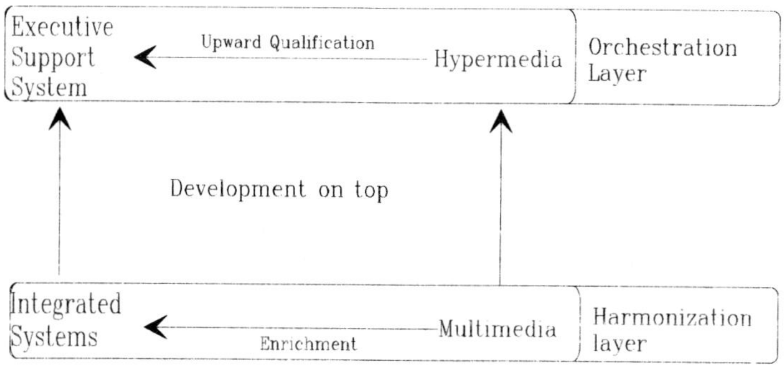

Fig. 1: Executive Support System Environment

Personal Computers and Intelligent Systems / F.H. Vogt (Editor)
Information Processing 92, Volume III
Elsevier Science Publishers B.V. (North-Holland)

ISDN for Multimedia Workstations

Rolf Wildhack

Stollmann GmbH, Gasstraße 18, 2000 Hamburg 50

Abstract

Multimedia is the next event which will arrive at desktop workstations, where computing power and graphical user interfaces are nowadays state of the art. The appropriate network for multimedia - Broadband ISDN - is still far away, but Narrowband ISDN is already on the way to the user. Its limited bandwith makes it crucial to implement multimedia applications. Nevertheless many companies and research groups are working on multimedia applications for ISDN. This paper gives an overview on developments and prospects concerning ISDN for multimedia workstations.

1. Multimedia

Multimedia will be one of the fastest growing market segments in the next years. Analysts predict multibillion dollar markets for multimedia applications by middle of the nineties. But it is not only multimedia, which has good prospects. Imaging with its single medium for example is a new technology, which shall also evolve into a big business in the same time.
Media within this context are: Data, Text, Graphics, Images, Video and Audio, where only the first three are already well-known on the desktop.

The driving force behind these developments is not only the hardware industry, which may need new software to sell new hardware. It is furthermore the challenge of new computerized applications, which may revolutionize complete lines of business. Another observation shows, that the introduction of personal workstations has brought lots of new productivity to the desk; new gains in productivity will be achieved not by personal computing but by interpersonal computing. The efforts in the area of groupware applications reflect this perception. Multimedia and appropriate networks are necessary to complete these applications.

Multimedia Computing is not longer the exclusive place for exotic start up companies. Well-known computer and peripheral manufacturers are working now on concepts for multimedia. Examples are IBM with its Person-to-Person/2-system and DEC with "Community Multimedia Networking".

2. Multimedia Workstations

Multimedia sets new requirements to workstations: An image of 1000x1000 pixels with 24 bits takes 3 Megabyte of memory uncompressed, an HDTV image takes even 45 Megabyte. So an older opinion tells, that multimedia workstations are defined by the four Gs: 1 Gigabyte memory, 1 Gigaoperations per second, Gigabytes of disk capacity and 1 Gigabit per second communications link. With these requirements, the technical problems of multimedia will be solved easily, but not the commercial ones. Fortunately some approaches were found, which can bring multimedia to lower equipped workstations. These approaches meet the workstation distribution of today very close: over 90% of the installed base are PCs running MSDOS. The remaining ones are Apple Macs and UNIX-workstations. So it is quite reasonable, to focus the following considerations mainly on the DOS-community.

For this PCs the additional multimedia requirements can be formulated as follows:

- High resolution color monitor
- Overlay card for video in windows
- Audio processing board
- Loudspeaker and microphone
- CD-ROM drive
- and lots of memory, disk space and processing power.

The operating system must show some realtime features for multimedia applications, especially the processing of time dependent data like Apple offers with quicktime.

1988 Microsoft released requirements for so called Multimedia PCs (MPCs), which are supported by leading PC manufacturers. These specify now a 386SX processor with 20 MHz, VGA-graphics, 2 MByte RAM, 30 MByte Disk, digital sound-board, MIDI-Interface, CD-ROM-drive and Windows. Microsoft is working on a multimedia upgrade kit for Windows. Other PC and Workstation manufacturers are more advanced in multimedia implementation e.g. Apple and Next, but the directions are similar.

One big problem for multimedia workstations is networking: even the speed of todays LANs is not very high, when images are transferred over the network. This becomes even more worse for audio and video, which require beside high bandwith isochronous transmission. That mixes with todays paket oriented data-networks "like oil and water" [4]. This is a problem to be solved, even though some implementations are already available, e.g. from Fluent Machines [4].

3. ISDN

The basic outlines for ISDN are well-known today. One driving force behind it is the digitalization of the telecommunication networks. The benefit for the user and herewith the other driving force is the price/performance relation: ISDN offers a basic rate access (BRA) with two 64 kbps B-channels plus one 16 kbps D-channel, that is significantly more than POTS offers (POTS: Plain Old Telephone Service), and one B-channel connection does not cost much more than an analogue telephone connection. An additional offer is the Primary Rate Access (PRA) with 30 B-channels and one 64 kbps D-channel, which may allow bandwith allocation on demand.

When ISDN started in Europe, the expectations concerning the speed of dissemination and the development of new applications were extremely high. Inbetween, the minds have cooled down, the network operators are working on the harmonization of signalling protocols and crossboarder connections for ISDN while the end-user-equipment manufacturers are distributing well-known applications for the new ISDN: that are PABX-connections to the public network and data communication applications like LAN-bridging, PC-host-coupling etc.. One discovery was common in the european ISDN community: the ideal ISDN terminal is the DOS-based PC. He is well suited for multifunctional desktop applications, and he is a quite reasonable tool for the implementation of ISDN-gateways. Small companies found this out early, the bigger ones followed later. The open architecture of the PC makes it very simple, to develop a PC-card for ISDN, adapt existing applications to it and utilize the benefits of ISDN (e.g. price/performance, see above).

Beside this well-known applications, first projects are showing up, which use the transmission of multimedia over ISDN. With its two 64 kbit/s transparent channels, ISDN offers a suitable transfer characteristic for multimedia, but the divergence to the transmission speed requirements of multimedia is still enormous. The key to this problem is compression.

4. Compression

The following table shows a comparison for requested transmission rates:

Media	Transmission - low quality	Speed high quality
Data	2400 bps	2 Mbps
Audio	16 kbps (AM)	64 kbps (FM) 1.4 Mbps (CD)
Video	10 Mbps (TV)	140 Mbps (HDTV)

Voice can be regarded as a low level subset of audio. ISDN uses now 3.1 kHz voice. A 7 kHz voice coding, which compares to AM quality, is planned for the future. Audio takes further problems into account, especially echo compensation combined with high quality in order to allow a comfortable hands-free operation.

Compression methods for images and video have made big steps during the last years. They target not only narrowband transmission of multimedia, but also the storage of these information on magnetical and optical disk drives and the processing in todays systems. Todays compression methods make use of the human factors in order to obtain a minimum loss of quality and a maximum compression. The main approaches combine the following techniques:

- Prediction: Subsequent pictures are predicted from previous ones. A further point here is motion compensation, that means moving objects are recognized and only the motion vector will be transmitted.
- Frequency-oriented compression: Humans have different sensitivities to various temporal or spatial frequencies, e.g. high frequencies cannot be recognized.
- Importance-oriented compression: Changes in brightness for example are more important than changes in color.

These methods result in losses during compression, that means the original picture or video cannot be reconstructed identically from the compressed information. But the differences may be very small. Lossy compression rates vary from 10:1 to 50:1 for still pictures, and from 50:1 to 200:1 for video, if greater losses are tolerated even more, see below. Lossless methods may yield only compression rates of 3:1 under average conditions.

An ISDN videophone may give an example for these compression techniques: The H.261-compliant videophones tested now in the german field trial offer a color monitor with 20 cm diagonal at maximum, the resolution of 576 x 720 pixels is compressed to 288 x 360, 8 pictures were sent per second with interpolation, intra and inter frame coding. This results in a compression rate of 800:1 and the presentation of limited motion.

In order to ensure the compatibility of terminal equipment and software, international standards are mandatory. For multimedia there are three available:

JPEG (Joint Photographics Expert Group), a standard proposed by ISO for still picture compression. JPEG considers a broad scope including lossy and lossless algorithms. The lossy baseline approach gives a compression of 10 to 100 (average 20-30) times while maintaining a high quality. A draft was submitted in 1991.

H.261 is a CCITT standard for smallband videophones and videoconferencing systems operating with transmission rates of p*64 kbps (p=1-32, for ISDN BRA: p=1 or 2). H.261 uses intra frame coding, predictive (interframe) coding, and optional motion compensation. The quality of H.261-based systems reaches from low with limited motion up to very high. CCITT approved recommendation H.261 in 1990.

MPEG (Motion Pictures Expert Group) is an ISO working group for compression of moving images for full motion picture compression on digital storage media. The considered transfer rates reach up to 1.5 Mbps. This aims at CD-Rom, Video Tape and T1-links. An improved version MPEG-2 is for transfer rates up to 10 Mbps. The MPEG algorithm works similar to H.261, but it must perform some more things like direct access, bidirectional access and fast forward and backward functions. MPEG covers three areas: Video, Audio (where CD-quality with 2x706 kbps is compressed to 2x128 or 64 Kbps) and System (TV-quality video and audio in 1.5 Mbps).

Due to the fact, that these standards cover only the very low levels of multimedia applications, a standard MHEG (Multimedia and Hypermedia Information Coding Expert Group) will be created to cover the higher layers of multimedia applications.

5. Base Technologies

The high sophisticated compression algorithms for multimedia require tremendous hardware efforts in order to perform in time. For still pictures the compression and decompression time is up to a certain limit more a question of taste. But for video, even with limited motion, the compression and decompression must be executed on the fly. Therefore todays H.261 codecs do not fit on the desk, but below it. The same is valid for their price. The solution to these problems will be low cost silicon. And several companies are working on that.
Examples for JPEG chip sets are C-Cube Microsystems, LSI Logic and Fluent with its JPEG chips for video on LAN and T1. On H.261 chip sets are working LSI Logic again and Graphics Communications America and probably several companies, which showed already H.261 codecs. Especially interesting for prestandard algorithms are the more general silicon approaches by Intel and UVC.

6. Applications and Products

Multimedia applications for ISDN are still in pilot state. But several projects in France, Germany, and other european countries utilize multimedia [3] and give some impressions of the impact of multimedia over ISDN on future applications. The implementations show an inhomogeneous manifold, but they can be divided into 3 groups depending on the basic technologies as shown in the following table:

Application	Media
Videoconferencing	Video, Audio
Videophone	Video, Voice
Picture Communication	Images
Document Image Communication	Images
Computer based Training	Voice, Data, optional Video
PC Desktop Conferencing	Data, Graphics

We discuss these groups a little more in detail:

6.1 Video

Narrowband videophones and videoconferences are the most exciting technologies in this area at all. Many of the leading telecom suppliers are working on solutions and present prototypes since several years. The reasons for this efforts are quite clear: videoconferencing is a technology, which has already prooven that it can save travel expenses, rise employee efficiency, and it can ensure rapid coordination of meetings from multiple sides, which results in quicker decisions, shorter time to market and other mission critical issues. Drawbacks for videoconferencing in the past were the high cost for equipment and for the broadband connections, which limited the usage to public studios or absolutely top level management. With the introduction of ISDN videoconferencing equipment, prices and connection charges will decrease rapidly, and open this technology to a wider user group. One problem for ISDN videoconferencing can be the limited quality. But nevertheless low speed codecs are catching up rapidly against high speed codecs in terms of market share. A solution to the quality problems can be bandwith allocation on demand.

The transmission and coding techniques are nearly the same for videophones and videoconferencing systems. For videoconferencing at least a Multipoint Control Unit (MCU) as defined in CCITT H.140 is necessary to coordinate the several distant partners. ISDN videophones on the other hand can be considered as a point-to-point videoconference with a probably lower quality for video and voice instead of audio. But they target a much wider market up to the private user. This can especially be seen at some product developments for videophones on POTS using transmission rates between 9.6 and 19.2 kbps, which are now entering the market. Of course, the very low transmission rate results in a very limited quality.

Applications for videophones are not only person to person calls, but furthermore surveillance of buildings, industrial areas, automatic teller machines and so on. And one can imagine, what the now evolving info-services on telephone networks can offer, if they utilize not only the common telephone but a videophone.

The integration of videophones and videoconferencing in workstations is of great importance. This is quite obvious, because a workstation is already on the normal desk, and it is able to present at least the video. Furthermore, the user wants to see his communication partners in windows, while the document, which may be the topic for the conference is shown in another window. So many of the now stand alone systems will be integrated in PCs or offer at least a PC integration kit.

Even a more important issue for the dissemination of videophones and videoconferencing is the compatibility and that must mean compliance to the H.261 standard. Companies who have already prestandard products in the market may praise the advantages of their products against the ones which

comply to the standards, but soon the customers will stick to the products, which offer the highest connectivity, and that will be the standard-compliant ones. In Germany, a field trial for videophones started this year and aims at the European Videophone Experiment (EVE), which should ensure compatibility of the products beside other targets like user feed back etc..
The prices for ISDN videophones shown at telecom 91 in Geneva varied from $ 7000 to $ 20,000. Future price developments can be deviated from the prices for available videophones on POTS, e.g. AT&T videophone 2500 for $ 1499 or Amstrad for $850. Entry level videoconferencing systems for ISDN cost now about $ 40,000.

6.2 Image communication

Image communication addresses a broad range of applications, while the applied technologies may vary from facsimile up to high resolution picture transmission. Applications areas are for example:

- Image data bases run e.g. by photographic news agencies. ISDN can shorten the delivery time from days to minutes.
- Medical images like X-rays or tomographies can be sent via ISDN much faster than via mail.
- Real Estate, travel or model agencies can obtain pictures, blue prints and further informations on objects from centralized data bases just in time, and that means furthermore: The information is very actual.

One example for an image communication product ist PictureView from PKI: PictureView is based on a 386 PC running windows equipped with a VGA card, a JPEG coded, an ISDN card, and an optional document camera or camcorder as picture input device. The system works with VGA-resolution and 16 bits per pixel. Compression and decompression of Pictures takes 3 to 7 seconds, transmission 7 to 8 seconds according to PKI [8].

6.3 PC desktop connection

It is difficult, to summarize the applications of this group. Examples are:

- Joint editing on documents generated by DTP or CAD tools via ISDN: One B-channel is used for data exchange, the second B-channel is for a voice connection, so the partners can talk and edit the document simultaneously.
- Interactive remote computer based training: The teacher and the trainees are equipped with PCs connected via ISDN. ISDN permits individual control of each trainees training program by the teacher, enriched by simultaneous telephone communication and screen sharing. Video can supplement this application.

- PC desktop conferencing: This application works with two PCs connected via ISDN and offers screen sharing and exchange of screen control between them. PC desktop conferencing via ISDN can shorten the time for contract negotiations or harmonization of other documents with distant partners very well.
  The Joint Viewing and Teleoperation Services (JVTOS) model of Race project 2060 (CIO) considers a multipoint solution for PC desktop conferencing.

Common for this examples are: they are based on PCs, they connect more or less common PC-tools via ISDN, and they address users which are used to work at PCs. So they are limited to a class of experts. It is obvious, that this group is in a very prestandard phase. Media can be all objects which the PC can handle from data and text up to graphics and images.

7. Conclusions

Multimedia is an exciting technology which will find for shure its markets. The integration of networking is important for the success of multimedia. Although Narrowband ISDN does not meet the bandwith requirements of multimedia applications very close, there are very interesting approaches for multimedia communication over ISDN, which will have a deep impact on future applications. The price/performance relation and the diffusion of ISDN will open these applications to a wide group of users.
The main emphasis in multimedia appplications will not be on overloaded systems which utilize all available media, but more likely in combimedia, that is the combination of 2 or 3 media. This meets the features which ISDN can offer for multimedia very well.

Literature

[1] Edward A. Fox: Advances in Interactive Digital Multimedia Systems, IEEE Computer 10/91

[2] Elliot M. Gold: Videoconferencing closes in on the desktop, Networking Management 1/92

[3] Fischer & Lorenz and Ovum: European ISDN Atlas 1991

[4] Malcolm Laws: Desktop Multimedia in Communications Week International, 9/30/91

[5] Norbert Hahn: Video-conferencing: A face-to-face communication, Communication Technology International 1992

[6] Nicholas C. Stanley: Building a telecommunications infrastructure for distant learning, Communication Technology International 1992

[7] Peng H. Ang, Peter A. Ruetz and David Auld: Video compression makes big gains, IEEE Spektrum October 1991

Personal Computers and Intelligent Systems / F.H. Vogt (Editor)
Information Processing 92, Volume III
Elsevier Science Publishers B.V. (North-Holland)

A Synthetic Media Architecture for an Object-Oriented Open Platform

Y. TANAKA[a], A. NAGASAKI[a], M. AKAISHI[a], and T. NOGUCHI[b]

[a]Electrical Engineering Department, Hokkaido University, Sapporo, Japan

[b]Electrical Engineering Department, Kushiro Technical Collage, Kushiro, Japan

Abstract

Computers as meta-media should provide us with an open integrated environment for all kinds of our intellectual activities, and hence need a unified framework for (a) the modeling, (b) the presentation, (c) the synthesis, (d) the sharing, (e) the coordination of user interactions, (f) the circulation / publication, and (g) the management of multimedia documents, system-provided functions, and application programs. The IntelligentPad system we proposed in 1989 provided a unified framework for (a), (b), (c) and (g). It represents everything as a pad. The pasting of pads on another pad defines a new composite pad. This paper further extends it for (d), (e), (f), and (g), to propose it as an open integrated platform for the next-generation OISs.

Keyword Codes: H.5.1; H.5.2; H.5.3
Keywords: Multimedia Information Systems; User Interfaces; Group and Organization Interfaces

1. INTRODUCTION

In his invited talk at IFIP Congress '89, N. Naffah predicted that OISs in 90s would come with the integrated support through hypermedia technologies [1]. We think that the key design concepts for the OIS in 90s might include the followings:

(1) unified treatment of intellectual resources including multimedia documents, server programs (database systems, file systems, mail systems, etc.), application programs, and their environments.
(2) functional integration of all kinds of intellectual resources.
(3) an open architecture for the export and import, or the circulation, of intellectual resources among different times and places.
(4) a generic toolkit for end-users to synthesize new intellectual resources.
(5) a shared space for the cooperative work with all kinds of intellectual resources. (The OISs in 90s cannot exist without CSCW facilities [2].)
(6) coordination of a sequence of user interactions with more than one intellectual resources, i.e., a script programming facility.
(7) integrated management of all kinds of intellectual resources, i.e., a database for media objects, which we call a media base.

Hypermedia systems today such as Analyst [3], NoteCards [4], and HyperCard fully satisfy (1), (2) and (6). Some of them partially satisfy (5) and (7). None of them however fully satisfy all the above concepts. They are closed in the sense that they provide no means for their users either to assimilate new tools developed elsewhere into their integrated environments or to compose new tools from existing ones. Tsichritzis pointed out that (3), (4), and (7) are fundamental to the next-generation software development [5]. We call such systems satisfying the above seven principles synthetic media systems. The first five principles would bring a new portable representation form for multimedia documents and application programs, which facilitates their distribution, stimulates their production and usage, and opens a new media business market. Wide-area computer networks will offer good infrastructures for such markets.

The adoption of media metaphors by computer systems began in early 80's with the DTP, which enabled us to layout various types of media on a single page. Around the mid 80's, video boards allowed the embedding of video clips in complex documents. Then people began to seek a way to treat different component types in a uniform way. This encouraged the object oriented system design, which allowed the embedding of programs. Such documents became dynamic media objects. The object oriented programming allows two different styles of programming, i.e., the class-hierarchy programming and the synthetic programming. Around the mid 80s, the synthetic programming paradigm developed various GUI toolkit systems for window systems. Among them are Xt of MIT [6], Andrew Toolkit of CMU [7], OPEN LOOK Toolkit, and Motif Toolkit. This trend encouraged our group to apply the toolkit approach to the design of dynamic media objects, which led to our proposal of the synthetic media, and resulted in the development of the IntelligentPad system.

In 1989, we proposed the IntelligentPad system satisfying (1), (2), and (4) [8], and showed a rough sketch for (7) [9]. It represents every intellectual resource as a pad, i.e., a sheet of paper. Figure 1.1 (a) shows its OIS application, while (b) shows its CAI application. The latter system provides not only a micro world of S. Papert, but also a construction set with which students can create or change his micro world. Pads are persistent. The system allows us to paste pads on another pad to layout them and to compose a new function by combining their functions. Various parts in (b) such as pullies and springs are animated on transparent pads, and combined through the pasting of their pads. In 1991, we further extended the system to partially satisfy (5) through the introduction of the shared copy operation [10]. Shared copies share the same state, but not all the events on them.

Here in this paper, we will show further extensions for (3), (5), (6), and (7), and propose the IntelligentPad architecture as a synthetic media architecture, i.e., as an integrated open platform for the next-generation OISs. For (3), the packaging technique has allowed us to export and import any pads to and from the public market. For (5), we have abstracted the event-sharing function from CSCW applications, and defined it as a special pad named FieldPad. Shared copies of the same FieldPad define a shared workbench. Similarly, we have abstracted the coordination function (6) and the media base function (7), and defined them as two special pads, i.e., the StagePad and the PadBasePad.

2. THE IntelligentPad AS A SYNTHETIC MEDIA ARCHITECTURE

Each primitive pad is defined as an MVC (Model, View, Controller) triple (Figure 2.1). Its model defines its internal mechanism consisting of its state and behavior, while its view and controller constitute its display object. Every pad uses a copy of the same controller object. The model part has a frame structure, i.e., a list of slots $[s_1, s_2, \dots, s_n]$, where s_i is a slot name. Each slot is accessed by either of the two messages, '**set** <*slot_name*> <*value*>' and '**gimme** <*slot_name*>'. Each of these two messages invokes the respective procedure

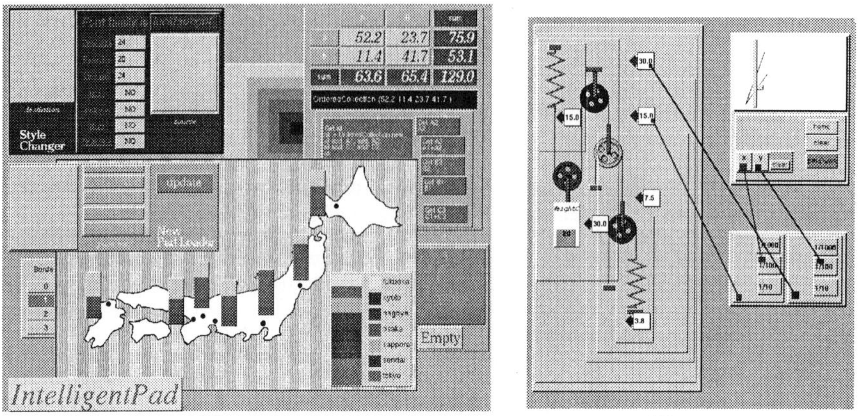

(a) (b)

Figure 1.1 A display snapshot of the IntelligentPad system.

attached to the slot. Each slot has two attached procedures, $proc_{i,\mathrm{set}}$ and $proc_{i,\mathrm{gimme}}$. The default for $proc_{i,\mathrm{set}}$ stores the parameter value into the slot, while the default for $proc_{i,\mathrm{gimme}}$ returns the slot value. Its slots and attached procedures define the internal mechanism of a pad.

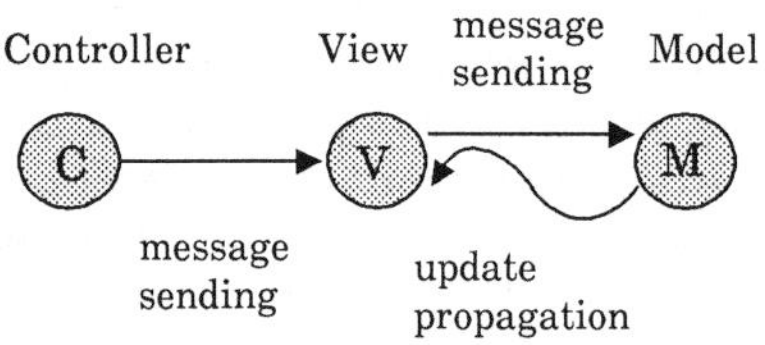

Figure 2.1 The internal structure of each pad.

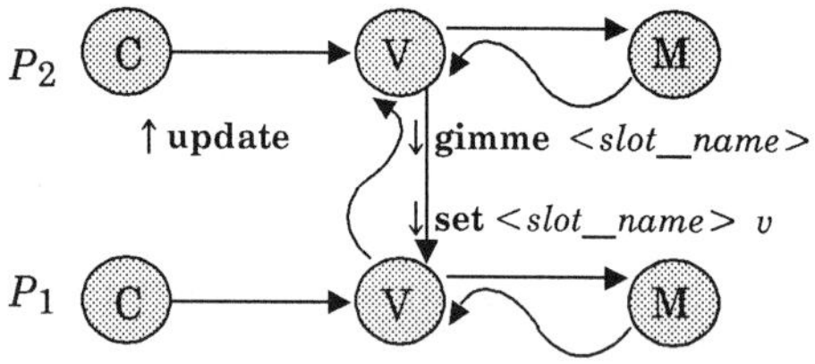

Figure 2.2 Standard message interface between pads.

The IntelligentPad does not allow pluggable MVCs. Its users can change the appearance of any media object only through pasting some other pads on top of it. When a pad P_2 or its icon is pasted on another pad P_1, the IntelligentPad constructs two paths between their views as shown in Figure 2.2. This defines a dependency from P_1 to P_2. The pad P_2 is a subpad of P_1, while P_1 is the master pad of P_2. No pad may have more than one master pad.

If P_1 has more than one slot, we have to select one of them to associate it with P_2. This selection can be specified on a connection sheet pad. The selected slot name is stored in a standard slot of the subpad P_2 named *connectslot*. A subpad can send either **set** ↑ *connectslot* <*value*> or **gimme** ↑ *connectslot* message to its master, while the master pad, when its state is changed, can send all of its subpads an **update** message without any parameter to propagate an update event. The up arrow before *connectslot* means that the slot name stored in *connectslot* becomes the real parameter. The two messages **set** s v and **gimme** s sent to a pad P are forwarded to its master pad if P does not have the slot s.

Besides the three standard messages, any pad can send some standard messages for geometrical operations to its master as well as to its subpads. Among them are move, copy, delete, hide, show, open, close, resize, and paste messages. The set of these standard messages defines a standard interface between pads. The programming of a pad with **set** ↑*connectslot* <*value*> and **gimme** ↑*connectslot* messages requires no knowledge about its master pad. Other standard messages between pads access no slots of each other. This allows the pad developers to program pads as generic reusable objects.

3. SHARED SPACE

The IntelligentPad allows us to make a shared copy of any pad as well as a nonshared copy. Shared copies of the same pad keep their bottom pads share the same model component. Shared copies distributed across a computer network may concurrently request their model component to update its state. IntelligentPad requests us to associate each shared copy with an arbitrary number as its priority level for the conflict resolution among concurrent model-update requests.

Shared copies cannot make one of them simulate paste operations performed on another. This requires the event sharing, which a FieldPad can perform. We may put any pads on a FieldPad to define a shared workbench. A shared copy of this composite pad has a nonshared copy of each pad on a shared copy of the field pad. The primary slot of a FieldPad stores the last operation performed in the area defined by this pad. A FieldPad can detect any user-event request over itself. The user events here includes mouse dragging, mouse clicking, and keyboard typing.

In the IntelligentPad, every mouse event is detected by the controller of the top pad at the mouse location. Every user event over a FieldPad, however, needs to be sent to this FieldPad. This requirement implies that each pad, when put over a FieldPad, has to replace its controller with a special controller used only over a FieldPad. This controller, when it detects a user-event request, sends its information to the view of the topmost FieldPad under this pad. The event information consists of the event type and the event location. The event location is given as the (x, y) coordinate relative to the FieldPad. When its state is updated, the FieldPad traces up the subpad links to find the topmost pad at the given event location. This is the same pad that sent the event information. The FieldPad then sends the view of the target pad the same message as its original controller would directly send. The same replay mechanism works in every shared copy of the same FieldPad, which realizes a shared workbench.

A FieldPad defines a space different from the desktop space. The IntelligentPad uses the metaphor of black holes and white holes to transport pads from one space to another. A BlackHolePad, when some pad is put on it, transports this pad to its corresponding WhiteHolePad. The transported pads can be dragged out of the WhiteHolePad into a new space. FieldPads can be hierarchically pasted on another FieldPad. This defines nested shared spaces as shown in Figure 3.1. The users X and Y share the same larger space, while the user Z shares the smaller space with X and Y. Every BlackHolePad and its corresponding WhiteHolePads are labeled with the same letter from A to C.

4. STAGE AND SCRIPT

In IntelligentPad systems, we can perform our jobs through synthesizing and manipulating various pads. Each pad when operated reacts to perform a subjob. In this sense, each pad may be compared to a stage actor who plays a role following

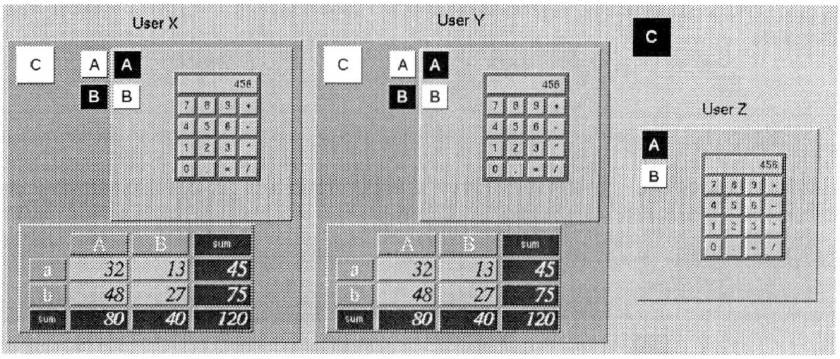

Figure 3.1 Nested shared spaces and warm holes.

the director's order. Some applications such as CAI and computer games need to program a sequence of operations on pads. In IntelligentPad philosophy, this script program should be represented as a pad. We call this a StagePad since it provides various actor pads with a stage on which they perform a play.

Our script programs differ from the HyperCard script programs in the following respects. They do not directly send messages to actor pads, but send them user events such as mouse clicks, mouse drags, and key strikes. They can not directly read or write any other observable slots of an actor pad than its primary slot. Script programs operate the actor pads in the same way as we operate them.

In an actual play, its script does not refer to any actor, but to his or her role. Any replacement of actors requires no rewriting of the script. The same is true to StagePad scripts. Each pad may have more than one operation point with different reactions. Hence, script programs refer to operation points instead of actor pads. Operation points are referred to through their role names. Each StagePad has a casting list, a table that associates operation points with their roles. A mouse click of a role in this list generates a new point mark, which we can put at any location on any pad over the StagePad. This location defines an operation point assigned to this role.

The performance on a StagePad allows user interruptions. Scripts are described as event-driven programs. The capturing of every user event over a StagePad is realized by making each pad send every executed user event on itself to the topmost StagePad below itself. Each StagePad has an event queue. The StagePad inserts the received event information at the front of its event queue, and transfer this information also to the topmost StagePad below itself. A script program is a collection of sentences of the form;

on <*condition*> **do** <*action*> **end.**

Each StagePad repetitively takes the first event from its event queue, and tries to find a sentence with this event in its condition part. If such a sentence is found, the sequence of operations specified by its action part is executed. Each operation adds their corresponding event at the end of the event queue.

A StagePad with some actor pads can be pasted on top of another StagePad. This allows us to define a play within a play. StagePads can be put over a FieldPad. When making copies of a FieldPad with a StagePad over it, the system disables the script of all copies of the StagePad except the one of the original.

5. PadBase & CONTEXT SEARCH

The increasing number of primitive and composite media objects require a media base. Media bases manage a large amount of different object types, while conventional databases can only manage a large amount of objects classified into a small number of different types. Media bases require new management and retrieval methods. In media bases, each unit to store is a dynamic media object consisting not only of its state and behavior but also with its appearance and its reaction against user manipulation. Conventional databases store for each object only its state, while abstract-data-type databases and object-oriented databases store for each object both its state and behavior. These databases consider that the appearance and reaction of objects are the matter of their human interface subsystems outside themselves. Such consideration works only for a small set of different appearance types and different reaction types. For a large number of different appearance types and reaction types, we need a media base.

The current version of IntelligentPad provides a pad base, a media base for all kinds of primitive pads and composite ones. In our daily conversation, we specify what we want by its name if we know the name. Otherwise, we partially specify it either by its category, by its substructure, by its context, or by some combination of these. We may describe fish as things in water. This specifies its context. We may describe a calculator as a thing with more than 10 buttons and a digital display. This specifies its substructure. Pad bases should allow us to specify the pads we want by any of these different methods. Since the IntelligentPad represents both contexts and components as pads, their structures can be specified in the same quantification method. We call a search based on such quantification a context search of pads.

The current version of IntelligentPad has the PadBasePad that works as an interface to GemStone object-oriented DBMS. As shown in Figure 5.1, a PadBasePad accepts a partially specified pad structure given in the left box, and returns search results in the large center box. These boxes are both structure-extraction pads. When a composite pad is put on this pad, it extracts the structure of this composite pad. We finished with the first implementation of the PadBasePad in 1990. Our experience with GemStone however has proved that its indexing technology can not sufficiently speed up the context search. The same problem lies in most OODBMSs available today. We need a new indexing method to speed up the context search.

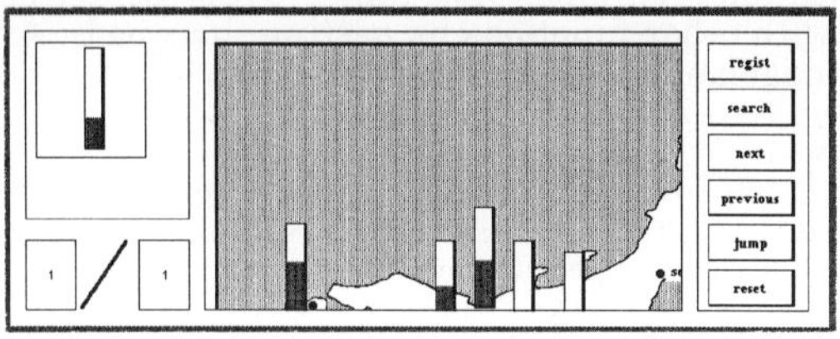

Figure 5.1 A PadBasePad retrieves a pad with the substructure specified in the left window.

6. EXPORT AND IMPORT OF PADS

In our society, each of us exports and imports his intellectual resources to and from the others. This is fundamental in the development of our culture. The newest version of the IntelligentPad system has enabled each of its installation to export and import any pads to and from its other installations. This facilitates the circulation of various primitive and composite pads, stimulates their production, usage and exchange, and opens a public market of pads. Each user may incrementally improve his environment starting from a minimal set of pads. System developers can improve the system facilities by releasing new pads that add new functions to the kernel system. Application developers can sell application modules in the form of pads or pad kits. User can publish their own combinations of pads as composite pads, which may carry business data together with its analysis tools, research reports with experimental data or simulation programs, stories with interactive animations and video clips, super computer programs with the visualization facilities, etc.

The export of an object instance *Obj* that is defined in a class hierarchy *H* to another installation with a different class-hierarchy *H'* requires some technology to send from *H* to *H'* all the class definitions in *H* necessary to define *Obj* and to make *H'* assimilate these classes. This is not an easy task. Some researchers think that class hierarchies are harmful in the circulation of objects. Our project adopted the packaging technology used in Common Lisp. It gives a package name to a subtree of *H* that is required to define *Obj*, and add this subtree to *H'* under a new branch from its root. Every class under this branch changes its name by adding the package name as its prefix, and rewrites its methods so that every class reference might use these new names.

The remaining question on the pad assimilation is how a pad base can assimilate newly imported pads. GemStone uses OPAL language to define all the classes of the stored objects. To assimilate an imported package of classes, the pad base has to automatically generate the corresponding OPAL definitions of these classes. It requires more research to answer this question.

7. CONCLUDING REMARKS

The IntelligentPad System as a synthetic media system is an open platform that can provide an overall integrated environment for human activities. An appropriate mapping of any specific application to a single pad or a set of pads will assimilate this application into the environment of pads. Any external object also can be assimilated by this integrated environment through the introduction of a pad that works as its proxy in this environment. The IntelligentPad System is open to any application programs. Once they are represented as pads, they can be easily combined with other functions by pasting their pads. A pad base provides an integrated management of all kinds of pads.

REFERENCES

1 Naffah, N., Proc. IFIP Congress '89, San Francisco, Aug. 1989, pp.745-750.
2 Schrage, M., Shared Minds : The New Technologies of Collaboration, Random House, 1990.
3 The Analyst User Guide, Xerox Special Information Systems, 1985.
4 Halasz, F.G., Morgan, T.P., and Trigg, R.H., Proc. of CHI + GI, 1987.
5 Tsichritzis, D., Proc. IFIP Congress '89, San Francisco, Aug. 1989, pp. 1033-1040.
6 Rao,R., and Wallace, S., Proc. of the Summer, 1987 USENIX Conference, 1987.
7 Borenstein, N. S., Multimedia Applications Development with the Andrew Toolkit, Prentice Hall, 1990.
8 Y. Tanaka and T. Imataki, Proc. IFIP Congress '89, San Francisco, Aug. 1989, pp. 541-546.
9 Y. Tanaka, Proc. of Deductive and Object-Oriented Databases, Kyoto, Dec. 1989, pp. 259-277.
10 Y. Tanaka, Proc. of Multimedia Information Systems, Sigapore, Jan. 1991, pp. 299-310.

Personal Computers and Intelligent Systems / F.H. Vogt (Editor)
Information Processing 92, Volume III
Elsevier Science Publishers B.V. (North-Holland)

Flexible Network Architectures for Personal Multimedia Communications

Bernd Heinrichs, Raschid Karabek

Aachen University of Technology
Informatik IV, Department of Computer Science
Ahornstr. 55, W-5100 Aachen, Germany

Tel.: +241/80-21410; FAX: +241/80-21429
e-mail: heibe@informatik.rwth-aachen.de

Abstract

This paper aims at pointing out the importance to increase network protocol processing performance in order to support the growing variety of new applications distributed across a multiplicity of personal computing systems (PCs and workstations) interconnected by numerous heterogeneous local and wide area networks. Future protocol architectures will have to offer a much broader range of services to meet the various requirements resulting from the never ending list of multimedia applications like real-time conferencing, cooperative design, medical imaging, publishing, distance learning, etc.. To build powerful and flexible controllers as well as fast routers and gateways for high speed interconnected networks we recommend a high modularization of protocol architectures and implementations in addition to the use of new designed protocols. We construct a multiprocessor based master-slave controller model. The kernel of this model is an intelligent control unit which recognizes protocol inherent parallelism during protocol processing and dynamically distributes the tasks to different processor elements. The implementation method is based on a special high level petri net language, which could be implemented in a very efficient manner on our master-slave controller model.

Keyword Codes: C.2.0; C.2.1; C.2.2
Keywords: Computer Communication Networks, General; Network Architecture and Design; Network Protocols;

0. MOTIVATION

Existing communication protocols (on network and transport as well as on session or presentation layer) [1] were conceived to accommodate and support specific network and user demands. We are convinced that we need a flexible protocol structure in which the protocols or protocol modules are available as elements of a matrix, from which the required protocols or protocol modules can be selected. It would be useful e.g. to build a vector of protocols consisting of the well-known and widely established TCP [2] accomplished by an improved High Speed Transport Protocol on transport layer. These protocols should be accessible and selectable by different applications through enhanced transport interfaces. Thus it will be possible to provide communication for an operating system distributed across a network as well as to provide high data rate communication. Integrating a combination of different approaches into today´s personal computing systems (PCs and workstations) will speed up the processing of protocols. The following approaches are proposed:

- adaptive protocols (regarding user and application demands as well as changing network conditions to adapt the quality of service),
- extended application layer protocols,
- optimized parametrization (timer, windows, rates),
- efficient algorithm design and new implementation strategies,
- powerful controllers with parallel protocol processing capability (multiprocessors),
- hardware support (VLSI) of selected protocol functions,
- lightweight protocols reducing the overhead of higher layer protocols,
- migration of high layer functionality to lower layers, if the functionality can be performed with minor overhead by lower layers,
- advanced operating system design.

Some specific applications and their requirements will be described in the following section. Coping with the arising problems not only requires a reconsidering concerning protocol design and functionality as illustrated in section 2 but also the use of an efficient implementation strategy. In section 3 our implementation approach will be described in which application services as well as the underlying protocol stacks are implemented as service or protocol library consisting of all relevant components to support multimedia applications. The single components of the library and protocols are specified by a standard programming language based on higher level Petri Nets. For our implementation strategy a specific type of Petri Nets, called Restricted Product Nets is used. As the name intimates, they are a restricted form of Product Nets [10]. In comparison to standard Formal Description Techniques (SDL, ESTELLE, LOTOS) the use of Product Nets simplifies the way to achieve an efficient protocol implementation in a straightforward manner out of a formal specification. Especially the suitability of Petri Nets to describe and uncover protocol inherent parallelism make them a powerful tool for advanced protocol processing. The resulting implementations are concurrently and efficiently executable on a dedicated hardware architecture, possibly as an add-on card for personal computer systems. The paper concludes with a short summary and an outlook on further work.

1. MULTIMEDIA APPLICATIONS

In spite of the upcoming demands of multimedia applications [3,4,5], adequate solutions to implement multimedia services in personal communication systems and to consolidate them onto recent and future LAN and WAN networks (FDDI [6], DQDB [7], CRMA II [8], Metaring [9]) are still under study. The main problems to support new applications result from the ***integration of real-time voice*** or ***video data streams***, which are isochronous in nature (video conferencing, video-on-demand). Such data can be considered as streams of finite sized samples of the original information, which should be generated, transmitted and received at fixed time intervals, observing strict timing constraints. Consequently the network has to supply in addition to a ***minimum throughput*** further requirements such as a ***limited end-to-end delay*** (especially for interactive applications) and ***limited delay variations*** (jitter). Excessive delay leads to perceptible reaction times in interactive applications. Large delay variations, which have to be removed at the receiver, necessitate large buffers and produce additional delay: The receiver has to introduce a certain delay before presentation to ensure that packets arriving later than the average packet do not have to be discarded on arrival. A large additional delay minimizes 'late arrivals' but should not be perceptible to the user, whereas with smaller delay the number of obsolete packets increases. Further requirements of new applications are e.g.:

- (reliable) multicasting,
- maintenance of the temporal synchronization among the different media in one multimedia application or
- simplified connection management.

Common error correction schemes like retransmission of lost packets are not feasible for continuous media (CM) applications [24] because the additional delay would void the data. On the other hand video and audio streams can suffer small packet loss (depending on the coding) without serious quality degradation (see below). Todays packet-switching networks do not meet these demands. A reasonable throughput, limited delay and jitter can only be maintained if at no point of the transmission path congestion occurs. Most work concerned with these issues adopt the view that in order to make CM-services feasible, networks should have to be able to provide reliable performance guarantees. Such networks are fundamentally different from todays networks. A rigid control and management of resources and more expensive scheduling strategies at each scheduling point are required

One important objection to this paradigm is, that todays networks do not guarantee performance and will not do so in the near future.Therefore simpler (and less robust) methods for multimedia support should be considered, which aim at supporting multimedia services with less or no change to existing networks using ***new rate***, ***flow*** and ***congestion control schemes*** combined with ***flexible traffic*** and ***application dependent priority schemes***.

We are currently working on a dynamic priority mechanism based on discrimination of data of different importance. Besides common ***static*** priority schemes which leave the priority of a stream constant during an entire transmission, more advanced ***dynamic*** methods that allow for changes of priorities, should be considered. Using static priority schemes means that packets having higher priority will be expedited at both the transmitter and receiver and every intermediate scheduling opportunity. A scheduler detects the priority of the receiving data and places it into the service queue according to its level. If data having higher priority is received during the processing of low level data, the processing of the actual packet will be preempted (that means a preemptive priority scheduling scheme is provided). The evaluation of more advanced scheduling methods is of great interest in the future protocol design. Dynamic methods based on deadline scheduling are a possible approach. Such methods use deadline-times, system clocks and time stamps. Each system the packet transits, including originating and intermediate systems, decrements the time field before forwarding the packet to network. A packet with an expired deadline timer which has not reached its destination will be served with lowest priority.

In our opinion an ***traffic*** and ***application dependent priority scheme*** would be much more appropriate to meet the needs of multimedia communications. When there is an intermediate system (router, gateway) which has to process incoming data according to its static priority value, it could happen that low priority packets do not get processed at all due to constant streams of high priority packets. Consequently the queues with lower priority data would overflow. To avoid such a situation we propose to loosen the static priority scheme. When the higher prioritized data tolerates a limited packet loss (acceptable error rates for audio and video-streams depends on the coding and compression algorithms used [4]) the scheduler can decide to serve a specified amount of data with lower priority and discard higher priority data according to a tolerable loss rate (with a maximum number of consecutive losses). At the time we are working on a detailed description and evaluation of our priority scheme. When congestion cannot be reduced by this operation the intermediate nodes should inform the continuous media sender to change its submission rate.

A certain amount of rate control can be accomplished by varying ***compression ratios*** [22], ***spatial, temporal*** and ***color resolution*** for video and ***sampling rate*** for audio streams. New low-bit-rate coding techniques like *ADPCM* (adaptive differential pulse code modulation [23]) effectively reduce the generated load. Even with effective rate control mechanisms short term overload of certain nodes by intermittent bursty traffic can occur. The result of such congestion situations is queue overflow and packet loss. Whereas for delay insensitive data, packet loss can be corrected by retransmitting the lost packets, audio/video data would suffer unacceptable additional delay by retransmission. To minimize quality degradation from packet loss (also usable as a means for congestion control), schemes for intentionally discarding certain packets in congestion situations are necessary. Such methods usually work by dividing audio/video-packets into classes with different priorities using embedded coding whereby audio and video quality degrades gracefully with the loss of information. High priority packets contain the 'essential' elements whereas low priority packets supply the additional refinements.

When there is sufficient bandwidth only for a restricted number of video streams and also the whole amount of possible rate adaptation does not help we believe that we need a model like the telephone service with call blocking for real-time packet services.

The requirements for individual data streams can be represented in a set of QoS (quality of service) parameters, which is a very difficult task in the case of multimedia documents. The problem to transmit audio, text and moving pictures upon the same connection (single session association) results from the different characteristics of the information types and thus ***different QoS requirements***. The whole information then has to be transmitted on a generally accepted low level of service. Therefore an approach which uses ***separate virtual connections (e.g. session associations)*** for the different coded data streams with the option to choose individual QoS parameters may be preferred. This offers the possibility to choose different maximum bit error rates for the transmission of multimedia objects. As mentioned above, voice and video data can suffer errors in transmission without service degradation, whereas errors in data transfer cannot be tolerated. Suitable ***synchronization mechanisms*** have to be available (in session or application layer) to coordinate the ordering in the time domain.

In current communication systems not only the adequate services to support the requirements are missing but also the possibility for an application to access the underlying protocol stack in a flexible and convenient way. To support multiple types of service, two things must happen, both a change from current practices: First, applications must be able to describe to the network what type of services they require. Second, protocol architectures must use this information to select the required services by composing them out of a number of given functions.

The setting up of different virtual connections may be based on the ***logical*** and ***layout structure*** of a document. The logical structure is the result of hierarchical subdivision of a document into increasingly smaller parts, on the basis of the human-perceptible meaning of the content, for example, into sections, chapters, paragraphs, footers, spoken and written comments, whereas the layout structure is the result of subdividing the content into increasingly smaller parts on presentation basis, for example, into pages, frames and blocks of different information types. Such subdivisions offer the possibility to treat the different information types of composed documents in <u>*parallel*</u> already on presentation layer.

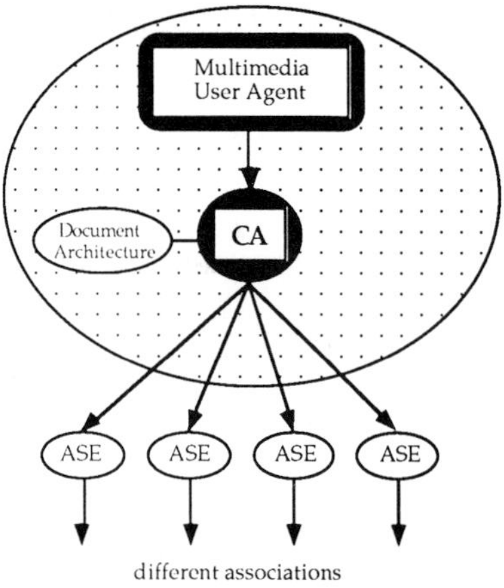

Fig. 1.1: Protocol Architecture Model

DTAM (Data Transfer and Manipulation [11]) currently is the only standard that combines a relatively complex information model as specified in ***ODA/ODIF*** (Open Document Architecture and Interchange Formats [11]) with services for the processing of composed documents in a heterogeneous environment. But only extensions of ODA/DTAM including the integration of audio, video or data and their distributed processing (***ODP***, Open Distributed Processing [12]) can fulfil the various requirements of multimedia applications. But the development of suitable standardized communication mechanisms and information models is running far behind the technological possibilities. Figure 1.1 illustrates a protocol architecture model, in which the various information types of a multimedia document are handled by a corresponding number of ***application layer service entities (ASE)***, that will be activated and further managed by a special ***control agent (CA)***, that supervises the multiple associations. Depending on the specific demands of the supported media each of the activated ASEs calls its own protocol suite. On top of these protocol stacks may be a presentation, session or transport layer entity. Especially the presentation layer may play an important role, since in multimedia environments many different media types have to be handled and converted. Conversion may be desirable, when it is cheaper to store or transfer information in a different format than the one in which it will be used. The whole scheme requires means for maintaining the synchronization of the different data streams. A control agent (CA) using application level synchronization [4], possibly supported by application level framing [13] is one possibility to solve these tasks. Such a protocol architecture also has to be based on an adequate hardware structure like for instance a ***multiprocessor system*** and high speed transport systems (layers 1 to 4) to get full processing power.

2. PROTOCOL FEATURES

In the last decade multiple new transport protocols have been developed which will contribute to the design of a new OSI HSTP (High Speed Transport Protocol [21]). The design of this protocol is mainly based on the following well-known protocols:

- **XTP** (Xpress Transfer Protocol [19])
- **VMTP** (Versatile Message Transaction Protocol [20])
- **TCP** (Transmission Control Protocol [2])
- **Delta-t**
- **NETBLT**
- **GAM-T-103**
- **URP** (Universal Receiver protocol)

Protocol performance mainly depends on the *syntax* and *semantics* of the protocols [18]:

The protocol syntax influences the complexity of parsing or generating of messages. It has an effect on the feasibility and cost of hardware implementation. Protocol designers should omit reverse parsing, backpatching of headers and variable length formats.

The protocol semantics controls the effectiveness of a protocol in various environments. Adequate sequence numbers are as important as the number of end-to-end handshakes for data transfers.

Our philosophy of protocol design to meet the requirements of new applications is the following:

Thesis: **Protocol Design Philosophy**

1) Performance
Protocols should have a fixed frame syntax to reduce the complexity of generating and parsing of messages, the protocol semantics should be success oriented

2) Flexibility
Protocols should be much more adaptive to react on changed network conditions or application demands

Since the XTP protocol design is mainly reflected in the new OSI HSTP in the following paragraphs some XTP protocol features to achieve higher performance and flexibility are illustrated.

XTP is a high performance protocol with the primary goal of hardware realization as a VLSI chip set. It is targeted at high performance distributed systems having real-time characteristics based on high speed LANs. One of the main advantages of XTP is that it covers the functionality of network and transport layer protocols. Thereby XTP is able, in contrast to standard transport protocols, to recognize and influence the phenomenon of congestion in high speed interconnected networks.The problems in the handling of congestion arise from the dynamic variation of throughput requirements and relatively long reaction times. Especially in high speed packet switching networks, data from all sources are statistically multiplexed on shared network resources; therefore the moment-to-moment throughput requirement often varies extremely. Mechanisms for handling congestion may be divided into congestion recovery and congestion avoidance. Congestion avoidance is preventive in nature whereas congestion recovery tries to restore an operating state, when demand has already exceeded capacity. In Internet hosts and gateways only a few mechanisms currently exist to avoid or control congestion: window flow control and Slow Start in TCP or source quench in ICMP (Internet Control Message Protocol used as error reporting mechanism between two Internet Protocol entities). In XTP a distributed rate control mechanism is used.

2.1. Rate Control

Standard rate control mechanisms should give the transmitter a permission to offer data to the network at a specific average number of bytes per second. XTP allows receivers and intermediate systems to specify the parameters RATE (bytes/second) and BURST (bytes/transmission), which the transmitter may not exceed. The length of burst intervals is given by the burst size divided by the rate. Fig. 2.1 shows the transmission of bytes during a one second period, where the BURST and RATE parameters are adjusted such that an inter-burst separation occurs.

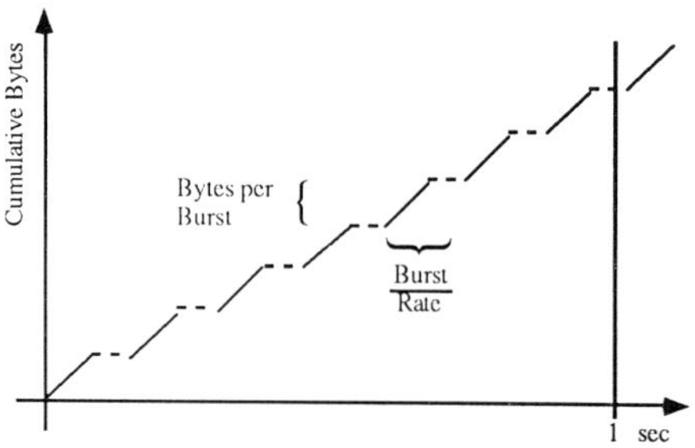

Fig. 2.1: Rate Control of an XTP Transmitter

Such pauses allow a slower receiver to get the data. Without specifying the BURST value rate control does not function, since back-to-back transmission would not be prevented.

2.2. Priorization of Packets

To support real time communications, a priority scheme is needed to discriminate among user data of different importance. XTP uses _static_ priorities (the priority level remains constant during the whole transmission) and a more advance _dynamic_ priority mechanism using deadline-times and system clock. The XTP priority schemes is very useful in high-speed interconnected networks, since the mechanisms are not only supported in sending and receiving but also in intermediate nodes since XTP covers the layers 3 and 4.

2.3. Packet Format

XTP first was conceived as a trailer protocol. This design decision did not last long, because the destination address, packet type, sequence number and other control information should be known before the data arrives. TCP is a header based protocol, the transport checksum is located in the header. For a VLSI realized protocol the position of the checksum field has a great impact on the protocol performance. When the data checksum is located in the header a hardware protocol processor is forced to backpatch the header to position the checksum. As a consequence, XTP uses a header/trailer combination with two checksums, one for the header, positioned at the end of the header, the other for the data part, positioned in the trailer. Then the whole packet needs to be parsed only one time and the checksums are computable on the fly. The computation of both checksums is not mandatory for each packet. Especially for media as video and voice overhead of calculating the checksum on data can be avoided since such kind of data is insensitive to single bit errors.

Another important factor of the packet syntax to achieve higher throughput is the use of fixed size control fields in the header and trailer (fig. 2.2), placed at fixed offsets in the packet.

Consequently the expenditure for parsing and internal packet transfer is reduced. The packet format is designed to allow pipelining of protocol operations.

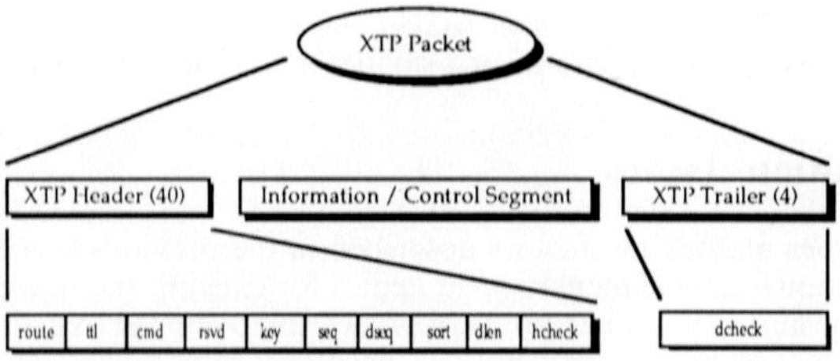

Fig. 2.2: XTP Packet Format

2.4. Connection Management

XTP and VMTP, unlike TCP with its three- and two-way handshaking mechanisms, offer the possibility to establish a virtual connection by an implicit setup mechanism using only a single packet. When the user wants to send a message, XTP has to check if a context associated with the specified destination address already exists. If not, a context structure will be created and a FIRST-packet containing the destination address and possibly all data is sent. If the receiving XTP entity is able to find an appropriate listening context, this context will be activated and the virtual circuit is set up.

In our opinion the overhead required to manage connections using handshake schemes is not significant for applications with high throughput demands. A good solution could be the handling of the handshake protocol out of band, perhaps on a separate signalling channel. Out of band signalling also is useful for applications with low-delay requirements, which often has only a small amount of data to transfer.

2.5. Error Handling

XTP uses a *selective acknowledgement* method in addition to the standard *go-back-n* method. Such a selective acknowledgement scheme combined with block acknowledgements is useful in high delay networks with a large bit error rate. When using the selective acknowledgement strategy the control packets contain up to 16 *spans*. Each span is an ordered pair of sequence numbers representing the correctly received data. Retransmission is based on the control information obtained from the receiver. XTP also offers the possibility to suspend the ordinary error control by using the NOERR-Mode. This is a useful operation mode for error insensitive data. When out-of-sequence data implies lost data XTP can use an aggressive error control (sending error reports just after detecting missing packets).

2.6. Address Schemes and Multicasting

XTP supports different addressing modes, using address formats from the ISO and the Internet world. Not every packet of the same connection must contain the complete address. This would waste a lot of memory space, increase the processing overhead and overload the network. The XTP approach caches the addressing data contained in the FIRST packet at both the sender and the receiver, and uses KEY as a lookup index into the cache to access the actual addresses as needed. To find the way through interconnected LANs, XTP data units contain predefined path indicators. Each router can perform a simple table lookup which maps the path indicator onto the preferred outband link and transmits the packet immediately. The appropriate tables are filled by the FIRST packet. In combination with the KEY value and the MAC address this path indicator identifies each context.

By setting the MULTI-bit (*cmd*-field) reliable multicasting will be supported. To reduce multicasting overhead control message traffic must be reduced by efficient acknowledgement and buffer control strategies. If a multicast-receiver recognizes packet loss, a REJECT-packet will be issued, which contains the sequence number of the first missed packet. The REJECT-packets are not exclusively addressed to the multicast sender but to the whole group. Consequently, the other members recognizes the control packet and can dequeue their control packet if the incoming control packet records the same or a smaller missed sequence number.

3. Implementation Issues

Besides various other reasons the factors described in the previous sections have led to the development of optimized implementation strategies for existing and new protocols. All these approaches have the aim to minimize protocol processing overhead (e.g. the number of packet exchanges, layer interactions, buffer operations, heavy usage of timers, interrupts and memory read/writes). Before introducing some major strategies to reach an efficient implementation, it is necessary to define the term *efficiency of an implementation*. Efficiency is a function of instruction path length to execute specific protocol functions, number of data moves inside processing nodes, delays due to the copying of data between adjacent protocol layers and delays resulting from imperfect synchronization between peer entities. The efficiency of parallel protocol processing can be defined as the quotient of the worst-case running time of the fastest known sequential solution and the product of parallel running time and number of processors. To optimize implementations, the following approaches are possible:

The most important inefficiency of many protocol implementations is the delay created by (unnecessary) copying of data between layers. This bottleneck can be overcome by passing pointers instead of data between adjacent layers. One of the most promising approaches is presented in [14]: the *buffer cut-through* method and *multi-task modules*. Data Units and Headers should be stored in separate memory areas to facilitate header insertion and since most operations are performed on the header. This reduces protocol processing to the actual protocol functions (creation of header, segmentation, reassembly etc.). Time-consuming operations like buffer space allocation and deallocation as well as copying between adjacent layers become unnecessary (for a complete descripton see [14]).

Another interesting strategy aims at increasing protocol performance by using micro and virtual protocols [15] and so called protocol graphs. This architecture is based on highly modularized protocols which offer the potential to configure to a communication system to precisely meet the demands of the various applications. An other asset of this approach is the possibility of processing several protocol modules in parallel. For an optimal support of the highly layered architecture a special operating platform has been developed [15]. The need for a special design of the operating system may be regarded as a drawback of this architecture.

3.1. Petri Net based Implementation

We take advantage of the idea of dividing the program code into small modules which can be executed in parallel. This approach is an attempt to combine formal specification techniques with highly efficient concurrent execution of protocol software. Since Petri Nets are well suited to describe and uncover protocol inherent parallelism we have developed a programming language based on the Petri Net concept. The Petri Net type we are using is based on **product nets** [10] which were developed especially for specification and analysis of protocols. We have introduced some modifications to product nets which result in the so-called **restricted product nets**. Since a detailed description of petri nets and especially product nets is beyond the scope of this paper, we omit this here

Product nets, roughly spoken, are nets with places consisting of typed tokens, erase and inhibitor arcs, combined with arc labels and transition inscriptions (called predicates) [10]. This kind of Petri nets is the base for the specification and implementation of our work. Having specified a protocol with higher level petri nets (as described in the following section) the step to implementation on a dedicated controller architecture is straightforward.

The implementation and execution of the protocols is subdivided into two levels. On the upper level the protocols are described with a programming language for the representation of the product nets, called **PENCIL/C** (**Pe**tri **N**et based **C**ommunication Protocol **I**mplementation **L**anguage) [16]. The used language is not a completely new programming language. It is designed as an extension of ANSI-C. The complete definition of this language is given in [16]. The only modifications to the ANSI-C grammar are the following:

The rule for the non-terminal symbol *external-declaration* is extended to

external declaration:
function-definition
declaration
transition-definition
state-definition

New introduced rules are:

transition-definition:
transition-header compound statement

transition-header:
trans *identifier (incidence list$_{opt}$) (expression)*

incidence-list:
incidence
incidence-list , incidence

incidence:
identifier
rdonly *identifier*

place-definition:
storage-class-specifier$_{opt}$ place-class-specifier type-specifier init-declarator-list;

place-class-specifier:
splace
mplace

The definition of places on external declaration level (*state-definition*) is comparable to an external variable definition. The keywords **splace** (single place) and **mplace** (multiple place) are followed by the type-specifier and a declaration and initializer list.

The transitions also are defined externally (*transition-definition*). The heading consists of the keyword **trans** and an identifier; in the following the identifier list enumerates all places incident to the transition. The header concludes with an expression, which covers the enabling condition for the transition. The transition description continues with the body consisting of local variables, declarations and statements. This is similar to the body of a function in ANSI-C. Places of both classes, splace and mplace, may be used and modified in the body of the transition, if their name occurs in the identifier list of the transition.

In [16,17] a method is introduced how to convert a restricted product net description of a protocol into its equivalent PENCIL/C program and examples are illustrated.

3.2. Petri Net based Protocol Execution

As mentioned above the execution of Petri Net based protocol implementations is subdivided into two different levels. On the upper description level it can be decided when to activate a transition. A transition in the product net will be activated as soon as the markings of the input places, the evaluation of transition predicates and arc labels, meet the enabling condition. When this condition is fulfilled, the second part of a transition, the body (protocol modules), consisting of definitions of local variables, declarations and statements, is executed. It is possible that several transitions in the same petri net can be activated concurrently. Subdividing or merging of transitions and places enables the implementor to define the granularity of the implementation. The protocol modules themselves are implemented like normal C-functions.

A dedicated controller architecture based on a multiprocessor system, which is well suited to handle protocol intrinsic parallelism, is required to achieve an efficient implementation. The **MDMA**-Controller architecture (**M**ultiple-**D**ecision-**M**ultiple-**A**ction) [16], depicted in fig.3.1, is a multiprocessor based controller model for the execution of protocols described by higher level petri nets.

Protocol modules can be executed by a number of so called action units (conventional processors with local memory for storing sequential program code and temporary variables). Each action unit can access a global memory which stores PDUs and global data. Action and decision units communicate logically via order queue and acknowledgement queue. Having found enabled transitions the decision unit offers tokens to the order queue which is scanned by inactive action units.

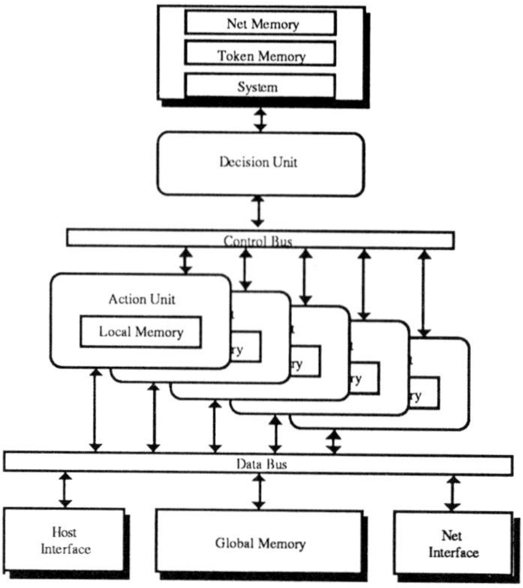

Fig. 3.1: MDMA Architecture

Action units return acknowledgements to the decision unit via the acknowledgement queue after completing their tasks. Then the decision unit manipulates the state of the petri net. In the meantime the decision unit looks for further enabled transitions. If there is only one decision unit and multiple action units, this model can be regarded as a central scheduler (decision unit) and a number of asynchronously attached workers. First experiences with implementing protocols using our implementation strategy are illustrated in [17].

4. CONCLUSIONS AND FURTHER WORKS

To develop communication subsystems which are able to support various application demands in an adequate manner, customer orientation is essential. Therefore we are analyzing the customer future communications needs in conjunction with the identification of trends in local and international market. This will provide the information required to maintain the focus of technical activities on the needs of the customers. Our aim is to build a service platform which provides an integrated set of multimedia services and is portable on every PC system across heterogeneous networks. To verify the suitability of our proposed traffic and application oriented priority scheme for multimedia communications we are currently working on simulations and analysis of various different strategies.

To support highest flexibility, the development of protocols and protocol machines which are optimized for specific applications is not the right approach. More appropriate will be general purpose controller architectures as the MDMA-architecture ([16]). The advantage of this dedicated petri net based controller results from the suitability of _petri nets to describe and uncover protocol inherent parallelism_. As a consequence future work will be focused on further development and optimization of the MDMA-architecture. Currently an emulator of the MDMA controller model and a compiler for petri net based implementations are being built. A multiprocessor based prototype realization with global memory will be built within the framework of the RACE project EUROBRIDGE. Development of XTP, VMTP and TCP/IP protocol implementations, as well as higher layer protocol implementations based on the Petri Net language are in progress. We want to implement a matrix of protocols and protocol modules which are selectable by the applications through intelligent interfaces since from a pragmatic point of view it is not realistic to assume that a new and perhaps better protocol will be able to compete against wide spread and well established protocol suites like the Internet protocol stack.

5. REFERENCES

[1] ISO 7498: Information Processing Systems - Open Systems Interconnection - Basic Reference Model, 1990

[2] D.E. Comer: *Interworking with TCP/IP, Volume I: Principles, Protocols and Architecture*, Second Edition, Prentice Hall International Editions, 1991

[3] Gerd Schürmann, Uwe Holzmann-Kaiser: *Distributed Multimedia Information Handling and Processing*, IEEE Network, vol. 4, no. 6, pp. 23-31, November 1990

[4] Cosmos Nicolau: *An Architecture for Real-Time Multimedia Communication Systems*, IEEE Journal on Selected Areas in Communications, vol. 8, no. 3, pp. 391-400, April 1990

[5] G.D. Flinchbaugh, P.L. Martinez, D.S. Rouse: *Network Capabilities in Support of Multimedia Applications*, Proceedings Globecom '90

[6] *FDDI Token Ring*, International Standard ISO 9314-1-3, 1989

[7] *DQDB Metropolitan Area Network P.802.6_/D12*, IEEE, Feb. 7, 1990

[8] H.R. van As et al.: *CRMA II: A Gbit/s MAC Protocol for Ring and Bus Networks with Immediate Access Capability*, Proceedings EFOC/LAN 91, pp. 262-277, London, 1991

[9] Israel Cidon, Yoram Ofek: *Metaring: A Full-Duplex Ring with Fairness and Spatial Reuse*, Technical Report, T.J. Watson Research Center, Yorktown Heights, 1991

[10] H.J. Burkhardt, P. Ochsenschläger, R. Prinoth: *Product Nets: A Formal Description Technique for Cooperating Systems*, GMD-Studien Nr. 165, September 1989

[11] *Open Document Architecture, Transfer and Manipulation*, CCITT-recommendations T.400-T.441, 1988

[12] ISO/TC97/SC21/WG7 N4883-4888, "Information Processing Systems - Open Systems Interconnection (OSI) - Open Distributed Processing (ODP)", June 1990

[13] David D. Clark, David L. Tennenhouse: *Architectural Considerations for a New Generation of Protocols*, SIGCOMM '90 SYMPOSIUM Communications Architectures & Protocols, pp. 200-208, September 24-27, 1990

[14] David D. Clark: *The Structuring of Systems using Upcalls*, 10th ACM Symposium on Operating System Principles, pp. 171-180, Washington, Dec. 1985

[15] S.W. O'Malley, L.L. Peterson: *A Highly Layered Architecture for High-Speed Networks*, Proceedings 2nd IFIP WG6.1/WG6.4 International Workshop on Protocols for High-Speed Networks, Palo Alto, California, Nov. 27-29, 1990

[16] Michael Rupprecht: *Implementierung und parallele Verarbeitung von Kommunikationssoftware*, PhD-thesis, Aachen University of Technology, 1991

[17] Bernd Heinrichs, Michael Rupprecht: *XTP - Efficient Parallel Software Implementation based on a Petri Net Specification Technique*, IFIP TC6 Workshop on Broadband Communications, Estoril, Portugal, 20/22 January, 1992

[18] Greg Chesson: *The challenge of workstations to networks*, Computer Networks and ISDN Systems 23, pp. 15-18, 1991

[19] *XTP Protocol Definition*, Revision 3.6, Protocol Engine Incorporated, January 1992

[20] *VMTP: Versatile Message Transaction Protocol*, Protocol Specification, Preliminary Version 0.7, February 1988

[21] Accredited Standards Committee: *High Speed Transport Protocol (HSTP) Specification*, September 1991

[22] M. Gilge, R. Gusella: *Motion Video Coding for Packet-Switching Networks - an Integrated Approach*,.SPIE Conference on Visual Communications and Image Processing,Boston, November 1991

[23] CCITT Recommondation G.721: *32 kbit/sec adaptive differential pulse code modulation*, Blue Book, Fascicle III.4

[24] B. Wolfinger: *A Continous Media Data Transport Service and Protocol for Real-Time Communication in High Speed Networks*, University of California, Berkeley

Personal Computers and Intelligent Systems / F.H. Vogt (Editor)
Information Processing 92, Volume III
Elsevier Science Publishers B.V. (North-Holland)

Support for PC/Workstation Interconnection to High Speed Data Networks

E.C. Foudriat(foudr_e@cs.odu.edu), K. Maly, C.M. Overstreet, L. Zhang, W. Sun
Computer Science Department, Old Dominion University, Norfolk, VA 23529

Abstract The bridge/gateway (B/G) system developed in this paper provides an effective interface between users and heterogenous interconnected networks. It brings distributed multimedia operations to the PC/Workstation class of computers. Critical features include effective message classification and receiver resequencing for supporting difference packet structures and data rates to be effectively coupled. The information used to enable resequencing is identical to that used for congestion control. A new lossless congestion control system is developed and its performance presented. The same system is used for link error correction which is more effective than end-to-end error correction. Finally, receiver and sender hardware systems are developed to show that the PC/Workstation bridge/gateway system is practical. The B/G features effectively enable connectivity through heterogenous network links and support many of the features normally found at the transport layer in OSI protocols.

Keyword Codes: C..2.1; C.2.2; C.2.4
Keywords: Network Architecture and Design; Network Protocols; Distributed Systems

I. Introduction Future networks will provide raw gigabit data rates for LAN to WAN distances. Users able to interconnect high range PCs or Workstations through these networks will have a wide range of distributed capability, such as video conferencing and "co-laboration" based on multimedia interchange of information. The Quality of Service (QOS) [13] or Types of Services (TOS) [29] which they provide must be supported over the range network systems.

The connection of PCs and Workstations to networks between end users will not be uniform. With evolution, users may be interconnected via a heterogeneous collection of mediums. A typical example illustrating these interconnections is shown in Figure 1. Users may connect to a LAN, MAN or WAN, may be directly connected to a public service network, or may be coupled to and through private "on-premise" systems. Each link may have vastly different operational parameters and protocols. The glue needed to make this coupling successful for PC/Workstation users is a bridge/gateway (B/G) which interconnects the physical networks and operates effectively with each one.

In this paper, we develop a B/G system for interconnecting a wide range of network systems and, thereby, providing effective support for a wide class of users. The features and architecture developed for the B/G system enable each network to maintain good operational efficiency supporting the QOS and TOS it is capable of providing.

The B/G system discussed in this paper is considerably different from previous ones. Present systems service connectionless networks usually via bridges or gateways [1]. Gateways, such as used in Internet, provide a compatible protocol at the network layer which forwards packets toward their destination on the selected "best route" and, where necessary, breaks up packets to conform to the media layer packet length restrictions [1, 2]. When gateways are not needed, e.g., coupling identical LANs, the transparent bridge approach is used. Bridge mainly handle routing to get packets to their destination [1, 2, 3, 4]. Typical interconnection between networks include those which support X.25, SNA, DECNet, XNS, etc., and span the data rate range from modems to LANs. DARPA's Internet [2] is a packet switched WAN network but its TCP/IP protocol has been used in many LANs also. These systems are connectionless as they handle data packets only.

High data rate networks, that is, systems directed toward the implementation of Broadband ISDN

[1]Support from Sun Microsystems, RF596044, NASA, LaRC; NAG-1-908, and Virginia CIT;INF-89-002-01

(BISDN) are mainly connection oriented although they are designed to handle packet like data. The connection takes the form of a virtual circuit and/or path [19, 20, 29]. The interface protocol handles the connectionless operations. For example, the OSI connectionless network protocol, CLNP, connects ISDN environments [6]. Another, frame-relay provides interconnection support but many of its critical QOS functions are supported at the end points only [7]. Other network interconnections include HUB, the scheme for Nectar [8], and direct ATM-to-host coupling [9, 10]. For the most part, these are end point-to-end point connections which do not span a range of different networks. Others have proposed transferring the protocol operations to the application level [7, 11] but, like frame relay, each host will have to implement TOS needs.

While there is no question that BISDN and its related systems provide capable, flexible network technology, they do not appear suitable for connecting PC/Workstations for multimedia services. First, they do not consider connection to vastly different formats or data rates. A recent paper [12] does consider an ATM - FDDI gateway but provides only minimal user support. Second, TOS appears to be enabled at the end stations as noted for frame relays [7, 11] and ATM systems [14]. Third, ATM packet size and protocol are inefficient when connecting to other networks [12]. Also, many network interconnection problems are considerably different when "on-premise" networks are included. It appears that interconnecting for multimedia applications can face a parcel of problems and possibly considerable expense if direct connection to high data networks is the only mechanism available. It may be eminently more practical to provide a single high performance B/G to interconnect a number of PC/Workstations, leaving intact their present coupling to a LANs. If each network segment, like those in Figure 1, must maintain effectivenss when connected, then the evolution of high data rate networking can be seriously slowed as all links must be changed or upgraded simultaneously.

In this paper, a B/G to interconnect heterogeneous networks and provide support for multimedia TOS is developed. In section 2, B/Gs requirements are presented. These lead to B/G features, presented in Section 3. First message classification features are developed to support the TOS requirements. Next, receiver handling features provides resequencing and restructuring to support diverse network interconnection. Sender handling features support reliability through a new lossless congestion control scheme and a more efficient error correction system. Architecture and preliminary performance estimates are described in section 4 to show the feasibility of implementing the critical B/G paths is hardware.

II. Bridge/Gateway Requirements Figure 1 illustrates a typical network configuration which would employ the type of B/G system considered here. The PC/Workstations are interconnected through B/G systems to other networks which may be LANS, MANs or public utility networks. The public utility networks may have intervening switching stations between B/Gs. Almost any combination of network interconnection can occur.

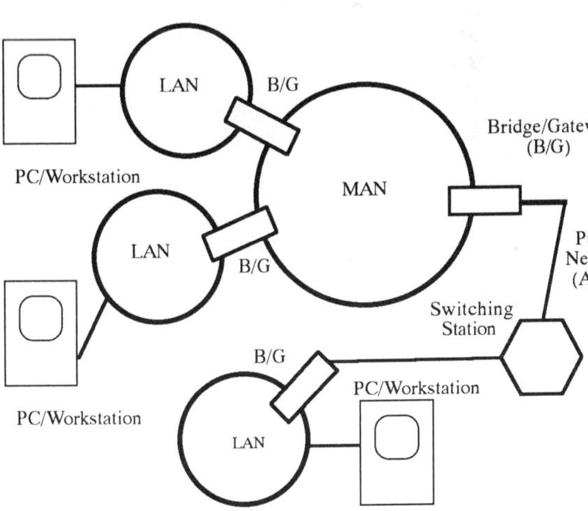

Figure 1 Network Configuration for Distributed Multimedia Applications

Requirements for B/Gs include:

1. interfacing to a wide range of data rates from

submegabit/sec. to gigabit/sec.;
2. handling a wide range of protocol and packet structures and sizes. This is further exacerbated by the different methods used to support integrated traffic components;
3. a wide range of connectivity and topology structures;
4. congestion and flow control;
5. error handling and error correction due to overflow and congestion [14, 21];
6. support for wide range QOS, e.g., sync, async, and bursty traffic, low latency messages, etc.

These requirements are similar to requirements proposed for new transport level protocols, namely, XTP [32]. Both provide support for traffic with a high degree of diversity, for congestion control, and error handling. The major difference is that the B/G structure deals directly with the media access mechanisms provided by each link whereas the XTP at the transport level ignores link operations by considering only the end-to-end requirement. As we show, the B/G system while providing the basic link interconnection is easily and effectively extended to support many transport layer features.

III. Bridge/Gateway Features To support the diverse requirements which enable multiple TOS, the B/G critical operational features are:

1. message classification - provides message and packet identity to enable packet related control;
2. receiver handling - provides for message restructuring for different data rates and/or different packet structure; enables reliability through error detection; and
3. sender handling - provides flow control and retransmission for error correction.

Although we do not list user interface as one of the critical features, it is an important part of making multimedia operations readily available to PC/Workstation clients. We note, however, that the B/G features developed enable a good user interface.

A. Message Classification A critical feature enabling QOS requirements and dictating much of the hardware/software packet handling in the B/G is the message classification structure. One message classification structure, synchronous and asynchronous, separates voice/video and data transfer service. Another scheme uses the concept of *congrams* [12] to support both connection and connectionless service (sync and async). This system is not suitable for networks using different access for synchronous and asynchronous data. Reference [29], in studying TOS, uses 4 types, reliable and unreliable; and low and high latency. This scheme, while applicable to ATM virtual circuit interconnection systems (VCI), is not directly relevant to connectionless networks. The message classification for the B/G system combines the first two systems above and supports both latency and reliability features of the last system. The message classes and their attributes are:

1. Synchronous messages which require call setup/termination at B/G nodes between source and destination. Typically, these messages are voice or video. Conditions for this class include known data rates, known route and known latency. This translates into operations where fixed size buffers are allocated and headers are built apriori. These messages are designated as Class A
2. Asynchronous messages which choose to establish control at B/Gs via call setup and termination. Typically, large data blocks and file transfers would use this class. Conditions for this class include unknown but source estimated data rates and known route. This translates into operations where fixed headers for each link are built apriori and where nominal buffer sizes are allocated. These messages are Class B.
3. Asynchronous messages which are self-contained. A typical member of this class is e-mail. Data rates are not considered and routing is either self-contained or inserted by the B/G from a fixed route table. No call handling operations are needed. These messages are Class C.

The message classification scheme provides the minimum number of classes needed to interface to a wide range of networks. Class A messages are unique since media access protocols to support synchronous (isochronous) traffic generally differs from those for Class B and C traffic. Although voice and video have significantly different data rates, both are effectively handled with a single access type system [30]. Note that the message classes, in themselves, do not support all QOS requirements, since reliable and low latency service for Class B and C messages are needed. In a future section, we discuss a lossless congestion and error correction system to provide reliable service. Hence this service can be provided for all classes of messages. For low delay service for asynchronous systems, priority within the Class B and C messages or selection of Class A can be used.

The B/G classification scheme is highly connection oriented. We justify this approach by noting that the new transport protocols, like XTP [32], are highly connection oriented since their goal is similar to the B/G's -- support for multimedia distributed systems requiring a range of QOS and TOS which cannot be supported by strictly packet switched systems.

B. Receiver Handling The critical receiver system feature is to provide message resequencing. Resequencing requires versatility, i.e., it must be able to handle an number of different formats depending upon the packet structural differences between the two networks that it interconnects..

For networks having significantly difference packet size and/or data rate (e.g., ATM to Ethernet), resequencing of Class A and B messages is required. Call setup provides the knowledge used in each B/G for allocating, monitoring and controlling resource for a message. Individual Class A and B messages may have different reliability needs and individual Class B messages different latency requirements. This is the key reason for supporting connections throughout the network.

Class C messages are lumped into a small number of resequencing structures based upon their priority class. Having individual buffer structures for each class enables the sender to best effect the priority handling for most media access protocols. However, each Class C message maintains its individual identity in the buffer since subsequent network may require different packetization.

For networks which have similar packet and data rate structures (e.g., ATM to DQDB) another resequencing structure is proposed. Here, resequencing is bypassed, Class A packets are accumulated in a single buffer, and all B and C packets into buffers according to their priority. Structures more typical of this type interconnection are discussed in reference [12, 31].

The requirement exits for all packets to be uniquely identifiable. It is assumed that packets arrive in the sequence from the link's receiver source. This assumption will be true for ATM which, as noted previously, uses VCI and virtual paths [19, 20]. Therefore, a packet arriving out of sequence indicates that a packet has been lost. With knowledge of the packet loss, the B/G can take immediate action for error correction. As noted above, error correction is one of the critical B/G features; its implementation and performance will be discussed in a later subsection.

C. Sender Handling The major sender operational feature for effective bridge/gateway performance is flow control. Flow/congestion control will be required for any B/G interfacing ATM systems [21, 22, 23, 24]. Further, congestion is likely between high and low data rate networks and will occur normally between heavily and lightly loaded networks.

ATM has a recognized congestion control problem. A number of congestion and flow control methods based upon statistical multiplexing have been proposed [21, 22, 23]. However, the ATM solution alleviate congestion by dropping overload packets thereby creating loss. Further, statistical multiplexing is not suitable for network links where a few users absorbing most of the capacity occur. Therefore, we propose a lossless flow and congestion control scheme.

Lossless Congestion Control System A lossless congestion control scheme is incorporated in the B/G system. It is similar to other schemes [26, 27] except that different feedback information to make it lossless is used. The system, more fully described in references [] allows the sender to limit its packets to those just needed to fill the receivers buffer. Thus, the system suffers no loss due to overflow at congested nodes participating in the control scheme. The information is also sufficient to enable error correction based upon a go-back-N scheme and with additions to use direct replacement.

Further, the lossless congestion control system is dynamic not only with respect to load but also resources, i.e., the receiver is able to adjust buffer space for the message based upon other resource demands after the message parameters have been established by the call setup. Additionally, the system is flexible with respect to potential loss. Although we have described the system as lossless, if the source wishes, it can send packets above those for which the receiver indicates it has free buffers.

It takes a chance that the buffer space will not be available upon packet arrival.

Performance of the lossless congestion control scheme is presented int references [25, 33]. Under congested conditions, i.e., intermediate nodes with overloaded capacity, the system is able to maintain a lossless condition while keeping the buffers sufficiently full so that access opportunities for the message are not wasted. Under overload conditions, this is the best performance which the message can expect to have.

Error Correction System The lossless congestions control scheme provides considerable improvement in reliability. However, if ATM drops packets to alleviate congestion should an overflow occur [26, 27], the question for error control for heterogeneous networks containing public service links becomes not whether but how. As noted previously, error correction is based upon end-to-end transport layer operations [14, 26, 27, 32]. While this mode is feasible, it is questionable whether it is capable of providing low latency service.

As noted previously, the flow control feedback is capable, using the error indicator bit and last received packet number, to alert the sender of loss regardless of cause. The error information is sufficient for the sender B/G to replace lost packets and reinstate the remainder of the message without further coordination with the receiver. We have called this method of error correction between B/Gs--link error correction.

Performance for the link error correction scheme is compared with the end-to-end error control implemented at the transport level. The results are shown in Figure 3 for the conditions where intermediate links are 100 km. Results for other lengths are similar. Conditions include processing time for the data link layer at each node and transport layer at each end. For end correction, two mechanisms are modeled, (1) where packet error is detected immediately at the receiver and (2) where messages time out. Time out is assumed as 0.5 times one way packet transfer time.

Link error correction, Figure 3, shows significant improvement in time to correct an error. For example, correction time is always less than 1/3 of that required for end-to-end correction and more important, is dependent upon internode length instead of overall network length. Hence, consistent QOS conditions can be supported independent of the end-to-end length of the communication. Also, link error correction does not use significantly more storage buffer space than end-to-end error correction, assuming similar packet sending rates. This is true since end-to-end round trip time approximates the sum of the individual link round trip times. However, buffers must be available at B/Gs instead of at the end nodes only.

IV. Bridge/Gateway Architecture Although this paper is directed toward the B/G features needed to interface PC/Workstations in a distributed multimedia environment, the question of hardware is addressed to demonstrate that the system is practical. Here, we present a hardware logic system which can implement the receiver resequencing and discuss the sender network interface.

Figure 4 shows the resequencing logic structure. Note, the resequencing system uses information generated in the data link layer for receiving packets. As packets arrive, they are sent to the message handler where the information is separated. The packet, stripped of header information, is sent to the resequence buffer. The packet id is sent to the associative memory which holds the pointer to the message structure in the update controller. The packet length is sent to the update controller and when the storage address of the new packet in the resequencing buffer is provided, the update controller information is updated and the data linked in the packet buffer. All these operation take place in a pipelined fashion using hardware for packet handling. When a new call request arrives, the setup handler, which is mainly in software, establishes a new cell in the active memory table of the associative memory and a new message structure in the update controller.

The resequencing architecture shows interesting symmetry, i.e., different activities related to a message are handled in distinct parallel elements. Call id and handling are directed to the associative memory , actual message handling to the update controller and actual packet data to the resequence buffers. This occurs on both the receiving and sending side of the resequencing system.

Outgoing messages are handled in a similar matter manner. The output controller selects the next message to be submitted to the outgoing channel and the control information is transferred to the associative memory and the update controller. The data packet is then moved to a buffer of the outgoing media access system A typical output buffering scheme for ATM is discussed in [31].

The system shown in Figure 4 is similar to systems being developed for ATM to host interfacing [9]. The major difference from the resequencing standpoint is that here a number of messages may exist simultaneously, that message classes require different handling than those to a host interface and that information obtained from the packet header is used to support both congestion and error control.

Processing speeds for the resequencing system are estimated from a preliminary design. The resequencing system should be able to handle arrivals at high megabit data rates if nanosecond logic circuits are used [28]. Handling times, i.e., from the time the packet is received until it is placed in memory and linked properly, are estimated to be in the microsecs time range. Transfer to the output buffer is estimated to add similar delay. While there is significant latency buildup when accumulating packets when the outgoing network has large block sizes, the actual added latency for the last bit due to the resequencing is only the packet processing time. The output buffer system does add the latency due to one copy. In further design, we will try to eliminate the need for output buffering.

V. Concluding Remarks A B/G system requires a number of features for interconnecting heterogeneous networks to support PC/Workstation distributed multimedia applications. In this paper, we have developed a message classification so that message packets can be effectively handled at B/Gs. Class A messages enable synchronous traffic while Class B and C handle the wide diversity of asynchronous traffic. Classification of messages into three classes is found to be the minimum by which B/Gs could support a wide range of traffic over a diverse set of networks. Priority within Class B and C messages is used to provide low latency TOS.

Message packet information used for resequencing is sufficient to implement reliable service. A form of flow and congestion control which is lossless is used in the B/G system because it is effective over a wider range of congestion control problems than statistical multiplexing. It is shown to be highly effective in maintaining full but not overflowed buffers and allows the sender greater freedom in packet submittal. Further, it can be easily extended to a leaky bucket like system where loss is possible but not probable.

With potential loss occurring in public service networks, reliability via an error correction is a requirement. Again the parameters for message packet handling enable link node error recovery between B/Gs. Data is presented to demonstrate that link node error control is able to correct errors within 1/3 the time for end-to-end error recovery systems.

The receiver resequencing and sender handling of packets is practical for high data rate interfaces . For both systems the critical path is implemented in high speed logic hardware for minimal latency. For example, the resequencing system is based upon an associative memory system capable of handling high megabit data rates with latency in the range of a few hundred microseconds.

With these B/G features, support for the wide range of TOS needed for distributed multimedia activity is provided. However, it is equally interesting, that within the context of the system necessary to provide effective interfacing between diverse network media, the B/G provides

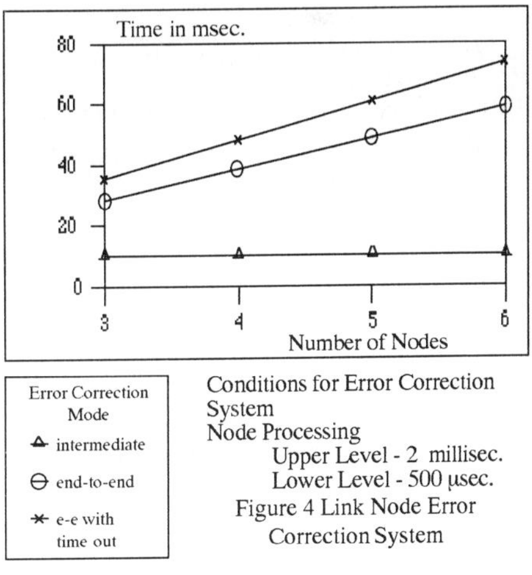

Conditions for Error Correction System
Node Processing
Upper Level - 2 millisec.
Lower Level - 500 μsec.

Figure 4 Link Node Error Correction System

support for requirements generally associated with the transport layer in an OSI system.

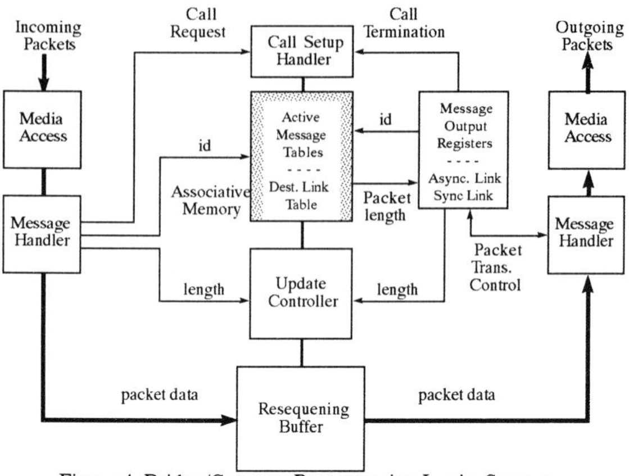

Figure 4 Bridge/Gateway Resequencing Logic System

VI. References

1. Seifert, W.: “Bridges and Routers,” *IEEE Network;* 2; (1); 1988.
2. Comer, D.: *Internetworking with TCP/IP*, Prentice Hall, NY. 1988.
3. Lin, Y.; Gerla, M.: “Brouter: The Transparent Bridge with Shortest Path in Interconnected LANs,” Proc. of 16th LCN; 1991; p 175 - 183.
4. Hamner, M.; Samsen, G.: “Source Routing for Bridged Local Area Networks,” *IEEE Network*; 2; (1); 1988; p 33- 36.
5. Perry, R.: “LAN/MAN Internetworking in the 802.6/SMDS Environment,” INFOCOM ‘90; p 639-648.
6. Braun, T.; Zitterbart, M.: “A Transputer Based OSI-Gateway for LAN-Interconnection Across ISDN,” Proc. of 16th LCN; 1991; p 158 - 165.
7. Chen, K.; Ho, K.; Saksena, V.: “Analysis and Design of a Highly Reliable Transport Architecture for ISDN Frame-Relay Networks,” *IEEE Jour. on SAC*; 7; (8); 1989; p 1231 - 1242.
8. Cooper; E.; Steenkiste, P.; Samson, R.; Zill, B.: “Protocol Implementation on the Nectar Communication Processor,” SIGCOMM ‘90; p135 - 144.
9. Traw, C.; Smith, J.: “A High-Performance Host Interface for ATM Networks,” SIGCOMM ‘91; p 317 - 325.
10. Davie, B.: “A Host-Network Interface Architecture for ATM,” Proc. of SIGCOMM ‘91; p 307 - 315.
11. Clark, D.; Tennenhouse, D.: “Architectural Considerations for a New Generation of Protocols,” SIGCOMM ‘90; p 200 - 208.
12. Kapoor, S.; Parulkar, G.: “Design of An ATM-FDDI Gateway,” SIGCOMM ‘91; p 173 - 183.
13. Little, T.; Ghafoor, A.: “Network Considerations for Distributed Multimedia Object Composition and Communication,” *IEEE Network Magazine*, 1990; p 32- 49.
14. Ohnishi, H.; Okada, T.: “Flow Control Schemes and Delay/Loss Trade-offs in ATM Networks,” *IEEE Jour. on SAC*; 6; (9); 1988; p 1609 - 1616.
15. Harita, B.; Leslie; I.: “Dynamic Bandwidth Management of Primary Rate ISDN to Support ATM Access,” SIGCOMM ‘89; p 197 - 210.
16. Foudriat, E.; Maly, K; Zhang, L. Sun, W.: “Gateway Resequencing in Multinode Networks,” ODU Tech Report; To Be Published.
17. Burren, J.: “Flexible Aggregation of Bandwidth fro Primary Rate ISDN,” SIGCOMM ‘89; p 191 - 196.
18. Clark, D. et. al.: “Analysis of TCP Processing Overhead,” *IEEE Comm.* 27; (6); 1989; p 23 - 29.
19. Gerla, M.; et. al.: “Interconnecting LANs and MANs to ATM,” 16th LCN; 1991; p 259 - 270.
20 Sato, K; Ohta, S; Tokizawa, I.: “Broad-Band ATM Network Architecture Based on Virtual Paths,” *IEEE Trans. on Comm.*; 38; (8); 1990; p 1212 - 1222.
21. Dighe, R.; May, C.; Ramamurthy, G.: “Congestion Avoidance Strategies in Broadband Packet Networks,” INFOCOM ‘91; p 295 - 303.
22. Fendick, K.W.; Mitra, D.; et. al.: “An Approach to High-Performance, High-Speed Data Networks,” *IEEE Communications Magazine;* 29; (10); 1991; p 74 - 82.
23. Shoraby, K.; Sidi, M.: “ On the Performance of Bursty and Correlated Sources Subject to Leaky Bucket Rate-Based Access Control Schemes,” INFOCOM ‘91; p 426-434.
24. Haas, Z.; Winters, J.H.: “Congestion Control by Adaptive Admission,” INFOCOM ‘91; p 560-569.
25. Foudriat, E.C.; Maly, K; et. al.: “A Dynamic, Lossless Feedback System to Solve Network Congestion and Error Recovery,” ODU Tech Report; TBP.
26. Mankin, A.: “Random Drop Congestion Control,” SIGCOMM ‘90; p 1-7.
27. Jacobson, V.: “ Congestion Control and Avoidance,” *ACM Computer Comm.*; 1990; p 553 - 573.
28. Goksel, A.; et. al.: “A Content Addressable Memory Management Unit with On-Chip Data Cache,” *IEEE Jour. of Solid-State Circuits*, 24; (3); 1989; p 592 - 596.
29. Cocchi, R.; et.al.: “A Study of Priority Pricing in Multiple Service Class Networks,” SIGCOMM ‘91, p 123-129.
30. Foudriat, E.C.; et. al.: “Combining Two Media Access Protocols to Support Integrated Traffic on High Data Rate Networks,” 16th LCN; 1991; p 442-451.
31. Davie, B.: “A Host-Network Interface Architecture for ATM,” SIGCOMM ‘91; p 307 -315.
32. Weaver, A.: "The Xpress Transfer Protocol," IWACA'92; 1992; p 253-260.
33. Foudriat, E.C. et. al.: "High Performance Interconnection Between High Data Rate Networks," IWACA '92; 1992; p 441-450.

SUBCONFERENCE: ENHANCING THE INTELLIGENCE IN INFORMATION SYSTEMS

Programme Committee and List of Referees:

Chair: G. Davis
Univ. of Minnesota, Minneapolis, USA

R. Benjamin
Rochester, New York, USA

J.P. Laurent
Univ. de Savoie, Chambery, France

M. Lundeberg
Stockholm School of Economics, Stockholm, Sweden

J. Motiwalla
National Univ. of Singapore, Singapore

A. Olivé
Techn. Univ. of Catalonia, Barcelona, Spain

Personal Computers and Intelligent Systems / F.H. Vogt (Editor)
Information Processing 92, Volume III
Elsevier Science Publishers B.V. (North-Holland)

Reflections On Effective Application Of Information Technology In Organizations... From the Perspective Of The Management in the 90's Program

Robert Benjamin[a] & Michael Scott Morton[b]

a. Robert Benjamin Consultants, Rochester NY, US & Visiting Research Associate, Sloan School of Management , MIT Cambridge Mass., US

b. Professor, Sloan School of Management, MIT Cambridge Mass., US

ABSTRACT

This paper examines the effectiveness of information technology applications in the context of organizational settings, from the perspective of the lessons learned from the MIT Sloan School, Management in the 90's research program.

Keyword codes: K.6.0, K.4.3.
Keywords: Management of Computing and Information Systems, General. Computers and Society, Organizational Impacts.

INTRODUCTION:

It is somewhat more than two years after the end of the Management in the 90's Program, a five year joint industry and MIT Sloan School of Management research program [Scott Morton, 1991]. It is a good time to take stock of what the program concluded, and what with the perspective of time we can now observe about how management can utilize information technology to improve organizational effectiveness, in the decade before us.

CONCLUSIONS OF THE 90'S PROGRAM:

The 1990's program provided evidence that supported the generally accepted notion that IT can and is changing work in specific settings in real organizations. These changes can be characterized as affecting both production work and coordination.

The physical production aspects of IT (as in robotics, or accurate sensor input to process control) are widely recognized. Less visible are the impacts on "mental" production work (such as loan officers in banks), where the use of powerful works stations has dramatically affected the quality and productivity of their work. This change in production work through the use of new IT tools extends to the way that production is being carried out. For example, the engineer in a design office now uses a powerful workstation to design a product, while at the same time draws on a library of successful prior designs, and accesses all relevant design data affecting the current design. The availability of such dynamic, current, information has in certain cases completely altered both the content and the process of the "production" job.

IT has also changed the nature of coordination work. Electronic mail is being used as a vehicle for keeping geographically dispersed members of a task force in touch. The new video-conferencing is allowing members of a firm to conduct budget meetings, or project reviews without leaving their geographic territories. These and numerous other examples of new coordination were described during the 90's program.

As production and coordination work changes for particular jobs within an organization, it can in turn enable greater degrees of coordination between groups within firms and different linkages between firms. In part this is due to the increasing percentage of relevant information now accessible in electronic form (thus leading to the so-called "informated" organization [Zuboff]), and in part it is due to the increasing breadth of the information technology infrastructure, within the firm and available to the firm through value added services. Thus the ubiquitous nature of PC's, the existence of an electronic network, and agreed standards and common data bases all form part of a necessary level of technology to permit easy flexible access between organizational units. This technical infrastructure which has been forming as a response to both personal and organizational computing requirements now provides the necessary base on which to easily build the inter and intra organizational links that lead to new levels of integration. This integration between departments within a firm, and between firms was seen in the 90's research as leading to whole new organizational forms. The shifting relationships between independent insurance agents and large insurance firms, the growth of electronic markets, and expansion of Just-In-Time networks, all demonstrate emergence of new organizational forms.

These two impacts of IT, the changing nature of production and coordination work, new levels of organizational integration were found to be present across a wide spectrum of international organizations. Where these impacts are linked to external competitive pressures such as higher quality product and leaner organizations, major shifts are visible in the competitive climate. American Airlines, and Baxter Health care are two well known examples where IT capabilities were used to resturcture work practices between firms to change the competitive arena. The 90's program found a wide array of industry changes that exploited new products and services where IT enabled new levels of inter-relatedness within and between firms.

These three findings described above in turn give rise to the fourth finding from the program. IT is presenting new opportunities to organizations who have to then to rethink their mission and objectives if they wish to survive in the competitive climate of the 90's. Business as usual, applying technology to existing ways of doing business, does not lead to success in turbulent environments. Despite this obvious fact, many organizations were found to be doing exactly that. Not surprisingly no real economic benefits were visible. Thus the apparent obvious need to rethink objectives, is not apparently obvious in the practices of current management.

The fifth finding was a paradox. While it is clear that IT can enable real change in organizations, the economic evidence of the payoff from IT is at best ambiguous. Ever since the original work in the 1990's program on this topic by Garry Loveman in 1985, the dilemma has been explored. There are a host of possible explanations. For example, the failure of economic measures to capture what IT has qualitatively done, improving quality, which permits the firm's survival. Another explanation is that the benefits go to the consumer, not to the producer of the goods. This is particularly true in a highly competitive industry that offers commodity like services. Thomas Theobold, Chairman of Continental Bank, Chicago expresses this view with some anguish:

> *"We would have 10 times as many employees, and half the quality of service if we didn't have the benefit of large computing, processing, and communications facilities. But I have been struck that ....nobody seems to come up with fantastic new business concepts on a scale that is relevant to our kind of business.*
> *Until the personal computer and inexpensive terminals came along there was some kind of a premium you had by having some information. It's been the improvement in global telecommunications that's taken the profit margins out of most ordinary foreign exchange or security trading"[Computerworld, 91]*

Theobold's and many other executives' frustration underlies another explanation, that most uses of IT are not for strategic advantage, but for putting band aids on old problems, or for strategic necessity. This thesis (for which there is also evidence) suggests that management has also been guilty of neglect and has permitted expensive technology to be applied to areas of low payoff.

This leads to the sixth finding, that IT does not provide significant impact on an organization (its strategy and operations) until there is a concomitant investment in its people, management processes and new organizational structures. This is shown diagrammatically in figure 1, and represents the need not to look for single quantitative answers to the "payback" question, but rather to recognize the inter-related systemic nature of organizations

(organizations that contain people with real feeling, skills, and aspirations, working with management processes and incentives that may be quite counter to the rational plans of senior executives and their IT collaborators). In short successful application of IT will require changes in management, people, and organizational structure.

The final, seventh finding, was that a major challenge for the 90's is for management to lead their organizations through the major change, the transformation, that will be necessary to meet the customer and competitive demands of the next decade. A transformation that can be enabled by IT, as part of a new style of organization the program described as "the flexible corporation". As we look forward we think a term that describes what the organization must become is "the learning organization"

THE LEARNING ORGANIZATION AND MANAGING CHANGE:

Today we realize that companies do not invest enough in managing change, "the ellipse" in figure 1, because they do not know the investment is important or they do not know how to manage change. To survive, they must learn to manage IT enabled change. On the surface it should be like all other kinds of change, and should be manageable under the tutelage of the organizational behavior discipline [Schein, and Beckhard, and Kochan].

There are some unique problems of IT enabled change that must be understood.

1. The 90's program instructed us that IT enabled new ways of working. As an example, consider an engineer able to design a product three dimensionally , mathematically analyze stress points, simulate behavior of components in motion, and more...all leading to reduction in number of prototypes required, shorter time to market cycle, lower cost, and higher quality. In order to achieve the benefits of the new way of engineering design, large shifts in organizational power, culture, process, and structure are required. Pivotal to this change, is the redistribution and diffusion of learning in the organization that a new way or working causes. If it is not managed, it is painful, and powerfully resisted.

2. IT has to a large extent become the engine that increased the magnitude of change in a number of important dimensions. Change has always been difficult to manage. IT enabled change adds a new dimension to the difficulty. First, the rate of change of the technology stimulates unprecedented change processes throughout the organization. Today it is not sufficient to change one element of the stovepipe .. one manufacturing plant...rather major multinationals are redoing entire processes such as distribution , affecting business unit value chains, country cultures, and supplier customer relationships.

Second, IT enabled change often results in shifting the location of knowledge in the organization (expert systems are illustrative), heightening power conflicts. Third, IT enabled change often modifies the natural time cycle of the organization from, for, example three weeks for an order to be processed and shipped, to one day, radically changing behavior in the process.

The result, as the 90's program saw early evidence of, is that IT enabled business processes are redistributing ownership of knowledge and task accountability , changing time and power relationships, across complex multi-national organizational cultures. Figure 2 [Short] illustrates the large number of systems, soft infrastructure, and hard infrastructure processes that must be changed and managed for a successful multi-national distribution project to be successful. Not only must processes be implemented across business unit and geographical lines, but soft infrastructure such as the reward system, and hard infrastructure such as data bases and technology architectures must also be implemented where typically the accountability and authority structure are counter to the needs of the project. To illustrate at each intersection of stove pipe and process shown in the chart, the issue of common good (the new process) versus hierarchical control is raised The chart also illustrates the issues raised by the need to implement infrastructure. Organizations will pay for process if it demonstrates added value, however funding of infrastructure which shows little short term benefits is in opposition to the short term orientation of units that must deliver the change. All the above, illustrates the magnitude of change management required.

3. There is little conceptual base or center of learning in the organization for how to do organizational change. Where it is consciously managed (and the number of instances is not very large) it is at the apex of the organization, and designed to achieve some long term goal such as Xerox to become a "quality company", and SAS to become a "moment of truth company". Generally these efforts are guided by a visionary executive, aided by one of a small group of organizational psychologists, who understand the dynamics of the change process.

The complex nature of change associated with integration of business process, and its frequency of occurrence in all organizations today, requires that the organization take the responsibility for learning how to manage change. Since IT inevitably takes the blame for bad implementation, IT needs to step up to the role of change manager to improve likelihood of successful results. It needs to develop change managers, to create the experiential learning that will improve the organizational outcome for successful change, to educate its business partners on its importance so that they are directly involved in the process, and to understand the implications of change before systems are implemented. To accomplish this we will have to learn:

- what change management is all about and organizationally learn how to control the process. Much as we do design reviews today we will have to do change management reviews, understanding who the stakeholders are in the change process, what they gain and lose, what resistances they have, what alliances must be formed to create a momentum for change, and other similar questions.

- when and how the organizational equilibrium shown in Figure 1. is disturbed by change and understand the processes for restoring its equilibrium.

- how to be clinicians of the change process, and become more than technology implementers.

4. Systems fail because the implications of change are not well understood. There are two primary reasons for this:

First, people resist change for many reasons, loss of power, mistrust of management, and many more. As noted above, the organizational psychologists have pointed the way to dealing with these change issues...and we must now learn how to apply their principles.

Second, systems fail because they are wrong. The policy embedded in them gives results counter to what was expected. In some cases the policy embedded in a system or process is explicit, in many cases it is implicit.

The 90's program described the new organizational forms. Several researchers, Malone for example [Malone] have pointed out that today's almost zero cost coordination transactions are changing the relative balance between production costs and administrative costs and are enabling new forms of organization. We are trying out these organizational forms as live experiments not understanding that they contain new complex policy feedback loops and will produce unanticipated results. In nearly all cases, as the modelers, and systems dynamicists [Forrester] have pointed out, large scale organizational processes are composed of many feedback loops, and it is counter-intuitive to understand how the complex feedback loops effects policy. Thus, we must learn how to model the effects of policy change both with modeling systems and with prototype organizational tests before these massive transformation projects become reality..Modeling systems for investigating policy in large complex feedback systems have been with us a long time, but have not been widely used. However today's powerful inexpensive technology permits a wider dissemination of systems dynamics models. AT MIT a learning laboratory has been established where companies study effects of feedback loops on important generic processes.

5. In the Management in the 90's project we foresaw an evolution from automated process to informated process (as described by Zuboff) and then to transformed process. In fact we are not seeing a rapid movement to informated process, let alone transformed process. There are a few good examples however:

- Frito-Lay has described a distributed managerial support system that provides field managers with detailed information on sales, promotion, and competitor activity throughout the US. The field managers are then able to learn from the data base and react quickly to their own markets without having to coordinate their activities with higher level management, who in observing the data are in a position to see overall trends and provide counseling to the field managers.

- Lithonia a manufacturer of industrial lighting have been through a sizeable transformation of how they view their business from internally oriented to a network of relationships centered on the agents who are their sales channel. This has been reflected in a multi-year transformational program starting with Lithonia's new vision, where incrementally new process to suit the vision was put in place. Lithonia's organization's focus on continual learning has enabled them build their new ways of doing things upon a base of learning developed at each incremental implementation stage.

To achieve an informated or transformed organization requires an organization with a capacity to learn, and learning how to learn is proving difficult. One of the reasons may be that we are attempting projects that are overbalanced with technology and we do not understand what people really need to learn ...what information they really need. We are aware of one organization that has equipped a service branch with a very low level of technology, cellular telephone transmission that one sees in taxicabs. However, the entire service team can hear each other as they talk with the dispatchers, and <u>information</u> is being passed along and remembered...."can you drop off a part, you are only a few blocks from me", "I remember you solved this problem ...did you do.." It apparently is a good fit to some information needs, and will have to be balanced with other requirements envisioned by IT staff and service management which may require a more powerful technology.

The leaner, more networked, more autonomous forms of organization we are moving towards, all have an empowering characteristic. Empowerment requires knowledgeable workers who rather than pass information up the hierarchy use that knowledge to manage their process as a feedback control system. This is illustrated in Figure 3., where a conventional view and an informated view of process are described. The figure is needless to say, an exaggeration, as it does not show information transfer from the people involved, and assumes it all is contained within the data base. Nevertheless it illustrates the magnitude of change and the sources of resistance to developing an empowered, learning organization.

Empowerment means that operational decisions will not be made hierarchically, that knowledge workers must feel comfortable in making decisions, that managers must learn to provide counsel rather than directives, and that information and our conceptual models of how to use it are the source of decisions. All of these will create resistances that must be managed if we are to successfully move to an informated stage for most organizations and then to a transformed state for the world class firm.

SUMMARY:

To summarize, we are at a crossroads today, where "the technology advances are moving us to a position of having a magic genie capable of satisfying almost any logically feasible information need.....exposing the really difficult part, what we want to get from the information system" [Emery]. Management in the 90's pointed out that the inhibitor to the "flexible organization", the "learning organization", to successful process implementation, and a benefits stream, was investing in managing change, in managing the equilibrium of the organization, the culture, the people and the management processes. As the technology pushes the demand for larger and more complex re-engineering, it is likely that successful implementation, and resultant benefits of the "genie" will be seriously slowed down if we do not invest in learning about change and its management in the context of IT.

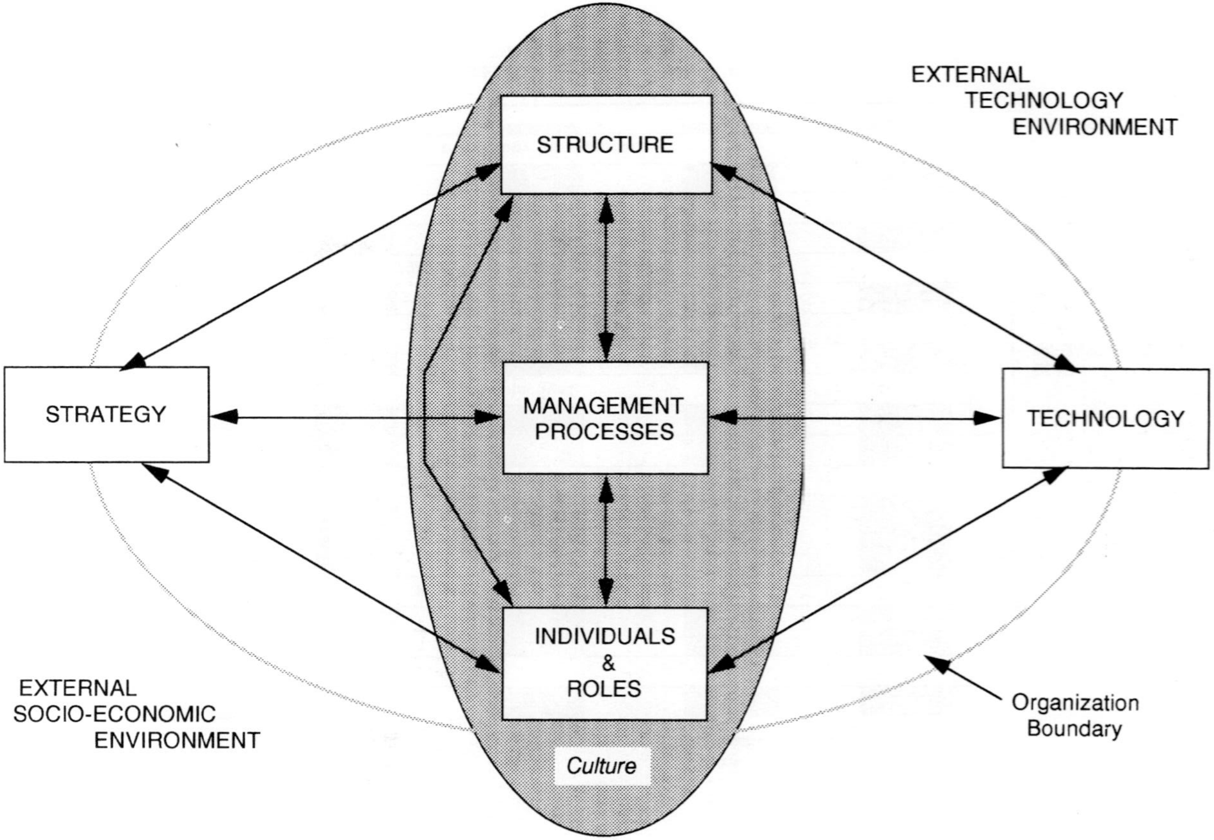

Figure 1. The MIT90s Framework

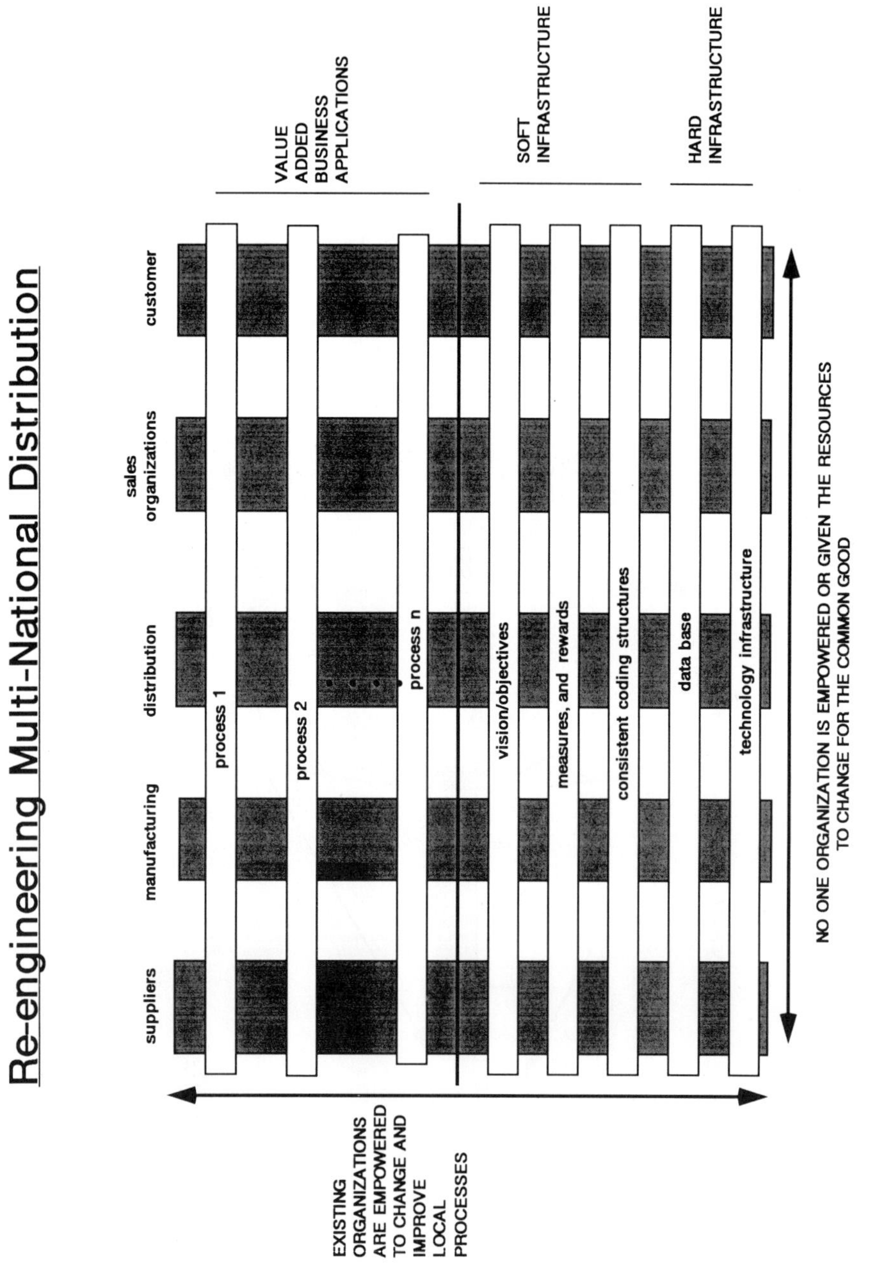
Re-engineering Multi-National Distribution
suppliers
manufacturing
distribution
sales organizations
customer
process 1
process 2
process n
vision/objectives
measures, and rewards
consistent coding structures
data base
technology infrastructure
VALUE ADDED BUSINESS APPLICATIONS
SOFT INFRASTRUCTURE
HARD INFRASTRUCTURE
EXISTING ORGANIZATIONS ARE EMPOWERED TO CHANGE AND IMPROVE LOCAL PROCESSES
NO ONE ORGANIZATION IS EMPOWERED OR GIVEN THE RESOURCES TO CHANGE FOR THE COMMON GOOD

– Figure 2 –

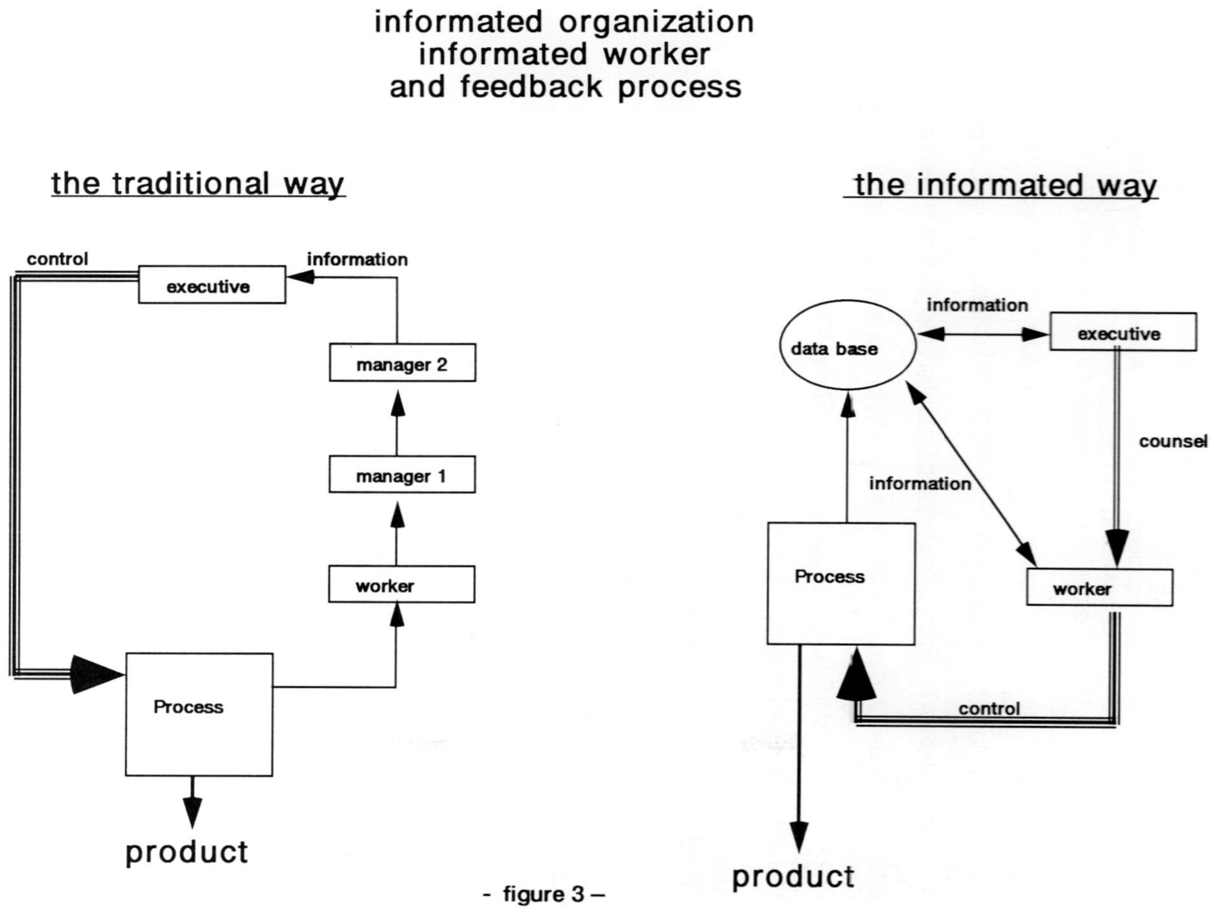
informated organization
informated worker
and feedback process
the traditional way
control
information
executive
manager 2
manager 1
worker
Process
product
the informated way
information
data base
executive
counsel
information
Process
worker
control
product

- figure 3 –

List of References

[Allen T, Scott Morton M Eds.] Information Technology And The Corporation Of The 90's, Oxford University Press, 1992
[Beckhard R,Harris R] Organizational Transitions, Addison Wesley, 1987
[Benjamin R, DeLong D, ScottMorton S] The Realities of Electronic Data Interchange: How Much Competitive Advantage; MIT CISR WP# 88-042, 1988
[Computerworld; 8/26/91]
[Emery J] , Information Technology in the 21st Century, MISQ, December 1991
Frito Lay HBR case
[Forrester J] Models and the Real World, 1990 ACM Conference on Critical Issues, ACM Press 1991
[Kochan T, Useem M, Eds.] Transforming Organizations, Oxford University Press, 1992
[Malone T, Yates J, Benjamin R] Electronic Markets and Electronic Hierarchies, Communications of ACM, June 1987
[Rockart J, Hofman D] Lithonia Lighting: Case Study, MIT CISR WP # 89-210], 1989
[Schein E] Process Consulting, Addison Wesley, 1987
[Scott Morton M, Ed.] "The Corporation of the 90's" ; Oxford University Press, 1991
[Short J, Benjamin R] MIT CISR Research Project in progress

Personal Computers and Intelligent Systems / F.H. Vogt (Editor)
Information Processing 92, Volume III
Elsevier Science Publishers B.V. (North-Holland)

Redesigning Information Production Processes for Controlled Production Time

Han Gerrits

Vrije Universiteit, Faculty of Economic Sciences, Business Administration and Econometrics
Dept. of Information Management and Information Technology
De Boelelaan 1105, 1081 HV Amsterdam, The Netherlands

Abstract
In this article we focus on organizations that manufacture products consisting of information. Examples of this kind of organizations are banks, insurance companies and parts of the government. We compare these information producing organizations with organizations that deliver material (tangible) products, like cars, electronic devices and clothing. The introduction of information technology in these latter organizations has led to measurably better performance; but these improvements are barely entangled in information producing organizations. In the article we try to understand why this is the case and how we can improve the performance of information producing organizations by looking at material production.

The first section discusses the research field and the problems faced. The second section suggests that the problems may arise from a lack of methodology to design information production processes. The last section takes the production control system for information production as an example to demonstrate an approach for redesign towards better logistic performance.

Keyword Codes: H.1.0, H.4.0, H.4.2
Keywords: Information Systems, Models and Principles, General; Information Systems Applications, General & Types of Systems

INFORMATION PRODUCTION: THE RESEARCH FIELD

Every organization has an operational process that gives it the right to exist, the process whereby it delivers something of value to its environment. This operational process needs inputs from the environment and converts them to outputs (products) that are more valuable to the environment. These products can be material, like cars or airplanes, or consist of information[1], like insurances or mortgages. Production of the first kind we call *material production* and production of the last kind we entitle *information production*. The information products in

---

[1]We will not make a difference between information and data in this article because that is not really needed for our discourse.

most cases do have some kind of physical appearance of course, but the real added value lies in the information that is the output of the primary process.

The last decade shows an improvement of the performance of material production organizations [Drucker91]. Most organizations can control the production times because better information systems give possibilities for better planning and controlling. Also, the flexibility of the operational process is enhanced by introducing flexible production systems [Groep87] and using logistic concepts for production system design [Goldratt91]. It should be clear that information technology is an enabler of these improvements: it gives the means to enlarge the information processing capacity of the information systems that is needed when the production systems get more complex [Porter85].

Some good examples of better control of production times and more flexibility are seen in the car industry: there are car companies that can tell you exactly when your new green car is coming from the production line, will be shipped and can be delivered to you. Also there are car companies that let you define your 'dream' car: you can choose the front, the kind of wheels, the roof, the engine, everything you wish.

However, in information production organizations these improvements are only partly realized[2] [Fortune91]. Which bank can tell you exactly when the mortgage offer for your new house will be ready? Which insurance company gives you the possibility to define your own insurance policy out of the components?

We are talking here about the logistic performance. Logistic performance indicators can be used to describe this performance. Main logistic performance indicators are the production time, the heigth of the stocks, the flexibility and the measure to which client orders are executed in time. As said, material production companies have improved their performance measured by these performance indicators through using logistic concepts to design the production processes and introducing information technology to support the control system.

It looks like information producing companies have not succeeded in achieving a better logistical performance. We believe that this is at least partly the result of using the wrong methods to design the information production processes and control processes. A redesign of processes is necessary to receive the benefits of using information technology.

---

[2]The research is done in financial companies in the Netherlands and may hence reflect a local situation.

PRODUCTION SYSTEM AND CONTROL SYSTEM

Every organization can be seen as being built up from two parts: the production system and the control system. In figure 1 this model is depicted, we discuss it here only shortly.

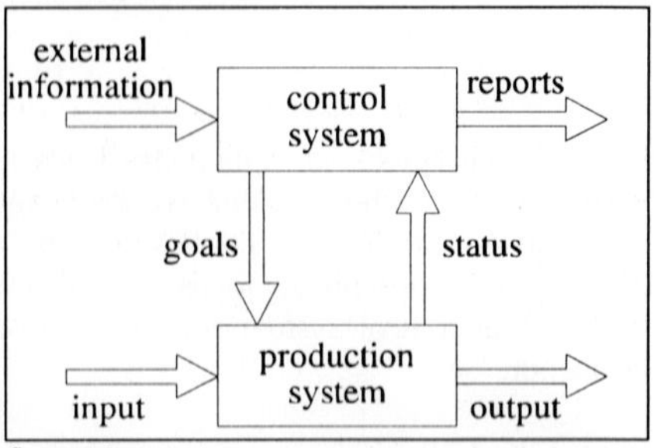

figure 1

The production system executes the operational process. Therefore it needs inputs to transform to the desired output. The production system needs to be controlled: it needs to know which products should be made when, which inputs should be bought, how the machines need to be programmed and so on. To achieve this, the control system sets goals or gives directives to the production system. Because in most cases the actual performance doesn't always conform to the defined goals, the control system receives status reports from the production system that describe the factual realization. Furthermore, the control system needs information from the environment to make the plans and set the appropriate goals for the production system. The control system reports to the environment about the achievements of the organization, for example by distributing the annual report.

It should be clear that every organization needs a production system: without that the organization would have no right to exist. Also, every organization needs a control system: in every organization there's a need for coordination of the different parts of the organization.

Notice that the control system is an information handling system: all the inputs and outputs are information. The production system on the other hand, is depending on whether the organization is producing material products or information products. In the first case the production system is a material handling system, in the later case the production system handles information. So, in material production the control system is an information system and in information production the control system *and* the production system are both information systems.
Now let's take a look at the concepts that are used to design the production and control systems. In material production the production system is designed according to theories and methodologies that take logistic performance into account. The control system for material production is designed with information system design methodologies that are focused on defining the data that is needed and the processes that process the data.

In information production however, we do not have theories or methodologies to design the production system from a logistic viewpoint: in most cases we let the information system designers use their methodologies. In figure 2 this is indicated by arrow 1. This implies that the production system for information production is designed using the methods that are suitable for designing control systems for material production. We think that we can improve the performance of information production by analyzing the way material production systems and control systems are designed and translating this knowledge to information production, as is depicted by the arrows numbered 2. This means using logistic concepts for designing information production [Ronen91].

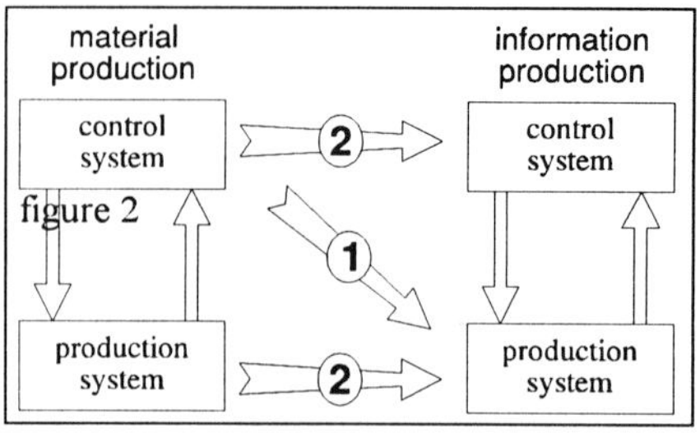

figure 2

First research results show that this leads to better insight into the problems we are facing in information production. To illustrate this, a case study is described, focussing on the design of a control system for information production.

A CONTROL SYSTEM FOR INFORMATION PRODUCTION

Before modern information technology made its entry in information production organizations, the production processes consisted of many different steps that were executed manually one after the other. The impulse to start the process was the reception of an order form with the data of the (potential) client asking for a product. Let's stay with the mortgage example: on the form the name and address of the client are written, the house for which the mortgage is needed and the amount is described. The processing of the form can start, resulting in a mortgage offer to the client. The introduction of information technology led to just automating the already designed production processes, leading to a less than optimal performance and leading to the problems we're facing now.

Looking at these processes with the design principles for material production in mind, we see some interesting points:

1. No explicit control system
In material production a special organizational unit is responsible for controlling the production. This unit receives all orders from clients and gives production orders to units in the production system. Organized this way, there's always one point in the organization that knows what's going on in the production system. How much workload is in the system, which capacities are almost exhausted and which ones are free.

In information production, in most of the cases there's no explicit control system. Orders are received directly in the production system and are forwarded to the next process after they are finished. This leads to situations where one unit has so much work that they need to work overtime to avoid the work gets piled up too high, while at the same time, another unit is just working very relaxed to prevent to run out of work. The result is not only a negative effect to the production times but also higher production costs than necessary. Another negative effect of the absence of a control system is that the orders can get stuck in the production system, without being noticed.

2. No registration of production
The production process consists of steps that are executed one after another, but in many cases there's no explicit registration of the execution of these steps. For a control system to be effective, it is necessary to have data about how the production is progressing: which jobs are ended, which are underway and which jobs are waiting, and why they are waiting. In material production, facilities are incorporated into the production system to provide the control system with these data. In information production this is only true in very few organizations. There are reasons for this: measuring the progress of production processes is only feasible if the registration doesn't cost too much extra time. Preferably, this registration is done automatically, and in material production with computer controlled machines this can be implemented quite easily. In manually executed information production this registration would cost extra handling of the employees and therefore isn't always implemented. When the process gets automated the same way as it was before automation, the registration is still not done. Also, in information production the processors are human beings that rather not exactly write down what they're doing.

Another reason to have data about the actual processing of orders is to get insight in the characteristics of the production. If, for example, there's a process that handles all mortgage offers, it's important to know if the characteristics of the orders are changing. There may be shifts in the orders from simple mortgages to more complex mortgages demanding more (human) processing capacity. One should be able to recognize these shifts in order to make changes in the capacity or the goals.

A last reason to have information about the actual performance of the production system is the rising need to have more flexibility in products. If the organization wants to have a broad product mix, the prices asked for those products should reflect the costs made for them[3]. Especially when products will be made according to clients' specifications, a cost accounting system (like activity based costing) that gives information about the costs of the different components of the products to be made, is necessary.

DESIGN OF A CONTROL SYSTEM

The implementation of the control system is aimed at controlling the production times of the production. Implementing such a system is not only a technical story: also the organization has to be restructured and the employees need to be trained in working another way than they were used to.
The control system should, among others, have possibilities for:
- setting standard production times for production processes and parts thereof (sub processes);
- reporting about the actual status of the production, giving actual performance versus standard performance, workload of the capacities, queues and so on,
- intervening in the production, for example taking orders out of queues for capacities that are overloaded and placing them in other queues;
- give alarm reports when processes are almost exceeding the standard time;

[3]For this article we ignore marketing considerations for product pricing [Kotler84]

- management reporting considering the performance of a period compared with other periods, and giving insight in shifts in production orders.

All of this wouldn't work if the organizational responsibilities for achieving production times are not clearly stated. On the basis of these responsibilities the information subsystem of the control system should be defined.

1. Responsibilities

The responsibility for achieving a standard production time is seldom explicitly stated. Managers in information production organizations are mostly judged by the costs their unit has made relative to the budget and quantitative performance of the unit. However, if production time achievement is a goal that should be achieved, managers must be judged on this performance aspect too.

The responsibility for the achievement of production times is broken down and pushed down into the organization. Somewhere in the top of the organization lies the responsibility for the complete production process, this responsibility is broken down in responsibilities for sub-processes.

Responsibilities only work out when there are instruments to steer with. One can't be responsible for achieving a standard production time if one hasn't mechanisms to influence the workload. The units in the organization should assess the new workload coming from the clients to decide whether the new workload can be guaranteed to be delivered in time. If this is not the case, the following instruments should be available:

- get extra capacity from other units that are not fully loaded;
- let the employees work overtime;
- lower the quality demands to the product, in order to achieve a lower need for capacity;
- decide to exceed the production time.

2. Reporting

Being responsible for the achievement of some goal means that there's a need to be informed about the actual performance. Every employee in the organization has got some kind of production time responsibility and should be informed. Decisions must be made concerning the detail of the reports. In the most detailed case, reporting is done per individual employee per process. The reports for management contain aggregated information and are aimed at recognizing trends.

3. Registration

To be able to produce the reports mentioned above, some kind of registration is needed. The control system must have a model of the production system. There are three moments that should be recorded:

- the moment a production order is placed in the queue of an employee;
- the moment a production order is taken from the queue and the processing is started;
- the moment the processing ends.

The control system needs the registration of these events to produce the asked reports.

CONCLUSION

Through using logistic concepts whose application is enabled by information technology, material production organizations have improved the control of their production systems resulting in short standard production times, while at the same more flexibility in the products is achieved.

Information production organizations have not achieved the same benefits by introducing information technology. This is partly due to a lack of methodology to design information production processes from a logistic viewpoint.

We think that looking at how material production systems are designed could help information production to overcome the problems we are facing now and achieve the same benefits. In this article we focused on the production time control of information products.

References:

[Drucker91] Drucker, Peter F., "The Emerging Theory of Manufacturing" in: The New Manufacturing, Harvard Business Review Paperback, 1991, Harvard Business School Press

[Goldratt91] Goldratt, Eliyahu M., Jeff Cox, The Goal, 1991, Gower

[Groep87] Groep sociotechniek, Het flexibele bedrijf, (The Flexible Organization, in Dutch), 1987, Kluwer Bedrijfswetenschappen

[Porter85] Porter, M.E., Millar, V.E., "How information gives you competitive advantage" in: Harvard Business Review, jul/aug 1985

[Fortune91] "The Service 500" in Fortune, June 3, 1991

[Ronen91] Ronen, Boaz & Israel Spiegler, "Information as inventory: a new conceptual view" in: Information & Management 21 (1991)

[Kotler84] Kotler, Philip, Marketing Management, 5th ed., 1984, Prentice Hall

Personal Computers and Intelligent Systems / F.H. Vogt (Editor)
Information Processing 92, Volume III
Elsevier Science Publishers B.V. (North-Holland)

COORDINATING AUTONOMOUS PROBLEM SOLVERS: THE 2 DIMENSIONS OF NESTED NEGOTIATIONS*)

Stefan Kirn **Gunter Schlageter**

FernUniversität Hagen, Applied Computer Science I, D-5800 Hagen, Germany

ABSTRACT. *Federative systems provide a framework to effectively support collaborative work by human experts. However, they also include difficult coordination problems. In this paper we develop the concept of nested negotiations, which applies to Durfees partial global plans. Planning their participation to a collaboration the agents take into account the task to be solved, their own goals and problem solving competence, their availability, and their (incomplete / time-dependent) knowledge about the global state of problem solving. This enables the agents to coordinate themselves in a completely decentralized, flexible and intelligent way.*

Keyword Codes: C.2.4., I.2.8.
Keywords: distributed systems, problem solving control methods

1. INTRODUCTION

Information technology is faced with the challenge to support human experts' collaborative work. Human experts work in complex and heterogeneous domains, and they use different types of intelligent aids (expert systems, active databases, etc.). In general, they work geographically distributed and collaborate in a flexible, task-dependent way [15]. They apply a significant portion of their work to coordinating themselves [12], while their aids are mutually unrelated and are not aware of any context sensitivity of human work at all [1]. Typically, CSCW-systems should be built up from distributed pre-existing systems that are developed independently from each other [14]. They should allow collaborative[1] work among the (software) agents as well as stand alone problem solving by one agent only. In such systems it is difficult or even impossible to control cooperative processes from a global point of view.

Much work has been conducted on cooperation. One approach deals with federations of databases to enhance the capabilities of conventional databases [16]. Distributed AI focuses on knowledge distribution and task allocation, coherence and coordination and on interaction languages [2]. However, there is no integration yet to fit the problems described above.

We applied the idea of federations to a group of knowledge based systems in FRESCO (FedeRative Expert Systems COoperation). FRESCO is a federative knowledge based system in banking. Its aim is to enhance the problem solving capabilities of distributed intelligent systems by introducing cooperative ability into the agents. This work is somehow related to that of [16]. However, instead *federated* we prefer *federative* to stress the agents *cooperative ability*. Also, this notion shall help readers to keep in mind the DAI-origin of our approach. In federative systems coordination must be based on decentralization. This led us to develop the idea of *nested negotiations* which helps to coordinate a group of autonomous problem solvers.

Section 2 discusses related work; section 3 introduces the FRESCO agent model and the idea of federative problem solving. Applying partial global plans and iterative negotiations section 4 considers the coordination task in FRESCO. In section 5 we discuss results and future work.

---

*) This work has been funded by the government of Northrhine-Westfalia, BASF AG and WestLB, Germany.

1 We use *collaborative* in a more general sense than the distributed AI-notion of *cooperative* (e.g., see [2]).

2. RELATED WORK

Federated databases are characterized by the basic aspects of the single systems. These are very complex, (more or less) independent from each other and the focus is on the autonomy of the agents [16], [13], [4]. Most approaches still include some centralizing aspects (e.g. global schema, centralized control). In contrast, [16] introduced a very flexible concept of a federated database. They substantially extend the conventional terminology of cooperating databases.

Distributed AI. Distributed AI (DAI) is divided in *distributed problem solving (DPS)* and *multiagent systems (MA)* [2]. In DPS the agents are faced with problems that are beyond their individual capabilities, so they must cooperate to achieve their goals. In MA the agents share an environment so they must act collectively to identify and resolve conflicts while taking advantage from the actions of other agents. Important shortcomings are: In most cases the agents are small, and they are not intelligent at all. Up to now there is no significant DAI-research on the cooperation of complex knowledge based systems. MA are designed top-down. Dynamically, they do not allow adding new agents or removing existing ones. MA use tight coupling in the following sense: The agents do not decide by themselves whether to cooperate or not. They are not allowed to really act just on their own. This is an inherent static aspect of MA.

Negotiations coordinate agents towards a common global goal. [3] introduced multistage negotiations to deal with incomplete knowledge. Their agents bargain on problems with a restricted global significance. They guarantee the overall system converging towards a global consistent solution. This has been improved further by [9] who extended the multistage negotiation protocol to solve resource allocation conflicts in distributed networks. [10] introduced a cybernetic model. Their agents generate goals that are communicated and allocated. Goals not being allocated are reorganized by starting a new cycle of goal formulation, communication, allocation and achievement. However, they did not explain how the agents can decide which one of them may process a goal and how to assess the achievement of a goal after having processed it. Also, they did not consider the consequences that arise from goal reorganisation.

Planning. Agents coordinate their behavior by exchanging plans before they start acting [2]. Usually one divides between multiagent planning (MP) and distributed planning (DP). While MP requires one agent having all relevant knowledge, DP requires all agents acting together on one single global plan. To overcome the shortcomings of both approaches, [5] suggested partial global plans (PGPs). Their agents possess only partial global knowledge. They start working by constructing local plans. These are processed to node plans which then are communicated among the agents to build up models of each other. Using them PGPs are constructed to specify how sets of agents will (inter)act, and to describe the cooperation style to be applied. Coordination is part of each agent's activities and is interleaved with local problem solving.

3. THE FRESCO AGENT MODEL

FRESCO agents determine by themselves whether there is any need to work together. They identify by themselves that part of a task to which collaboration shall be applied. They evaluate which of them might be the best one to solve a task under consideration. They also choose the collaboration style that is the most promising one. The overall solution path is determined by "the most appropriate" task decomposition, cooperation style and task allocation. However: None of the agents can control the global process of problem solving. There is no centralized global knowledge on the capability and availability of any agents. Task allocation is based on abstract (unprecise) descriptions of tasks and agents capabilities (therefore, task allocation may fail), and problem solving may require to dynamically modify the cooperation style.

Each agent applying for cooperation is responsible for some portion of the coordination task. The agents are autonomous in the sense that they may join a collaboration taking into account their own egoistic but inherent constructive aims. As a consequence, we implemented a cybernetic approach to the agents' problem solving behavior (fig. 1). Such an approach includes difficult problems: the assessment of the appropriateness of task decompositions; the agents self-assessment of their competence and the acceptability of results. For details see [7], [8a].

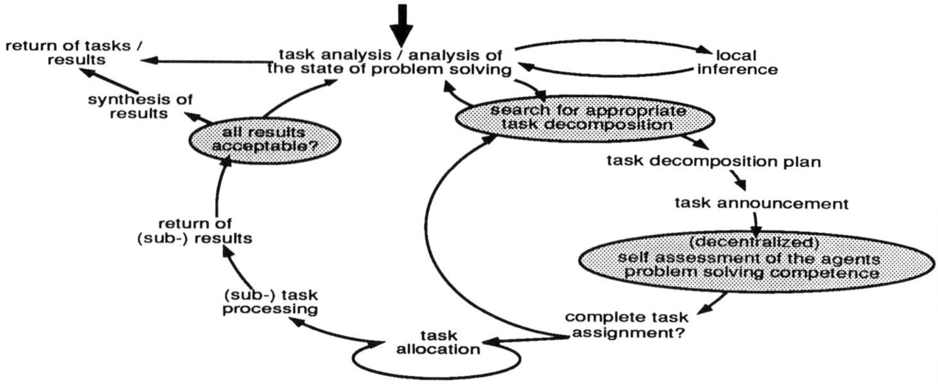

Fig. 1: Cybernetic Model of the Agents Decision Process

The agents are benevolent and competitive. A detailed discussion of their architecture and collaborative behavior can be found in [7].They coordinate themselves by nested (one-, multi-stage) negotiations on partial global plans. Two predicates describe the basic lines of their behavior:

(1) *Need_For_Collaborative_Approach(Task)* ---> *Init_Collaboration(Task)*
(2) *Expect_Promoting_Global_Probl_Solving(Task)* ---> *Apply_Collaboration(Task)*

4. COORDINATING AUTONOMOUS PROBLEM SOLVERS

Nested negotiations work on partial global plans describing the agents intended behavior. They enable the agents to initiate negotiations within other, already active negotiation processes. They provide a framework to deal with the interrelationships mentioned above. They allow to dynamically introduce agents into a collaboration, even if they are not (directly) visible by one of the partners. Finally, they allow the agents to ask others for collaborative support improving their own arguments within an ongoing negotiation process. Collaboration competence means, that an agent can reason about collaborative processes, (its own relationships to) other agents, (parts of) the state and dynamic behavior (evolution) of the global system etc.

4.1. Using Partial Global Plans in FRESCO

Suppose a task T which needs to be decomposed. Decomposition results in a local decomposition plan (TDP_T) which is to be negotiated to construct the task allocation table (TAT_T). If all subtasks have been assigned to at least one competent agent, the TAT_T is to be processed to generate the local task allocation plan TAP_T. Otherwise, the agent must change the TDP_T using the knowledge received from the preceding negotiation process. Then, the TDP_T and the TAP_T are aggregated to form the nodes task plan (NTP_T) which specifies the agents activities solving T. Generalizing the NTP_T, the agent constructs the partial global plan PGP_T of T which serves as a communication unit (fig. 2). If the manager of T agrees with the PGP_T submitted by KBS_j, that agent is requested to process NTP_T. The decomposition D_T of T is a function

$$D_T\colon D(T) \rightarrow TD_T;\ with\ TD_T := (T_i, \langle synth\_info \rangle_i, REL_{ik})^n$$

n indicates the number of subtasks. <synth_info>$_i$ describes how to integrate the result of T_i into the overall result. REL_{ik} defines the relationships between T_i, T_k. Bargaining subtasks requires to add further knowledge to them. This is done by DESCR

$$DESCR_T\colon DESCR(T) \rightarrow (\langle type \rangle, \langle semantics \rangle, \langle requirements \rangle)_T$$

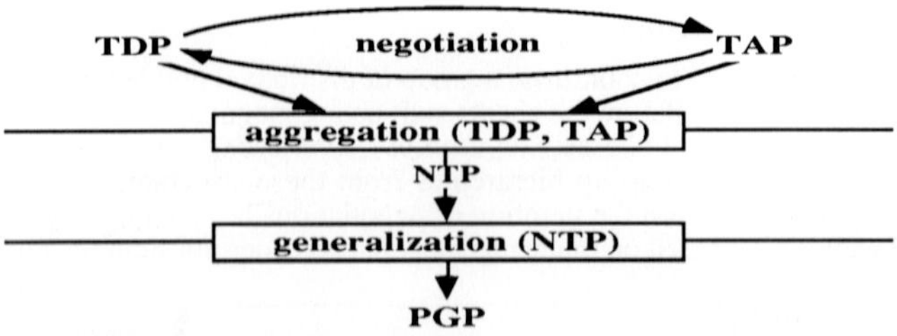

Fig. 2: The FRESCO Concept of Partial Global Plans

Type indicates the cooperation style (e.g., distributed or multiagent problem solving, teamwork etc.) and the problem solving type of a task (e.g., diagnosis, configuration). *Semantics* includes the task definition, its input data or goals. *Requirements* include the problem solving strategies needed, the knowledge representation formalisms, the definition of the task's search space and the resources that are needed to solve T. To construct the local task decomposition plan TDP_T DESCR applies to all T_i included in TD_T. So, the TDP_T can now be defined as:

$$TDP_T := (T_i, (\langle type\rangle, \langle semantics\rangle, \langle requirements\rangle)_{T_i}, REL_{ik}, \langle synth\_info\rangle)^n$$

The competence evaluation function $COMP_T$ of an agent is given with:

$$COMP_T\colon COMP(KBS_j, DESCR_T, C_{min}, E_{min}) \rightarrow (C, E)_{j,T}$$

where m indicates the number of agents of the overall system and $j \in \{1, .., m\}$. KBS_j identifies agent j. C stands for the expected amount of competence to solve T. E defines the evidence of C and$(C, E)_{j,T}$ stands for the result of the competence evaluation of KBS_j.
In short, C is represented by a vector. Among others, the values of the components of that vector describe the ability of an agent to deal with the classes, instances and problem solving strategies, with the knowledge representation formalism, the resources and task description language required by T. Obviously, these components correspond to the characteristics of a task being included in the function $DESCR_T$. For details see again [7], [8b]. Now we introduce the process of negotiating task allocations $NEGOTIATE\_ALLOC_T$.

$$NEGOTIATE\_ALLOC_T\colon NEGOTIATE\_ALLOC\ (DESCR_T) \rightarrow TAT_{(T)}$$
$$TAT(T) := (T_i, \{(KBS_j, C_{ij}, E_{ij}) \mid (C_{ij} \geq C_{i,min})\ AND\ (E_{ij} \geq E_{i,m})\}^n$$
$$success(NEGOTIATE\_ALLOC_T) :\Leftrightarrow \forall T_i\ \exists KBS_j\colon (C_{ij} \geq C_{i,min})\ AND\ (E_{ij} \geq E_{i,min})$$

Bargaining introduces (temporal) global knowledge. If $[\exists\ T_i \in TDP_T$: there is no KBS_j with $C_{ij} \geq C_{i,min}]$ the actual TDP_T cannot be satisfied. In that case, the evaluation of the above condition triggers a modification changing the actual TDP_T. After having generated a complete and consistent TAT_T task allocation TA_T takes place to construct the local task allocation plan TAP_T

$$TA_T\colon TA(TAT_T) \rightarrow TAP_T\ ;\ with\ TAP_T := (T_i, KBS_j, C_{ij}, E_{ij})^n$$

$C_{ij} := \max\ \{C \mid j \in \{1, ..., m\}$ AND $C_{ij} \geq C_{min}\}$ indicates the competence of $KBS_j \mid T_i$. The aggregation AGGR of the TDP_T and the TAP_T forms the nodes task plan NTP_T.

$$AGGR_{TDP,\ TAP} : AGGR(TDP_T, TAP_T) \rightarrow NTP(T);$$
$$NTP(T) := (T_i, \langle synth\_info\rangle_i, REL_{ik}, KBS_j, C_{ij}, E_{ij})^n$$

Generalizing the NTP_T leads to the partial global plan PGP_T:

$$GENERALIZE_{NTP}\colon GENERALIZE\ (NTP_T) \rightarrow PGP(_T)$$
$$PGP(T) := ((local\_agent\_id, T, C, E), (T_i, KBS_j)^n)$$

Local_agent_id identifies the local agent. T identifies the current task T. C indicates the expected competence of an agent to solve T and E indicates the evidence that holds for C.

4.2. Nested Negotiations

Negotiations provide a model to coordinate a group of distributed problem solvers. As conventional negotiation takes place before the agents start acting, negotiation-based cooperation can be divided into three separated phases: *negotiation - contracting - acting* (fig. 3). Typically, distributed problem solvers build up hierarchies from these structures (e.g., see [17], [6]). Multistage negotiations focus on the iteration of negotiations between two agents before they start acting. Mostly, acting based on multistage negotiations does not suppose any contracting.

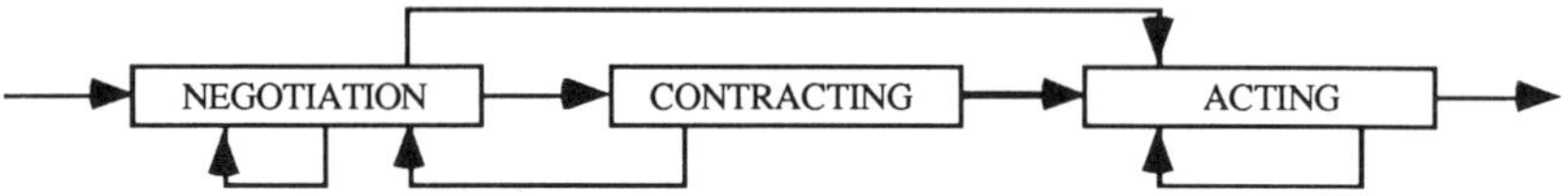

Fig. 3: General Model of Negotiation Concepts

This negotiation model has been based on the assumption, that the ACTING phase can be anticipated completely, and that in the case of a cooperation abort or of a system crash the cost of re-initializing cooperation is not from significant importance. Both assumptions do not hold when considering cooperative autonomous problem solvers in productive Open Systems. Instead, we are faced with multi-user access to cooperative information systems and with the fact, that cooperation processes within such systems may perform complex and interrelated operations. In general, they also may take a significant time to succeed[2]. Considering cooperating problem solvers we have to state, that (1) in general, they solve tasks by inferencing. It is already well known, that there does not exist any general solution how to predict, for example, the exact ordering of rules which will fire during an inference process. (2) Local inferences may take some time to generate a solution. So, in general, the costs of re-initializing cooperative processes must expected being rather high. (3) Dynamic knowledge base updates (by maintenance, adaption or learning) provide a lot of severe consistency problems. In the case of an unexpected cooperation abort, it is important to strictly control the consequences arising from them. (4) Applying cybernetic models to the agents behaviour requires to completely control their involvement into a collaboration process from its very beginning up to its end. We still lack concepts to fit these requirements. The more, Open Systems introduce new problems:

Applying the contract net protocol a group of agents may bargain on the allocation of some task T. If none of them feels competent, T is rejected. However, if there is at least one agent A participating to two different cooperative systems, there is still a chance to find a solution.

Considering PGPs provides further insights. First, PGPs represent the agents intended behavior. Negotiating PGPs leads to a representation of the agents globally accepted (and expected) behavior. Sometimes, they may become invalid (e.g., arising by changes to any of the PGPs). Finally, PGPs will be deleted from the system (e.g., problem solving completed). So, we must divide between these four states. In addition, every agent only knows a subset of all PGPs within the overall system. Due to the dynamics of federative systems, the agents knowledge about these states becomes inconsistent over time. However, the agents knowledge on the PGPs currently living within the system determines their problem solving and collaborative behavior. That means, changing PGPs requires communicating (and: negotiating) the changes that are intended before realizing them[3]. Searching for a negotiation-based solution the most important aspect will be on the adaption of the negotiation model to the agents cybernetic behavior. Looking at the Open Systems-example a first idea can easily be identified:

Solution: *By providing Agent A with the ability (and the right!) to negotiate T before answering to the competence assessment request, the "visibility / accessibility-problem" can be solved easily. This can be implemented by a simple extension to the contract protocol.*

---

2 I.e., we are faced with problems that are similar to those in design databases and object oriented databases.

3 Prominent example: The consistency-problem arising from dynamic updates in federated databases.

More general, the application of the negotiation paradigm to the intitial phase of a collaborative process only seems to be too restrictive. Instead, the concept of negotiations should be extended to the collaboration processes from their very beginning up to their end (fig. 4).

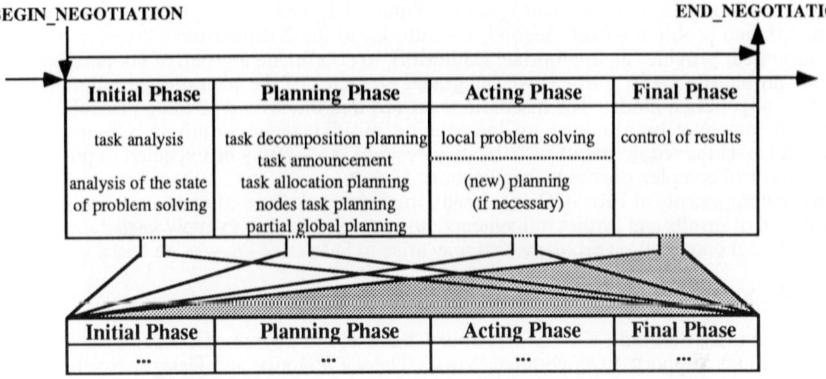

Fig. 4: The General Concept of *Nested Negotiations*

4.3. The FRESCO Collaboration Management

We now detail the FRESCO collaboration management. Suppose, KBSj applies to some task T. Processing $COMP_T$ the task analysis component first evaluates the local competence to solve the task. Depending on the result $(C, E)_{j,T}$ the agent decides on how to approach T. If T requires collaborative problem solving [i.e., $(E < E_{min})$ **OR** $(C < C_{min})$] the agent generates its task decomposition and task allocation plans. If the situation arises that negotiating will not contribute to complete the TAT_T, the agent can choose among different alternatives:

1. *Choose another contractor and restart the process of (sub-) task allocation.*
2. *Constraint Relaxation: Reducing the value of E_{min}:* This relates to the DAI-discussion on trusts and expectations. $Agent_j$ now trusts his "colleagues" more than before. This may arise from missing alternatives, but also from learning from experiences in the past.
3. *Constraint Relaxation: Reducing the value of C_{min}:* Suppose, that there is no agent with a strong competence with respect to T. That may lead the agents to reduce their expectations and to accept partners with a minor qualification.
4. *Nested Negotiations:* Suppose, none of the agents is able to fit the $C_{min,T}$-constraint, and that constraint relaxation has not been allowed. In that case the manager of T selects $agent_j$ calling for a collaborative solution. I.e., $agent_j$ *collaboratively* develops local TDPs and TAPs to enhance its own C_j by collaboration means. Being successful ($C_{j,\ collaborative} > C_{min,\ T}$), it generates the NTP and the PGP, and returns the latter to the manager of T. This concept of *nested negotiations* provides facilities to dynamically establish task forces to approach tasks that are beyond an agent's local capability. Furthermore, nested negotiations can be used to coordinate a dynamic network of collaborating agents.

CONCLUSIONS

As a starting point, we introduced FRESCO, a federative knowledge based system in banking. The federative approach has its roots in the field of federated databases as well as in the distributed problem solving paradigm being developed by recent DAI-research. One important concern of federative systems is on the coordination problem.

FRESCO includes very complex intelligent agents while at the same time combining multiagent facilities with distributed problem solver characteristics. This makes the coordination problem much more complicated than it is in classical DAI-systems. One of the most interesting approaches to the coordination problem are partial global plans, which in the original version has been applied by [5] to multiagent systems. Within FRESCO, partial global plans are applied to a distributed problem solver. Second, we introduced the 2-dimensional concept of *nested negotiations*. It provides an appropriate framework to coordinate a group of cooperating autonomous problem solvers. Further, we integrated elements of the planning paradigm with an advanced negotiation model. The discussions proved that this would be quite possible. Further improvements may be obtained by introducing multistage negotiations. Obviously, this approach meets the requirements of federative systems, and it may be expected to promote the development of complex distributed applications further.
The basic components of FRESCO are already implemented. Current work now deals with the exploitation of results and further refinements. It is intended further to apply *nested negotiations* to the different coordination problems that may arise in federative knowledge based systems.

REFERENCES

[1] Bannon, L.; Schmidt, K.: CSCW: Four Characters in Search of Context; in: Studies in Computer Supported Cooperative Work - Theory, Practice and Design, North Holland, Amsterdam 1991, ed. by J.M. Bowers and S.D. Benford.

[2] Bond, A.; Gasser, L.: Readings in Distributed Artificial Intelligence, Morgan Kaufmann Publishers, San Mateo, CA., 1988.

[3] Conry, S.E. et.al.: Multistage Negotiation in Distributed Planning, in [2], pp. 367.

[4] Deen, S.M.: Research Issues in Federated Knowledge Based Systems, British Computer Society Workshop Series: R&D in XPS V, Proc. of XPS, Cambr. 1988.

[5] Durfee, E.H.; Lesser, V.R.: Using Partial Global Plans to Coordinate Distributed Problem Solvers, IJCAI 1987, pp. 875.

[6] Findler, N.V.; Gao, J.: Dynamic Hierarchical Control for Distributed Problem Solving, Data & Knowledge Engineering, 2(1987), pp. 285-301.

[7] Kirn, St.: Collaborative Ability of Intelligent Agents in Federative Environments, PhD thesis, Hagen 1991.

[8a] Kirn, St.; Schlageter, G.: Federated Expert Systems: Concepts and Implementation, in Deen, M. (ed.): Cooperating Knowledge Based Systems, Springer Verlag, 1991.

[8b] Kirn, St.; Schlageter, G.: Competence Evaluation in Federative Problem Solving - How to Make Expert Systems Cooperative, 11th Conf. on 2nd Gen. XPS, Avignon, 1991.

[9] Kuwabara, K.; Lesser, V.R.: Extended Protocol for Multi-Stage Negotiation, 9th Workshop on DAI, Bandera, Texas, October 23-27, 1990.

[10] Lâasri, B. et.al.: An analysis of negotiations and its role for coordinating cooperative distributed problem solvers, 11th Conf. on 2nd Generation Expert Systems, Avignon, France, 1991, pp. 81.

[11] Lesser, V.R.; Corkill, D.D.: Functionally Accurate, Cooperative Distributed Systems, IEEE Trans. on Systems, Man and Cybernetics, SMC-11(1), January 1981, pp. 81.

[12] Malone, Thomas, W.; Crowston, K.: What is Coordination Theory and How Can it Help Design Cooperative Work Systems?, Proc. Conf. on CSCW, Los Angeles, CA, 1990.

[13] Navathe, S.B. et.al.: Federated Information Bases: A Loosely Coupled Integration of Database Systems and Application Subsystems, Gainesville, FL 32611, 1990.

[14] Nolan, R.L.; Pollock, A.J.; Ware, J.P.: Toward the Design of Network Organisations, Stage by Stage, 9(1), Lexington, MA, 1989.

[15] Schmidt, K.: Analysis of Cooperative Work - a Conceptual Framework, Tech. Report, Cognitive Systems Group, Roskilde, Denmark, 1991.

[16] Sheth, A.P.; Larson, J.A.: Federated Database Systems for Managing Distributed, Heterogeneous, and Autonomous Databases, Bellcore, ACM Computing Survey, 9/1990.

[17] Smith, R.G.: A Framework for Distributed Problem Solving, IJCAI 1979, pp. 836.

Personal Computers and Intelligent Systems / F.H. Vogt (Editor)
Information Processing 92, Volume III
Elsevier Science Publishers B.V. (North-Holland)

Integration of telephony into dp applications: a building block for intelligent information systems

Peter F. Pawlita

Siemens Nixdorf Information Systems AG
Dpt. SP VNS 13, P.O.Box 830951, W-8000 Munich 83, Germany

Abstract

*C*omputer *s*upported *t*elephony (CST) is a promising data/voice integration conception and enhances the intelligence of information processing systems. CST integrates computer functions, data and telephone switching functions on DP application level. This paper explains basic ideas and building blocks of CST, CST applications and their ability to improve the efficiency of telephone usage, decision-making herein, and office/business procedures. It describes a concrete implementation and mutual influences of CST and intelligent information systems.

1. INTRODUCTION

After data/voice integration having only moved slowly into practice so far, recently interest in a promising straight-forward data/voice integration technique has grown: *Computer supported telephony* (CST). CST integrates computer functions, computer data and telephone switching functions on DP application level. CST applications can manage and optimize daily telephone usage and integrate voice communication into office and business procedures. CST enhances the intelligence of information processing systems and workstations. This leads to improved efficiency of telephone usage and decision-making herein, office and business productivity, as well as synergy and rationalization effects.

Technically CST both is a data/voice integration conception and a conception of function sharing between a computer and a telephone switching system, primarily a PBX (*p*rivate automatic *b*ranch exchange). It enables computer applications, so-called *CSTA*s ($\hat{=}$ *CST* applications), to directly initiate, accept and manipulate calls. CST uses computer intelligence to enhance telephone usage by contributing application logics, dialing informations from directories, or call-initiated display of business informations from databases; on the other hand, it expands system intelligence to handle voice communication.

Basic ideas of the CST approach are the following [1]:

- CST aims at improvement of productivity of office or business telephone users
- with CST, application programs can *directly* address and exploit PBX switching functions and - vice versa - PBX users can access computer applications
- the integration landscape of CST according to Fig. 1 consists of:
  - computer and telephone switching system (here: PBX) with their resources
  - user workplaces (display terminal, PC or workstation, plus telephone)
  - the networks for connection of display terminals to a computer and for connection of telephones to a PBX, plus the public telephone network
- CST protects existing customer investment, especially in terminal, computer, PBX, and network equipment, computer data and (if expandable) applications;

basicly, CST is independent of ISDN and ISDN terminal equipment
- CST does not affect existing computer or PBX kernel technologies.

2. IMPLEMENTATION

CST requires implementations of at minimum four basic *building blocks* (Fig. 1):
1) opening of the PBX switching kernel by implementing a *direct switch access* by which commands, messages and transparent data can be transferred
2) provision of a *computer< - > PBX interconnection system* for data exchange of those data mentioned before, e.g., a dedicated channel
3) provision of a high-level *API* (≙*a*pplication *p*rogram *i*nterface) within the computer. By it, computer applications can directly address PBX switching functions and vice versa can be addressed by PBX-attached telephones
4) *application programs:* adaption of existing applications to the application interface to use the new functionalities or provision of new applications.

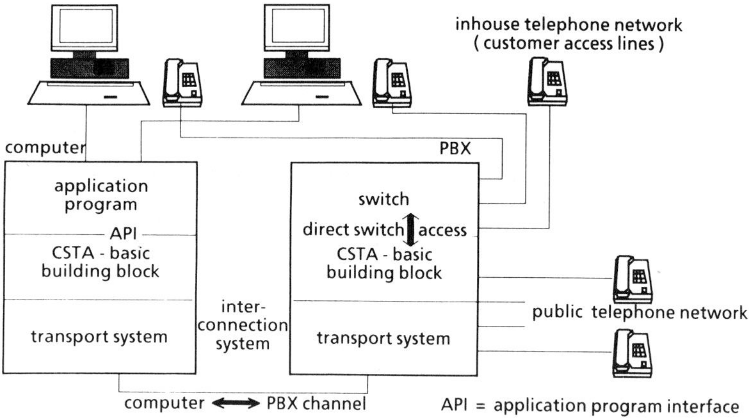

Figure 1. CST - general architecture. Basic building blocks

Emphasizing the computer side of CST, important architectural *requirements* for a universal-type CST implementation are (Fig. 2): building block principle, a stable API decoupling applications from telephone-oriented functions, system-independent design (to ensure independence of PBX type and of computer platform), and a client /server architecture of CST computer software.

An example of a highly universal CST implementation is the Siemens Nixdorf *Tel*ephone *A*pplication *S*ystem TELAS described in more detail in [1]. TELAS is a product conception and a product family. Its implementation meets the requirements mentioned above; its building block principle incorporates (cf. Fig.2) 1) a basic building block (TELAS-BAS) offering CST monitor and protocol engine and an API called ITBAS playing the role of an application platform, 2) standard applications atop of TELAS-BAS, and branch- or customer-specific applications.

The client/server architecture enables TELAS-BAS to be split into client and server part; thus, the client carrying the API can be spread on distinct systems. Currently, TELAS is available on Siemens Nixdorf SINIX® multi-user computers and workstations, and (as a client) on MSDOS/Windows computers. It supports two digital ISDN-PBX, Siemens Hicom and Siemens Nixdorf 8818, and (with reduced functionality) non-CST-equipped PBX and public telephone networks.

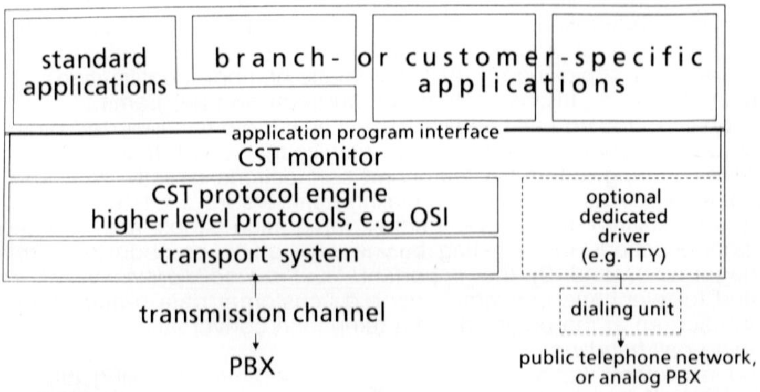

Figure 2. Example of a universal - type CST implementation

The high-level API ITBAS offers all important services to applications to address and control PBX switching functions directly. ITBAS supports:

- organizational commands, e.g., for opening, operation and closing of logical "CSTA sessions" between CST entities in computer and PBX
- commands for *call-related services* ("call management"), e.g., make call, answer call, conference call, make consultation, alternate, redirect, hangup, ..
- control of customer access lines
- input/output of data at push-button telephone terminals
- commands for PBX administration functions, import of PBX accounting data.

3. CST APPLICATIONS

At present, first products are available or in development which represent the basic CST service consisting of the first three building blocks mentioned in section 1. Product implementations from computer vendors have become known, besides Siemens Nixdorf, also from Digital Equipment, IBM, etc..That means basic platforms exist to build applications upon and to realize complete solutions.

The manifold *principal CSTAs* [2 - 5] can be classified into 5 application fields:

a) *incoming call handling*

- "service center"-type applications (e.g., "help desk" for maintenance), where "service request" calls for a special but unknown expert/technician arrive. Possible problem solutions are 1) using ACD (automatic call distribution) the incoming call is routed automatically to "1 of n" experts whose line is not busy. This expert picks up the call, draws up the problem and forwards the call and associated documents to the real expert, 2) incoming calls are routed automatically and specificly to the unique competent expert, by using second order-dialing of"problem number", or 3) automatic ring back
- message center/message handling applications, like 1) unattended message acceptance, e.g., in 24-hour service, or 2) integrated message handling, e.g.,

automatic "message waiting"-alerts to terminals, automatic delivery of messages via alternate message systems, etc.
- emergency call applications, e.g., industrial or fire alarm management employing notifications to selected persons and automatic provision of alarm plans
- inbound telemarketing: by number of caller and comparison with customer files the nature of a call is detected and a customer-related document is displayed before picking up. ANI (automatic number identification) is useful.
- opinion polls, e.g., in conjunction with broadcasting programs.

Incoming *plus* outgoing call handling as a mixed case is supported by a so-called
- individual telephone agent support (intelligent "comfort telephone" via data screen), offering automatic telephone connections directly from an interactive computer application and taking dialing numbers from a telephone directory or from an existing data base. Further integration steps are 1) integration of telephone actions into existing business or office procedures (e.g., workflow management), and 2) the important *"just-in-time" provision of documents* related to telephone conversations: e.g., customer data required are provided on the screen at the beginning of a telephone conversation

b) *outgoing call handling*
- outbound telemarketing: according to a programmed calling plan, i.e., serial calls according to a customer list plus document provision, a customer collective can be addressed (fresh products service, brokers, etc..)
- customer-friendly debt collection, i.e., "warning by telephone before warning by registered letter", initiated by computerized term control
- market research (opinion poll)

c) *data transfer service* for simple terminals, e.g.,
- unattended read of customer data files , e.g., daily order data at pharmacies
- simple data collection via push-button telephones, e.g., referring to orders, flexible working time, factory data, document requests from archives

d) *PBX operation/data handling*
- data transfer, e.g., reading and evaluation of call accounting data,
- control of customer/configuration data, e.g., blocking of undesirable calls

e) *mixed applications* combining several application areas, e.g., in hotels (wake-up service, room status, charging), or hospitals (telephone authorization for patients, distress call routing, room status, retrieval of patient history files, etc.)

CSTA software development means programming of a sequence of API commands, like the ITBAS commands in sect. 2. Applications can be expected primarily from software houses as well as vendors or customers. Currently, only few CSTAs atop of CST platforms exist; one major reason is the usual "chicken and egg"-problem in the entry phase of new information technologies. The number of standard applications will be limited. One example of a standard application broadly applicable is the Siemens Nixdorf-developed "Telephone manager" TELAS-MAN atop of the application platform TELAS-BAS for individual telephone agent support of SINIX terminal users; it offers functions like computer-based call management and call-initiated provision of documents and memos.

CST allows to automate many office/business procedures where computer displays and telephones are involved; for it, a computer application undertakes the "call management" which is the organisation and high-level procedure logic for complete courses of calls and substitutes many manual operations. CST allows

- to integrate telephone support into computer applications
- to take advantage of existing computer intelligence, data and data management to make telephone usage more effective and convenient
- integration of telephone terminals into DP procedures
- control and accounting procedures for PBXs done by computer applications.

Main *CST benefits* are:

- improvement of productivity at office/business workplaces, relieving from routine actions, e.g., searching for telephone numbers/documents, dialing, waiting
- rationalization/cost saving, by time saving of users, additional uses of existing equipment (terminals) and data, and further synergy effects
- organizational benefits by computer-aided workflow and information flow and improved decision support.

4. CST AND INTELLIGENT INFORMATION SYSTEMS

This section discusses the mutual influence of CST and intelligent systems. First, we ask which intelligent information system functions are common to the CST applications in section 3. These emphasize the computer part of CST and the user´s point of view and his practical expectations in system intelligence:

- relieving from routine actions, more automatism, by supporting pure voice- (or: generally: telecom-) oriented functions, like 1) call management of connections between objects, with objects being telephone customers ($\hat{=}$ persons or programs), or 2) handling of other telecom functions like fax, video telephone, or messaging, or conversions between telecom and other services
- call-related support for decisions, by
  - provision of relevant information "just in time", for decisions and improved competence, e.g., by knowledge-based or learning techniques
  - relieving from routine decisions,eg. selecting, filtering, addressing, routing,..
  - help to manage information, to reduce information volume and redundancy, relieving from information overflow ("right information at the right time")
- appropriate information storage and access for programs, computers or telephone users, e.g., for decision making just mentioned
- powerful user interface including voice communication (displaying objects, status, message lamp..), creating a "changing face of telephone usage"
- management of integration (data/voice, computer/PBX, "single system image")
- hiding of system complexity, supporting
  - naming and associating (X.500 directory usage, association objects <-> telephone numbers/terminals, considering of organizational relations),
  - transparency, e.g., users do not realize computer/PBX function sharing
  - hiding of configuration change, mobility of users
- automatic event processing (messages, responses, alarms,..) and workflow management, including voice communication, and offering intelligent dynamic linking between events, objects, processes, etc.
- "human-like" behavior of computer if the callee is a computer
- additional advanced techniques/building blocks for special purposes, like automatic call distribution (ACD), automatic number identification (ANI), caller identification, authentication (by voice recognition) and authorization, voice-response, support of further telecommunications services like fax or video, and transaction service for calls that must not get lost.

Based on this analysis, we can conclude regarding the *impact of intelligence of* information systems on CST: The basic CST technology (covering the first three technical building blocks explained in sect. 1) is of course a *necessary precondition* for call management and control by the computer, but the *key* to improved efficiency is the ability of CST applications to link events, functions and objects intelligently. Further, the majority of intelligent functions belong to non-voice computer technology. Thus, the CST key is the intelligence of the application itself and its ability to exploit existing system intelligence. CST *takes advantage of intelligence of information systems* (as an ability not only to process, store and manipulate data but to control flows, to link, and to make ruled-based decisions)

- to create new intelligent applications or voice-enhanced applications
- to combine existing elements to create a synergistic new system
- to offer an appropriate voice-enhanced interface for the computer user.

On the other hand, we can conclude on the *role of CST for intelligent systems:* CST (mainly its applications) can expand the intelligence of systems in many respects. CST is a field where system intelligence can demonstrate high effects in everyday life of the large telephone user community. In this context, the basic CST technology is a necessary precondition.

Typical future information processing architectures will be distributed. Applications will consist of a relatively small control body while most of common generic functions will be carried out by a "lego" of services, the basic *CST service* being one of them (Fig. 3). Thus, CST is a useful new building block in the architecture of future information systems. Typical "windows" to the intelligent information system and its services including CST will be appropriate workstations and PCs. The CST service generally is a multi-stage service (cf. Fig. 3), where from the data terminal user´s point of view a CST client, a primary CST server (a multi-user computer) and a secondary server (switching server like PBX) cooperate.

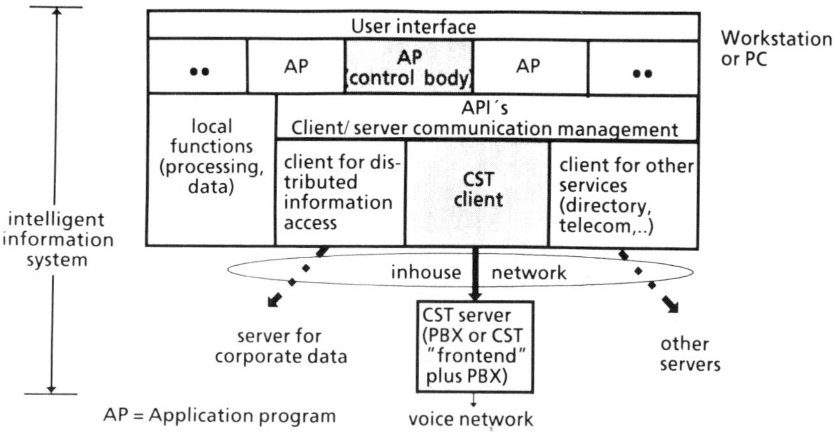

Figure 3. Role of CST in intelligent information systems

We have seen the mutual influence and synergy between CST and intelligent systems. A challenging integration and evolution process can be expected.

For CST to become successful, further developments should consider:

- CSTAs should offer system-independent or portable services for telephone users (like in TELAS) at workstations, PC and traditional terminals
- architecture and design of CST applications should be suitable to exploit intelligent functions as building blocks, e.g., in a service-oriented way
- CST will be an essential factor in multi-media, workgroup and enterprise communication, value added services, and communication of hypertext users. Thus, CST technique and applications must cowork with these techniques.
- CST applications must take advantage of existing mainframe or corporate data
- CST application architecture should be invariant to introduction of a closer data/voice integration, broadband communication or other function sharing techniques; this is also a requirement for standardization.

Regarding intelligent systems, the following is recommended:

- broad consciousness of the advantages of CST
- integration of CST service into information system architecture and into concrete applications based on a defined CST API
- experimentation with intelligent functions and verification of efficiency gains.

5. CONCLUSIONS AND OUTLOOK

CST opens up a new but evolutionary field of data/voice integration, because

- for the first time DP applications broadly can integrate telephone handling
- the integration approach is a very natural one and the technical/economical hurdles for vendors and customers are relatively low
- improvements of office/business communication productivity can be expected.

The key issues for CST success will be the following:

- productivity gains must be verified in practice and perceived by customers
- early availability of a standardized application platform, e.g., of ECMA
- availability of a critical mass of applications
- fruitful cooperations between DP and TC people at customers, computer and PBX vendors, and between customers, vendors and/or software houses.

Standardization: Perhaps the most important current CSTA standardization from computer point of view is at ECMA TC 32; several European and North-American computer and PBX vendors are involved. This standardization aims at functional definition of an application layer interface and protocol between computer and PBX [2, 6, 7]. The other important standardization effort is at ANSI T1.

It was shown that CST takes advantage of intelligence in information systems and - vice versa - CST should be a building block in future information systems enabling the integration of voice communication or other telecom functions and expanding the sphere of action of information processing and data. The CST integration conception at the application level is useful where computer intelligence and computer data can improve office communication and personal or unattended communication via telephone. CST is an evolving field, where many new applications are emerging and practical use is in the initial stage. CST fills a gap in covering many types of IT procedures, communications and objects by system intelligence and thus will be a necessary building block of future IT systems.

6. REFERENCES

1 P.F.Pawlita, Computer supported telephony: concept of a possible future mass application field, Proc. Int. Conf. on Computer Comm., New Delhi 1990, 21-27
2 ECMA TC-TG11, Computer supported telephony applications, Technical Report 4th Draft, Nov. 1989
3 Yankee Group,Computer-integrated telephone systems,Boston, MA, April 1989
4 P. Pawlita, How computers can improve the efficiency of telephone usage, Siemens Review 58 (1991), No. 6, 16 - 19
5 Jenkins, A., Giving Voice to Applications, Datamation Int. Ed. Vol. 35, No. 17, Sept. 1, 1989, 57-59
6 ECMA TG 11/91/185 + /186, CSTA services + protocol, final draft std., 1991
7 J. Piggott, The status of CSTA, Commun. Intl., Dec. 1991, 12-14

Personal Computers and Intelligent Systems / F.H. Vogt (Editor)
Information Processing 92, Volume III

Elsevier Science Publishers B.V. (North-Holland)

Building The Intelligent Island

Juzar Motiwalla[a] and Michael Yap[b]

[a]Institute of Systems Science, National University of Singapore, Heng Mui Keng Terrace, Kent Ridge, Singapore 0511

[b]National Computer Board (Singapore), 71 Science Park Drive, NCB Building, Singapore 0511

Abstract

Singapore is developing a vision of an Intelligent Island for the year 2000. This vision proposes a framework whereby information flows across and within key economic sectors will be harnessed to enhance economic competitiveness. It envisages a pervasive National Information Infrastructure (NII) where the general public can easily access national on-line information not only for direct utilitarian purpose, but also to enhance their individual potential and improve quality of life. This paper outlines the research issues being addressed to meet this challenge of public information access, and sketches the architecture of the information infrastructure required to realize the vision.

Keyword Codes: H.4.0; H.5.0; I.2.0
Keywords: Information Systems Applications, General; Information Interfaces and Presentations, General; Artificial Intelligence, General

1. INTRODUCTION

The development of physical infrastructures such as rails, roads, powers, canals and telecommunications, have tremendous impact to a nation's ability to succeed. Today, there is a new infrastructure challenge. Just as the highway system is needed to facilitate movement between locations, a nation-wide information infrastructure is needed to move vast quantities of data and to propel the innovative use of information.

Singapore has recently embarked on a determined effort towards the development of such a pervasive information infrastructure. In this paper, we highlight the national level planning issues examined and the research issues investigated in the specific goal of making large amounts of information accessible and useful to the general public.

2. IT2000 - A VISION OF THE INTELLIGENT ISLAND

With the establishment of the National Computer Board (NCB) in 1981, Singapore has deliberately prepared itself to meet the challenges of the Information Age. The last decade of concerted national computerization efforts have paid off, creating a very positive environment for the private and public sectors to collaborate in exploiting IT for national competitive advantage.

The World Competitiveness Report has in the recent years, consistently placed Singapore among the top nations in the world to effectively exploit IT. The broad-based approach in spearheading the nation into the Information Age has resulted in good progress on various fronts. The IT industry registered a compound annual growth rate of 30% between 1982 and 1990.

The NCB initiated the IT2000 Study in January 1991 to examine how IT can be further exploited to stimulate national competitiveness and to enhance the quality of life. The goal is to transform Singapore into the Intelligent Island where an advanced national information infrastructure interconnects every home, office, school and factory. In our vision, the computer will evolve into an information appliance, combining the functions of the telephone, computer and TV, to provide a rich array of communication modes and access to services. Text, sound, pictures, video, documents, designs and many other forms of media will be transferred and shared through the infrastructure reaching all homes and offices.

The approach taken at the onset of the IT2000 has been very much demand driven. The first stage of the effort calls for an extensive study of the needs and strategic application of IT in various sectors of Singapore over the next decade. 11 sectoral study groups, comprising some 200 knowledgeable and influential senior executives and academics from both the private and public sectors, were formed. The sectoral groups were in turn supported by over 50 NCB IT professionals, who have researched into the state-of-practice of IT in the various sectors. After months of intensive study, the groups have surfaced more than 60 major projects that will help bring the nation to the next phase of its development, and whose implementation will be facilitated by the availability of the national information infrastructure. Studying the proposals of all the sectoral groups, we recognised a set of common themes that collectively describe the IT2000 vision. The 5 themes include.

2.1 Developing a Global Hub.

The infrastructure will help turn Singapore into a highly efficient switching centre for goods, services, capital, information and people, enhancing its role as the global business, services and transportation hub. Potential applications that would support this theme include remote collaborative work, remote delivery of expertise, integrated transportation networks and electronic marketplace for information services.

2.2 Boosting the Economic Engine.

The potential benefits of the infrastructure to the economy are immense, generating greater productivity and new business opportunities. It will help to strengthen inter-firm coordination, both within and across national borders, and enable flexible and just-in-time business operations. Applications suggested include integrated networks to support the exchange of documents, payments and drawings, and a nation-wide multimedia leisure information and reservation system.

2.3 Enhancing the Potential of Individuals.

By providing more opportunities and bringing education to the convenience of the individuals, we hope to facilitate interactive and self-paced learning. The focus will be to greatly improve access to cultural digital repositories in Singapore and around the world, and to provide extra help for the disabled. Applications suggested include multimedia training, distance learning and adaptive computer technology.

2.4 Linking Community Locally and Globally.

An appropriate infrastructure can facilitate the creations of various community-based networks linking people with common causes or interests. It will help to support civic and cultural networking, and with overseas extension, helps to promote international goodwill.

2.5 Improving the Quality of Life.

The emphasis here is to enrich the lives of the people by supporting many conveniences, increasing discretionary time and generating more opportunities and choices in the kinship, social, work and civic spheres. It will help facilitate living in an increasingly more congested, vibrant and cosmopolitan Singapore, by shielding some of the complexity. Applications suggested include one-stop, non-stop government and business services, cashless transactions, dynamic transport information, round-the-clock healthcare information and telecommuting.

3. ACCESS TO SERVICES

The Intelligent Island portrays a scenario of immense information flows. The National Information Infrastructure must promote, capture, integrate and exploit these information flows. With the unleashing of the communications bottleneck through gigabit networks, there is a natural tendency to conjure a vision of numerous classes of trade documents, multimedia educational and reference material, large amounts of public information and a host of transactions being readily made available to consumers in the Intelligent Island. However, without "intelligence" in the infrastructure this vision is unlikely to happen.

One of the opportunities presented in the Intelligent Island is to put the national information on-line. The challenge is to make the information easily accessible and useful to the general public. Such access will go a long way towards meeting the objectives listed in Section 2. Specific activities that are critical in meeting this challenge include the following.

(1) A methodology and architecture that supports input and structuring of information.

(2) Intelligent routing of information.

(3) Intelligent initiation of transactions.

(4) Intelligent retrieval of information.

(5) Natural language interface to support access to information services.

This set of activities must accomplish 2 critical objectives. They must reduce information overload and allow easy access, manipulation and viewing of information by the general public.

4. KEY RESEARCH ISSUES IN INFORMATION ACCESS

In order to achieve the goals of enabling information access for the general public, research on building a flexible architecture, agent-based interaction, handling of multimedia information, natural language processing and user interfaces are being actively pursued. Research is being carried out in Singapore, with a substantial amount at the Institute of Systems Science, on several of these topics.

4.1 Natural Language Interfaces

The focus here is in developing intelligent multilingual interfaces, with an emphasis on Asian Languages. Work is underway on easy-to-use input methods for ideograph-based languages. It is noted that input of characters for such languages is notoriously slower than for languages with a manageable alphabet size. Major enhancements will come from investigation into a combination of these input-based methods with speech and pen-based entry. Another feature will be intelligent prompting and improved productivity of information entry through methods of text generation and composition.

In a multilingual society like Singapore, it is important to allow the general user to formulate his query in one of the main languages in use. Further, as the system must be in interactive mode, intelligent determination of the domain of discourse is required quickly so that the appropriate database search is narrowed.

There will be a need for translation of user queries at the keyword and phrase level where indexes to the collections of information that have been generated are of a different language. To allow broader linking of individual users, it may be useful to have translations at a coarse level for e-mail and short notes.

4.2 Multimedia Interfaces

A consistent way to represent, structure and navigate multimedia information is required. A standard method of composition and viewing by information providers and users will greatly enhance the success of this endeavor. A key feature will be a text-to-hypertext engine, which will automatically enable appropriate representation of information in a form which allows sensible navigation.

To achieve our aim of bringing the magic of the Information Age to the masses, significant effort has to be invested in producing easy to learn and easy to use interfaces. New interaction paradigms will have to be explored. Users must be allowed to utilize vocabulary and concepts they are already familiar with.

Further, as multimedia information is expected to be a pervasive feature of the Intelligent Island, the interaction paradigm and its implementation must consider the manipulation of multimedia objects. However, from a phasing and feasibility point of view, the initial emphasis will remain on text.

4.3 Search Engine

While there has been considerable work on search, and there are established methods of effective search for fairly focused collections of data, the challenge posed in the Intelligent Island is enormous. Not only is there a massive amount of information that could possibly be accessed, the information is continuously being updated, it is in distributed locations and covers a wide variety of domains. Semantic coherence across such a "database" is critical. The work so far has intially focused on free-text search. As in the Intelligent Agent scheme, there will need to be continuous updates of user profile and automated responses to further refine queries.

As queries will often not be precise, and data models are heterogeneous as described later, cost-effective methods for retrieving closest match responses and for allowing continuous query refinement must be designed. To allow for retrieval based on closest match, consideration will be given to indexing, clustering and similarity measures for objects.

4.4 Intelligent Agents

The concept of the Intelligent Agent is an extremely powerful vehicle to exploit for integration of the activities listed in Section 3, and in ensuring economical and effective implementation of these activities.

In this paper we emphasize the provision of Information Services by Service Providers to Users. A Service Provider will register its service with a Distributed Encyclopedia. A User Agent formulates a request, while a Service Agent will perform various operations to meet the needs of the request, including transfer of tasks to other Service Agents, Billing Agents, etc.

A key issue is that, in order to react to stimuli and interact intelligently with other agents and its environment, an agent needs knowledge about its environment. We need to address the capture of appropriate expertise, user profiles and the goals to be accomplished in processing queries.

4.5 Global Directories and Multidatabases

The success of the Intelligent Island concept may very much rely on the existence of a Distributed Encyclopedia that contains description of all the classes of services that are provided (it may just be indexes to actual implementation). The construction of such a global database hierarchy is indeed unprecedented and requires much consensus-building and research.

To support the execution of a query, each Service Provider may have to agree to the encyclopedia definition so that it would be able to translate and map into its own database. Ideally, the service providers' databases should be modelled on the Distributed Encyclopedia. However, given that providers are likely to have already established their own databases, the solution may be to encapsulate them within a framework consistent with the Distributed Encyclopedia. Naturally, there will be a need to map the envelope layer to the implementation. In addition, each Service Provider will also be required to provide an environment to support the execution of a query, namely, to support the Service Agent.

Here we are confronted with the issue of multidatabase system interoperability. Initial work will be carried out on limited multidatabase problems, involving few organizations and sites, existing collections of data and established database systems. The first set of research issues will include object-oriented global data model, definition of query language and algorithms for query processing and concurrency control.

5. THE INFRASTRUCTURE FOR THE INTELLIGENT ISLAND

As outlined above, the vision of an Intelligent Island for the year 2000 proposes a framework whereby information flows across and within key economic sectors will be harnessed to enhance economic competiveness and solve challenging organizational problems. A nation-wide infrastructure to promote, capture, integrate and exploit these information flows will be required.

It is an infrastructure consisting of efficient transport mechanism, information processing and service facilities that combine both computer and communication technologies. From it anyone, anywhere, at anytime could easily, quickly, and inexpensively get information services that they want.

Such an infrastructure to handle massive transfers among multiple economic sectors as well as public and governmental use is unprecedented with no past experience to learn from. We believe that Singapore provides a viable test bed for this concept, and the National Computer Board in Singapore will spearhead a multi-agency effort to implement it.

Figure 1 below shows the major components of the NII. **Applications** are specific end-users systems which are constructed on the Application Architecture and use the facilities provided by the Common Object Layer. The value of developing applications based on the Application Architecture is the improved ability to integrate transparently with other applications and extensive reusability.

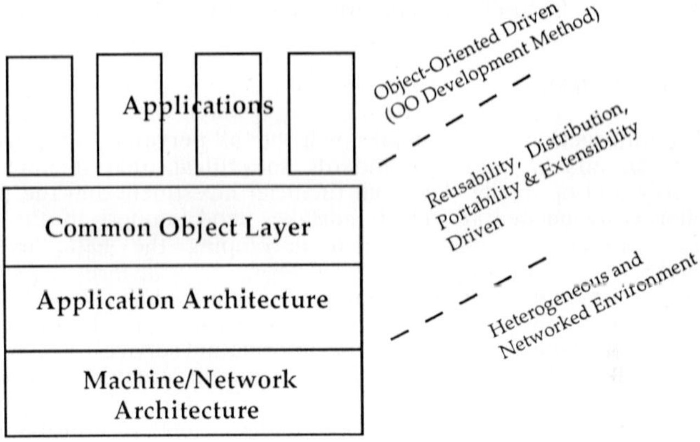

Figure 1 : Major Components of the NII

A common development method supported by the necessary tools is proposed for all applications. The method shall support effectively the construction of a wide range of large applications. It promotes the implementation of applications that are consistent with the architecture, increases productivity and enhances seamless integration.

The **Common Object Layer** comprises of facilities that are useful in many application domains and are available through the Application Architecture-compliant object interfaces. They include electronic mail facility, support for cooperative work, reusable user interfaces, billing, object query facilities and intelligent agent facilities such as knowbots. In addition, the developers may define subclasses to enrich or customize the functionality of these common objects. For application developers, it means greater productivity. The Common Object Layer exemplifies a key concept the object-oriented paradigm promotes - class reusability.

The **Application Architecture** defines a computing environment following a consistent object paradigm that provides a platform-independent capability for data exchange and code reuse. Externally, the application architecture determines how applications of the NII can be constructed. It provides the structure so that design and implementation decisions can be made effectively. Internally, it describes the structure of interconnections of the NII. It specifies component interactions, and ultimately the details of the interface among interoperating components. The Application Architecture assumes that underlying services provided by a platform's operating system and lower-level basic services such as network computing facilities are available.

To support the Intelligent Agent concept above, the Application Architecture of the NII would need to be distributed, providing transparency to data access and system interoperability. Global data objects are automatically available to all clients. The execution of objects can be distributed among heterogeneous clients and the process of object migration is transparent. The NII must support the passing of code to remote nodes for execution as well as data. This would implicitly demand that Service Providers support execution within their own environments.

The Machine/Network Architecture constitutes the physical layer (and associated protocols) of the NII and includes the carriers of information such as the fibre optics lines and wireless networks. It also includes all user-access systems such as smart cards, hand-held computers and HDTV.

6. CONCLUSIONS

The information infrastructure will be all-pervasive, and its needs for communication and computing standards so critical, that it might not arise spontaneously and optimally. The high financial investment and the possibility of even higher costs needed to rectify mistakes lend support to the need for a disciplined approach in planning and developing the national information infrastructure.

The government would be required to play a leading role in facilitating the realization of the Intelligent Island. However, it must be emphasised that it is not the intention to centralize and monopolize information services. The building of the National Information Infrastructure is to promote greater innovative use of information. It is a concept established to make it easier for individuals and enterprises to provide information services and exchange of information, bringing Singapore closer to the enjoyment of the full benefits of the Information Age.

The NII will bring a wealth of information resources to draw from. The implementation of the concept of "intelligence" and provision of infrastructure as discussed above provides the means to bring to the general public relevant information. The gap between the information "haves" and have nots" need not continue to widen. The system can augment the information disadvantaged with broader and easier access.

ACKNOWLEDGEMENT

Numerous people in Singapore are contributing to the realization of the vision of the Intelligent Island. Ideas in this paper have evolved with contributions from Ko Kheng Hwa, Foong Tze Foon, Robin Hu, Low Hwee Boon, Desai Narasimhalu, Jonathan Priddey and Wong Seng Hon.

Personal Computers and Intelligent Systems / F.H. Vogt (Editor)
Information Processing 92, Volume III
Elsevier Science Publishers B.V. (North-Holland)

Knowledge Base Management Systems using Description Logics and their role in Software Information Systems

Alex Borgida
Dept. of Computer Science, Rutgers University,
New Brunswick, NJ08904, USA
borgida@cs.rutgers.edu

Premkumar Devanbu
AT&T Bell Laboratories, Murray Hill, NJ 07974, USA
and Dept. of Computer Science, Rutgers University
prem@research.att.com

Abstract

Description languages and logics form the basis of a new family of knowledge base management systems, which are beginning to have practical industrial applications. This paper presents a brief outline of description logics, and then shows that they can be used in a variety of ways in order to obtain more flexible information systems – ones that perform inferences, deal with incomplete knowledge, and help organize information. Once class of applications for such systems is managing information about software, and we give throughout examples from the world of Software Engineering.

1 Introduction

Information Systems can be viewed as mechanisms that support users in developing and maintaining *models* of their application domains. One trend in Information System research has been towards developing languages and tools that support a more "natural" modeling of the problem domain. Though quite successful in many ways, one obstacle which has hitherto not been surmounted has been the efficient yet proper treatment of *incomplete information* – we are all aware of the shortcomings of null-values in SQL, for example. A more recent trend has been increased support for "inference": the system's awareness of truths that are not explicitly told to it. However, this inferential mechanism has only rarely been applied to the querying process itself, as it should be if we are to support data exploration (e.g., [1]).

Our first intent is to survey a new class of "data models" (called Description Logics (DLs)) and demonstrate how these can be used to address some of these issues.

In order to ground our discussion, we will consider Software Information Systems (SIS). Large software systems are probably the most complex artifacts built by people, and their construction involves the management of enormous amounts of information. SIS attempt to capture this information in a computer, in order to promote access and sharing, thereby facilitating maintenance tasks. As argued in [16], there is a variety of information that surrounds the software development process, including information about: (i) the environment within which the proposed software system will function, and how the system is expected to interact with or relate to that environment; (ii) the design/architecture/implementation of the software system, and the decisions that lead to it; (iii) the development process itself that led to the software system, including the methodology used, the team of developers involved, schedules, etc.

Such information can evidently be useful throughout the software life-cycle (especially maintenance), but in addition may be used in training new personnel or supporting software reuse. A second purpose of the paper is then to show how DLs can be used to manage and retrieve knowledge about software.

2 What are description languages?

Description languages are descendants of the KL-ONE knowledge representation system [6, 7]; they have been used in many AI applications such as the representation of the meaning of natural language sentences. (See [20] for a review.)

DLs start with the intuition that for describing many situations it is useful to think of various kinds of *individuals*, related by *relationships*, and grouped into *sets/concepts*[1]. This intuition is of course shared with a great many other formalisms such as semantic networks, semantic data models, object-oriented languages, etc.

The fundamental observation underlying DLs is that there is a benefit to be gained if languages for talking about these kinds of things are *compositional,* and *structured.*

As an example, Figure 1 contains a description of some C functions. Its intended reading would be *"a C-function, which has one or more* `args` *(arguments), and all of its* `stmts` *(statements) are instances of C-statement."* In this description, `args` and `stmts` are binary relations (called roles or set-valued attributes), while `C-FUNCTION` and `C-STATEMENT` are concept names defined elsewhere.

```
(and
        C-FUNCTION ,
        at-least(1, args) ,
        all(stmts, C-STATEMENT) )
```

Figure 1: A description

We believe it is instructive to view DLs as special languages obtained by term composition. All DLs therefore have (at least) two sorts of terms: concepts (intuitively, denoting collections of individuals), and roles (intuitively denoting relationships between individuals). Therefore the syntax of DLs consists of rules for creating composite terms from atomic symbols (identifiers of various sorts) and *term constructors.*

The above example was in fact valid according to the following syntax of a very simple language, $\mathcal{DL}_1$:

< conceptDesc> := **thing** | **nothing**
| **primitive**(< atomic-concept-id>) *;; concepts without "iff" conditions*
| **and**(< conceptDesc>$^+$) *;; concept intersection/conjunction*
| **all**(< roleDesc> ,< conceptDesc>) *;; restricting the range of roles*
| **at-least**(< pos-int> , < multiroleDesc>) *;; lower bound on number of fillers*
| **fills**(< roleDesc> , < individual-id>) *;; a particular filler is present*
< roleDesc> := < multiroleDesc > *;; binary relationships*
| < functionalRoleDesc > *;; functional relations*
< functionalRoleDesc > := < attrib-id>
| **compose**(< attrib-id> ,< attrib-id>$^+$) *;; composition of binary relations*

[1]In our examples, we follow the convention that concepts are written in capital letters, relationships in lower-ca and individual's names have their first letters in capitals.

The description in Figure 2 would also be syntactically valid in this term language. It denotes C-functions having at least 2 arguments, all of whose type is some kind of array.

```
(and
 C-FUNCTION ,
 at-least(2,args) ,
 all(args,all(has-type, ARRAY-TYPE)) ,
 all(stmts, C-STATEMENT) )
```

Figure 2: Another description in $\mathcal{DL}_1$

In summary, DLs provide languages for building (composite) terms from identifiers using term constructors; these terms denote several sorts of things, including *concepts* (sets of individuals) and *roles* (relationships, which are often, but not necessarily, binary).

3 The logic of DLs

A description, as presented above, is just a variable-free first order term. To give them meaning, we need rules of manipulation which allow us to infer/deduce new descriptions from old ones or relationships between descriptions.

3.1 The subsumption ordering

Since concept and role descriptions can easily be thought of as unary and binary predicates, it is natural to consider an entailment relationship between them based on the notion of subset for their denotation (e.g., we would want **at-least(2,args)** to entail **at-least(1,args)**).

The technical term for this is the *subsumption relation* between descriptions: if C and D are of sort "concept", then we want B to subsume C (written as C $\Longrightarrow$ B) when every individual denoted by C is in the denotation of B; similarly for descriptions denoting relationships. Given a description language, we therefore always start by looking for the subsumption relation between concepts ($\Longrightarrow$). The specification of the meaning of $\mathcal{DL}_1$ would therefore indicate, among others, that if the restriction on the role is stronger, then the whole term is more specialized. This could be presented as a rule of inference for example:

$$\frac{\vdash C \Longrightarrow B}{\vdash \mathbf{all}(r,C) \Longrightarrow \mathbf{all}(r,B)}$$

Given appropriate rules for reasoning with $\mathcal{DL}_1$, we would then expect the description in Figure 1 to subsume the description in Figure 2.

Given its origins in set containment, the *sine qua non* of the subsumption relation is that it be reflexive, transitive and anti-symmetric. Since there are descriptions that subsume each other, such as **at-least(3,args)** and **and(at-least(2,args),at-least(3,args))**, we introduce a derived equivalence relation on descriptions, $\equiv$, defined as (C $\equiv$B) iff both (C $\Longrightarrow$ B) and (B $\Longrightarrow$ C), and in fact consider the space of descriptions modulo this equivalence relation.

Every DL usually introduces concept constructors **thing** (the universal concept), **nothing** (the inconsistent concept), and some constructor like **and**, whose semantics is that of concept intersection. As a result, the space of descriptions, partially ordered by $\Longrightarrow$, becomes a semi-lattice with **and** being the meet operation. In all practical cases, this semi-lattice is in fact a lattice: we can find for every pair of descriptions a least common subsumer. This lattice is then the source of a number of operations on dscriptions, as we shall see below.

4 Using DLs in Knowledge Base Management

A language, even with an entailment relation and some operations defined over it, is just an abstract mathematical entity. The question then facing us is how to use this language.

To explain our answer, it is useful to adopt a formal view of KBMS. Let us start from Levesque's functional view of a knowledge server [13], treating a KB as an abstract data type on which one can perform two *kinds* of operations: TELLs and ASKs. TELLs are used to build or modify the "domain model"

$$\text{TELL:} \quad \mathcal{L}_{\text{Tell}} \times \text{KB} \rightarrow \text{KB}$$

while ASKs retrieve information

$$\text{ASK:} \quad \mathcal{L}_{\text{Query}} \times \text{KB} \rightarrow \mathcal{L}_{\text{Answer}}$$

The proper specification of a KB management system and its behavior therefore requires the definition of four things:

- $\mathcal{L}_{\text{Tell}}$: a language for describing what we know about the world;
- $\mathcal{L}_{\text{Query}}$: a language for describing questions that we wish to learn about;
- $\mathcal{L}_{\text{Answer}}$: the language in which answers will be phrased;
- Query answering: how answers to queries are related to what has been told to the KB.

For example, an abstract Relational DBMS could be described by setting $\mathcal{L}_{\text{Tell}}$ = {positive and negative ground atomic formulae} — these are the tuple inserts and deletes; $\mathcal{L}_{\text{Ask}}$ = {formulae of First Order Logic} — these are the SQL queries; $\mathcal{L}_{\text{Answer}}$ = {positive ground atomic formulae} — these are the tuples in the answer; and defining the answer to some question Q(x) as the set of values b for which Q(b) is entailed by the facts told the KB.

Without any loss of generality, and with considerable gain in convenience, we allow a whole host of TELL and ASK operations, each with possibly different associated languages.

Experience with building large software systems of all kinds, including knowledge bases, has taught us that it is an error prone process. Some ways in which errors can be more easily detected is to allow named abbreviations, to insist on identifiers being declared (so that simple typographical errors can be detected), and to allow assertions delimiting valid states of the knowledge base. For this purpose, we distinguish two special kind of TELL operations, DECLARE and CONSTRAIN. With this enhanced view of knowledge bases, the relational data model introduces the relation and attribute names using , DECLARE, while CONSTRAIN specifies the domains of attributes, as well as keys, referential integrity, etc.

With the above terminology in hand, we can now make an important point:

> Description Languages can be used in any of the languages associated with a KBMS, including $\mathcal{L}_{\text{Tell}}$, $\mathcal{L}_{\text{Ask}}$, $\mathcal{L}_{\text{Answer}}$, $\mathcal{L}_{\text{Constrain}}$, as well as $\mathcal{L}_{\text{Declare}}$. In each of these situations, the logic associated with this Description Language is used to define the meaning of question answering.

In what follows, we will elaborate on this assertion and its implications, by considering the problem of developing a knowledge base that helps manage information about software.

4.1 A simple database-like SIS

Let us start with a very simple KBMS, whose functionality is less than that of an ordinary relational dbms. To talk about the domain, we will first need to introduce some single-valued attributes (e.g., `maintained-by`) and some multi-valued roles (e.g., `args`). We will also need some collections of individuals that correspond to natural kinds (e.g., `FUNCTIONS`, `TYPES`, `VARIABLES`). This information can be communicated to the KBMS through suitable simple declarations.

In order to describe the state of the world, we will need to tell the KB about new individuals, e.g., introduce a new individual, `Sort-func45`, by invoking an operator: `Sort-func45 := CREATE-IND()`. These individuals will then be made instances of primitive concepts, using an operation INSERT-IN, e.g., `INSERT-IN(Sort-func45,C-FUNCTION)`; and their interrelationships will be described by stating what are role fillers, using the operator FILL-WITH, e.g., `FILL-WITH(Sort-func45, maintained-by, Hoare)`, `FILL-WITH(Sort-func45, args, list--length)`,....

In the natural course of things, descriptions first arise when we consider queries: queries are characterizations of the objects that satisfy their conditions, and DLs are well suited for this. For example, suppose we are looking for initialization routines; we might then want to locate *"functions with no arguments, which modify only global data, and are called only in one place"*. The description for this would be

```
and(FUNCTION,
      at-most(0,args) ,
      all(compose(assignment-stmts,lhs),GLOBAL-DATA) ,
      at-most(1,called-by))
```

The answer to such a query would be a list of individuals that satisfies the conditions of the description[2].

Continuing with the functionality of simple database management systems, we might find it useful to give names to some queries, because users frequently refer to them (e.g., they represent some subset of the data or some reorganization of it). These named queries are traditionally called *views* in the database world. Such queries may even be "materialized" – i.e., their answers are maintained up-to-date by the KBMS, rather than being evaluated every time someone looks at them. To introduce such views – named and composite concept descriptions – we can use an additional operation, say DEFINE.

We have therefore seen here that DLs are naturally suited for expressing queries (i.e., $\mathcal{L}_{\text{Question}}$) and for defining terminology (i.e., $\mathcal{L}_{\text{Declare}}$). Papers like [2] and [18] have investigated the use of DLs for querying data and knowledge bases.

Even in querying the KB, we find interesting and novel applications of the fact that descriptions form a lattice. "Data exploration/mining" is essentially the activity of looking for interesting correlations or patterns in large sets of data accumulated for other purposes. This activity involves asking very many queries, possibly by teams of people, over an extended period of time. The DL-based KBMS can *automatically organize* this large set of queries through the subsumption lattice, thereby providing similar advantages to those claimed for object-oriented software development. This is one reason why a standard operation performed by DL-based systems is *classification* of a given new description with respect to some set of previously given descriptions.

Moreover, in many situations a query that returns an empty set as answer is anomalous – a "miss"; it is reasonable to consider "generalizing" it slightly until a non-empty answer set is obtained. The infinite lattice of possible descriptions provides the obvious space to search

[2]The conditions for an individual satisfying a composite description are a second aspect of its semantics.

for such generalizations, and therefore the system can provide a helping hand in this task, as illustrated in [1].

4.2 A more powerful KBMS: using DLs in TELLS

The first step towards a more powerful KBMS is the simple observation that an operation such as FILL-WITH(Sort-func45,args, List-to-be-sorted) can be rephrased in a DL-like notation by introducing a decription constructor **fills**:

INSERT-IN(Sort-func45,**fills**(args, List-to-be-sorted)).

In fact, we can associate arbitrary descriptions with an individual:

```
INSERT-IN(Sort-func45,
        all(responsible-persons,fills(department,DataProcessing)))
```

But this small step has enormous impact: it allows the KBMS to maintain *incomplete information* about individuals. For example, in the above case, we do not yet know the exact identity of the person who will be responsible for the function's maintenance, but we can already gather information about her: she is in the DataProcessing department. In fact, there may be several such persons, and we now know something about all of them! If we now learn that they share an electronic mail address where bug complaints need to be reported, we can add this information by stating

```
INSERT-IN(Sort-func45,
        all(responsible-persons,fills(login,'sortbugs@down.net.com')))
```

Note that this kind of information can already be used in query processing: Suppose we ask a question like "Find all functions maintained by people in London departments":

ASK-KB(**all**(responsible-persons,**all**(department,**fills**(location,London))))

Now, if DataProcessing is known to have location London, then Sort-func45 can be returned as long as question answering involves checking whether the descriptor of an individual is subsumed by the query.

To appreciate the significance of this, observe that no database system can represent the kind of indeterminate information presented about Sort-func45 above. DBMS can only handle "null values" for atomic facts such as strings and integers, and even then not for unique identifiers (e.g., the name of a person); nor can they reason properly about such null values. In contrast, a system such as CLASSIC, whose subsumption algorithm is low-order polynomial time, answers its questions correctly and completely (of course, it does limit the kinds of views one can define in other ways!)

This expressive power of DLs is also related to a second problematic aspect of databases: so-called "view updates". Because DBMS translate updates to views into updates to the "base concepts" from which the views were defined, the set of views that can be updated is extremely restricted. In contrast, asserting in a DL that some individual belongs to a defined concept — a view — is maintained as just another fact about it, and this fact is reasoned with fully.

It is this aspect of KBMS based on DLs which explains their success in problems dealing with configuration management [17]: configurations are incomplete designs, which are slowly being built up, yet we want to find out about problems with them before everything is fully known.

4.3 DLs in answers

Traditionally, questions such as "Who is responsible for Sort-func45?" are answered by printing some individual value(s), looked up in the database. The fact that we can associate arbitrary descriptions with individuals allows us to produce easily *descriptive answers*, representing the terms we have been told or deduced about these values. For the above questions we might now get answers such as **and**(PROGRAMMER,**fills**(department,DataProcessing)).

In fact, this facility is useful not just when there is incomplete information, but also whenever we don't want to give back lists, as in the case when the list is too long: it is then possible to use the least common subsumer [8] of a set of individuals as a description of what is common to them, and return this instead. (This is related to the notion of intensional answer, introduced in [11] for FOL-based systems).

4.4 Different DLs in different languages

In order to make it easier for people to learn to use a DL-based KBMS, some systems (e.g., CLASSIC [5]) use the *same* syntax (i.e., description constructors) in the various kinds of languages associated with a KBMS. It is however not necessary to do so. In fact, because of computational costs, it may be desirable to allow different languages for different operators. This should not be too surprising, as we saw this happen in Relational DBMS. Such an approach has been advocated in [13, 12], and has been practiced in systems which use DLs as query languages (e.g., [2]).

In the case of SIS, a more powerful query language allows us to ask a whole new range of useful questions. For example, we can enrich $\mathcal{L}_{\text{Ask}}$ by adding to $\mathcal{DL}_1$ a new constructor

<roleDesc>::= **restr**(<roleDesc >, <conceptDesc>) *;;role with restricted range*

The **restr** construct builds a sub-relation of the original role (binary relation), by restricting the range (e.g., daughters might be defined as **restr**(children,FEMALES)). The query "functions which contain assignment-statements" can then be written as:

```
and(FUNCTION,at-least(1,restr(stmts,ASSIGNMENTS)))
```

Based on this, the more complex query "functions containing an assignment statement with a function call on the left hand side[3]" can be written as:

```
and(FUNCTION,
      at-least(1,restr(stmts, and(ASSIGNMENTS ,all(lhs,FUNCTION-CALL)))))
```

Note that these constructors make it possible to express descriptions for which deciding subsumption is computationally intractable. However, we may chose to implement only an incomplete version of the subsumption test between queries, while maintaining complete reasoning about the individuals being retrieved — reasoning about individuals which don't have partial information is much easier.

4.5 DLs as components of other languages

We need not be limited to using a single description when telling the system some information. Thus, we may want to associate with a concept *necessary conditions (integrity constraints)* that would have to hold of its individual instances. For example, suppose we want to require that in switch statements where the switching expression is an enumerated type, the body of the switch *must* contain cases that handle all the members in the enumeration. We can first show the definition of concept ENUM-SWITCH; it has a switch-expression that it switches on, and a set of cases to choose from; in turn, the cases each have labels and bodies:

```
and(SWITCH-STATEMENT ,
      all(switch-expression,all(has-type,ENUMERATED-TYPE)) ,
      all(cases, all(label,IDENTIFIERS)) ,
      all(cases, all(body,STATEMENT)))
```

[3] This might be case where a function returns a pointer, for example.

Given a CONSTRAIN-type operator such as CONSTRAIN(**<on-class> , <constraint--condition>**), where both arguments are descriptions, we can impose the desired integrity condition by stating

```
CONSTRAIN(ENUM-SWITCH ,
          same-as(compose(switch-expression,has-type,members)
                  compose(cases,label)))
```

Here, the constraining concept uses another powerful constructor, **same-as**, which states that two relations are identical. Then, whenever a new function is added, if one of its statements is matched by **ENUM-SWITCH** but is inconsistent with the constraint description associated with it, an error message would be generated by the system, and the update would not be allowed.

A more "active" KBMS can be obtained through the addition of an operation such as ASSERT-RULE(**<lhs-description>,<rhs-description>**), e.g., ASSERT-RULE(**FUNCTION--WITH-GLOBALS, ERROR-PRONE-CODE**). This would have the effect that any time an individual is recognized as a function that accesses global variables, it would be added to the set of things that might be likely to have errors. Such rules have been offered in systems such as LOOM [14] and CLASSIC [5], with the claimed added advantages that the subsumption hierarchy of the left-hand sides for rules can help organize the rule set, and also manage the rule firing process.

In conclusion, descriptions can be used in a natural way as specifiers of conditions and actions, for a variety of rule languages, including integrity constraints, triggers, defaults, etc.

5 Domain-dependent DLs

The above framework is quite general. "Individuals" can be not only simple objects, but also programming language values (e.g., arrays, procedures), or composite values (e.g., lists or trees of others kinds of individuals). And there is freedom in choosing the constructors in the language syntax, and their intended interpretation.

Illustrative of the kind of benefit one gains from this freedom is the work on CLASP [9], a language for describing plans. Many real-time systems, such as telephone switches, are best described by patterns of user-system interactions, or *features*. Consider a plain ordinary phone call (an example of a feature): it is usually described by a sequence of events and event patterns such as "user picks up a phone, gets dial tone, dials 4 or more digits, then gets an arbitrary number of rings, ...". CLASP considers sequences of specific actions — called "scenarios" — as individuals occurring in their world, and then describe classes of such individuals through regular expressions constructed from basic action classes. The regular expressions are built up using new description constructors. For example,

```
sequence(action(DIAL),
         alternative(loop(action(RING)),loop(action(BUSY-SIGNAL))))
```

describes a pattern of occurrence of events where a dial event is followed by either an arbitrary sequence of busy signal or ringing events.

A large telephone switch supports a great many features and CLASP can be used to describe such features. An SIS can then be used to manage collections of such descriptions, which are retrieved and inspected by programmers working on switching software.

Of course, there is a price to be paid for inventing new constructors: we need to specify how to reason with them and implement this specification! For this reason, and others, we believe it it useful to consider some of the following ideas in designing DL-based KBMS:

- *Provide an "escape-hatch" in the language.* It is possible to introduce one or more constructors in the language whose semantics are "opaque" for subsumption reasoning (e.g.,

CLASSIC's test-defined concepts which are passed a Lisp or C function in order to determine memberships of individuals). Such constructors are of course open to abuse, but they have proven to be extremely useful in practical applications of the CLASSIC system.

- *Use a KBMS architecture that makes it easy to* extend *the description language and its logic.* The idea is that when the user runs into the boundaries of the limited language, she can have them expanded sufficiently to accomplish the task at hand. This approach requires a modular architecture for DL reasoners which is as easy to extend as, for example, a syntax-directed translation scheme used in a programming language compiler. Such an architecture is in fact presented in [4], and the methodology of providing extensions is illustrated in [3].

6 Two example SIS based on DLs

We describe here briefly two substantial systems, LASSIE [10] and COMET [15], which use the services provided by DL reasoners, including classification, rules, and constraint mechanisms, to assist software engineering.

The LASSIE system (a now defunct prototype) has a KB containing knowledge about the software controlling a PBX telephone switch. The KB uses a description logic (CLASSIC plus CLASP) to model different aspects of knowledge about the system, including the domain of application (a PBX telephone switch), the architecture of the system, and some details of the code. The primary intended use of the system is as an interactive retrieval facility: a user can explore the knowledge base to search for modules that can be reused or to learn about the system. Subsumption is used in this process to assist retrieval since the user can describe a module in a variety of different ways, and still retrieve it. For example, the user may ask for a module using architectural information (information at the process level, such as "what operations are performed by the `Call-manager` process when it gets a message from the `User-manager` process?") or domain information ("which modules can perform a hang-up operation on an outgoing trunk?"). Subsumption allows equivalent formulations to be detected. In a sense, this reduces the cognitive burden on the user: she does not need to know exactly what is in the knowledge base, before she begins searching for information.

In addition, because of the presence of definitions and rules in the knowledge base, and their accessibility to users, they can learn useful information about the architecture of the system, the model of the domain used therein, and the relationship between the two. For example, the definition of the `TRUNK-DIALOUT-ACTION` might have a constraint such as **`fills(instigator,Attendant)`**; from this, the LASSIE user learns that only the attendant is allowed to dial out on trunks. Rules are also useful: For example, there may be a rule connecting `TRUNK-OPERATION` with `CONSOLE-LOG-EVENT`. This is a requirement on the system that says that every trunk operation is also an event that is logged on the console. The user may not have been aware of this, and may simply have been searching for examples of trunk operations; however, the firing of this rule alerts her to an existing commitment that any trunk operation she implements must log a message on the console.

Commitments are precisely what COMET system is concerned with. Its authors take the position that making and keeping track of commitments is of primary concern in developing large software systems, if we are to support the new paradigm of software development through the reuse and modification of existing programs and their specifications.

For example, a binary search module has a commitment that it's input be sorted; any re-user or modifier of this module had better be aware of this. A frequent and crucially asked question is: "how will a change in this module affect or be affected by the rest of the system?" Answers to such questions are found in COMET by reasoning with commitments in a description logic, LOOM [14]. COMET is concerned with the domain of tracking systems (such as radar systems). and its knowledge base stores description of several *modules* and the commitments associated with them. A user synthesizes the design of a new module (or a new design for an existing module) by retrieving information from the knowledge base, perhaps by subsumption, and constructing a new definition. The COMET system guides the user to construct the definition to be able to reuse existing modules in a way that will cause minimal disruption in the existing system. The system comprises a user interface that uses the underlying LOOM mechanism to help the user as she constructs a LOOM definition of her new design, by constraining the choices she has at various decision points. This limited set of allowable changes is computed by COMET "on the fly" through the use of subsumption reasoning in the hierarchy of defined concepts. And it is this limitation of the changes allowed that provides COMET the opportunity to be very helpful and knowledgeable.

7 Conclusions

DLs provide a special syntax for expressing information about individuals, definitions, and questions, with a limited choice of description constructors. The systems built on them exploit these limitations in order to provide effective solutions to such difficult problems as view updates, and reasoning with partial information, as well as facilities for descriptive/intensional answers. Through the use of the classification mechanism (which is based on the subsumption lattice) DL-based KBMS can *organize* information entered into the system, such as queries, rules, etc. thus supporting interactive work.

As a result, KBMS based on description logics are emerging as useful practical tools in a variety of situations, including interfaces and exploration of traditional databases, configuration management, and software information systems. Our examples have hopefully given the reader some insights into the last of these problem domains.

Acknowledgements: We are deeply grateful to Ronald Brachman for his collaboration in many aspects of the work discussed here.

References

[1] Anwar, T.M., Beck H. and Navathe S., "Knowledge Mining by imprecise querying: classification-based approach", *Proc. 8th Conference on Data Engineering'*, Tempe, Arizon. February 1992, pp.622–630.

[2] Beck, H. W., Gala, S. K., and Navathe, S. B., "Classification as a Query Processing Techniqu in the CANDIDE Semantic Data Model," *Proc. Fifth IEEE International Data Engineerin Conference*, February 1989, pp. 572–581.

[3] Borgida, A. "Towards the systematic development of terminological reasoners: CLASP recon structed", submitted for publication, April 1992.

[4] Borgida, A., and Brachman, R., "A Customizable Knowledge Base Management System", sub mitted for publication, March 1992.

Borgida, A., Brachman, R. J., McGuinness, D. L., and Resnick, L. A. "CLASSIC: A Structural Data Model for Objects," *Proc. 1989 ACM SIGMOD International Conference on Management of Data*, June, 1989, pp. 59–67.

Brachman, R. J., "What's in a Concept: Structural Foundations for Semantic Networks," *Intl. Journal of Man-Machine Studies*, **9**(2), 1977, pp. 127–152.

Brachman, R. J., and Schmolze, J. G., "An Overview of the KL-ONE Knowledge Representation System," *Cognitive Science*, **9**(2), April–June, 1985, pp. 171–216.

Cohen, W., Borgida, A., and Hirsh H., "Computing Least Common Subsumers in Description Logics", to appear in *Proc. of AAAI'92*, San Jose, CA., July 1992..

Devanbu, P., and Litman, D., "Plan-based Terminological Reasoning," *Proc. KR'91*, Boston, MA, 1991.

Devanbu, P., Brachman, R., Selfridge, P., and Ballard, B., "LaSSIE: A Knowledge-Based Software Information System", *Communications of the ACM,34*(5), May 1991.

Imielinski, T., "Intelligent Query Answering in Rule Based Systems", *Journal of Logic Programming 4*, pp. 229-257, 1987.

Lenzerini, M. and Schaerf, A., "Concept Languages as Query Languages", *Proc. AAAI'91*, pp. 471-476.

Levesque, H. 'Foundations of a Functional Approach to Knowledge Representation', *Artificial Intelligence 23*(2), 1984, pp. 155–212.

MacGregor, R. M., "A Deductive Pattern Matcher", in *Proceedings AAAI-87*, St. Paul, Minnesota (1987) 403–408.

Mark, W., Tyler, S., McGuire, J., and Schlossberg, J., "Commitment-Based Software Development", *IEEE Transactions on Software Engineering*, Special Issue on Knowledge Representation and Software Engineering, to appear in 1992.

Mylopoulos, J., Borgida, A., Jarke, M., and Koubarakis, M. "Telos: Representing Knowledge about Information Systems", *ACM Trans. on Information Systems 3*, 1990.

Owsnicki-Klewe, B., "Configuration as a Consistency Maintenance Task," in W. Hoeppner, editor, *Proc. of GWAI-88*, Springer Verlag, September, 1988, pp. 77–87.

Patel-Schneider, P. F., Brachman, R. J., and Levesque, H. J., "ARGON: Knowledge Representation Meets Information Retrieval," *Proc. First Conf. on Artificial Intelligence Applications*, Denver, CO, December, 1984, pp. 280–286.

Schewe, K.D., " Variant Construction using Constraint Propagation techniques over Semantic Networks.", In *Proceedings of the 5th Austrian AI Conference*, Insbruck, 1989, Springer IFB208, pp. 188–197.

Woods, W. A., and Schmolze, J. G., "The KL-ONE Family," *Computers and Mathematics with Applications 23*(2-5), Special Issue on Semantic Networks in Artificial Intelligence.

Personal Computers and Intelligent Systems / F.H. Vogt (Editor)
Information Processing 92, Volume III
Elsevier Science Publishers B.V. (North-Holland)

THE ODISSEA APPROACH TO THE DESIGN OF INFORMATION SYSTEMS FROM DEDUCTIVE CONCEPTUAL MODELS

Maria Ribera Sancho
Facultat d'Informàtica, Pau Gargallo, 5, E 08028 Barcelona Catalonia, email:ribera@lsi.upc.es

Abstract

This paper describes the general framework and some details of the ODISSEA approach to conceptual modelling and design of information systems. We use a logic-based language for the specification of conceptual models and apply logic-based techniques for the generation of a system design from a conceptual model. The main originality of our work is that our language is based on the "deductive" approach to conceptual modelling, instead of the usual "operational" approach. Deductive conceptual models (DCM) show a number of significant advantages, but are much more difficult to design and implement. We deal with the problem of generating a design for a given DCM. We present a new method for generating transactions from a DCM. The method uses the SLDNF proof procedure and can be implemented in Prolog environments.

1. INTRODUCTION

A general trend in informations systems is the adoption of knowledge engineering techniques to enhance existing methodologies as well as to introduce new and more productive development paradigms, methods and supporting tools [Bub86].

This paper describes the general framework and some details of the ODISSEA approach to conceptual modelling and design of information systems. The main originality of our work is that the ODISSEA language is based on the "deductive" approach to conceptual modelling, instead of the traditional, "operational" approach. Both approaches can provide a complete specification of the static and dynamic aspects of an information system, but they differ in the way the dynamic aspect is modelled.

A detailed comparison of the operational and deductive approaches can be found in [BuO86, Oli86]. The main conclusions are that DCMs provide more local definitions, are easier to change and to accomodate new requirements, and provide more design freedom. However, DCMs are much more difficult to implement than operational models. The reason is that an operational model already embeddes some architectural design decisions, which are not made in DCMs [Oli89].

The main design decisions required to implement an information system from a DCM are data base design and transaction design. Usually, many valid alternatives in data base design exist, and the designer must choose the alternative that he/she considers most appropiate. Complete automation of this decision is not possible, but there is a place for CASE tools that aid the designer by confirming the consistency of his/her decisions and by evaluating their impact in terms of performance.

In transaction design, the designer must decide which transactions will exist and, for each of them, when will be executed, its pre-conditions and the actions to be performed, including data base updates and output production. Contrary to data base design, transaction design from a DCM can be completely automated. Transaction pre-conditions can be determined from the integrity constraints defined in the DCM. Data base updates can be determined from an analysis of deductive rules, and output production can be determined from queries definition. We present a new method for generating transactions from a DCM. The method is based on the use of the SLDNF proof procedure and, thus, it can be implemented easily in Prolog environments.

The paper is organized as follows. Section 2 briefly introduces the main components of a DCM, including an example that is used throughout the paper. Section 3 describes the internal architecture of the system that we would like to be able to generate from a DCM. Section 4 presents the Internal Events Model (IEM), a key concept in our approach to design generation. Section 5 discusses the use of the IEM in transaction generation. Section 6 provides an overview of the ODISSEA design environment, showing the context in which transaction generation can be done. Finally, Section 7 summarizes the results of our work and points out future research.

2. DEDUCTIVE CONCEPTUAL MODELS

A deductive conceptual model (DCM) of an IS consists of five sets: A set B of base predicates, a set D of derived predicates, a set IC of integrity constraints, a set Q of predefined queries, and a set A of alerts

In the following, we briefly describe each of these sets. Figure 1 shows an example that will be used troughout the paper. The example is written in a simplified syntax of the ODISSEA language [QuS91].

Base predicates correspond to the external event types. We assume, by convention, that the last term of a base fact gives the time when the event occurred and was communicated to the IS. If $p(a_1,..., a_n,t_i)$ is a base fact we say that $p(a_1,..., a_n)$ is true or holds at t_i. All times are expressed in a unique time unit small enough to avoid ambiguities. In the example of figure 1 we have four base predicates: start, end, assign and mng. A base fact start(p,t) means that project p started at time t. A base fact end(p,t) reports that project p ends at time t. A base fact assign(pg,p,t) means that at time t, programmer pg is assigned to project p. A base fact mng(pg,t) means that at time t, programmer pg becomes a manager. We take as time unit a second.

Derived predicates model the relevant types of knowledge about the Universe of Discourse. Each fact of a derived predicate, called derived fact, represents an information about the state of the UoD, at a particular time point. We also assume that the last term gives the time when the information holds. Each derived predicate is defined by means of one or more deduction rules. A deduction rule of predicate p has the form $p(X_1,..., X_n,T) \leftarrow L_1,..., L_m$, where $p(X_1,..., X_n,T)$ is an atom denoting the conclusion and $L_1,..., L_m$ are literals representing conditions. Each L_j is either an atom or a negated atom. Variables in the conclusion or in the conditions are assumed to be universally quantified over the whole formula. The terms in the conclusion must be distinct variables, and the terms in the conditions must be variables or constants.

Condition predicates may be ordinary or evaluable ("built-in"). The former are base or derived predicates, while the latter are predicates, such as the comparison or arithmetic predicates, that can be evaluated without accessing a database. In the example, there are five derived predicates, with their corresponding (and hopefully self-explanatory) rules.

Integrity constraints are closed first-order formulas that base and/or derived facts are required to satisfy. We deal with constraints that have the form of a denial $\leftarrow L_1,..., L_m$, with $m \geq 1$, where the L_j are literals and variables are assumed to be universally quantified over the whole formula. We associate to each integrity constraint an inconsistency predicate icn, with at least a time term, and thus it has the same form as the deductive rules. We call them integrity rules.

Outputs from an IS may be requested by the user (queries) or triggered internally by the system when some condition holds (alerts). Each query is defined by a name, a number of parameters, to which the user will give values when he makes the query, and a body. The answer to a query is the set of values that satisfies the conditions given in the body. (In order to focus on our objective, we omit in this paper alert definition and handling). In the example, there are two queries. When query q2(p,t) is issued at time t, with parameter p, the system will provide the programmers assigned some time to project p. Note that this query requires the system to know the complete history of predicate assigned.

base start(Project,Time)
base end(Project,Time)
base assign(Programmer,Project,Time)
base mng(Programmer,Time)
derived project(P,T) ← start(P,T1), T1 ≤ T, not(completed(P,T))
derived completed(P,T) ← end(P,T1), T1 ≤ T
derived assigned(Pg,P,T) ← project(P,T),assign(Pg,P,T1), T1 ≤ T
derived active(P,T) ← leader(Pg,P,T)
← assigned(Pg1,P,T), assigned(Pg2,P,T), Pg1≠Pg2
derived leader(Pg,P,T) ← assigned(Pg,P,T),mng(Pg,T1), T1 ≤ T
inconsistency ic1(T) ← start(P,T), project(P,T-1)
inconsistency ic2(T) ← end(P,T), not(active(P,T-1))
inconsistency ic3(P,T) ← leader(Pg1,P,T),leader(Pg2,P,T),Pg1≠Pg2
query q1(T) **is** active(P,T)
query q2(P,T) **is** assigned(Pg,P,T1), T1 ≤ T

Figure 1. Example of Deductive Conceptual Model

3. INTERNAL ARCHITECTURE

In ODISSEA, we aim at designing and building information systems with simple and conventional architectures. The only notable feature is that we build the systems on top of a Deductive DBMS (DDBMS). Currently, we are using a system coupling Prolog to a Relational Database system (RDBMS) [CGT90], but other DDBMS could be used as well. On the other hand, it would also be possible to use a RDBMS.

The main components of a generated IS are: The User Interface Management System (UIMS), the Extensional Data Base (EDB), the Intensional Data Base (IDB), Base Transactions (BT), the Transaction Manager, and the the Query Processor (QP).

The UIMS handles all input/output interaction. The emphasis of our project is not in this (important) component and, therefore, we only have simple menu-driven dialogues.

The EDB comprises all facts explicitly stored in the data base. These facts do not need to be the base facts defined in the DCM. Indeed, it is quite usual to store in the EDB some derived facts, and not to store all base facts. In our example, we could store in the EDB the current state of predicates project and active, and the full history of predicates assigned and mng.

The IDB comprises the rules that relate the DCM predicates to the facts stored in the EDB. Not all DCM predicates may be derivable from the EDB; this will depend on the designed EDB schema. We call Accessible Predicates (AP) those DCM predicates that may be derivable from the EDB. We also say that we have a Full History AP when the complete history of the predicate is derivable from the EDB, and that we have a Current State AP when only the current facts of the predicate are derivable. There are one or more rules in the IDB for each AP. In our example, the APs are: mng, assigned, leader (Full History), and project, active (Current State).

Base Transactions update the EDB when a new base fact is received. There is a BT for each base predicate defined in the DCM. Typical actions performed by a BT are: receive the corresponding base fact from the UIMS, check integrity constraints satisfaction and update the EDB. We give in Section 5 a procedure to derive the BTs from a DCM.

The Transaction Manager is a general module that handles all base transactions. We describe it in more detail in Section 5.

The QP handles two types of queries: predefined and ad hoc queries. The former are those defined in the DCM, while the latter are queries whose definition must be given by the users at execution time. Users issue ad hoc queries in terms of predicates defined in the DCM, just as predefined queries, but only accessible predicates and facts can be requested.

4. THE INTERNAL EVENTS MODEL

We have seen, in the previous Section, the internal architecture of the IS that we would like to be able to generate. Now, we start to describe our approach to the design and implementation of such IS from its DCM. The key concept of our approach is the Internal Events Model (IEM). This model was presented in [Oli89,San90], and has inspired novel solutions to the problems of integrity constraints enforcement and view updating of deductive databases [Oli91,TeO92]. In the following, we briefly describe the main concepts of an IEM, and show its application to the example.

4.1 Internal events

The concept of internal event tries to capture in a natural way the notion of change in the extension of a predicate. We associate to each predicate p an insertion internal events predicate ιp and a deletion internal events predicate δp defined as follows:

(1) $\forall X,T\ (\iota p(X,T) \leftrightarrow p(X,T) \wedge \neg p(X,T\text{-}1))$

(2) $\forall X,T\ (\delta p(X,T) \leftrightarrow p(X,T\text{-}1) \wedge \neg p(X,T))$

If p is a derived predicate, then ιp facts and δp facts represent induced insertions and deletions of derived facts, respectively. If p is an inconsistency predicate, then ιp facts that occur at time T will correspond to violations of its integrity constraint. Note that, for inconsistency predicates, δp facts cannot happen in any transition, since we assume that the IB is consistent at time T-1 and, thus, p(X,T-1) is always false.

We also use the internal events concept for base predicates. In this case, ιp facts facts represent the external events (given by the environment) corresponding to insertions of base facts. We use sometimes the term "event" to denote either an internal or external event.

4.2 Transition rules

Let p(**X**,T) ← L_1,..., L_m be a deductive or inconsistency rule. The rule defines the extension of p at time T in terms of the extensions at time T, or before, of the predicates appearing in the body of the rule. A transition rule for p is a rule that defines the extension of p at time T in terms of the extensions at time T-1, or before, of the predicates appearing in the body of the rule, and the internal events of these predicates that occur at time T. We obtain the transition rules substituting each L_j, j = 1...n, by its equivalent expression (see [Oli89,San90])).

4.3 Internal events rules

An internal event rule is a rule that defines the conditions upon which an internal event happens. Thus, internal event rules allow us to deduce which internal events happen in a given transition. For example, the rules: ιproject(P,T) ← ιstart(P,T)

δproject(P,T) ← ιcompleted(P,T)

are an insertion and a deletion internal event rule, respectively. The first states that the occurrence of an ιstart fact (in this case, the insertion of an start base fact) induces a corresponding ιproject fact. The second rule states that the occurrence of a ιcompleted fact induces a corresponding δproject fact.

We get the internal events rules using a procedure based on the definitions (1), and (2), replacing p(**X**,T) by its transition rules, and applying a set of standard simplifications, that may involve the integrity constraints. Figure 2 shows (part of) the result obtained by the application of the procedure to the DCM example of figure1.

IDR.1 δproject(P,T) ← ιcompleted(P,T)
IDR.2 ιcompleted(P,T) ← ιend(P,T)
IDR.3 ιassigned(Pg,P,T) ← ιassign(Pg,P,T), not(δproject(P,T))

IDR.4 ιleader(Pg,P,T) ← assigned(Pg,P,T-1), not(δassigned(Pg,P,T)), ιmng(Pg,T
IDR.5 ιleader(Pg,P,T) ← ιassigned(Pg,P,T), mng(Pg,T1), T1 < T
IDR.6 ιleader(Pg,P,T) ← ιassigned(Pg,P,T), ιmng(Pg,T)
IDR.7 ιic3(P,T) ← ιleader(Pg1,P,T),leader(Pg2,P,T-1), not(δleader(Pg2,P,T)), Pg1 ≠ Pg2

Figure 2. Part of the internal events model of the DCM example.

5. DERIVING BASE TRANSACTIONS

5.1 The approach

In this section we will focus on one aspect of the ODISSEA internal architecture: the Base Transactions. We show the use of the IEM to derive the set of actions that each BT should perform.

As we mentioned before, there is a BT for each base predicate defined in the DCM. A BT will receive the corresponding base fact from the UIMS, check integrity constraints satisfaction and update the EDB. We can also derive composite transactions, corresponding to the simultaneous occurrence of two or more base facts, but this extension will not be considered here.

Let TR={ιb(**k**,t)} the transaction corresponding to the insertion of a base fact b(**k**,t), where **k** is a vector of constants denoting the transaction parameters, and t the occurrence time. We derive its effects in the following way: For each integrity constraint icj specified in the DCM, we can check its violation by evaluating the internal event predicate ιicj. In the same way, for each stored predicate p(**X**,T), we can derive the induced insertion (resp. deletion) of a fact p(**x**,t) by evaluating the internal event predicate ιp(**X**,t) (resp. δp(**X**,t)). As IEM rules are defined in terms of accessible predicates extensions at time t-1 or before, to evaluate internal event predicates we also need the IDB rules, which relate accessible predicates to the facts stored in the EDB.

To obtain these evaluations we use the standard SLDNF proof procedure. More precisely, let I=i(**X**,t) be the internal event predicate to be evaluated. We say that TR induces I if goal {←I} succeeds from input set IEM ∪ IDB ∪ EDB ∪ TR. If every branch of the SLDNF-search space for IEM ∪ IDB ∪ EDB ∪ TR ∪ {←I} is a failure branch, then TR does not induce I.

Obviously, the evaluation can be completely done at execution time, when the concrete values of EDB and transaction parameters are known. However, we can do some preparatory work at compilation time, by partially evaluating IEM ∪ TR wrt I [LlS91]. The result of the partial evaluation is a set E of n rules (n≥0):

I ← C_i i = 1..n, where C_i is a conjunction of literals and such that evaluation of {←I} at execution time from E∪IDB∪EDB gives the same result as the evaluation of {←I} from IEM ∪ IDB ∪ EDB ∪ TR. If n=0 then TR does not induce I. Applying this procedure to our example case, at compilation time,we have to partially evaluate, for each possible transaction, internal event predicates ιic1(t), ιic2(t), and ιic3(P,t), corresponding to the integrity checking conditions, and ιproject(P,t), δproject(P,t), ιactive(P,t), δactive(P,t), ιassigned(Pg,P,t), and δassigned(Pg,P,t), to derive the update conditions.

Take, as an example the transaction: TR={ιstart(p,t)}. These are the sets of rules obtained at compilation time:

ιic1(t) ← project(p,t-1)

ιproject(p,t) ←

5.2 Example

We will try to illustrate our approach with an example (a formal description of the method can be found in [OS92]). Assume that we want to derive the transaction TR={ιassign(pg,p,t)}. We have to partially evaluate IEM ∪ TR wrt ιicj, corresponding to the integrity constraints. Consider, for example, the partial evaluation wrt ιic3(t). Possible sets of conditions C_i that would lead to the violation of ic3(t) are obtained by having some failed derivation of IEM ∪ TR ∪ {←ιic3(t)} succeed. Figure 3 shows this derivation tree.

←ιic3(P,t) — STEP

IDR.7 — 1

← ιleader(Pg1,P,t), leader(Pg2,P,t-1), not (δleader(Pg2,P,t)), Pg1≠Pg2

IDR.5 — 2

← ιassigned(Pg1,P,t), mng(Pg1,T1), T1<t, leader(Pg2,P,t-1), Pg1≠Pg2,
not(δleader(Pg2,P,t)), Pg1≠Pg2

IDR.3 — 3

← ιassign(Pg1,P,t), not(δproject(P,t)), mng(Pg1,T1), T1<t, leader(Pg2,P,t-1),
leader(Pg2,P,t-1), not(δleader(Pg2,P,t)), Pg1≠Pg2

TR — 4

← not(δproject(p,t)), mng(pg,T1), T1<t, leader(Pg2,p,t-1), not(δleader(Pg2,p,t)),
pg≠Pg2

← δproject(p,t) fails — 5

← mng(pg,T1), T1<t, leader(Pg2,p,t-1), not(δleader(Pg2,p,t)), pg≠Pg2

← δleader(Pg2,p,t) fails

←mng(pg,T1), T1<t, leader(Pg2,p,t-1), pg≠Pg2

7-10

[]

C={mng(pg,T1), T1<t, leader(Pg2,p,t-1),pg≠Pg2}

Figure 3

Steps 1,2 and 3 are SLDNF resolution steps, using rules of IEM as input clauses. At step 2 we have several alternative rules to resolve with. IDR.4 or IDR.6 could have been used instead of IDR5, and each one of them may lead to a different set of conditions C. Nevertheless, in this concrete case, branches corresponding to IDR.4 and IDR.6 fail. At step 4 the selected literal is an external event literal ιassign(Pg1,P,t) that can be resolved with the base fact in TR. At steps 5 and 6 the selected literals are not(δproject(p,t)) and not(δleader(Pg2,p,t)) respectively. In order to get a successful derivation, SLDNF-search space must fail finitely for {←δproject(p,t)} ∪ IEM ∪ TR and for {←δleader(Pg2,p,t)} ∪ IEM ∪ TR. The failure for δproject(p,t) is shown in Figure 4(a), δleader(Pg2,p,t) fails in a similar way. From step 7 to 10 the selected literals correspond to stored predicates (mng(pg,T1)), to accessible predicates (leader(Pg2,p,t-1)), or to evaluable predicates (T1<t and pg≠Pg2). Observe that none of them can be evaluated at compilation time because they depend on the concrete values of the EDB facts at time t. As a consecuence, this literals are included in the condition set C and its evaluation is delayed until execution time. The set of conditions obtained for ιic3(P,t) adds the following rule to the BT definition: ιic3(p,t) ← mng(pg,T1),T1<T,leader(Pg2,p,t-1),pg≠Pg2

Rules for ιic1(t), and ιic2(t) can be obtained similarly.

We also have to derive, for each stored predicate p(**X**,T), the set of conditions to be checked at execution time, in order to induce an insertion or a deletion of a fact corresponding to this predicate, by partially evaluating IEM ∪ TR wrt ιp(X,t) and δp(X,t). Consider, for example, the partial evaluation for ιassigned(Pg,P,t).

Possible sets of conditions C that would lead to the insertion of a base fact assigned(pg,p,t) are obtained by having some failed derivation of IEM∪TR∪{←ιassigned(Pg,P,t) } succeed. Figure 4(b) shows this derivation tree.

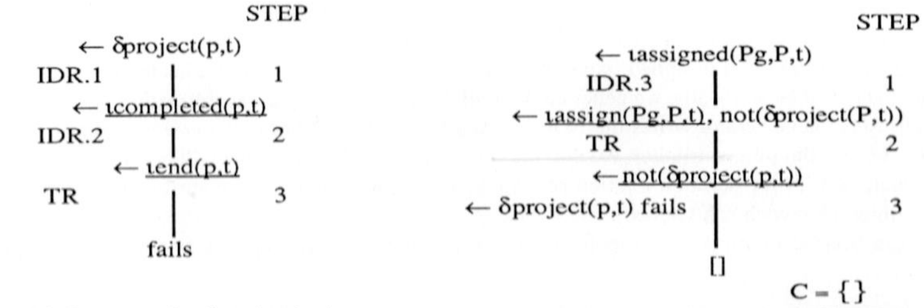

(a) failure tree for δproject(p,t) (b) derivation tree for ιassigned(Pg,P,t)

Figure 4

The derivation ends with the empty clause as a result and C={}. This means that the transaction ιassign(pg,p,t) induces inconditionally the insertion of a fact assigned(pg,p,t) to the EDB. As a consecuence, the following rule will be added to the BT definition: ιassigned(pg,p,t) ←

5.3 The Transaction Manager

Once we have outlined the transaction generation method, we describe now how Base Transactions are treated at execution time by the Transaction Manager.

When an external event occurs in the real world, it is received by the UIMS, and the corresponding BT have to be evaluated by the Transaction Manager. As we have seen before, BT rules follow the general pattern:

ιicj(**x**,**Y**,t) ← C(**x**,**Y**,t) for the integrity constraints, and

ιp(**x**,**Y**,t) ← C(**x**,**Y**,t) and δp(**x**,**Y**,t) ← C(**x**,**Y**,t) for stored predicates

At execution time, constants **x** and t take its values from transaction parameters, and the body C can be completely evaluated given that facts stored in the EDB are available at this time. After receiving the transaction, and once the corresponding BT rules are known, the Transaction Manager acts in the following way:

1- For each rule ιicj(**x**,**Y**,t), checks if there exists any value **y** of **Y** such that C(**x**,**y**,t) evaluates to true. This means that the transaction violates the integrity constraint icj. In this case, an error message is sent to the UIMS and the transaction execution is stopped.

2- For each rule ιp(**x**,**Y**,t), find all possible values **y** of **Y** such that C(**x**,**y**,t) evaluates to true, and for all of them: If p is stored "current" INSERT tuple p(**x**,**y**) into the EDB. If p is stored "full history" INSERT tuple p(**x**,**y**,t,∞) into the EDB.

3- For each rule δp(**x**,**Y**,t), find all possible values **y** of **Y** such that C(**x**,**y**,t) evaluates to true, and for all of them: If p is stored "current" DELETE tuple p(**x**,**y**) from the EDB. If p is stored "full history" SET tuple p(**x**,**y**,ts,∞) to p(**x**,**y**,ts,t)

We have implemented the Transaction Manager using the Prolog language.

6. THE ODISSEA DESIGN ENVIRONMENT

We have seen in Section 4 the concept of Internal Events Model, and we have discussed, in the previous Section, the role it plays in transaction generation. We now briefly describe our design environment and show the context in which transaction generation is done. The ODISSEA design environment has five main components: The IEM Generator, the Reasoner, the DDB Designer, the EDB Schema Generator and the Transaction Generator.

The IEM Generator derives the IEM corresponding to the DCM, by using the procedure described in Section4.

The Reasoner is the component of our environment for DCM validation. The Reasoner can answer two kinds of queries from the designer (see [CoO91] for details):

a) Given an initial and target states of the Information Base, together with a sequence of external events, check whether the sequence is able to perform the transition between both states.

b) Given an initial and target states, obtain one or more sequences of external events (plans) to perform the transition between both states.

The Deductive Database (DDB) designer is the component that generates the set of Stored Predicates (SP), the set of Accessible Predicates (AP) and the IDB rules. Usually, there are many valid alternatives of SP sets and, thus, the designer must choose the one that he/she considers most appropiate

Once the SP set has been designed, we determine the AP set, that is, the predicates whose facts can be derived from the stored facts. Finally, we generate the IDB rules with a simple transformation of the DCM.

The EDB Schema Generator writes the EDB schema for the set SP. For each current predicate we define a relation scheme with the same attributes, except the time attribute, since the time will be implicit. For each full history predicate p(**X**,T) we define a relation scheme p(**X**,T_start,T_end), where attributes T_start and T_end represent the interval in wich p(**X**) holds.

The Transaction Generator is the component that generate the Base Transactions, as described in the previous section.

7. CONCLUSIONS

We have presented the ODISSEA approach to the design of IS from a DCM. We have discussed the main decisions involved in this process: data base design and transaction design. Data base design can not be completely automated, but we provide some tools that help the designer in alternatives generation and analysis.

Transaction design can be completely automated, assuming a given hardware/software execution environment. We have presented a method to derive the transactions from the DCM. The method is based on the use of the SLDNF proof procedure and, thus, it can be implemented easily in Prolog. We hope that our method will facilitate the implementation of DCM and, thus, it may help to overcome the main disadvantage of the deductive approach. We plan to build an additional component, which transforms our Base Transactions into a procedural language. In such a way, we can improve the performance of the generated system.

Acknowledgment

The author wish to thank A. Olivé for the ideas, comments and support, received while writting this paper, and also to the ODISSEA group for their suggestions on earlier drafts. This work has been supported by the CICYT PRONTIC program, project TIC 680.

REFERENCES

[Bub86] Bubenko,J.A. "Information system methodologies - A research view". In [OSV86], pp. 289-318.

[BuO86] Bubenko,J.A.;Olivé,A. "Dynamic or temporal modelling?. An illustrative comparison". SYSLAB Working Paper No. 117, University of Stockholm, 1986.

[CGT90] Ceri,S.;Gottlob,G.;Tanca,L. "Logic programming and databases", Springer-Verlag, 1990.

[CoO91] Costal,D.;Olivé,A. "A method for reasoning about deductive conceptual models of information systems", to appear in Proc. CAISE'92.

LlS91] Lloyd,J.;Shepherdson,J.C. "Partial evaluation in logic programming". J. Logic Programming, 1991, No.11, pp. 217-242.

[Oli86] Olivé,A. "A comparison of the operational and deductive approaches to conceptual information systems modelling". Proc. IFIP 86, North-Holland, Dublin, 1986, pp. 91-96.

[Oli89] Olivé,A. "On the design and implementation of information systems from deductive conceptual models". Proc. of the15th. VLDB, Amstedam, 1989, pp. 3-11.

[Oli91] Olivé,A. "Integrity constraints checking in deductive databases", Proc. of the 17th. VLDB, Barcelona, 1991, pp. 513-523.

[OS92] Olivé,A.; Sancho,MR. "The Odissea approach to the design of information systems from deductive conceptual models". Technical Report, Univ. Pol. Catalunya, Barcelona, 1991.

[OSV86] Olle,T.W.;Sol,H.G.;Verrijn-Stuart,A.A. (Eds.) "Information systems design methodologies: Improving the practice". North-Holland, 1986.

[QuS91] Quer,C.;Sistac,J. "ODISSEA: a language for deductive information systems". Proc. 2nd. Intl. Workshop on the Deductive approach to IS and DB, Aiguablava(Catalonia), 1991, pp. 22-49.

[San90] Sancho,M.R. "Deriving an internal events model from a deductive conceptual model". Proc. Intl. Workshop on the Deductive approach to IS and DB, S'Agaró (Catalonia), 1990, pp. 73-92.

[TeO92] Teniente,E.;Olivé,A."The events method for view updating in deductive databases", Proc. EDBT92, Vienna, Austria, 1992

Personal Computers and Intelligent Systems / F.H. Vogt (Editor)
Information Processing 92, Volume III
Elsevier Science Publishers B.V. (North-Holland)

A Knowledge Based Information System

E.Bertino[a], S.Bottarelli[b], M.Damiani[b], M.Marcadella[b], M.Migliorati[b],P.Randi[b]

[a]Dipartimento di Informatica e Scienze dell'Informazione
Universita' di Genova Via L.B. Alberti, 4 - 16132 Genova (Italy)

[b]Datamont R&D Centre Viale Restelli 1/A - 20124 Milano (Italy)

Abstract
A data management system is presented combining knowledge representation techniques, with database techniques, and with hyper-textual techniques. The goal of the system is to support large-scale knowledge bases.

Keyword Codes: I.2.0; I.2.4; I.2.5
Keywords: Artificial Intelligence, General; Knowledge Representation Formalisms and Methods; Programming Languages and Software

1. INTRODUCTION

Advanced data management systems are characterized by increasing expressive power of their data models. The reason for this is that information is becoming an increasingly important resource for many organizations. It is therefore important to provide high-level data modeling tools to adequately describe information encoded as data in databases. Research and development in the area of databases is evolving along several directions, such as object-oriented databases [1], knowledge bases, deductive databases [2], extensions to relational systems. Despite differences among the approaches found in all those directions, most proposed systems provide highly expressive data models able to directly represent real-world entities and to convey a large amount of intensional knowledge about the stored data.

In this paper we describe a data management system, developed as part of the ADKMS project[1], which makes a step towards providing advanced modeling and reasoning capabilities. However, rather than developing a new data model, we took the approach of starting from an existing knowledge representation model and extending it with various features to make it suitable for the development and management of large scale knowledge bases. Special attention in the development of the system was paid to provide different environments for different types of users. To this purpose, the system combines the techniques of visual programming, which we believe to be a proper interaction paradigm for knowledge acquisition and usage, with a rapid prototyping approach, which allows an initial prototype to be quickly developed to be used by domain experts and end-users for evaluation, validation and assessment purposes.

The core of the system is the BACK representation language [5], a KL-ONE like representation system. BACK is object-based in the tradition of frames and semantic nets. The effectiveness of BACK in capturing the domain semantics greatly simplifies the task of building domain models, since it allows the domain conceptualization to be directly represented. A second important feature of BACK is its ability to compute on the represented knowledge by inference algorithms. Therefore, BACK can be used to answer queries, issued by using the BACK query language, about a domain working directly on the represented knowledge modeling the domain. The richness of the BACK language implies a high degree of usage complexity. It is therefore important to provide some higher level, easy-to-use languages and tools for the users of the system. The system provides different environments for different types of users. We distinguish between end-users, and knowledge engineers. However, while the main tasks of the knowledge engineers are to insert/modify concepts, facts, or other relevant information, and to monitor system operations (such as inferences), the end-users interact with the system mainly to extract all relevant information they need to carry their own tasks. Therefore, their interactions are mainly retrieval-oriented. Moreover, those users are often non-computer experts and therefore they require a friendly and comfortable interaction style to access the knowledge base. Based on those requirements, two different user environments have been developed: the BACK Interface Tools (BIT), directly based on the BACK model, providing a set of tools to support the tasks of knowledge engineers and of domain experts; the end-user environment providing hypertextual capabilities for querying and navigating through knowledge bases.

Finally, we note that performance is a crucial issue in making the system usable in real applications. BACK, while being fully adequate from the representational point of view, is quite inefficient, especially in the case of queries. The main reason we observed was that, while the BACK query language is set-oriented, the internal processing of queries is instance-oriented. In order to overcome this problem, an efficient coupling with a relational DBMS (RDBMS) supporting the SQL language has been designed and implemented. It turned out that many BACK queries can be directly translated into SQL, which is also a set-oriented query language. The SQL optimizer can then generate efficient set-oriented strategies to execute such queries. Therefore, significant gain in performance is achieved. In this paper we focus on the strategy used to couple BACK with the RDBMS and we present some results from performance testing. The user interfaces and tools are presented in [3].

2. THE BACK REPRESENTATION LANGUAGE

The BACK language distinguishes between terminological (TBOX) and assertional (ABOX) knowledge. Terminological knowledge captures the intensional aspects of a domain and consists of a set of *concepts* and *roles* (properties of concepts) organized in subsumption taxonomies. Concepts are used to intensionally collect relevant entities of a domain; roles are used to specify properties of instances of concepts and thus model the relationships between concepts; assertions are used to specify the extension of a concept. A distinguished feature of the language is the possibility of specifying *definitional* properties (i.e. properties expressing necessary and sufficient conditions for an individual to be a concept instance). Through the *classification* inference concepts are placed automatically in the net of concept descriptions depending on the specified properties, while instances are automatically completed with the most specific description. Figure 1 presents a small portion of a terminology example drawn from an application in the business area [4] (the complete terminology include 500 concepts). In the used graphical notation, similar to that used by other KL-ONE languages, an ellipse represents a concept. Bold arrows denote subsumption links. A role is represented by a little box into a circle with arrows from the domain concept and to the range concept. A simple box denotes value restriction.

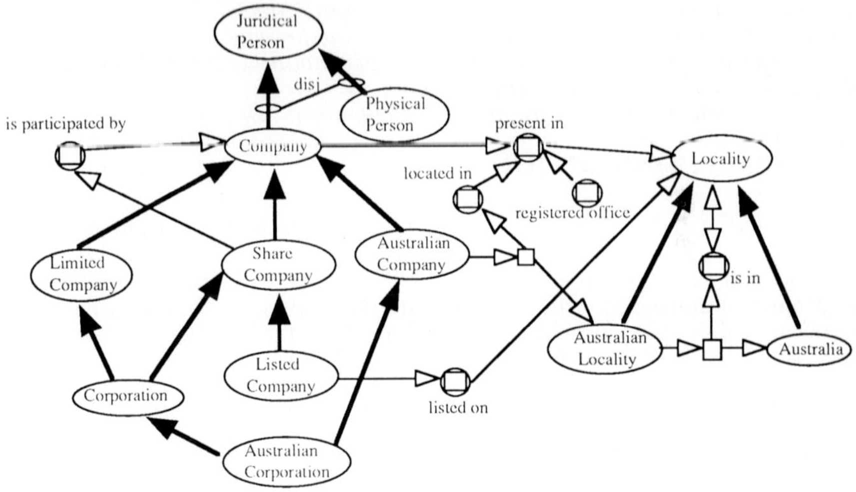

Figure 1. Graphical description of a sample terminology

The example shows several aspects of BACK. The central concept is "Company", a *primitive concept* (i.e. only necessary conditions can be defined on it) which is a specialization of "Juridical Person" but *disjoint* from "Physical Person". A relevant property is expressed by the role "present_in" with *range* "Locality"; this role can be further specialized into the roles: "located_in", "registered_office", and describes the location - in its different forms - of a company. The "Company" concept subsumes the *defined concepts*: (necessary and sufficient conditions can be defined on them): "Limited Company", "Share Company", "Australian Company", defined using *value restrictions* on roles. For example, the concept "Australian Company" is defined using a value restriction on role 'located_in': the restriction constraints this role to take as values only instances of the concept "Australian Locality" (in other words, "Australian Company" is defined as a "Company" located in an "Australian Locality"). Concept and role definitions are expressed using the BACK Tell Language (BTL). Given the above description, the insertion of a new company with, for example, the registered office in Sydney, listed on New York, and which is participated by Montedison S.p.A. is performed by the following BACK Assertion Language (BAL) expression:

X = Company with registered_office: 'Sydney' andwith listed_on: 'New York' andwith is_participated_by: 'Montedison S.p.A.'

The above assertion entails a number of classification inferences that allows to infer that company *X* is an *Australian Corporation*. We now present an example of ABOX query expressed in the ABOX Query Language (AQL):
%which are the names of the chairmans of all Italian companies engaged in both the chemical and the agricultural sectors and having some installation in a nation in which a company participated by Montedison is also present?
[rf(firstname), rf(surname)] for
getall Physical_Person with inv has_in_office:
some(chairman with inv has)body: some(Italian_Company with engaged_in:
some (Chemical_Area) and some (Agricultural_Area)
andwith Installation: some(Nation with inv present_in:
some(Company with has_capital: some(Capital with subdivided_in:
some(Participation with belonging_to:
some(Company with named: `Montedison')))))

3. RDBMS CONNECTION

The use of a DBMS as repository for the BACK system offers several advantages, including efficient query processing, concurrent accesses, and transactions. However, in order to take full advantage of DBMS functionalities a proper coupling is crucial. An important aspect, which affects the performance, is the "mapping strategy" used in translating the knowledge representation data model onto the database model.

One of the initial versions of the system already provided a coupling strategy for a RDBMS. The RDBMS was actually a main-memory RDBMS simulated in Prolog. The mapping strategy (called *disaggregated scheme*) used in this initial version consists of allocating a relation for each concept. The relation associated with a given concept consists of a single column and contains the internal identifiers of all instances of the concept. Moreover, for each role two relations are allocated. One holds the fillers of objects for that particular role, the other the cardinality information of the role filler's set of objects. An additional relation is allocated to store all aliases defined for the instances. Therefore, the number of relations needed to store the instances of a concept with a number n of roles is $2^*(1 + n)$.

From this kind of scheme an inefficiency soon emerged. The problem is that the number of relations to be allocated increases quite rapidly with the complexity of the modelled domain, and that the information about a single instance is spread over several relations. Moreover, as we observed in developing the business application [4], many relations are usually empty or filled with only a few concept instances, especially those of very general primitive concepts. Therefore, this mapping strategy resulted in a very large number of relations with few tuples each. Using so many relations resulted in substantial overhead due to the large number of relations to access for solving an AQL query. Therefore, the overall performance of the system was quite unsatisfactory even for small knowledge bases.

In order to overcome this problem, an alternative strategy for coupling has been investigated and implemented. Two main principles appeared to be important. It is necessary to define and use mapping strategies which minimize the number of relations to be opened when executing an AQL query. Some kind of compromise between the number of relations composing the relational scheme and their size seems, however, to be useful. The translation strategy from AQL into SQL must be able to generate SQL queries that directly reflect the semantic meaning of the corresponding AQL queries. That is, a single complex SQL query must be generated, whenever possible, for a given AQL query, rather than generating several simple SQL queries. This translation strategy has two main benefits: the number of RDBMS queries issued drastically decreases; the optimization capabilities of the RDBMS are fully exploited.

The mapping strategy we adopted is similar to that defined in [6]. The main goal of this strategy is the minimization of the number of allocated relations. The resulting scheme consists of three relations plus an alias relation. The relations have the following schemes. (Instances are internally identified by an identifier consisting of the symbol "uc_" concatenated with an integer number: for example uc_1, uc_2,...., uc_123, etc.)

1) **instances (concept, uc)** : a tuple <concept_i, uc_j> of this relation indicates that uc_j is an instance of concept concept_i
2) **values (role, uc, value)**: a tuple <role_i, uc_j, value_k> of this relation indicates that value_k is a known role filler for the role whose name is role_i for the instance uc_j.
3) **cardinalities (role, uc, cmin, cmax, numvals)**: a tuple <role_i, uc_j, cmin_k, cmax_h, numvals_l> of this relation indicates that the instance uc_j has a number numvals_l of known fillers for role role_i; cmin_k and cmax_h hold the minimum and maximum restrictions on the number of role fillers.
4) **abox_uc_alias (alias, uc)**: a tuple <alias_i, uc_j> of this relation indicates that alias_j is an alias for instance uc_j.

Figure 2 shows the relation contents for some of the concepts in Figure 1.

instances

concept	uc
company	uc_1
company	uc_2
corporation	uc_10
locality	uc_18

values

role	uc	value
present_in	uc_1	uc_18
present_in	uc_2	uc_20
has_capital	uc_1	uc_30

cardinalities

role	uc	cmin	cmax	numvals
present_in	uc_1	0	in	1
present_in	uc_2	0	in	1
has_capital	uc_1	1	in	3

abox_uc_alias

alias	uc
Montedison	uc_1
Himont	uc_2
Italy	uc_18

Figure 2. Example of relation contents[2]

This mapping strategy, called *fully aggregated schema*, has several advantages. First of all, it uses only four relations as the repository of all information needed by the ABOX. Unlike the previous relational scheme, this approach reduces the number of relations to be accessed and simplifies the AQL/SQL translator. Moreover, the scheme does not need to be restructured upon modifications to the TBOX. We note that it is possible to define an intermediate approach (called *partially aggregated schema*), which consists of partitioning the whole TBOX into *clusters* of concepts, and then adopting the previous mapping strategy for each cluster. For example, the TBOX in Figure 1 could be partitioned into the following clusters:

C1: {Juridical_Person, Physical_Person, Company, Australian_Company, Share_Company, Limited_Company, Corporation, Listed_Company, Australian_Corporation}

C2: {Locality, Australian_Locality, Australia}.

The performance of the partially aggregated schema is strongly influenced by the TBOX partition into clusters. A good conceptual partition should be able to keep small the number of relations, while at the same time avoiding an excessive growth of relations. We note that the partially aggregated scheme may be further enhanced by considering the possibility of adopting different mapping strategies for different clusters. A conceptual partition divides the TBOX into several distinct portions. These portions may have different characteristics, either in terms of topology, or in terms of instances, or in terms of access patterns. Therefore, it should be possible to handle each cluster in a different way, adopting for it a particular, customized relational scheme. In some cases, for example, some clusters should be handled by using the disaggregated scheme, while others by using the complete aggregated scheme or yet another to be defined.

The current version of the system uses the fully aggregated scheme as mapping strategies. Based on this mapping scheme, an AQL/SQL translator has been designed and implemented in Prolog. An important result is that when no defined concepts are involved, an AQL query can be mapped in most cases on a single SQL query. When defined concepts are involved, an AQL query must be mapped on a sequence of SQL queries. However, the number of SQL queries generated is much lower than the number of queries generated under the disaggregated scheme. These results show that a high level mapping from AQL to SQL is indeed possible. Figure 3 reports some sample results obtained measuring the performances of the original -in core - version of the BACK system and of the BACK system extended with the AQL/SQL translator. The y-axis records the time needed to execute an AQL query; the x-axis the number of nested *all* operators involved in AQL queries. From the diagram we can see that the time needed to execute an AQL query using the approach based on the AQL/SQL translator is very close to and sometimes lower, especially when dealing with complex queries, than the original in core BACK system. We evaluated also the overhead due to query translation. This overhead is between 5% and 10% of the overall time required to execute a query. It can be further reduced by implementing the translator in a language different than Prolog.

4. FINAL REMARKS

We have presented a knowledge based system which provides various tools to support the tasks of the knowledge engineers, and at the same time an easy-to-use end-user environment. The system also includes a RDBMS which is used to store all instances contained in the knowledge base. An efficient coupling between BACK and a RDBMS has been designed and implemented. The system has been developed in an environment consisting of SUN and Apple Macintosh machines and is based on a client-server architecture. The server runs on the SUN workstation and hosts the BACK representation system, the RDBMS, and the knowledge engineer environment. The end-user environment runs as a client application on the Apple Macintosh and is implemented in the Hypercard environment.

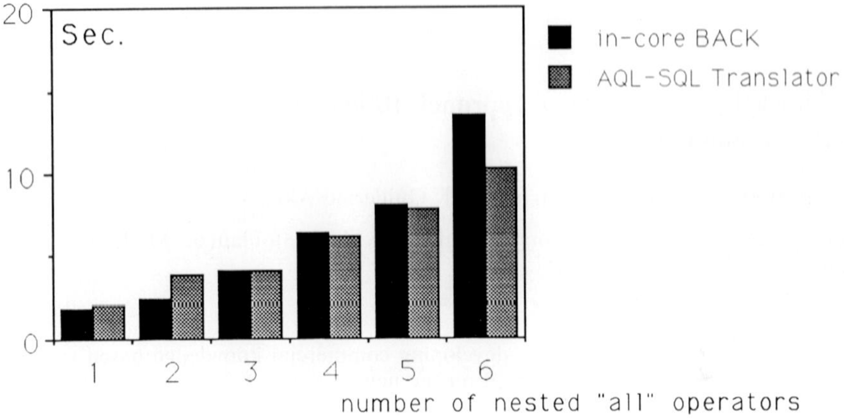

Figure 3. Time needed to extend a query depending on the number of *all* operator

5. REFERENCES

1 Bertino, E., and Martino, L. Object-oriented database management systems: concepts and issues. *Computer*, Vol. 24, No. 4, pp.33-47, April 1991.

2 Bertino, E., and Montesi, D. Towards a logical-object language for databases. *Proc. of Third Int. Conference on Extending Database Technology (EDBT90),* Vienna (Austria), March 23-27, 1992.

3 Bertino, E., et Al. The ADKMS knowledge acquisition system. *Proc. of Second Far-East Workshop on Future Database Systems*, Kyoto (Japan), April 26-28, 1992.

4 Damiani, M., and Bottarelli, S. A terminological approach to business domain modeling. *Proc. of Int. Conf. on Database and Expert Systems Applications (DEXA90)*, Vienna (Austria), August 29-31, 1990.

5 Nebel, B. Computational complexity of terminological reasoning in BACK. *Artificial Intelligence*, Vol. 34, No. 3, pp. 344-348, April 1988.

6 Nixon, B., et Al. Implementation of a compiler for semantic data model: experiences with Taxis. *Proc. ACM-SIGMOD Conference on Management of Data*, San Francisco, May 27-29, 1987.

---

[1] The work reported in this paper has been partially supported by the European Economic Communities under the ESPRIT project P311 (II phase). Partners in this project were: Nixdorf (D), Datamont (I), Olivetti (I), Technische Universitat Berlin (D), Quinary (I).

[2] In table **cardinalities** a value 'in' for the column **cmax** indicates that the number of role fillers does not have an upper limit

Personal Computers and Intelligent Systems / F.H. Vogt (Editor)
Information Processing 92, Volume III
Elsevier Science Publishers B.V. (North-Holland)

A Knowledge Engineering approach to overcome elusive problems in KBS development

Idoia Alarcón, Jose Luis Zaccagnini and Guillermo Alonso

Instituto de Ingenieria del Conocimiento, UAM Cantoblanco, Modulo C-XVI, planta 4, 28049 Madrid, SPAIN.

Abstract

A methodological approach for developing commercial knowledge based systems is described. The methodology, based on the new concept of "maquette", has arisen from the experience in developing several KBS projects at the Knowledge Engineering Institute (IIC) at Madrid, and is oriented to deal with elusive problems that usually affect time and cost limitations, clients requirements, and user interface efficiency. Finally some case studies are briefly discussed.

Keywords Codes: I.2.1, I, D.2.

Keywords: Artificial Intelligence Applications and Expert Systems, Computing Methodologies, Software Engineering.

1. INTRODUCTION

Although methodology is assumed to be an important issue within any engineering process, its use for developing Knowledge Engineering (KE) applications is not usually followed. Two causes could be appointed: the lack of a widely accepted methodology and the fact, frequently assumed, that expert systems development is much of an art. From this point of view, it seems impossible to formalize the tasks and steps that will lead to the final success of knowledge based applications. Sometimes, this confusing situation comes out from mistaking pure Artificial Intelligence (AI) research with Knowledge Engineering practices. But in KE commercial applications time and cost constraints as well as the commitment to match clients requirements play an essential role. Then, in addition to technical correctness, there are a set of topics in KE that should be methodologically addressed to guarantee the achievement of quality commercial products.

Several proposals have been presented in the last years attempting to include the specific KE tasks into Software Engineering methodologies [3,5]. Most of the authors agree that some of the problems presented along the development of a KBS are elusive and can produce its failure, after an unrecoverable spent of time and resources. The IIC, facing this kind of problems, has developed a methodological approach oriented to avoid the associated risks. It also facilitates some of the knowledge related tasks.

2. OPERATIONAL KBS DEVELOPMENT PROBLEMS

Some of the difficulties to achieve the final success of KBS are:

- Bad and late users identification.
- Ill-defined integration and communication requirements.
- Fuzzy definition of project goals and objectives.
- Lack of participants commitment.
- Poor criteria of real feasibility.
- Erroneous cost estimation and assignment of resources.
- Initial communication difficulties between knowledge engineers, experts and users.
- Mixture of handicraft and methodologically structured tasks.
- Bad design of the user interface.
- The project never finishes.
- More expert than user-oriented system validation.
- No criteria for maintenance plans.

3. THE IIC METHODOLOGICAL FRAMEWORK

The **I**nstituto de **I**ngenieria del **C**onocimiento (**IIC** - Knowledge Engineering Institute) was set up in 1989 by the Autonomous University of Madrid and nine leading Spanish companies: Banco Español de Crédito and Banco Hispano Americano (banking), Iberia (Spanish airline), Informática El Corte Ingles (computers and professional services), INH-Repsol (integrated oil co.), IBM (computers), Renfe (Spanish railways) Tabacalera (food), and Union Electrica Fenosa (electricity: production and distribution). Around 70 persons work in AI and KE R&D at the IIC, which specially promotes the transfer of technology to industry. Both the Spanish Ministry of Industry, Commerce and Tourism, and the Ministry of Education and Science also contribute to the funds of the IIC.

From the experience obtained, and taken into account the state of the art of proposed methodologies for KBS development [e.g. 2,3,5,9], a methodological framework of the IIC has been defined. This methodology is oriented to commercial applications. Therefore, great importance is attached to concepts such as time and resources constraints, user requirements, integration with the real environment, user interface quality and maintenance [10]. The framework consists of four standard phases - *Study, Development, Implantation, and Follow Up* - that cover sequentially the whole life-cycle of a project (figure 1, left side). In addition two global activities are defined along the whole project life-cycle: *Project Management* and *Testing & Validation*

4. THE MAQUETTE APPROACH

The Development phase is the core of any methodology, and deals with the solution to the problem from a technical point of view. In the IIC-Maquette approach, this phase is formed by two main tasks running in parallel: the *Development of the Maquette and the Development of the System.* This is the main novelty brought by our methodology, by splitting this usually single task into two parallel activities.

The *maquette* is a system that models the final application aiming to show the main features of the complete system to be developed. It has a similar appearance to the final system but not all its capabilities. It is installed in the user environment in a very early stage. Usually, it is extremely helpful to develop and test the integration with the real environment in the maquette: it will be dealing with real data right from the beginning. The *system* is the complete application developed following more standard software and knowledge engineering methods, but taken advantage from the permanent use of the maquette. Both the maquette and the system development are carried out in parallel (although the maquette has to be finished earlier), with a continuous communication between them.

One of the main goals of this approach is to try to include most of the handicraft and ill-defined activities of the development phase into the tasks of development of the maquette. This preserves the usual activities ready to be structured and performed according to the usual knowledge and software engineering methods. The most important component in this approach is the "methodological orientation" that allows to avoid many of the elusive risk factors discussed above. The most accurate definition of *maquette* that can be proposed at the moment is the following: a demo-like application *the most similar to the desired appearance of the final product* that can be *installed earliest* in the user environment. The achievement of this compromise will be reached with different kinds and sizes of maquettes in each project. In some cases it will be possible to build a maquette even without any kind of knowledge based modules. It is also possible to point out the main characteristics that must be present in the maquette based on maquette development:

- It must have the most realistic emulation of the user interface desired for the final user interface. This includes hardware, software and I/O supports.
- It must have the communications and integration modules needed to be installed and run in the user environment.
- It must be installed and tested by the users as soon as possible
- It must grow in parallel and permanent interaction with the System
- It must be substituted by the full System at the end of the development phase.

4.1 Benefits in all the methodology phases

From our experience, the use of the maquette approach from the very early steps of a KBS project avoids many of the elusive problems listed above and provides a number of methodological advantages along all the life-cycle.

Study phase: Many risk factors, analyzed during the first feasibility studies, can be detected and evaluated very early and accurately if this task is performed with the immediate aim of building the first maquette version.

Development phase: In the *analysis and design tasks* the design of the maquette provides the best way to characterize the real goals of the system to be developed. The possibility of emulate a model of the full system drives very efficiently its modularization. In addition, it allows to obtain a more accurate estimation of the

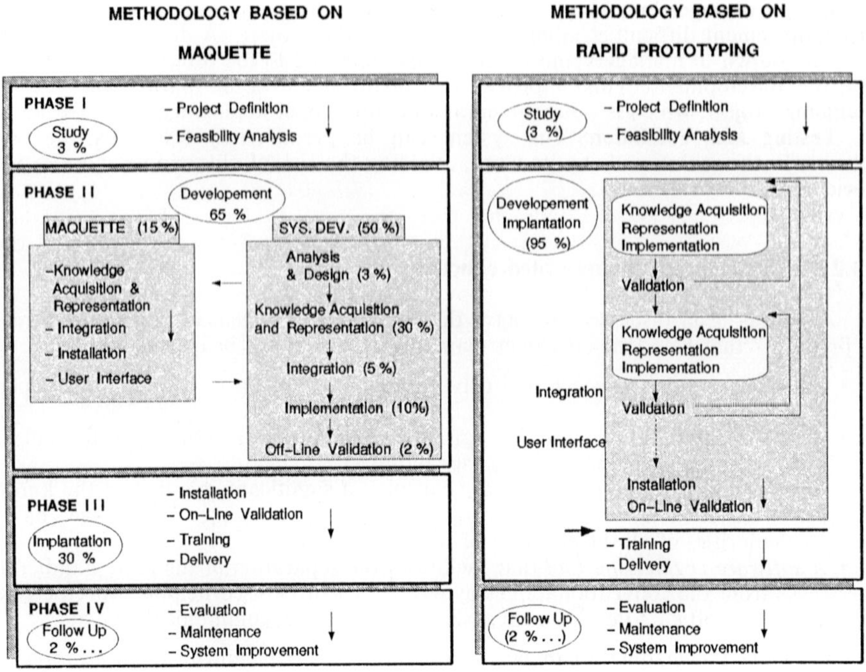

Figure 1. Maquette and rapid prototyping approaches

modules size and the resources needed. The user interface is designed at the first moment and can be tuned very carefully, with the the users along all the phase.

During the "bottle neck" of the initial *knowledge acquisition tasks*, the maquette is used as a common reference for experts and knowledge engineers to discuss about the general structure and the final goals of the system.

It is clear that the nature of the approach forces to identify and test, early in the *integration tasks*, the actual environment characteristics that the future system will face. Something similar can be said about the *implementation tasks* to test modules of the final software, and their interaction. Possible errors in the design of the system are detected at an early stage of the development and can be easily solved providing on and off-line *validations* from experts and users.

Implantation phase: The installation of the operational system is strongly facilitated by the previous use of the maquette: many of the possible problems of integration would have been detected and solved at this stage. This approach makes the delivery and final acceptance of the system just a formal procedure.

Follow-up phase: The early feed-back with experts and users allowed by the maquette provides good criteria to evaluate the success of the final system. Its integration in the real environment of the user facilitates the forecasting of the maintenance problems.

Project management: Many of the elusive problems mentioned are closely related to management difficulties along all the steps of the project. A demo of the system can be shown to managers and other instances related to the project at early stages of the development. This improves the involvement of all participants in the ongoing project, which is a fundamental issue for proper deployment of the system.

Testing and Validation: The system can be permanently tested by the best "tester": the real user doing its work, avoiding the risk of obtaining a more expert oriented validation.

4.2 The maquette: a many-syded concept

As it has been discussed, we have discovered that the *maquette* is more than a "program" that helps the developer team in its work, it can be considered also

- *A methodological approach* that drives the procedures for developing a full operational KBS
- *A sub-phase of the life-cycle* that can be completely characterized and formalized with its own development phases (see figure 1).
- *A knowledge engineering tool* that can play a significant role during the knowledge acquisition tasks. It also allows to handle the knowledge based particularities of all the elements of the full system.
- *A software engineering tool* that facilitates the separation of the more handicraft tasks from the conventional ones as well as it can be used helping specific conventional software development tasks (user interface, communications, etc.)

Typically the maquette can be described vs the well known *rapid-prototyping* incremental strategy for building expert systems [4,7,9], that is an evolution of the iterative trial-and-error research approach. In fact, there is not a *standard* rapid prototyping method, although its general process flow can be sketched (see right of figure 1). The key issue is that to end up with an application that meets client demands within the time and resource constraints is not easily reached when using a not formal methodological approach biased towards the technical matters, as rapid-prototyping is. In fact, the experience shows that this usually causes delays, increases costs and even may end up with applications that users will find useless. Some of the reasons are:

- The lack of a formal methodological approach, replaced by a weak tactic.
- The loop-back strategy (re-prototyping), a very time consuming activity that obstructs project cost estimations. Often, there is no clear "finishing" point: incremental development is continued until available resources are exhausted.
- The "handicraft" tactic disables the possibility of using conventional software methodologies and makes difficult the maintenance.
- The trial-and-error approach delays the managers, experts and users final acceptance of the actual system functionalities almost to the end of the development / implantation phase.
- The tightly experts oriented system development, with end-users oblivion.
- The lack of adequate focus on user-interface issues resulting in non-ergonomic applications: a crucial aspect with respect to system acceptance.

In summary, all these problems may have a negative incidence in developing commercial applications, as long as time, costs and client satisfaction become crucial topics. To overcome some of these problems and most of the mentioned above, IIC is developing the maquette approach [11] where most benefits of the "rapid-prototyping" are kept, but without interfering with the more conventional knowledge and software engineering developing practices. Figure 1 shows both "rapid-prototyping" and "maquette" approaches, within the knowledge based systems development methodological framework.

Table 1. Maquette and rapid prototype: main differences.

PROTOTYPE	**MAQUETTE**
Partial subsystems development	Full application development
Experts oriented	Experts and users oriented
Late testing of system integration	Early testing of system integration
Late user interface design	Early user interface design
Fuzzy goals definition	Clear goals definition
Difficult requirements redefinition	Easy requirements redefinition
Late risk factors detection	Early risk factors detection
Partial subsystems evaluation	Full system evaluation
Difficulties to finish the project	Clear finishing conditions

5. CASE STUDIES AND FUTURE WORK

The IIC is developing operational KBS for different application areas. Some of the projects have used a prototype approach, running into the difficulties discussed beforehand. In other cases, different approaches of the maquette-oriented procedures have been performed with a significant success overcoming the elusive problems discussed.

The MIP System (Intelligent Process Monitoring), described in [1], is a real-time expert system developed at the IIC for assistance to the control of a petrochemical reactor in an acrylonitrile plant of REPSOL, the largest Spanish integrated oil company. The MIP system has been deployed and is in satisfactory current use since March 1991. MIP is an integrated system based on the blackboard concept and formed by several modules. The maquette approach helped in facing the constraints in the environment from the very beginning, improving the communication between knowledge engineers and experts, defining clearly end-users characteristics and requirements, guaranteeing the user acceptance, and obtaining an early "demo" of the system able to be shown to managers, experts and users.

The PCUBO System: is an advisor expert system for human resources management, is to assist in the taking of decision about the promotion of personnel, and optimizing the selection of candidates for a specific job. This system is described in [12]. The advantages obtained from using the maquette approach were very useful for many of the risk factors discussed in this paper: rapid debugging process in the final design, experts motivation, and early clarification and statement of specifications.

In conclusion, we propose the maquette approach and its own role in a structured methodology framework for developing full operational, problem oriented, efficient and robust knowledge based systems. Nevertheless, we are aware of the need of validating this methodology with a larger number of projects coming from other sectors and/or other development centers. The IIC is currently doing this validation and has started up a project to develop a software tool for supporting the maquette approach activities. This will facilitate the use of the methodological approach discussed in this paper and will be very useful in many of the knowledge and software engineering tasks.

6. ACKNOWLEDGEMENTS

This project has been partially supported by Spanish Ministry of Industry, Commerce and Tourism (PEIN II). We want to thank Sesh Murthy, Jesus Regaño, Erik de Pablo, Jaime G. Enríquez and Xavier Alaman for their involvement in the development of the IIC Methodological Framework.

7. REFERENCES

1. X. Alamán, S. Romero, C. Aguirre, P. Serrahima, R. Muñoz, V. Lopez, J. Dorronsoro and E. de Pablo. "MIP: A Real Time Expert System for Assistance to Process Control". 8th. Conference on Artificial Intelligence for Applications (CAIA'92), 1992.
2. R.D. Bowerman and D.E. Glover. *Putting Expert Systems into Practice.* Van Nostrand Reinhold Company, New York, 1988.
3. J.S. Edwards. *Building Knowledge-Based Systems. Towards a Methodology.* Pitman, 1991
4. S. Harker. "Rapid Prototyping as a Tool for User Centered Design". In G. Salvendy (Ed.), *Cognitive Engineering in the design of human-computer interaction and expert systems.* Elsevier S.P., 1987.
5. F.R. Hickman, J.L. Killin, L. Land, T. Mulhall, D. Porter and R.M. Taylor. *Analysis for Knowledge-based Systems: A Practical Guide to KADS Methodology.* Ellis Horwood Limited, England, 1989.
6. T.J. Laffey, P.A. Cox., J.L. Schmidt, S.M. Kao, and J.Y. Read. "Real-Time Knowledge-Based Systems" *AI Magazine.* Spring 1988, pp. 27-45.
7. D.S. Prerau. *Developing and Managing Expert Systems*, Addison Wesley Pub. Co., USA, 1990
8. M. Stock. *AI in Process Control*, McGraw-Hill, New York, 1989.
9. D.A. Waterman, *A Guide to Expert Systems*, Addison-Wesley, USA, 1986.
10. J.L. Zaccagnini, I. Alarcón, G. Alonso, J. Regaño and S. Murthy. "Marco metodológico de proyectos del IIC para el desarrollo de Sistemas Basados en el Conocimiento (v. 1.0)". Inf. Tec. del IIC, A04-91.
11. J.L. Zaccagnini and I. Alarcon, "Metodologia para S.B.C.: La Estrategia de Desarrollo Basada en Maqueta", Spanish National Conference on Artificial Intelligence, AEPIA-91, Madrid, October 1991.
12. J.L. Zaccagnini, J. G. Enriquez and J. Casas "PCUBO: Sistema Experto de ayuda en la toma de decisión para la promoción de personal" Inf. Tec. del IIC, A12-91.

Personal Computers and Intelligent Systems / F.H. Vogt (Editor)
Information Processing 92, Volume III
Elsevier Science Publishers B.V. (North-Holland)

An Architecture for Intelligent User Interfaces

F. Ramparany and E. Minor
Cap Gemini Innovation
7 Chemin du Vieux Chêne, 38240 Meylan, France

Abstract
Computer systems supporting complex human activities or complex processes require user interfaces that can build and maintain explicit models of the user, the process, and the system itself. Such interfaces could adapt to the user, and could provide focused advice and guidance support at any point during the process. We qualify such adaptive user interfaces as "intelligent".

Benefits which are expected from intelligent interfaces include a drastic reduction in the learning time required to efficiently use the environment, and efficient teaching of how to conduct the process for novice users.[1]

In this article, we propose a generic architecture for designing intelligent user interfaces. The main components of this architecture are:
- a task scheduler
- an activity selector
- an activity configurer
- a process context modeler
- the interface with the domain process specific modules and functions.

These components and their organization are described. An implementation of an intelligent user interface using this architecture will be presented. This user interface was built for the Knowledge Engineering Workbench (KEW), developed within the Esprit project ACKnowledge [1]. KEW is a workbench that integrates complementary tools and techniques dedicated to knowledge acquisition.

keywords codes: H.1.2; I.2.0; D.2.2
keywords: user/machine systems; artificial intelligence; tools and techniques

1 Introduction

Building computer environments to support human activities absorbs much of the effort of the information processing industry. In some cases these activities are too complex to be fully automated by the environment and thus require intensive interaction with the user. Examples of such activities include creative processes, where the purpose of the processes is to construct an object or produce a situation that didn't exist prior to the process. Need for creativity requires that humans remain strongly involved in the process. Another example of interaction intensive activities is in safety critical environments, where important decisions should be left to responsibility only of humans, and the role of the system is limited to providing relevant information upon which the human will base his decision.

The increasing complexity of activities to be supported, together with the requirement for a friendly user interface, has brought to the fore the need for powerful advice and guidance facilities to assist users. These facilities must be fully integrated into the environment in order to help the user make decisions about: *what to do next*, and *when, why, and how to do it.*

The two facets of today's and future computer based environment, which are the complexity of supported activities and friendliness of user interface, have contradictory implications. On one hand, the complexity of the activity to be supported implies that the computer environment needs to provide numerous, sophisticated functions, and that the user must be an expert in the use of these functions. On the other hand, a friendly user interface should minimize the effort the user will allocate to the interaction with the environment, so that he can concentrate on the process itself rather than on the computer environment.

The above analysis will be refined in the section 2.

To mediate the gap between the complexity of the computer environment and the user friendliness of its interface, we propose an architecture for designing intelligent user interfaces. The architecture, including its components and their organization, is described in section 3.

Finally, we describe how we have used this generic architecture to design the advice and guidance module of the knowledge engineering workbench (section 4).

2 User interface supporting complex processes

Complexity is difficult to characterize. In the following paragraphs we present our definition of complexity as applied to processes, and review current research on UI support for complex processes. We then summarize the main requirements for an intelligent support for such processes.

Dimensions of process complexity

If we refer to the definition of processes in its widest meaning (as found in Webster): *"a natural phenomenon marked by gradual changes or a series of actions or operations that lead toward a particular end"*, processes may be qualified as **complex** due to various features:

- the *number of parameters* to be taken into account when deciding on *the series of actions*

is enormous
• the number of *potential actions* and the *size of their series* needed to meet the end(s) is enormous
• the *end of the process* is difficult to define.
• there are *many ends* and eventually some of them are *conflicting.*

Computer systems have often been seen as the natural solution for reducing the effort of humans when they are involved in the management of complex processes. This is particularly true when the two first features apply. Using computer systems to support such processes can lead to solutions ranging from full automation of the process, to intensive cooperation between the computer system and the human.

Moreover, when the last two features apply as well, intensive interaction between systems and humans remains the only solution. In this case, efficiency and usability of the user interface are fundamental issues.

Current issues in designing user interfaces

Until recently, effort in improving user interfaces to complex systems has tended to focus on the so called "look and feel" of the interface. "Look and feel" deals with how information should be presented and with the techniques and conventions used to interact with graphical elements in the interface. Examples of "look and feel" are menu structures and conventions for making menu choices, control of position and size of windows, and transfer of control between windows.

Increasing effort is now being directed toward support for the process aspects of user interfaces. Much of this research is focused on issues of integration, cooperation, and distribution for complex systems [2], and on reducing what HCI experts call the "cognitive loading" of the interface. Cognitive loading is a measure of the number and complexity of different things which the user must keep in mind at the same time. By concentrating on the cognitive aspects of the interface, rather than simply the "look and feel", HCI research is moving in the direction of developing intelligent user interfaces.

Two powerful tools for analyzing and controlling the cognitive aspects of interfaces are *user models* and *task models.* User models aim at detailed characterizations of how the users of specific complex applications behave. There are important differences between the users of different types of systems, and even between the users of a particular system. For an interface to react "intelligently" it should contain a number of different user models, and attempt to classify each user into one of them. An example of user modeling is the determination of a users experience level [3] . By analyzing user commands a system can place the user in one several categories, for example "novice", "intermediate", or "expert". This information can then be used by the system to select help information of the appropriate level of sophistication.

Task models structure the modes of use of a complex system into goals, and activities needed to achieve the goals. As a user concentrates on a particular goal while using a complex system, he will tend to carry out the activities related to the goal. An interface designer, by modeling the task, can group the activities needed for a certain task in ways that make them easier and more natural to use. An example of task modeling is presented in [4], where knowledge representation techniques were employed to add a task model to an interface for an existing complex application.

Through user and task models, HCI research is beginning to concentrate on support for the processes involved in using complex systems. This support often takes the form of advanced help, and of interfaces structured to lead naturally to the goals which users want to accomplish. From now on, we will use the terms *"advice and guidance"* when referring to this specific kind of process support.

Requirements for an intelligent advice and guidance system

Our experience in different application domains is that an advice and guidance (A&G) module should satisfy the following requirements:

1. it should take the goals of the user into account. This means that the goals of the user are well defined and the A&G module knows about them and takes them into account to derive its recommendations
2. it should be able to update the goals if they change during the process
3. it should be able to manage unusual situations. It should be able to revise its recommendations if the situation is not the one expected. Thus it should monitor the state of the process
4. it should know about the resources that are available (functions, persons, data) for the process to progress

To summarize, A&G modules should be highly flexible, sensitive to the context of the process and capable of adapting their behaviour depending on the profile of the user and his own way of performing the activity.

3 An architecture for active advice and guidance

In this section we introduce the functional architecture of a user interface which supplies advice and guidance. We will identify the main functional components of this architecture and the useful and desirable properties of those components based on the requirements analysed in section 2.

Decomposition is a natural approach to complexity management that has been commonly used in computer science. Advice and guidance should provide ways to decompose the overall goal of the process into more tractable subgoals. Subgoals that require some work from the user, or from the system, or from both, should correspond to tasks. In our

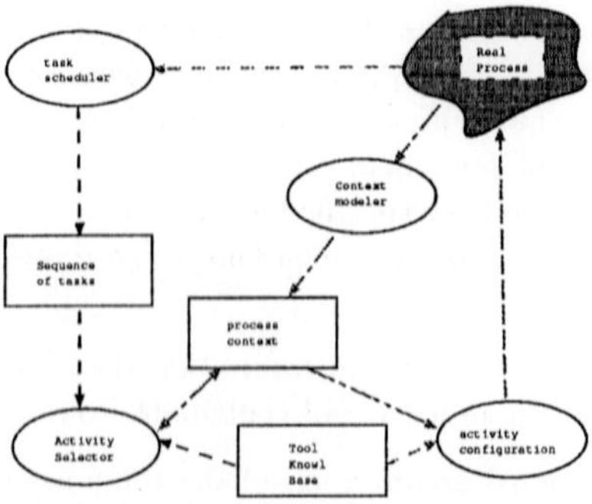

Figure 1: Functional architecture for user interfaces

terminology, a task embodies the concept of work to be carried out to achieve some specific goal. Unlike a goal decomposition structure, a task decomposition structure captures temporal constraints (sequencing among tasks), and logical constraints (input/output relations among tasks).

Thus, we propose that a task scheduler be provided by the advice and guidance module (see figure 1). This task scheduler should take into account user goals (requirement- 1), in particular at the early stage of the process. During the course of the process it should be capable of reacting to changes in goals due to modification in the process environment, or in user intentions (requirement- 2). From the specification of goals, the task scheduler will identify a set of tasks organised into a temporal network that will organise the various activities of the user and the system.

Although it is possible to plan tasks in advance, it is sometime impossible to specify in detail how these tasks will be realised (requirement- 3), since some of the information needed to determine these details is only available at the time the task is started. This suggests that relevant information concerning the process and its environment be stored explicitly by the advice and guidance module. This information provides the basis for more elaborate guidance to the user.

To this end we propose that a process context modeler be an integrated part of the advice and guidance module. The process context modeler will create and maintain a description of the process status, including up-to-date information about the objects manipulated by the process, and information about the process environment (requirement- 3). We can interpret this context description as an abstract view of the process state, where only information relevant for A&G has been retained.

Armed with information about the process status and knowledge about the resources available to the system, the A&G module can select the most appropriate resource (tool, person, data), to achieve each task (requirement- 4). This selection is performed by the activity selector.

Once resources have been identified, the activity configurer analyzes the process context description and sets the details of using the selected resources to achieve the current task. This might involve additional activities, such as adaptation of the result of using a specific tool to fit the requirements of the global process. For example, in our application after the knowledge engineer has used one specific technique to acquire knowledge he will have to reformulate this knowledge into a common knowledge representation and integrate it into the final knowledge base.

The intention of configuring activities is to ensure that the effect of the activity is consistent with the global goal of the process, and contributes to its achievement.

Figure 1 displays the functional organisation of the components described above. This functional architecture is generic as it could be used for designing UI modules for a variety of applications. In the next section, we instantiate this generic UI architecture in the context of an Advice and Guidance module for a knowledge engineering workbench.

4 Advice and Guidance in the Knowledge Engineering Workbench

The Knowledge Engineering Workbench (KEW) has been described in detail in a previous publication [5]. Here we will simply mention that the aim of the workbench is to provide numerous tools for the use of knowledge engineers when they acquire knowledge from domain experts or from raw materials such as books, cases and so on. The goal of the knowledge engineer when using KEW is to capture the acquired knowledge into an operational knowledge base. The resulting knowledge base is then delivered to end-users for solving their problems. Key activities of the knowledge acquisition process include the extraction, analysis, structuring and formalizing of knowledge.

We will now explain how the generic components of the UI architecture introduced in section 3 have been instantiated, and will outline ways in which they are specific to the knowledge acquisition process.

The task scheduler defines the knowledge acquisition tasks which must be performed by the knowledge engineer. In KEW the process of knowledge acquisition is guided by the model of problem solving which the target knowledge based system will adopt [6]. This model is used to decompose the ultimate goal of the knowledge acquisition into subgoals corresponding to specific KA tasks [7]. In the process step shown in figure 2 there are two independent tasks with the goals, respectively, *"Elicit domain knowledge for partition* `observable`*"*, and *"Elicit domain knowledge for partition* `solutions`*"*. It is up to the user to select which task he wants to engage in first.

Once a task has been selected, contextual information about the nature of the task is formulated. This includes the kind of knowledge to be acquired and the name of the knowledge base partition where the new knowledge will be stored.

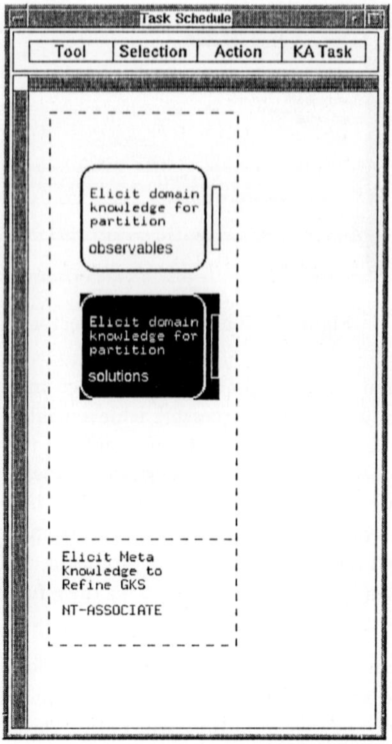

Figure 2: KEW task scheduler

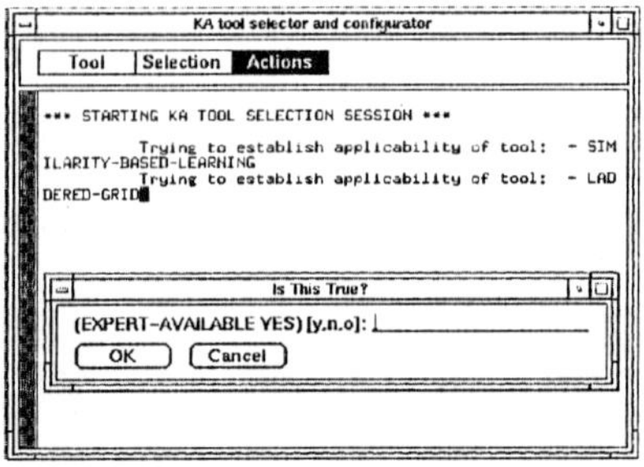

Figure 3: KEW activity selector

The contextual information can be exploited by the advice and guidance module to derive the most promising tools to apply for successful achievement of the task. Figure 3 shows how the A&G module asks for additional information from the user in order to refine its description of the KA process context. The system asks whether *a domain expert will be available* while carrying out the current KA task. This information is quite relevant, because some KA tools require intensive contributions from the expert [8],[9]. Another source of information used for selecting the most promising tools is knowledge about the tools (that are available in the workbench), such as their functions, the format of data they work on, and the format of data they produce.

Once the recommended tool has been identified, the knowledge engineer may decide to use it. This will generate a KA activity which specifies which KA tool will be involved, which input will be used, and which output will be produced. In addition the system will *configure* the activity in such a way that the knowledge acquired can be properly integrated into the target knowledge base. As mentioned in section 3 the intention of configuring activities is to ensure that the effect of the activity is consistent with the global goal of the process, and contributes to its achievement. Thus the *configuration* process may involve additional activities such as *transforming the knowledge acquired into a specific knowledge representation* or *integrating the knowledge acquired into an existing knowledge base partition.*

KA activities are stored in the agenda which is displayed in figure 4. The lower browser of the agenda (left of figure 4) displays the configuration of an activity (`P-CST-PLAN-1`) involving a tool called `CST`. This configuration has planned a transformation of the output of `CST` specified as activity `P-TRANSF-TOOL-PLAN-1`, followed by the intregration of the output into the target knowledge base specified as activity `P-KIT-PLAN-1`.

The upper browser of the agenda displays the current activities (those the knowledge engineer is presently performing). In the KEW session corresponding to this agenda two activities are carried out by the knowledge engineer, one involving the *ka-task-scheduler*, and the other involving *gdm-manipulator*.

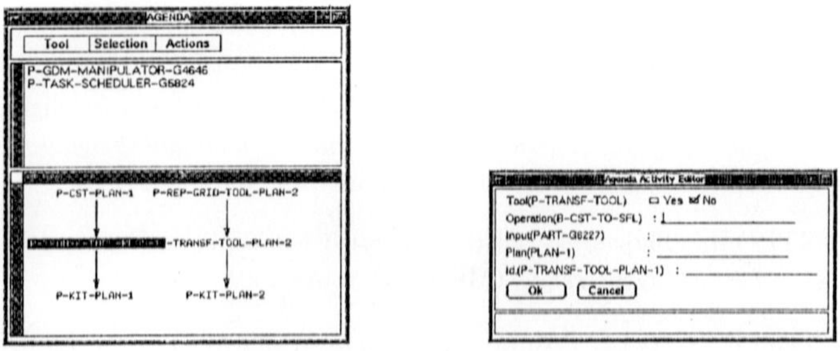

Figure 4: KEW agenda structure

5 Conclusion

In this paper we have shown that an intelligent user interface which supports complex processes could significantly enhance efficiency, particularly when these systems require intensive interaction with their users.

We have proposed a generic architecture for designing intelligent user interfaces, offering more user support for the process. This architecture includes four main components:
• a task scheduler that organizes the process at the highest level of abstraction
• an activity selector that determines details of how to achieve sub-tasks
• an activity configurer that adapts activities to satisfy the goals of the global process
• a process context modeler that provides an abstract description of the process state, and makes it available to the other components

We have stressed some properties that these components should exhibit to make the support more intelligent. We have pointed out the need to adapt the interaction to the profile of the user and to the specifics of the situation. In particular we need an explicit representation of the contextual information about the process and about the users goals.

This architecture has been adapted to fit the requirements of an advice and guidance module of the knowledge engineering workbench. This workbench has been developed within the ACKnowledge project, and is designed to support knowledge acquisition in the development of knowledge based systems.

Acknowledgement

Support for this work has been provided by the Commission of the European Communities under project P2576. The authors are grateful to Christer Fernstrom and Laurence Hubert for their valuable comments on earlier drafts of this paper. Special thanks to Gertjan Van Heijst who has greatly contributed to the development of KEW advice and guidance module.

References

[1] J.-C. MARTY, N. SHADBOLT, and B. WIELINGA, "The acknowledge project improving the knowledge acquisition process.," in *Results and Progress of ESPRIT Projects in 1989, XIII/416/89*, November 1989.

[2] C. FERNSTROM, "The eureka software factory: Concepts and accomplishments," in *Proceedings of ESEC Conference*, (Milan), October 1991.

[3] R. SPALL and R. STEELE, "An investigation into quantitative user modelling of user interactions for the purpose of predicting user expertise," in *Interact '90, Proceedings of the IPIP TC 13 Third International Conference on Human-Computer Interaction*, (Cambridge, U.K.), August 1990.

[4] J. JUNGER, G. BOUMA, and P. LETANOUX, "Intelligent user interface for a conventional program," in *Interact '90, Proceedings of the IPIP TC 13 Third International Conference on Human-Computer Interaction*, (Cambridge, U.K.), August 1990.

[5] F. RAMPARANY, M. ABEN, and L. SOLORZANO, "An integrated knowledge engineering workbench," in *Proc. of the IEEE conf. on Developing and Managing Expert System Programs*, (Washington, D.C.), pp. 170–177, September 30-October 2 1991.

[6] J. BREUKER, B. WIELINGA, M. V. SOMEREN, R. de HOOG, G. SCHREIBER, P. de GREEF, B. BREDEWEG, J. WIELIMAKER, J.-P. BILLAULT, M. DAVOODI, and S. HAYWARD, "Model driven knowledge acquisition: Interpretation models," task A1 D1, University of Amsterdam and STL Ltd, 1987.

[7] G. v. H. R. d. H. F. R. H. R. N. S. B. W. Peter Terpstra (editor), A. Anjewierden, "Ka process support in kew," Tech. Rep. ACK-UvA-A2-DEL-001, July 5, 1991.

[8] N. SHABOLT, "Knowledge elicitation - the key to successful expert systems," *Expert System User*, pp. 22–25, October 1988.

[9] A. BURTON, N. SHABOLT, G. RUGG, and A. HEDGECOCK, "Knowledge elicitation techniques in classification domains," in *Proceedings of the 8th European Conference on Artificial Intelligence*, (Munich, Germany), pp. 85–90, August 1-5 1988.

Personal Computers and Intelligent Systems / F.H. Vogt (Editor)
Information Processing 92, Volume III
Elsevier Science Publishers B.V. (North-Holland)

Using Metaphors to Enhance Intelligence in Information Systems: Rationale for an Alternative to Rule-Based Intelligence

Julie E. Kendall

School of Business, Rutgers University, Camden, NJ 08102, USA

Abstract

Metaphors are everywhere we look in the spoken and written language, and this ubiquity sometimes blinds the users of metaphors to their importance and potential for use in enriching the intelligence in new information systems. It is argued here that systems analysts and knowledge engineers not only model rule-based decisions, but that they should also model political, metaphor-based intelligence as well. Our understanding of the importance of metaphors, our advances in modeling capabilities, and worldwide changes in societies prompt the realization that the time has come to put different metaphors to use. The first recommendation is one of increasing analysts awareness of the importance of a multiplicity of metaphors being used by systems designers, experts and users. The second recommendation is to incorporate different, reactive metaphors such as organism, journey, war, zoo and jungle into intelligence in information systems. The third recommendation is to begin modeling how humans actually use metaphorical networks to solve complex problems.

Keyword Codes: I.2.0; K.4.2; K.3.2
Keywords: Artificial Intelligence, General; Computers and Society, Social Issues; Computers and Education, Computer and Information Science Education

1. INTRODUCTION

The methods and training currently open to knowledge engineers and systems analysts enable them to proceed in logical fashion in eliciting knowledge from experts in order to build rule-based systems (Harmon and King, 1985; Rich, 1983). The major metaphors entailed in these methods and subsequently built into the new information systems are those of the machine and the game.

The machine metaphor is perhaps the most widely-used and widely-acknowledged rule-based metaphor in information systems development. The metaphor of the machine is aptly characterized by thinking of its predictability. Equally important is the notion of a designer of the machine, who in some ways may believe in their own omniscience. The machine metaphor assumes that because each component is designed with a purpose, all events involving components should proceed smoothly. The machine metaphor exalts uniformity over creativity, praises the standard and predictable rather than the unique. Thus humans involved with the machine metaphor are considered as replaceable parts, just cogs in the wheel. Individuals are unimportant in their individual contributions, and only are valued if they contribute to the whole.

A second extremely common rule-based metaphor is that of the game. Those analysts using the traditional systems development life cycle are using the game metaphor (Kendall & Kendall, 1991) which emphasizes teamwork, a coach, and the importance of rules. In the game, rules are strictly observed, and if not, penalties ensue to the infringer. There is a coach whose reputation rises and falls with that of the team. All of the members work toward a common goal.

In addition to the machine and the game, there are other, less-frequently used, rule-based metaphors which should be considered for inclusion: organism, society, and the family. Additionally, there are many reactive metaphors including war, jungle, and zoo that are used to describe organizations by people in them, but are not acted on by analysts. Currently, it appears that analysts, perhaps unknowingly, limit the kinds of metaphors they use and incorporate into information systems.

Major organizational metaphors have been identified by Clancy (1989) and confirmed and extended by Kendall and Kendall (1990). Table 1 summarizes the main metaphors found, the environments in which they exist (order or chaos), and whether they are rule based or reactive.

2. MOVING BEYOND RULE-BASED METAPHORS

Based on the foregoing analysis of the problem, and on many different studies of metaphor usage done over the past twenty years (Boland, 1989; Kendall & Kendall, 1990 and 1991; Lanzara, 1983; Madsen, 1989; and Schon, 1979), it is clear that what needs to be done is to expand the cluster and connectivity of metaphors used by systems analysts and knowledge engineers in analysis, design and development of intelligence in information systems.

There are number of practical ways in which this can and should be done. First is that systems analysts need to be educated in the existence of the importance of considering multiple metaphors. The second is for systems analysts and knowledge engineers to consciously using methodologies to create intelligent information systems that enact metaphors that are not limited to those that are rule-based, but include a diversity of metaphors. The third way to address this need is much more long term and much more theoretical, that is to begin to work

Table 1
Organizational metaphors are anchored in different environments and thus differ in their rules and reactions

Metaphor	Environment	Comments regarding rules and reactions
Machine	Order	Rules specify how a machine operates
Game	Order	Rules govern how points are tallied and who wins
Society	Order	Rules decree what is not acceptable social behavior
Family	Order	Rules suggest how to act and compromise
Organism	Both	Rules govern growth while reactions nurture development
Journey	Chaos	Reactions suggest goal adjustments and weathering the storm
War	Chaos	Reactions imply killing the enemy
Zoo	Chaos	Reactions imply interacting with dissimilar entities
Jungle	Chaos	Reactions relate to survival

with linguists in determining the underlying structure of metaphorical thinking and strive to model metaphors' web of highly interconnected associations for inclusion in intelligent information systems.

3. EDUCATING ANALYSTS AND KNOWLEDGE ENGINEERS

Educating professionals who are still in school can take place during their regular courses of study in business, engineering, and computer science departments before students graduate. At a very basic level, students must be introduced to alternative metaphors such as the organism, the journey, war, society, family, zoo, and the jungle, which have been found to be prevalent in groups of information systems users and in alternative design methodologies (Kendall & Kendall, 1991).

It is recommended that students be instructed about what metaphors are and how they function, then asked to use them as a method for determining information requirements or as a method for knowledge elicitation as discussed in Kendall, (1991).

Briefly, this method gets students involved in determining key metaphors of experts and/or users during information requirements phases systems development. It uses metaphors along with more traditional approaches thus enlarging, rather than artificially narrowing, the scope of what is considered in designing a new system.

Educating professionals who have graduated is also important, given the pervasiveness of CASE tools and the rule-based metaphors that are being inculcated without a second thought. Seminars that discuss CASE tools can also discuss the metaphors that are implied by their use and offer analysts some expanded ways of thinking about problems of enhancing information systems that go beyond using workbench technologies. Some of the new Group Decision Support System software can be used to aid analysts in reframing their conceptualizations of what metaphors should compose the system.

4. USING METHODOLOGIES THAT OFFER ALTERNATIVES TO RULE-BASED METAPHORS

Many of the old methodologies, and several of the new methodologies available for systems analysts and knowledge engineers in CASE tools, are based on metaphors which are rule-based. These include the standard systems development life cycle which has its root in the game metaphor (Kendall & Kendall, 1991).

Analysts seeking to expand the types of intelligence included in new information systems would do well to consider using methodologies which depart from the game or machine metaphor. For example, this might include trying Checkland's soft system methodology which appears to have at its base a zoo metaphor; Mumford's ETHICS methodology that seems to have the family metaphor as its metaphorical underpinnings; and Avison and Wood-Harpers' Multiview, which has appears to use the root metaphor society (Kendall & Kendall, 1991).

It is suggested here that use of these and other development methodologies based on alternative metaphors will help analysts and knowledge engineers reframe the situations being experienced. By allowing analysts to conceptualize problems in new ways, and not to become trapped in the necessity of reducing all system intelligence to a series of rules, they will go beyond simply reproducing rule-based intelligence for information systems to thinking of promising alternatives.

5. MODELING METAPHORICAL NETWORKS

In seeking to determine the underlying structure of metaphorical thinking, linguists, systems analysts, knowledge engineers and information systems researchers will be working cooperatively to model the web of highly interconnected relationships that metaphors use. This is a challenge that must be met with a broad-based interdisciplinary approach if computer-based metaphorical associations are to have the look and feel of human metaphorical use.

What must be conveyed to researchers and practitioners is the importance and usefulness of including metaphorical associations, (beyond rule-based metaphors), in intelligent systems. It is suggested that the mere act of recognizing multiple metaphors and their associations will help researchers to reconceptualize systems and their approaches in new ways. One way to begin is to attempt to tap into the work that is already being done on neural networks (Tank and Hopfield, 1987), which, at least superficially, seem to away to start thinking about how networks of metaphors interconnect.

Another way to proceed is to implement experiments with development teams, providing them with overarching metaphors within which to develop new systems. For example, using a desktop metaphor as the pervasive metaphor, developers at Apple Computers came up with the Macintosh which eventually revolutionized the use of screens and iconography of PC-based information systems. It proved to be a persuasive and meaningful metaphor for the users of many systems that followed and copied the Macintosh. Other metaphors may work better for development and use at different times in an organization's culture, phase in its life cycle, or even during a country's particular point in history.

A third way to proceed is on a more theoretical level, that is first collecting, then classifying and finally providing a taxonomy of metaphors and the subsequent metaphors which they most frequently entail. This is work that is partially begun in psychology and organization science (Morgan, 1986) but now for the first time we have a common interest in intelligent systems to pull together diverse disciplines in a collective effort to determine what metaphors are, how they function, how they can be modeled, and how they can be embodied in new systems.

6. IMPLICATIONS OF USING METAPHORS IN INTELLIGENT SYSTEMS

Much is changing quite rapidly. We must not let this opportunity to improve and enhance the intelligence in our systems pass unnoticed. There is a peculiar urgency in trying to explore alternative metaphors and bring them to bear in developing new systems.

One reason for this pressure is that there appears to be widespread and almost unquestioning adoption of CASE tools to create new systems. Although it is too early to judge this as a negative development, it should be noted that most CASE tools are built upon rule-based metaphors such as the game. One implication that must be drawn from the foregoing discussion is that the game is but one metaphor necessary to face a changing world. A modest assessment is that rule-based metaphors are not the best ones for developing systems in all situations. In order to enhance the intelligence in our systems we must begin and extend the work on several different aspects of metaphors.

Organizations and societies worldwide are in greater flux than we have seen in the past seventy years. These changes cannot be adequately addressed by one metaphor repeatedly used to design and characterize our information systems. Rather, world changes are better acknowledged through use of multiple metaphors, modeled in useful ways, and included in new information systems with interfaces that have the look and feel of the way people use metaphors productively every day.

Modeling techniques have advanced to the point where discussions of modeling metaphorical networks for use in intelligent systems is no longer merely theoretical speculation. Researchers must see that modeling metaphors is difficult but important work whose time has come. The rewards for creative expansion beyond use of single, unrelated metaphors will be great.

The convergence of new tools, world change, and advanced modeling capabilities have put researchers and practitioners in an excellent position to improve the intelligence in new information systems through expanded use of metaphors for analysis, design and application.

7. CONCLUSION

In conclusion, after recognizing the usefulness of metaphors in expanding the intelligence of information systems, there are several tangible ways of proceeding that must be contemplated. The first is awareness that using many metaphors, rather than limiting oneself to one or two metaphors that underpin traditional and CASE methodologies, will help analysts and users to reframe the problem in new ways. Using different design methodologies with alternative metaphors can move the analyst toward improving the intelligence encapsulated in a new system.

A second way to proceed is to actually incorporate different metaphors into the "logic" of the systems themselves. So that rather than having intelligent systems grounded exclusively in rule-based metaphors, the analyst and knowledge engineer may seek to develop systems that include reactive metaphors such as the organism, journey, war, zoo, or jungle.

Thirdly, we may seek to model the ways that humans use metaphors to help them problem solve. In essence, this means using one root metaphor to resonate associated metaphors which in turn help inform users about otherwise obscure situations. This will be accomplished by making accessible the new intelligence that comes from illuminating the interrelationships and interconnections of large networks of metaphors. Multiple metaphors can be productively introduced into development methodologies, participation in user- analyst systems design, and applications of new information systems to enhance intelligence in all phases of systems practice.

8. REFERENCES

Boland, R. J., Jr. (1989) Metaphorical traps in developing information systems for human progress. In H.K. Klein and K. Kumar (Eds.), *Systems development for human progress* (pp.277-290). New York: North Holland.

Clancy, J. J. (1989) *The invisible powers; the language of business*. Lexington, MA: Lexington Books.

Harmon, P. and King, D. (1985) *Expert systems*. New York: John Wiley & Sons, Inc.

Kendall, J.E. (1991) Using Metaphors for Knowledge Elicitation During Expert Systems Development, *Proceedings of the First International Meeting of the Decision Sciences Institute*, Brussels.

Kendall, J.E. and K.E. Kendall (1990) Existence of predominant organizational metaphors and their implications for information systems development, working paper, University of Cambridge.

Kendall, J.E. and K.E. Kendall (1991) Metaphors and methodologies: Living beyond the systems machine, working paper, University of Cambridge.

Lanzara, G.F. (1983) The design process: Frames, metaphors, and games. In U. Briefs, C. Ciborra and L. Schneider (Eds.), *Systems design for, with and by the users* (pp. 29-40). New York: North Holland Publishing Company.

Madsen, K. H. (1989) Breakthrough by breakdown: Metaphors and structured domains. In H.K. Klein and K. Kumar (Eds.), *Systems development for human progress* (pp. 41-53). New York: North Holland.

Morgan, G. (1986) *Images of organizations*. Beverly Hills: Sage Publications.

Rich, E. (1983) *Artificial intelligence*. New York: McGraw-Hill.

Schon, D. (1979) Generative metaphor: A perspective on problem setting in social policy (254-283). In A. Ortony (Ed.) *Metaphor and thought*. Cambridge, U.K.: Cambridge University Press.

Tank, D.W. and Hopfield, J. J. (1987) Collective computation in neuronlike circuits. *Scientific American*, October.

Personal Computers and Intelligent Systems / F.H. Vogt (Editor)
Information Processing 92, Volume III
Elsevier Science Publishers B.V. (North-Holland)

The Formalization Of Knowledge-Based Systems Validation And Verification: Promises And Pitfalls

Erik Hollnagel

Principal Scientist, Ph. D.,
Computer Resources International A/S, Space Division, Bregnerødvej 144, DK-3460 Birkerød, Denmark

Abstract
The growing practical application of knowledge-based systems (KBS) has increased the need for reliable and efficient verification and validation (V&V). This paper discusses the use of formal methods and specifications as a solution to the need. It is argued that the use of formal methods is based on a number of assumptions which, on closer inspection, are very similar to the assumptions underlying informal methods. Caution in the use of formal methods is therefore advised. The paper describes the EPSRIT project VIVA which aims to improve KBS V&V by enlarging the range of V&V functions and increase the scope of application to all steps in the KBS life-cycle. This approach complements the use of more demanding formal methods.

Keyword Codes: I.2, D.2.4
Keywords: ARTIFICIAL INTELLIGENCE, Program Verification

1. INTRODUCTION

As the use of Knowledge-Based Systems (KBS) or expert systems is steadily growing and spreading into new areas, so is the need to insure that a given KBS actually performs as it should. As long as KBS were used either in large scale research programmes as demonstrations of what information technology and computers might eventually achieve or in relatively small and uncritical applications, the needs for explicit Validation and Verification (V&V) were manageable - and in most cases performed in a rather perfunctory way. But with the increasing (planned or actual) application of KBSs in industrial size problems the need for a proper V&V must be taken very seriously. If a KBS is integrated in an industrial application, it may well be critical for the safe and efficient functioning of the system. Every precaution must therefore be taken to ensure that the functioning of the KBS is adequate. One way of doing that is to perform a thorough V&V of the KBS before it is being used.

For those who know how difficult it is to perform V&V for "conventional" software systems the prospect of doing something similar for KBSs is indeed a daunting task. During the last half of the 1980es there have been long and heated discussions about the nature of KBSs - in particular about whether a KBS could be seen as similar to a "conventional" software system or whether it was a different beast altogether. Although this issue probably not has been resolved to everybody's satisfaction, the consensus seems to be that KBSs can indeed be treated as other software systems, in particular with regard to guidelines for development and implementation.

2. TERMINOLOGY

Verification and validation are terms which have a general usage, and they are therefore easily understood by most people. The disadvantage of this is that they terms may be understood in very different ways by different people - even within a technical sub-field such as software engineering. The denotations may be well-defined but the connotations may be many and varied.

The "classical" definition, attributed to [1], refers to the distinction between building the right system versus building it the right way. Validation is the process of determining whether the system is the right system; verification is the process of determining whether the system has been built in the right way, i.e., according to specifications. This notion has been formalised further by the IEEE, which has provided the following definitions for the key terms:

> **Verification**: the process of determining whether or not the products of a given phase of software development meet all the requirements established during the previous phase.
>
> **Validation**: the process of evaluating software at the end of the development process to ensure compliance with software requirements.

Regardless of whether one accepts this definition in full, it is important because it identifies the requirements as the basis for the validation and verification. The definition could probably be made even more precise by distinguishing between the requirements and the specifications; validation would then refer to the requirements, whereas verification would refer to the specifications. This is in good agreement with Boehm's notions of building the right system versus building it in the right way.

The objection sometimes raised against this definition is that it assumes the development follows the well-known waterfall model. The basis for the objection is that the development of KBSs may not comply with the waterfall model, and that the definitions therefore are inapplicable. But the definitions really refer only to the case where one phase or stage follows another, i.e., where one does not go into work helter-skelter.

From a pragmatic point of view there will always be a stage of specification before a stage of implementation. The specification may be more or less explicit, but unless the implementation is guided by Divine inspiration - which in the case of software development is an unreliable foundation - there will necessarily be some kind of specification which then can serve as the basis for the following verification. Regardless of whether the overall development method matches the waterfall model or is a more iterative prototyping process, there will always be a "local" coupling between phases of specification and phases of implementation. It is, in fact, highly desirable that the specification is made as explicit as possible, and software development without specifications should be strongly discouraged.

Another way of defining the terms refers to a distinction between the various people who are involved in the building of a KBS: the Customer and the Builder [2]. The Customer is the person who is the future user of the system (and presumably also the one who pays for it); the main objective of the customer is to get a good product, i.e., to get the right system. The Builder is the person who actually creates the system; the Builder therefore usually includes several distinct roles such as the domain expert, the knowledge engineer, and the software engineer. The main goal of the Builder is to produce a system that performs correctly. In terms of the definitions the notion is that the Customer performs the validation by examining the behaviour of the system whereas the Builder performs the verification of the KBS by examining the syntactic properties. Although this definition approaches the terms from a different angle, it is in good agreement with the ones discussed above. It adds the dimension of different types of users which may be important when the notion of the Validation Knowledge is introduced below.

3. Verification: Formal Specifications And Formal Methods

One of the main problems with V&V is that it cannot be achieved by an algorithmic solution. The V&V of a KBS does not have an algorithmic solution but demands AI-based or KBS-based approaches. A proper procedure for KBS V&V must take into account the different nature of KBSs and their strong dependence on the application area, the different KBS development styles (life-cycle models), and the fact that many KBSs are used in hybrid systems. The verification might, in principle be achieved by applying a pre-defined set of procedures or heuristics - and the application of these could conceivably be automatic. If the specifications were provided by means of a formal representation, then the checking of whether they were met by the implemented system could, in principle, be done without human intervention. In practice, however, the problems are beyond the scope of automation as we can achieve it at present.

Validation, on the other hand, clearly requires an approach which goes beyond algorithms. Because validation addresses the problem of whether the system is the right one, the process of validation is based on interpretation; interpretation of the requirements as well as interpretation of the system's performance. Despite all the promises and advances of AI, automatic interpretation is still a dream. I shall discuss the interpretation problem of validation in the section on Validation Knowledge (cf. below).

Turning towards verification one tempting solution lies in the notion of formal specifications and formal methods. The appeal of formal specifications is that they can be expressed using classical logic. Take, for instance, the specification that "the arity of the attribute LEGS is four". Arity is defined as the maximum number of a value for a given instance; the example is, of course, true for mammals only - with some notable exceptions. The verbal statement is usually considered to be an informal specification, but it can be also expressed as:

$$\forall\ O \in \text{FactBase},\ \text{Cardinal}\ (\{v,\ \text{LEGS}(O) = v\}) \leq 4 \qquad (1)$$

in which case it is considered to be a formal specification. That it is expressed in classical logic is in itself of little importance. The important thing is that because the specification can be expressed in classical logic, then a number of other things are taken for granted. For instance, that it is possible to prove that an expression in classical logic is true or false because classical logic is complete and consistent. Furthermore, that it is possible to do this in an algorithmic manner because classical logic is decidable. Unlike informal specifications, and other types of expression, a formal specification is self-contained; it does not refer to anything else. Classical logic constitutes the basis and therefore also provides a set of powerful methods and procedures. That, at least, is the general assumption.

The translation from the informal specification to the formal specification is usually not trivial and not all informal specifications can be turned into a formal specification. An example is the informal specification "on-line explanations must be adequate." This could be put as a specification to the system, and even as a requirement, but the problem is how it is possible to determine whether it has been achieved.

One solution is to define an **operational measure** which can be applied to the specification. We may, for instance, define "on-line explanations" as the explanations that are given by the system under certain well-defined circumstances; these may be divided into passive explanations given on request, active explanations given when the system detects a need, explanations of overall features, explanations of specific parts of the reasoning, etc. It is important to describe the criteria that are used to define "on-line explanations." Similarly, the term "adequate" may be defined as meaning, for instance, that the user is satisfied with the explanation in at least 80% of the cases, or that the user does not ask for additional explanations but rather returns to the task. (It is further assumed that there is a way to determine whether or not the user was satisfied with an explanation.)

In this way the informal specification "on-line explanations must be adequate" can be represented as:

$$E_s(P)\ /\ E_t(P) >= 0.80 \qquad (2)$$

where

E_s is the number of satisfactory explanations in situations of type P, and

E_t is the total number of explanations in situations of type P.

Consider now what the difference is between expression (1) and expression (2). Expression (1) is considered as an expression in classical logic and the truth or falsehood of the expression can therefore be determined in a closed form, i.e., totally within the system. Expression (2) is seen as referring to external events and therefore depends on other operations, i.e., the truth or falsehood cannot be determined in a closed form: some kind of interdependence or interaction is necessary. Yet the difference is really not so great.

In both cases the correctness of the expression can be ascertained by a simple algorithmic process which consists of either finding the value {v, LEGS(O) = v} for all objects of type O in the FactBase and then compare it with the number 4, or finding the value of E_s and E_t in the database of events for situations P, calculating the ratio, and comparing it with 0.80. In both cases a number of more elementary operations are involved, but these are assumed to be an integral part of the system, hence reliable and available. On this level there is therefore little difference between the two expressions.

If we consider the objects of the operations, there is a clear difference between expression (1) and expression (2). In the first case one object is {v, LEGS(O) = v} which refers to an entity (a slot value) in the FactBase. LEGS(O) in turn refers to a fact which at some time and in some way has been entered into the FactBase. How this has happened seems to be irrelevant for the operations that are part of expression (1). On the other hand, E_t is defined as the total number of events of type E for situations P, whereas E_s is the accumulated number of events (of type E for situations P) which are marked as "satisfactory"; this mark can in itself be a symbol associated with the event representation. Neither E_t nor E_s are part of the FactBase, hence not part of the KBS either. In that sense they are externally derived values and depend on external operations. But given that these operations can be defined algorithmically, there is really no principal difference in the way the verification takes place.

The difference between the formal and informal specifications as well as between formal and informal methods is therefore a matter of degree of elaboration. The closed system of classical logic is only closed at a certain level of elaboration. If we move beyond that considering, for instance, how the values of LEGS(O) were introduced in the system, then we must refer to external operations, and the formal method is no longer different from the operations by which the informal specification is verified. The operations that go into determining the values of e.g. E_s and E_t may, in principle, continue *ad infinitum* - although in practice they will stop pretty soon. The importance is really whether the outcome is open to interpretation or not. The less ambiguity, the more formality.

If the desired value can be measured reliably, then a specification such as $E_s(P) / E_t(P) >= 0.80$ can be applied exactly. Either the value is higher or equal than .80 or it is lower. This in itself can be determined with full certainty. It is only if the value is known with uncertainty (e.g. upper and lower bounds) or if the data behind it are open to interpretation (a distance from the raw data to the constructed measurement) that informal method breaks down. The value of LEGS(O) has the convenient feature of always being a positive integer, hence the uncertainty is neglected. But it is there, nevertheless. Determining what the number of legs is involves some operations (observation and counting) and the outcome may be wrong. The formalized concept makes it look as if is a datum, but establishing that datum, hence instantiating the test, requires operations - by the machine, by the user, or by both together. The uncertainty that was suspected in the informal approach can therefore creep in the formal approach as well.

4. VALIDATION: REQUIREMENTS, INTERPRETATION, AND SEMANTICS

There general view seems to be that validation deals with the semantics or the meaning of KBS or of what it purports to do, while verification deals with the syntax, i.e. whether the rules have been applied properly and consistently, whether the inference engine works properly, etc. It is often assumed that the syntax can be checked by the system itself if it is given a set of principles to do it by - although this introduces a dangerous element of recursion, because these principles would have to be validated themselves. As I argued in the preceding section, this is not always as simple a matter as it may seem.

The semantics, however, clearly require that some kind of interpretation is made. In most cases this interpretation is provided by a human expert in the form of the so-called **Validation Knowledge**. A considerable number of the systems described in e.g. [2] do, in fact, imply and require the assistance of a human expert - either to provide the basis for the validation or as the final arbiter when discrepancies have been found. This does raise the additional question of how much of the validation is performed by machine and how much by hand.

The validation is concerned with determining whether the system is the right system, and / or whether the outcome of using the system is the expected outcome. This implies that the results must be compared against something else. Therefore either the results must be interpreted or the "something else" must be the result of an interpretation. That something else can either be general knowledge that must be appropriate for the KBS in question, or specific knowledge that refers to the application. The former may be called the **Conceptual Model** (the C-model) and the latter the Validation Knowledge.

4.1 The Conceptual Model

As an example of the Conceptual Model consider the situation where we may want to check the properties of a set of facts in the KB, to determine whether they are incoherent. We may have the following set of facts:

X is_a rectangle *and* breadth_of X > length_of X

The result of applying the conceptual model to this would be that the facts were incoherent. The incoherence arises because a rectangle always is longer than it is broad; or conversely, that the longest side always denotes the length while the shortest side always denotes the breadth. A more complex example would be:

room(X) & area(X) = 40 m^2 & length(X) = 6 m

In this case there would also be incoherence between the facts. The conceptual model would contain the fact, or the definition, that {breadth_of X < length_of X}. Since this would be something that applied to all rectangles, the fact would not be kept in the application KB.

An other example is the following:

o There are three children in a line.

o At least one child is a boy and at least one child is a girl.

o Does a boy stand next to a girl?

Formal reasoning systems are defeated when called upon to make an inference of this nature. But it can easily be solved by humans because they have access to additional knowledge - the Validation Knowledge.

The conceptual model will in general contain the common sense facts that must be obeyed by the application KB (and rule base) and it is therefore necessary for the validation process. If the conceptual model is incomplete or missing it is the evaluator's task to define the required facts. In terms of efficiency, and ultimately also reliability, it would be preferable if the conceptual model was defined independent of the specific application - although, of course, relative to the class of applications (since there otherwise would be not natural limitation on the facts that should be included in the conceptual model).

Constructing the conceptual model is a task that takes time and can involve considerable resources. The advantage of the conceptual model is that the facts it contains can be validated by a processes of consensus of domain experts. To take the example of the rectangle, if there was disagreement about the appropriateness of this fact, it would be a simple matter to change the definition. In cases like this the important thing is that the definition is agreed to between the experts, rather that it is correct in an absolute sense.

4.2 Validation Knowledge

The notion of Validation Knowledge means that the human evaluator (the customer, the expert) provides the examples of what a correct outcome of the system should be, hence defines the semantics of the system. It also serves to focus the validation on important aspects, defined as those which might lead to serous unwanted consequences if they fail. The main problem in V&V is to determine the meaning of what the system does, i.e., whether the solutions reached are indeed the right solutions. This is evident from broad definitions of validity to mean e.g. "the ability to find a legal solution to any problem which deserves it" [3]. In general, a solution is right if it complies with the system requirements. It is, however, not a simple matter to determine if this is the case. Unlike system specifications, system requirements are usually described by means of informal concepts or by means of concepts that refer to the operating conditions and the operating context. The requirements can therefore not easily be brought on a form which is amenable to systematic treatment. An additional problem is that for each question or set of input given to the system there may be several solutions i.e., the chaining or the tree may produce multiple results. The system will not itself be able to determine which of these results is the correct one or which of them is the better solution. Furthermore, if the correctness of the results could be determined on a purely syntactic basis then it would require that all the rules and facts in the system had been proven correct. But if this was possible a KBS would by definition not be needed in the first place.

Describing the requirements is an act of interpretation and matching the outcome with the requirements is another act of interpretation. The effort is to make the matching as strict as possible; this may be a feasible undertaking if the basis for comparison has been established. It is this basis which is referred to as the Validation Knowledge. The Validation Knowledge could, for instance, describe the effects of specific events in the real application (error modes or fault modes) as well as the event or failure itself. The Validation Knowledge would, in other words, define the expected outcome, and that definition would be based on an understanding of the specific requirements. (It would clearly be in addition to the Conceptual Model discussed above.)

It would naturally be preferable if the results could be matched directly to the requirements. But to achieve that one needs an automated semantic analysis. This leads head-on to the problem that is known from natural language processing: a computational semantics is only possible if the context is defined (which in a sense makes the whole thing syntactical again). Yet determining the context is an order of magnitude beyond what we can achieve or perhaps even grasp. It is therefore necessary to use Validation Knowledge as an intermediate solution, i.e., to include the user as a semantic interpreter in the task. Although it may not bring the much wanted revolution to KBS V&V it will significantly enlarge what can be done computationally. It does, ultimately, leave the semantic (= validation) problem unsolved and untouched because the interpretation is deferred to a system which cannot itself be checked.

The validation knowledge serves to determine whether the KBS's reasoning is correct. It might be warranted to assume that the reasoning was correct if the reasoning was restricted to elementary logic, because the mechanization of this type of logic is a trivial matter and the very foundation for digital computers. The experience from other software systems nevertheless suggests that errors may occur and remain hidden for long periods of time even in fundamental logical or arithmetic functions. Moving on to other and more sophisticated types of logic and reasoning, as required by various types of inference engines, will almost certainly introduce failures - simply because the programs (the rule interpreters and their control) are written by fallible humans.

A KBS basically carries out its reasoning following a set of rules or procedures but the underlying logic of the reasoning is difficult to externalize and to comprehend. One problem is that it may be difficult to establish test cases where one can define what the right reasoning is. And testing by making sure that each rule has been fired at least once does not contribute much to substantiate the chains of inference. Evaluating decision alternatives is different from logical deduction and syllogistic reasoning, and even here, as many psychological experiments have demonstrated, people are very bad at reasoning in a consistent way if the problem is only moderately complex [4]. There is consequently no basis to believe that they will do better in understanding how a complex reasoning mechanism works. We therefore seem to be trapped in an impasse: reasoning mechanisms are introduced to compensate for the shortcomings of human reasoning, but these very shortcomings make it extremely difficult to determine whether the reasoning mechanisms work correctly. The problem of proving and evaluating the correctness of the reasoning obviously gets harder the more difficult it is for the user to understand the functioning of the system, i.e., the less transparent the KBS is.

5. VIVA

A number of projects have addressed the problem of V&V of KBS, either as joint research projects or as activities within individual organizations. There is, however, still a clear need to provide an integrated and powerful V&V tool-set, supported by a method for application, which can be used for industrial sized KBSs, which can be applied at various stages during the system life-cycle. The recently started ESPRIT Project 6125 VIVA (Validation, Interpretation, and Verification of Knowledge-based Systems) has the purpose to provide such a toolset.

Most V&V tools require specific application knowledge to be applied; VIVA will provide a systematic approach to the identification of the knowledge required by these tools, but will not perform an automatic translation. In VIVA, the actual V&V tools will be supplemented by tools which assist in the interpretation of the results as well as in the refinement/improvement of the KBSs being analyzed. VIVA will also provide a Common Knowledge Representation (CKR) to serve as an intermediate knowledge representation for the purpose of V&V. The CKR will make use of existing common knowledge representation formalisms and developing standards.

The VIVA project is driven by user application needs rather than by formal issues of V&V and proof of functioning (e.g. provably correct systems). The purpose of the VIVA project is to develop a set of tools and the associated VIVA method for the V&V of KBSs. The VIVA Toolset and method will support a user in the following tasks:

- o select and follow a suitable KBS development paradigm (life-cycle model);
- o select V&V tools appropriate for each stage in the life-cycle;
- o elicit the specific application knowledge ("Validation Knowledge") required for some of the selected tool(s);
- o carry out V&V of the relevant aspects of the KBS by applying the selected tools to the Common Knowledge Representation;

- o investigate and advise on the cause of any noted discrepancies or anomalies; and
- o carry out necessary refinements of the knowledge.

The project will provide a comprehensive toolset comprising both adaptations of existing tools and newly developed tools. The toolset will be developed using the software engineering standards of the European Space Agency. It will include tools that allow off-line V&V (static + dynamic checking) and on-line V&V (testing), as well as interpretation (finding causes of anomalies) and refinement (changing to remove anomalous effects). The project will also produce and deliver a VIVA method which will enable the user to choose the right tool for the purpose throughout the KBS life-cycle.

The toolset will be developed and tested using applications mainly from the aerospace area as test cases. The applications will represent systems at various stages of development. The toolset is aimed at KBS design rather than post-event analyses. The toolset is not primarily intended to serve as a metrication / quantification tool, although it is possible that pertinent feedback may be obtained from using some of the VIVA tools in this way.

SUMMARY

In the field of KBS V&V the need to develop improved methods is notable. There are two aspects of this need: firstly, to be able to improve the quality of KBS V&V, i.e., to be able to increase the scope of the V&V process as well as the reliability of the outcome; secondly, to improve the efficiency of the V&V process, i.e., making it easier to perform and by making the V&V procedure more reliable in itself.

The need can partly be seen as the issue of depth and breadth of KBS V&V. The premise is that the V&V necessarily must be of limited scope - like most other analyses e.g. of risk and reliability - simply because exhaustive analyses of even moderately complex systems are practically impossible. Verification is capable of going into breadth, e.g. looking for consistencies, contradictions in a chain of reasoning, etc. throughout the KBS. The restriction is that verification can only look for well-defined problems or relations, and this may limit the depth. Validation, on the other hand, more goes into depth. The validation is clearly of limited scope from the start - it does not address the whole system but selected aspects of its performance as defined e.g. through the validation knowledge. On the other hand, validation should aim to be exhaustive in investigating these aspects. The breadth therefore depends more on the preceding analyses which specify the foci, than on the validation itself.

A good answer to the practical need would be a V&V procedure which achieved both breadth and depth. The strength of current V&V methods is that they are very powerful when used with a precise target, but less useful when used without a clear idea of what one wants to address or achieve. As any other highly specialised tool V&V methods must be used knowingly - not necessarily by an expert, but certainly by a person who has a specific purpose in mind and who is trying to solve a precise or specific problem. The quality of the outcome is therefore to a large extent determined by the quality of the preceding identification of V&V foci. The promises or attractions of formal specifications and formal methods are that they seem to achieve an increase in depth and breadth at the same time: the formal specifications increase the depth while the formal methods increase the breadth. The reliance on formal specifications and formal methods is, however, a mixed blessing. The seemingly unambiguous representation language may be misleading because the semantics are hidden by the syntax. The formal methods appear to be self-contained but the dependence on the C-model and the validation knowledge remains. Formal methods are only closed if the assumptions behind them obtain. Too strong a faith in formal methods is therefore a pitfall. The real world is much too unwieldy to yield to the assumptions of formalisms - whatever they are.

A more pragmatic solutions is the emergence of a coherent and integrated approach as demonstrated by VIVA project. Rather than relying on the strength of formalisms *per se*, VIVA will extend both the range of V&V functions - from capture of validation requirements to interpretation and refinement - and the scope of application, to cover different steps in the KBS life-cycle. Solutions of this nature recognise the practical needs and can therefore supplement the efforts to improve the power of a more rigorous formal approach to KBS V&V.

ACKNOWLEDGMENTS

The work described in this paper is sponsored by the CEC DG-XIII through ESPRIT project 6125: VIVA. The VIVA project is carried out by a consortium consisting of CRI A/S (DK), CISI Ingenierie (F), European Space Agency (NL), Lloyd's Register (UK), Logica Cambridge (UK), University of Abderdeen (UK), and University of Chambery (F). The support of the CEC and the exchange of ideas with the partners in the consortium is gratefully acknowledged.

REFERENCES

1 Boehm, B, W. Veryfying and Validating Software Requirements and Design Specifications. *IEEE Software*, *1*(1), 75-89, 1984.

2 Ayel, M. & Laurent, J.-P. (Eds.) *Validation, verification and test of knowledge-based systems*. Chichester: John Wiley & Sons, (1991).

3 Mazas, P. Design knowledge validation through experimentation: The SYSIFE system. In M. Ayel & J.-P. Laurent (Eds.) *Validation, verification and test of knowledge-based systems*. Chichester: John Wiley & Sons, (1991).

4 Wason, P. C. & Johnson-Laird, P. N. *Psychology of reasoning*. B. T. Batsford, Ltd, 1972.

Personal Computers and Intelligent Systems / F.H. Vogt (Editor)
Information Processing 92, Volume III
Elsevier Science Publishers B.V. (North-Holland)

Verifying knowledge-based systems using the COVER tool

A. D. Preece[†], R. D. Bell[‡] and C. Y. Suen[†]

[†]Centre for Pattern Recognition and Machine Intelligence, Concordia University, 1455 de Maisonneuve West, Montréal, Canada H3G 1M8 (email preece@cenparmi.concordia.ca)

[‡]Network Operations, Bell Canada, 100 Dundas Street, London, Canada N6A 4L6

Abstract

Knowledge-based systems (KBS) are complex software systems; they must be evaluated thoroughly to ensure their reliability. Many faults in KBS can be revealed by checking for logical anomalies in the knowledge bases of these systems. Such anomalies include redundant, conflicting or missing knowledge, and can be detected automatically and efficiently by a knowledge base verification tool. This paper describes the COVER knowledge base verification tool, emphasizing those features which are designed to make COVER practical for use in real-world KBS projects. Use of COVER is illustrated by examples from the verification of a large KBS for telephone switch maintenance.
Keyword Codes: I.2.1
Keywords: Artificial Intelligence Applications and Expert Systems

1. KNOWLEDGE-BASED SYSTEMS VERIFICATION

A knowledge-based system (KBS) is a type of software system that uses an explicit representation of a body of real-world knowledge—the knowledge base (KB)—to solve complex problems. In recent years, many KBSs have entered routine use in a wide variety of domains. As with all complex software, KBSs must be evaluated thoroughly to ensure their quality and reliability; however, many of the evaluation techniques of conventional software cannot be applied easily to KBSs [7]. Conventionally, much of software evaluation consists of *empirical testing*: feeding inputs to the system and comparing the system outputs with the required outputs. Although most KBSs undergo such testing, there are a number of difficulties. For example, a minimum requirement for testing conventional procedural software is that each path through the system (defined by the branching of control statements) is exercised. For a complex KBS, there will usually be far too many paths to meet this requirement [5].

The important part of the KBS evaluation activity is ensuring the reliability of the KB. Typically, this is the only complete formal specification of the functionality of the system; therefore, its correctness and completeness cannot be formally checked against any higher-level specification. However, its own self-correctness and self-completeness should be checked: this is the verification process for KBSs. Manual verification of a complex KB is error-prone; therefore, an automatic verification tool is desirable.

2. THE COVER VERIFICATION TOOL

COVER is a KB verification tool which combines ideas from previous verification tools [2, 4, 8] with a number of novel features [6]. COVER checks KBs consisting of rules and facts written in a generic rule language. So far, application KBs written in a variety of different commercial knowledge representation languages have proven straightforward to convert into the extensible language checked by COVER. COVER has been used experimentally to verify five real-world application KBs, and has lead to the detection of faults in each; the most substantial of these experiments is described later in this paper.

COVER is used interactively by KBS builders to check KBs in various stages of completeness. When used this early in development, it becomes part of the knowledge acquisition process, highlighting needs for more knowledge and checking the specification of the existing knowledge. It can also be used during KB maintenance, to detect if faults arise from system modifications.

The representation language checked by COVER is rule-based and is a subset of predicate logic. It is powerful enough to capture the rule and frame expressions of several commercial knowledge representation languages.

The basic knowledge statement is a *rule*, in form equivalent to a Horn clause in first order logic: a single unnegated literal in the consequent, a conjunction of literals in the antecedent (disjunctive antecedents are handled using separate rule expressions). Rules with empty antecedents are called *facts*, and are used to represent declarative information such as primitive data items and relations (such as "frame-like" taxonomies).

COVER assumes negation-by-failure. A restriction currently imposed on literals is that only a single level of predicate nesting is allowed within a literal; that is, the literal $\mathtt{P}(\mathtt{Q}(x,y),z)$ is allowed, but $\mathtt{P}(\mathtt{Q}(x,\mathtt{R}(y)),z)$ is not (this restriction prevents the creation of infinite data structures).

COVER is only able to check the *logic* of the KBs. This means that some of the features of commercial rule languages are ignored by COVER. For example, a useful practical feature is the ability to perform procedural tasks as side-effects of firing a rule. The following rule is written in the Level 5 expert system shell rule language. If it succeeds, it assigns the value *true* to the boolean fact COM_PWR_CCT_PROB. As side-effects, it also displays a screen of text associated with the identifier REPLACE_QPC85.

```
IF FLOW8A_FUSE IS NO
AND FLOW8A_VOLTAGES IS NO
AND FLOW8A_REPL_CONV IS YES
THEN COM_PWR_CCT_PROB
AND DISPLAY REPLACE_QPC85
```

COVER ignores such side-effects; it considers only the logical meaning of the rules. In other words, it considers the rules as having the sole purpose of establishing some value for the data item (or items) appearing in the conclusion.

2.1. Checks performed by COVER

COVER detects logical *anomalies* in a KB—these are unusual structures that suggest the presence of faults. By detecting the anomalies and presenting them to its users,

COVER leads to the detection and elimination of subtle logical errors in KBs. COVER detects four types of anomaly: redundancy, ambivalence, circularity, and deficiency. Each of these is discussed below (more formal definitions appear in [6]); real-world examples follow in Section 3.

Redundancy A KB contains redundancy if there are expressions within it that are not necessary to the inferring of any conclusions by the KBS. For example, in the propositional logic KB

$p \rightarrow q \qquad q \rightarrow r \qquad p \rightarrow r,$

expression $p \rightarrow r$ is redundant.

Ambivalence A KB is ambivalent if it is possible to infer mutually-incompatible conclusions from some set of inputs. For example, in the KB

$p \rightarrow q \qquad q \rightarrow r \qquad p \rightarrow \neg r,$

both r and $\neg r$ will be inferred from input p: the model is ambivalent.

Circularity A KB contains circularity if it is possible to enter an endless loop while following some chain of inference. For example, in the KB

$p \rightarrow q \qquad q \rightarrow r \qquad r \rightarrow p,$

p is dependent upon itself, and, unless q or r can be provided as inputs to the system, p will never be inferred.

Deficiency A KB is deficient if there is some set of inputs for which it will infer no conclusion. For example, in the KB

$p \rightarrow q \qquad \neg p \rightarrow r \qquad q \rightarrow \neg r,$

if $\neg q$ is a permissible input, then the system is deficient for this input (because it will not infer anything, which suggests that knowledge is missing).

2.2. COVER verification procedures

COVER performs four anomaly-detection procedures: the integrity check, the rule check, the environment check, and the deficiency check. This division gives the user of COVER more flexibility than would be possible from a single procedure, because it is possible to select the most appropriate level of verification appropriate at each stage in development.

The integrity check Viewing the KB as a graph, the integrity check establishes the basic "connectivity" of the KB, as follows: for each rule expression, the integrity check procedure ensures that each antecedent literal unifies with either a declared input or the consequent literal of some other rule, and that each consequent literal unifies with either an antecedent literal or a goal declaration. This check detects so-called "dead-ends" in the KB. It has the advantage of being a very efficient check, with computational complexity $O(n)$ for n rules. Full details of this algorithm appear in [6].

The rule check The rule check looks for special cases of redundancy and ambivalent rules concerning *pairs* of rules. Each pair of rules is compared to see if:

—the two rules are identical (after renaming variables, if necessary);
—one rule subsumes the other (same consequents, subsuming antecedents);

—the two rules are in conflict (same or subsuming antecedents and conflicting consequents).

This check was the only check for redundancy and ambivalence performed by the early verification tools [4, 8], and remains a useful, relatively inexpensive procedure for detecting many anomalies—such as the examples in the next section. The theoretical computational complexity of this check is $O(n^2)$ for n rules—details of the algorithm appear in [6].

The environment check The environment check detects subtle anomalies by tracing and analyzing inference chains through the KB; it computes the *extension* of the KB, which it then checks for anomalies.

This procedure is very expensive computationally, proportional to the number of paths through the rule base, b^d, where b is the average size of rule antecedents (breadth of search), and d is the length of inference chains (depth of search) [6]. Nevertheless, experiments with this method show that it is feasible for large real-world knowledge bases [2, 6] because inference chains are very often quite short in rule-based expert systems due to the heuristic nature of the knowledge. Sample algorithms for the procedure are described in [2, 6].

In the worst case, this method is intractable; for this reason, recent research has proposed methods which make use of heuristics to focus the search for anomalies [3, 6]. The main idea behind this work is to generate only a partial extension for parts of the knowledge base where anomalies are likely or expected.

The deficiency check The deficiency check finds missing rules using a generate-and-test method: the program generates combinations of data items and values and tests to see if the situations indicated by these combinations are not covered by rules in the KB. This procedure is very expensive for complex KBs—the number of combinations grows exponentially with the number of data items and values [8]. To overcome this combinatorial explosion, COVER employs a novel method which makes use of the existing domain knowledge to control the search for *likely* missing rules. For example, by using information about which data items appear together in rules or inference chains, COVER can decide if certain data items are likely to appear together in missing rules; these are called *relevant* data items. Then, instead of generating combinations of all data items and values, it can restrict the generation to combinations of the relevant data items and their values. More details of this procedure appear in [6].

3. EXAMPLE OF COVER IN USE

In order to demonstrate the utility of this approach to verifying rule-based KBSs, COVER was used to verify a KB developed by Bell Canada. The DMS1 advisory system offers diagnostic advice to field technicians in the repair of the DMS1 telephone switching apparatus [1]. The system was written using the commercial expert system shell package, LEVEL 5, and consists of approximately 550 production rules. The rules are invoked in a conventional backward chaining strategy, and represent the heuristic experience of an expert DMS1 technician. DMS1 is in operational use by field technicians in the province of Ontario, Canada.

Prior to the application of COVER to the DMS1 KBS, the DMS1 system had undergone extensive empirical testing. The aim of this testing was to attempt to test all of the paths through the KB, as defined by the various combinations of data items (fault symptoms) that the user can enter. Following this testing, the KB had been further refined during its operational life, through corrections and enhancements requested by the users of the system.

COVER was run on the DMS1 KB on a Sun Sparc/2 Workstation. The entire checking procedure took approximately 3.5 hours. In total, 61 cases of redundancy, 10 cases of ambivalence, and 17 cases of deficiency were reported (no circularity was detected). Representative samples of these anomalies are presented below.

Duplicate rules Although some of the cases of duplicate rules in DMS1 were due to simple editing errors (the knowledge engineer inadvertently entered the same knowledge twice), the duplication in the following example is potentially more serious. COVER determined that these two rules are logically identical because the logical conclusion of the rules (the boolean fact `RING_DIST_PROB`) is the same. However, these rules display different conclusion text to the user as side-effects of their firing (`QPP421AB` and `QPP420`), which suggests a fault. Note that, because Level 5 has a backward-chaining inference engine, which selects rules for firing based upon the order in which they appear in the KB, the second of these two rules will never fire. The expert determined that the first rule was the correct one, so the second was removed.

```
IF FLOW13_ALM_CHECK IS YES
AND FLOW13_QPP_FUSE IS YES
AND FLOW13_FUSE1 IS YES
AND FLOW13_FUSE2 IS NO
AND FLOW13_ALM_AGAIN IS YES
THEN RING_DIST_PROB
AND DISPLAY QPP421AB
```

```
IF FLOW13_ALM_CHECK IS YES
AND FLOW13_QPP_FUSE IS YES
AND FLOW13_FUSE1 IS YES
AND FLOW13_FUSE2 IS NO
AND FLOW13_ALM_AGAIN IS YES
THEN RING_DIST_PROB
AND DISPLAY QPP420
```

Subsumed rule All of these cases were similar, and the example below is typical. The intention of the designer in writing these rules was to assign values (via the `:=` operator) to string variables (`POINTA` and `POINTB`) as side-effects of establishing the fact `DONEIT`. This is a common method of forcing procedural operations in backward-chaining systems. This works in Level 5 because the rules are entered into the KB in order of antecedent specificity. The inference strategy employed by Level 5 of selecting rules in order of appearance means that the most specific rule applying in a given case will always be the one that fires.

```
IF MA_LAMPS IS 1.DGP FAIL A
AND MA_LAMPS IS 2.DGP FAIL B
AND MA_LAMPS IS 3.LINE FAIL A
AND MA_LAMPS IS 4.LINE FAIL B
THEN DONEIT
AND POINTA := "A & B Cards"
AND POINTB := "A & B Cards"
```

```
IF MA_LAMPS IS 1.DGP FAIL A
AND MA_LAMPS IS 2.DGP FAIL B
AND MA_LAMPS IS 3.LINE FAIL A
THEN DONEIT
AND POINTA := "A & B Cards"
AND POINTB := "A Card"
```

For this reason, no error results from these subsumed rules, although such implicit dependencies between rules make understanding and maintaining the system unnecessarily difficult.

Ambivalent rules In the following rules, the data item TROUBLE_REPORT is declared as being able to take multiple simultaneous values, to model the concept of there being more than one type of problem in the trouble report. The user could enter the values CUTS_OFF and FALSE DIALING for TROUBLE_REPORT, in which case *both* of the rules below would be satisfied, inferring the conflicting conclusions DMS1_TROUBLE and NOT DMS1_TROUBLE (in Level 5, use of backward-chaining means that only one of the rules would actually fire, but this does not change the fact that logical ambivalence is present). This was corrected by restructuring the rules so that they cannot be simultaneously true.

```
IF TROUBLE_REPORT IS RINGS, DOESN'T ANSWER
OR TROUBLE_REPORT IS NOISE
OR TROUBLE_REPORT IS RINGS, TRIPS
OR TROUBLE_REPORT IS CUTS_OFF
OR TROUBLE_REPORT IS NO DIAL TONE
THEN DMS1_TROUBLE

IF TROUBLE_REPORT IS FALSE DIALING
OR TROUBLE_REPORT IS CAN'T BREAK DIAL TONE
THEN NOT DMS1_TROUBLE
```

Missing rule COVER reports pseudo-conditions for rules which it determines to be logically necessary for the completeness of the KB, but which are absent. One such set of pseudo-conditions appears below.

```
IF FLOW8B_COM_PWR_FUSE IS NO AND
FLOW8B_REPL_FUSE IS YES AND
FLOW8B_VOLTAGES IS NO
THEN ...?
```

In actuality, this case does not require a rule to be added to the KB because of the procedural semantics of the rule: establishing the first condition to be true requires that the user investigates whether a fuse has blown; if this is not so (the query is answered NO) then there is no need to investigate the second condition, which involves *replacing* the fuse! Although COVER has no way of knowing this, it is obvious to the designer that this is not really a missing case. Note that the data items F6B_FUSE_BLOWN, F6B_RESET_FAIL and F6B_CT_FUSE_AGAIN in the above rule were determined to be relevant to one another using the *relevance* heuristic described in the previous section.

4. CONCLUSIONS

This paper has sought to demonstrate the value of KBS knowledge base verification. To this end, it has presented an experiment in which a KBS in current use by Bell Canada was checked by an automatic verification tool, and anomalies were revealed to be present which empirical validation did not detect. Furthermore, some of the anomalies detected clearly represent faults. This result should not be taken as implying that empirical validation is ineffective; on the contrary, the small number of logical anomalies detected in this system must largely be attributed to the efforts of the knowledge engineers who performed the validation, and also to the field technicians who have used the system. Verification and empirical testing are complementary activities [5]. Many faults which were detected during testing would have been revealed more efficiently if COVER had been available during early development of the DMS1 KBS. On the other hand, COVER is not able to check whether the conclusions produced by the KBS are correct; this must be established by careful testing involving the human experts.

Acknowledgements This work was funded by Bell Canada. Level 5 is a trademark of Information Builders Inc. Sun Workstation is a trademark of Sun Microsystems Inc.

References

[1] R. D. Bell. Diagnostic and administrative expert systems at Bell Canada Network Services. In C. Y. Suen and R. Shinghal, editors, *Operational Expert Systems in Canada*. Pergamon Press, 1991.

[2] A. Ginsberg. Knowledge-base reduction: A new approach to checking knowledge bases for inconsistency & redundancy. In *Proc. 7th National Conference on Artificial Intelligence (AAAI 88)*, volume 2, pages 585–589, August 1988.

[3] J. P. Laurent and M. Ayel. Off-line coherence checking for knowledge based systems. In *IJCAI-89 Workshop on Verification, Validation and Testing of Knowledge-Based Systems*, 1989.

[4] T. A. Nguyen, W. A. Perkins, T. J. Laffey, and D. Pecora. Checking an expert systems knowledge base for consistency and completeness. In *Proc. 9th International Joint Conference on Artificial Intelligence (IJCAI 85)*, volume 1, pages 375–378, 1985.

[5] A. D. Preece. Towards a methodology for evaluating expert systems. *Expert Systems (UK)*, 7(4):215–223, November 1990.

[6] A. D. Preece, R. Shinghal, and A. Batarekh. Verifying expert systems: a logical framework and a practical tool. *Expert Systems with Applications (US)*, 3(2/3), 1992.

[7] J. Rushby. Quality measures and assurance for AI software. NASA Contractor Report CR-4187, October 1988.

[8] M. Suwa, A. C. Scott, and E. H. Shortliffe. An approach to verifying completeness and consistency in a rule-based expert system. *AI Magazine (US)*, 3(4):16–21, Fall 1982.

Personal Computers and Intelligent Systems / F.H. Vogt (Editor)
Information Processing 92, Volume III
Elsevier Science Publishers B.V. (North-Holland)

An overview on the VALID project[1]

Pedro Meseguer, Enric Plaza
Institut d'Investigació en Intel·ligència Artificial, CEAB-CSIC,
Camí de Santa Bàrbara, 17300 Blanes, Catalunya, Spain.
[e-mail: plaza@ceab.es, pedro@ceab.es]

Abstract

We summarize the work and the approach of the Esprit-II VALID project, the aim of which was to develop methods an tools for the validation of Knowledge-Based Systems. The project has developed a validation environment in which different KBS can be validated. It includes a validation toolkit comprising seven tools, ranging from inconsistency detection to KBS inspectors. The knowledge engineer can interact with the validation toolkit using windows and menus. Validation tools produced by the VALID project have been tested on real KBS and have been useful in improving their performance. Also some results about KBS quality assurance are reported. A number of conclusions regarding KBS validation extracted from our experience close the paper.

Keywords Codes: I.2.1
Keywords: Artificial Intelligence, Applications and Expert Systems, Verification, Validation, Testing, Knowledge-Based Systems.

1. INTRODUCTION

Knowledge-Based Systems (KBS), like any other piece of software, should be validated after their construction to assure their compliance with the initial requirements. This statement is justified by years of experience in software engineering. However, specific issues in KBS development reinforce even more this necessity for validation. First, KBS development languages do not incorporate enough guards to prevent error introduction. For instance, in the rule-based paradigm, errors can be easily introduced when a new rule is added to a large rule base, because it is quite difficult to be aware of all potential interactions that this new rule can cause. Second, the success of KBS technology in fields like medical diagnosis, troubleshooting, credit authorization or equipment configuration has generated an increasing industrial demand of these systems. But industry requires high levels of quality in KBS, at least as high as it requires for conventional software. And third, KBS are well-suited for applications in which safety is critical. For instance, a KBS for troubleshooting of satellite faults working on-site and in real time. An error in this KBS can cause the satellite to fail, so an exhaustive validation is mandatory prior to KBS release.

Current KBS are composed of hundred or even thousands of objects (facts, rules, metarules, integrity constraints, etc.). At this scale, manual KBS validation is almost impossible, because the extremely large amount of different situations that can occur. Then, KBS validation should be supported by tools, which perform the mechanical work and provide the knowledge engineer the information required for validation. These tools, denominated from

[1] This work has been obviously supported by ESPRIT-II 2148 VALID project.

now on validation tools, are of great help for the knowledge engineer or expert in charge of performing the validation task. Validation tools are not autonomous, in the sense that their results should be analyzed and interpreted by the validation team.

Many shells have a large set of similarities. Considering production rules, the most widely used knowledge representation for KBS, the basic mechanisms underlying rule satisfaction and rule firing are general. This cause that many verification problems (subsumption, redundancy, circularity, unfireable rules) are shared by different shells. This family resemblance of rule-based shells suggests the possibility to integrate them on a common representation. Validation tools will work on this common representation, instead of on specific KBS. Working on a common representation (instead of on specific KBS) validation tools will be shell-independent, facilitating their reuse on KBS developed with different shells with similar characteristics.

These were some of the motivations causing that, at the year 1988, an European consortium set up a validation proposal to the Esprit II program of the Commission of the European Communities. This proposal turned out to be the VALID project (#2148), entitled "VALIDATION METHODS AND TOOLS FOR KNOWLEDGE-BASED SYSTEMS", with a duration of 3 years (from January 89 to December 91), with a budget of 4.000.000 ECUS, and requiring an effort of approximately 29 man/year. The VALID consortium was formed by the following partners:

- *Cognitech*, coordinator (prime contractor), an IT french company dedicated to AI products and services.
- *CRI*, a leading Danish software technology company that applies new techniques to software engineering, including the application and integration of AI techniques.
- *Centre d'Estudis Avançats de Blanes*, an AI research institute established in the KBS validation area, belonging to the Spanish Council for Scientific Research (CSIC) the largest research organization in Spain.
- *Universidad Politecnica de Madrid*, a university team heavily involved in software development methods.

This paper aims at describing the approach and results achieved by VALID, with the following organization. In section 2 the main ideas supporting the VALID approach are exposed. Section 3 contains a description of the VALID environment, the basic software developed to build validation tools. In section 4 the set of implemented validation tools are explained. Section 5 contains a brief description of other results achieved in the project. Approach and results are evaluated in section 6. Finally, section 7 contains some conclusions and future trends in validation.

2. THE VALID APPROACH

The general aim of the VALID project was to advance to the state of the art on validating *existing* KBS. That is to say, the main restriction VALID had was that its scope were expert systems implemented in currently available shells and languages and designed and developed using industrial knowledge engineering methodologies (e.g. rapid prototyping). The significance of this restriction is that we forbid ourselves the possibility of taking an a *normative stance* on KBS validation; i.e. we could not prescribe how knowledge acquisition should be preformed, what kind KBS shells (or aspects of KBS languages) were recommended or discarded, etc so that KBS validation is feasible or easier. This option had more consequences that we anticipated at the beginning.

The VALID approach was mainly concerned on the fact that currently available methods and tools for KBS validation assumed such a simplified model of a KBS that they were (i) either not applicable to real life KBS, or (ii) applicable to one specific KBS, but it was not known if it could the method (if not the tool) could be applied to other KBS's and in what circumstances it could (could not) be applicable. We use the notion of *method* as an algorithm that uses some knowledge (about a KBS, or about restrictions on KBS behavior, or domain knowledge about the KBS application domain) to achieve some validation goal (e.g. that an inconsistent situation cannot be achieved). A *tool* is a computer program that embodies such a method.

We committed the VALID project to select a subset of different KBS, implemented in a variety of shells, in order to investigate to which extend validation methods (and even validation tools) could be used by different sorts of systems. Certainly, not all methods would be expected to be useful for a wide scope of systems: as a general rule, the more assumptions about an expert system a validation method poses, the less generic it would be. However, we were interested in developing validation methods that could be useful for more than one KBS, and this approach forced us to take into account several KBS instead of one. In summary, the specific goals of VALID were (1) generality, i.e. a comprehensive approach to validation that comprised different kinds of validation problems and the corresponding methods and tools; (2) genericity, i.e. the development of methods and tools that were to be applicable to a set of KBS, and (3) integration, i.e. a programming environment that supported the developed toolkit for validation.

Therefore VALID has followed a metalevel approach to validation. This approach involves two aspects. First, that the structure and behavior of a KBS, viewed as a program, would be represented by a model expressed in CCR (Common Conceptual Representation). Second, that the validation method would know about and work upon the KBS model in CCR. Essentially, the metalevel approach to validation is the view that a validation tool is a program working upon a model of another program, the KBS (analogously, a debugger is a program that works upon (the representation of) another program). In order to support the development of validation programs, the validation metalanguage VETA, was developed [2] [4]. VETA works upon a model of a KBS language and offers abstraction, support and flexibility for the implementation of validation tools. It includes facilities for managing versions of knowledge bases, cases and traces and has built-in primitives for computing relationships among the objects of a KBS. The model VETA has of a KBS is that which can be expressed in the CCR.That is to say, some aspects of the KBS structure and behavior are *reified* into CCR objects, and upon this objects work the validation tools. The objects in CCR are those existing in a KBS, like rules, rule-sets, metarules, attributes, etc., but also objects needed for validation that not necessarily exist in the KBS but are needed for validation purposes [4]. For instance CCR includes contexts (the values of attributes in a given instant of problem solving), different versions of a knowledge base, and traces (containing the information of the solution and the problem-solving behavior of a given KB version upon an specific problem). In the next section we describe VETA and the programming environment that supports the validation toolkit.

3. THE VALID ENVIRONMENT

The architecture VALID environment integrates the different aspects of validation for the knowledge engineer: a set of validation tools implemented in VETA and a KBS application translated to CCR. The validation actors (the knowledge engineer, usually accompanied by the domain expert) interacts with the VALID environment GUI. Presently we will explain in detail this architecture. The VALID environment offers a toolkit for validation where the knowledge engineer is able (1) to select a KBS application that is translated by an interfacing program to a format readable by the validation environment, and (2) to execute a validation tool upon that KBS application. The VALID environment manages several versions of knowledge bases of that application, the cases that represent domain problems, and the traces that represent the behavior of a KB version when solving a specific case.

A KBS implemented in a language can be included in the VALID environment when a interface program translates the KBS objects into CCR objects. The VALID project defined the CCR from modeling three KBS languages: KOOL (a frame-based language), MILORD (a metalevel rule-based architecture) and OPS83 (a production system), and three interfaces were built. The contents of a KB version is translated by the static interface, while the dynamic interface generates traces (files representing the behavior of the KB version solving a specific case). The compilers translate those files into internal CCR objects to be manipulated by validation tools using VETA primitives. The compilation process computes relationships that are of general utility for validation purposes, e.g. computes cross-references between CCR objects. The compilation already performs useful analysis of the KB structure: for instance if two rules have the same conditions (or the same actions), the compiler reifies into a unique object, so that those two rules share their common part. This compilation process speeds up the checking procedures performed by the validation tools.

The tools are implemented upon VETA, a validation metalanguage that works upon the CCR objects that model the structure and the behavior of a KBS application. VETA is implemented as an extension of Lisp, so that the programs for validation can use the general capabilities of Lisp to work with numeric data (as in the PENIC tool below) or list and graph structures (as in the IN-DEPTH tool). The extension of Lisp consists of the VETA primitives and a library if VETA functions. The VETA primitives are the basic functionality needed to manipulate the CCR objects and assure their coherence (e.g. assuring that traces correspond to the currently loaded KB version etc). The library of functions are higher level functions used for general purposes by more than one tool, e.g. computing all rules that modify a specific attribute).

The VALID environment allows that several validation tools are able to work upon the same KBS application, and furthermore that their analysis can be performed to the same KB version and to the same state of the KBS (when working on the problem-solving steps represented by the traces). The validation actor can switch from the analysis performed by CONKRET tool to the inspection services provided by Execution Visualizer to browse thru the states and objects reported as involved in a failure by CONKRET. The VALID environment also provides general facilities to load KB versions, cases and traces, to execute VETA functions upon the current state, and a query window for inspection (a modified version of the CURRICULUM-KB tool).

4. VALIDATION TOOLKIT

Seven validation tools have been developed on the valid environment, ranging from inconsistency checking, execution visualization, KB inspection or KB refinement. Some of them are based on new theoretical developments, representing significant improvements with respect to the current state of the art on automated KBS validation. These tools are CONKRET, CONTROLLER, CURRICULUM KB, EXECUTION-VISUALIZER, IN-DEPTH, PENIC and WITNESS. They are briefly described in the following.

The CONKRET tool [3] [13] supports KB refinement and revision of the strategic knowledge. This tool automatically processes a set of example cases, analyzes the reasoning process for the failed cases, and shows to the knowledge engineer the set of potential errors which are more likely responsible for these failed cases. Moreover, CONKRET has some heuristics in order to give advice about the corrections on the KB that may solve these errors. CONKRET requires the KB control knowledge to be translated into CCR metarules. This tool is intended for the tuning stages of KBS building, when knowledge acquisition is pretty well finished but the behavior of the system is not as expected.

The CONTROLLER tool [3] is used by the development team in order to verify with a set of cases the coherence of KBS input (initial data plus the data acquired during the KBS session), the coherence of KBS output and the coherence of KBS output with respect to its input. CONTROLLER verifies integrity constraints, which express domain-dependent knowledge (written by the expert) or implicit or common sense knowledge (written by the knowledge engineer).

The CURRICULUM KB tool [3] helps knowledge engineers to inspect the KB and to see the evolution of the fact base. This tool is used during KBS implementation and testing. Objects contained in the KB (rules, rule sets, instancies, etc.) can be inspected. CURRICULUM KB is used to filter a set of objects regarding different criteria; moreover, it provides facilities to detect malformations within the KB structure. CURRICULUM KB can be used for any KBS. It is particularly suited for inspecting KB in first-order logic.

The EXECUTION-VISUALIZER tool [3] assists the knowledge engineer in examining a trace of a KBS execution for a particular input case. It is designed to retrieve information about the KBS dynamic behavior. For instance, it can be used to determine the rules and metarules that have been instantiated and fired (including the firing order), the rules that have not been fired and the item templates that have not been instantiated. It also allows the user to locate trace points (steps) involving specific information. This tool is intended to be used on KBS producing a faulty output in one or more input cases. This tool is generic in the sense that it consists of a generic kernel operating entirely on CCR. This kernel may be tailored with shell language specific front-ends that make the tool easier to use for knowledge engineers working with particular shell languages.

The IN-DEPTH tool [3] [15] checks for consistency a KBS including uncertainty management and metacontrol capabilities. The tool reads a set of integrity constraints for the KBS and determines all possible KBS inputs satisfying them. Integrity constraints not only model logical contradictions but also semantical incompatibilities. IN-DEPTH is an step forward with respect to consistency checkers because it can deal with the explicit representation of uncertainty and control knowledge in KBS. It uses an extension of ATMS labels [9]. This tool requires the set of functions used in the specific uncertainty management, plus the set of constraints to be tested. It can be used on implemented KBS, from prototypes to finalized systems. IN-DEPTH is suited to work on batch, since in occasions it can delay its response for a while (because its exhaustivity).

The PENIC tool [3] [14] is an efficient consistency checker for propositional KB. It is based on Petri Nets: the KB written in CCR is translated into a Petri Net representation, and an algebraic method is used to detect the reachability of any inconsistency state. PENIC requires the declaration of the potential contradictions to be tested.Its main advantage consists on its efficiency, and it can be used from implemented KBS prototypes.

The WITNESS tool [3] aims at providing a medium to record the opinions of different people involved in KBS development and usage (knowledge engineers, experts, end users). This process continues from implementation to exploitation. The method underlying WITNESS consists of building a database by recording the comments from the mentioned actors. This database is used by the development team in order to propose well-founded modifications of the KBS. WITNESS works on the following components: versions, sessions, questions/answers and messages. WITNESS scope is restricted to KBS developed on top of KOOL shell.

5. OTHER RESULTS

In order to assess the feasibility to include KBS developed in languages other than the three initial ones, a study on the possibility of interfacing the VALID environment with the KEE language was performed. This study was centered on evaluating the translation of KEE constructs into CCR. Some aspects as the object attribute value representation, the rule representation, and the object hierarchies are easily covered by CCR aspects. However the complete translation from KEE to CCR is not possible because of some slight differences. Some changes on CCR will allow to map properly the declarative constructs of KEE into CCR. The procedural facilities of KEE could not be mapped at all, since CCR does not represent procedural knowledge. A document describing the type and importance of the proposed changes has been made [16]. Finally, an interface between KEE and VALID was developed as the first example of the future possible extensions to the VALID environment.

Also a quality manual aiming at the definition of the possible quality actions that can be performed during the whole KBS life-cycle was produced. The description of these actions are complemented with the validation tools that can be used in these actions. The quality manual [5] is the result of interviews with knowledge engineers from Cognitech and reflects their experiences in quality assurance for KBS.

6. EVALUATION

In the following a set of project aspects are evaluated. For a more detailed evaluation of the project results see [8].

Metalevel approach. VALID has followed a metalevel approach for validation tools, which have been implemented in the validation metalanguage VETA. This idea has been previously used in the RM refinement metalanguage developed by Ginsberg [11] [12]. In parallel and independently to VALID, a similar approach has been taken in the EVA project [1] to develop a validation environment with generic purposes. This metalevel approach provides a level of abstraction from which validation tools can be developed hiding specific implementation details. From a set of elementary primitives, new functions can be incrementally added as the combination of these elementary primitives. VETA provides an integrated way to access, compare and manipulate CCR objects (representing KBS elements). The level of implemented VETA primitives is relatively low, since their functionality is mainly focused on accessing CCR objects. The main effort has been put on integrating three shells with quite different characteristics (MILORD, KOOL and OPS83), while the most desirable would have been developing a more powerful set of primitives for validation.

Genericity. The most challenging aspect of the VALID project was its genericity aim. In a syntactic aspect a global genericity has been achieved, given that all the information contained in KBS belonging to three different shells has been represented into CCR objects. However, a global semantic genericity has not been achieved, because of the presence of certain expressions with particular semantics for specific shells. The integration in a common ground of these particular semantics has not been possible. In a more global analysis, to solve the genericity problem a non-ambiguous description of the procedural semantics for the considered representation languages is required. This is not the case for the shells currently in use for commercial KBS development.

Generality. Another challenging goal of VALID was its aim of developing very different validation tools in the same environment. This goal has been clearly achieved, given the wide range of implemented tools. However, this generality aim was based on an implicit assumption: to validate a KBS is enough to faithfully represent the knowledge contained in it. This assumption turned out to be false. Validation tasks may require significant amount of extra knowledge with respect to the considered KBS. For instance, integrity constraints modeling incompatible situations are extra knowledge required for verification purposes. In general, the knowledge contained in a KB can be enough to provide a solution that happens to be correct, but it could be not sufficient to *validate* the correctness of the achieved solution.

Tool utility. Tools were selected by each partner according to their specific needs or preferences. Industrial partners were guided by their current needs on developing KBS. Non-industrial partners were guided by their research on KBS validation. Every tool has practically shown its utility in the specific validation task for which it was designed. For a more extended description see [6].

Tool integration. All the validation tools have been integrated in a common environment, facilitating their usage. Interaction is based on windows, menus, on-line helps and other facilities. This environment is developed on Open Windows running on SUN-4 machines. For a detailed description see [7].

Tool reuse. Several tools have been tested on KBS developed on different shells with good results. On the contrary, other tools assume knowledge about specific aspects of the shell. This is explained by the lack of a total semantic integration of the proposed shells, causing that when a tool needs to fix a particular semantics it becomes shell-dependent. These aspects have been carefully recorded. For a more extended description see [3].

7. CONCLUSIONS

From the three year experience in the VALID project we can draw the following conclusions:

- It is possible to verify and validate a variety KBS in a common environment.
- Global genericity for validation tools requires a semantic integration of knowledge representation languages.
- The metalevel approach is a valuable framework for validation,
- Integrated models of different KBS languages is a long-term goal, but integration of narrower families of these languages seems more feasible.
- Validation may require extra knowledge with respect to the KB contents.
- The VALID project has been a first attempt at a comprehensive approach to the KBS validation problematic. We now consider that future work in this area can proceed along some of the following lines:
- Specifications: there is a wide consensus among researchers [10] that a true validation can not be achieved without clear and precise specification of the KBS task.
- Validation in the life-cycle: validation tasks have to be integrated along the life-cycle development of KBS, both regarding knowledge acquisition for validation and validation

of KBS during intermediate development stages.

- Testing methodologies: testing is an unavoidable stage in KBS validation but no substantiated KBS testing methodology exists yet.
- Learning components: validation can be enhanced by including machine learning techniques that use examples to refine the knowledge base contents.
- Better KBS languages: KBS languages should include capabilities helpful for validation, such as type-checking, modularity, anomaly detection, etc.
- Verification by construction: Combining a KBS development methodology (including specifications) and a KBS language with verification capabilities, we can approximate the ideal of verifying the KBS in the incremental process of building it.

Acknowledgements

We thank the Commission of the European Communities for project funding, our partners in the VALID project for their very valuable work, and the VALID reviewers for their useful comments and criticisms.

REFERENCES

[1] Chang C.L., Combs J.B., Stachowitz R.A. A Report on the Expert Systems Validation Associate (EVA). *Expert Systems with Applications*, **1**(3), 217-230, 1990.

[2] Esprit II 2148 VALID project. *Deliverable D4: Veta Definition.* CEAB/D/1.1, 1990.

[3] Esprit II 2148 VALID project. *Deliverable D5: Validation Tools.* CEAB/D/3.1, 1990.

[4] Esprit II 2148 VALID project. *Deliverable D6: Veta Implementation.* CEAB/D/4, 1991.

[5] Cognitech. *Deliverable D8: Quality Manual.* COG/D/5.1, 1991.

[6] Esprit II 2148 VALID project. *Deliverable D9: Report on Validation Tools Evaluation.* COG/D&3.2, 1991.

[7] Esprit II 2148 VALID project. *Deliverable D10: The VALID Environment.* CRI/D/4.3, 1991.

[8] Esprit II 2148 VALID project. *Deliverable D12: Final Report,* COG/D/4.2, 1991.

[9] deKleer, J. An Assumption-based TMS. *Artificial Intelligence* 28:127-162, 1986.

[10] Jenkins, P , Plaza E. Co-chairman introduction. In *Proc. of the European Workshop on Verification and Validation of KBS.* 22-24 July 1991. Cambridge, Engand.

[11] Ginsberg A. A Metalinguistic Approach to the Construction of Knowledge Base Refinement Systems. *Proceedings AAAI'86*, 436-441, 1986.

[12] Ginsberg A. *Automatic Refinement of Expert System Knowledge Bases.* Pitman Research Notes in Artificial Intelligence, 1988.

[13] Lopez B.:"CONKRET: A Control Knowledge Refinement Tool", in *Verification, Validation and Test of Knowledge-Based Systems*, Ayel and Laurent eds., John Wiley and Sons, 1991.

[14] Meseguer, P.:"A New Method to Checking Rule Bases for Inconsistency: A Petri Net Approach", *Proceedings of ECAI-90*, pp. 437-442, 1990.

[15] Meseguer P.:"Verification of Multi-Level Rule-Based Expert Systems", *Proceedings of AAAI-91*, pp. 323-328, 1991.

[16] UPM, Comparative Analysis of the VALID-KEE environment, UPM/W/7/TK2/1, VALID project library April, 1991.

Personal Computers and Intelligent Systems / F.H. Vogt (Editor)
Information Processing 92, Volume III
Elsevier Science Publishers B.V. (North-Holland)

Intelligent Access to Data and Knowledge Bases via User's Topics of Interest

S. CAZALENS and R. DEMOLOMBE

ONERA-CERT, 2 Av. Edouard Belin, 31055 Toulouse, France.

Abstract
Retrieving relevant information in Data and Knowledge Bases containing a large number of different types of information is a non trivial problem. That is the reason why, in areas like Decision Support Systems, or Computer Aided Design, users need the help of Intelligent Systems. Such Intelligent Systems must be able to provide the users with useful information which is not explicitly requested. For this purpose, we consider a method where the user's needs are represented in terms of their topics of interest. This kind of user representation is integrated in an appropriate modal logic, that allows the system to reason about the user's representation, the user's query and the DKB content, in order to determine the useful information. The main contribution of the paper is to present a first attempt to the formalization of the concepts of topic, interesting topic and interesting piece of information. Several criteria are investigated for these definitions, in particular to define a partial order on interesting pieces of information.

Keyword Codes: H.3.3; H.5.2; I.2.4
Keywords: Information Search and Retrieval; User Interfaces; Knowledge Representation

1 Introduction

The aim of an Intelligent System when accessing large Data and Knowledge Bases (DKB) is to help users to retrieve **useful** information. In many cases, a user's query characterizes only part of the useful information for two possible reasons: first, in Data and Knowledge Bases containing hundreds of relations, there are so many different types of information that the user may ignore the existence of some of them. Second, it is generally too boring for users to entirely describe all the information they want. So, the system must be able to reason about the description of a given situation defined by: 1) a query or a dialogue, 2) a user representation, and 3) a DKB content, in order to determine the useful information. To define such reasoning methods we have to make precise what we mean by useful information. Roughly speaking, useful information is information that is needed to reach a given goal, or information that helps the user to select or refine a goal, or information that is logically related to the query. We briefly sketch three kinds of reasoning methods associated to these three definitions of useful information.

(i) The plans and goals method [1, 4]: plans are sequences of actions representing users' typical behaviours in order to reach a given goal. In that case useful information is information which is needed in order to achieve a relevant plan. For example, in order to take a train, one has to buy a ticket and go to the platform. Hence, he has to know the ticket price, the platform number and the departure time. So, by reasoning from the plans and the user's goal, the system can derive information to provide the user with.

(ii) The topics of interest method [5]: When the system fails to recognize what the user's goal is, it may be the case that, in fact, the user needs to refine his goal definition. In such a situation, if the system can determine what the user's topics of interest are, it can provide him with information related to these topics. For example, if a user wants to know the price of a return ticket to New-York, then the system can infer that expenses are one of his topics of interest, and it can also provide the user with the possible special fares.

(iii) The logical links method: in that case, useful information may be the information that explains why a direct answer holds. For example if the direct answer is "there is no flight to Milano this morning", the explanation may be "because there is fog". Useful information may also be the information one has to make sure by himself, when querying an incomplete DKB, in order to get a direct answer. An example of such conditional answer could be: "there is a flight to Milano today if there is no fog". In general, useful information, in the context of a query q, is of the form: $q \leftarrow p$ and p, for explanations, or: $q \leftarrow p$, for conditional answers.

These three methods are complementary, and it would be very convenient for an intelligent system to have a formal description of each of them in the same formalism. There already are several proposals to formalize the Plans and Goals method in modal logic (Epistemic and Dynamic modal logic), [8, 7, 4]. However, as far as we know, there is no formalization of the Topics of Interest method in the same modal framework. The objective of this paper is to contribute to define such a formalization. We do not consider here any implementation, or efficiency aspects. In the following, we first recall what the topics of interest approach consists in, and we show where the problems of formalization are. Then we show how the topics, the topics of interest, and the interesting pieces of information are defined in this approach.

2 The Topics of Interest Method

Some works like [5] have already underlined how much it can be useful to take into account the user's topics of interest, when answering cooperatively to a user's question. Here, we summerize the main ideas. The user's topics of interest are one of the components of the user's model, together with his beliefs, goals, and may be other information. Roughly speaking, the topics are used to represent information about the meaning of words and sentences used in the description of the world. Of course, they capture only part of their meaning. In a Data and Knowledge Base context they mainly inform about the meaning of the predicates and formulas. For example, the predicates *departure-time* and *arrival-time* belong to the topic **timetable**, while *frequency* and *validity* belong to the topic **condition of validity**.Their use is very simple: if a user asks a question about the *departure-time* of a given flight, then he may also be interested by the *arrival-time* of the same flight. Note also that the topics can be organized into a hierarchy: for example, the topics **timetable** and **condition of validity** belong to the more general topic **time**. Within this hierarchy, the links are of type "is-a".

It is worth noting that the link between a sentence and a topic is independent of the truth value of the sentence. For example, the fact that "the predicate *Departure-time* is related to the topic **Timetable**", is independent of the truth value of the sentence "the *Departure-time* of flight AF001 is 1 pm". The first sentence is about the meaning of the predicate; it is linguistic information, while the second one describes the real world. The hierarchy of topics is also independent of any truth value. This is the basic reason why the concept of topic is not easy to formalize in standard logic. Indeed in standard logic two formulas having the same truth value in every world state are equivalent, and they can be substituted one each other, even if their meanings are completely different. However, as it is said in the introduction we want to adopt a common theoretical framework with the Plans and Goals method, to keep the complementarity of the two approaches. For this reason we have tried to integrate the concepts of topic and topic of interest into an Epistemic Logic.

3 Formalization of the topics

The Epistemic Logic semantics is defined in terms of possible worlds. Possible worlds represent different states of the world compatible with the user's beliefs, or in general with an agent's beliefs. It is a non trivial issue to represent topics, and topics of interest in this framework. Indeed, the links between topics and formulas, and the topic hierarchy are not part of the application domain description. They are linguistic information and then they are independant of what is true in a given world. Hence, we have to adapt standard Epistemic modal logic to represent this information. Another issue is to define the structure of the sets of formulas related to a given topic. These sets of formulas are called topic extensions.

3.1 Topic Extensions

In the simplest approach, we can define no structure at all on a given topic extension. In that case, the set of formulas in a topic extension should be explicitly defined. That would be extremely heavy, and even impossible if the set is infinite. A more realistic approach is to define a structure on a topic extension. We have defined two kinds of structures where a set of primitive propositions (not necessarily atomic formulas) is explicitly given for each topic. In addition, general rules are defined to characterize, for each topic, how the overall topic extension is defined from the set of primitive propositions. We have considered two kinds of general rules (i) and (ii):

(i) A formula F belongs to topic T iff each subformula of F belongs to T or is a primitive proposition. Topic extensions defined by this rule have a structure similar to that of "production fields" defined by Siegel and Bossu in [2]. The contraints imposed by this rule are quite strong. For example, if in a formula like $A \vee B$, formula A belongs to T, but formula B does not belong to T, then $A \vee B$ does not belong to T. The consequence is that if we want to retrieve all the formulas related to the topic T, we do not get A ∨ B.

(ii) A formula F belongs to topic T iff at least one of its subformulas belongs to T. According to this definition, the formula A ∨ B of the previous example belongs to T. In our mind, the justification for this rule can be found in the analogy between topics and key-words in the area of Information Retrieval. Indeed, in Information Retrieval, if a key-word is associated to a chapter of some book, or to a section of a paper, then, it is associated to the overall book, or to the overall paper. Here we consider that subformulas play a similar role as chapters or sections in a document.

3.2 Topic Hierarchy

Topic extensions can also be structured via a structure on topics themselves. If a topic T1 has a more general meaning than T2, then T1 extension must contain T2 extension. This corresponds to the general idea of structuring object types via an "is-a" relation. In the following, we adopt the notation: T2 $\prec$ T1 to represent the fact that T1 is more general than T2.

4 Topics of Interest and Interesting Formulas

In a given situation, a user is interested in information related to some particular topics. These topics are called the user's topics of interest. There are different possible methods to determine what they are. However it is not the purpose of this paper to present these methods, and we assume that the system knows what the current topics of interest are.

Our idea in formalizing topics of interest and interesting formulas, was to take inspiration from the formalization of the Logic of General Awareness by Fagin and Halpern in [6]. Indeed the concepts of interest and awareness share an important common feature which is their independence with respect to the truth value of the sentences. The fact that one is aware of sentence p does not depend of the truth value of p, and, in the same way, the fact that one is interested by p does not depend on the truth value of p. In the following, we present our formalization, assuming the reader is familiar with basic notions of Modal Logic as explained in [3].

4.1 Formalization of the Interesting Formulas

A Kripke model capturing the concept of Interest is a tuple:

$$\mathrm{M} = (\mathrm{S}, \pi, \mathcal{T}, \mathcal{B})$$

where S is a set of states, π(s,p) is a truth assignment function for each state and each primitive proposition p, $\mathcal{B}$ is a relation on S × S. $\mathcal{B}$ is serial, transitive and euclidean. It represents the accessibility relation for the user's beliefs. $\mathcal{T}$ is a function associating to each state s, a set of topics $\mathcal{T}$(s), representing **the current topics of interest at state s**. We have considered that the set of topics a user is interested in may depend on what he has in mind, that is, it may depend on his belief state. We have adopted a very intuitive structure for $\mathcal{T}$(s), defined by the rule: **if a topic T is a current topic of interest, then all the topics which are more specific than T are also current topics of interest**: interest is inherited in the hierarchy of topics. The truth relation for the logical connectives and the beliefs is defined by:

M,s $\models$ *true*,
M,s $\models$ p where p is a primitive proposition, iff π(s,p) = *true*
M,s $\models \neg\varphi$ iff M,s $\not\models \varphi$
M,s $\models \alpha \wedge \beta$ iff M,s $\models \alpha$ and M,s $\models \beta$
M,s $\models B\varphi$ iff M,t $\models \varphi$ for all t such that (s,t) belongs to $\mathcal{B}$.

We introduce the notation Iφ to represent that φ is an interesting formula. There are several possible variants for defining the truth of Iφ in a model M, at some state s. All of the following definitions refer to $\mathcal{T}$(s), assuming that $\mathcal{T}$(s) gives a complete description of the user's state of mind with regard to his topics of interest at state s.

A first possible definition is: "φ is an interesting formula" iff at least one of the current topics of interest contains φ :
$M, s \models I\varphi$ iff $\exists T(T \in \mathcal{T}\ (s)\ and\ \varphi \in T)$
According to this definition, any formula in the extension of a topic of interest is an interesting formula. Of course this definition may lead to a too large set of interesting formulas. To prevent this drawback, we can define a partial order on the interesting formulas, in order to select the most interesting ones, as presented in the following section.

Another alternative definition is to make explicit the topic with regard to which the formula is interesting. That leads to slightly change the syntax, and incorporate the name of the topic in the operator I, using the notation : $I_T\varphi$. In that case, the definition is:
$M, s \models I_T\varphi$ iff $\varphi \in T\ and\ T \in \mathcal{T}\ (s)$
Because of the structure of $\mathcal{T}$(s), we can deduce the following rule, which reflects a kind of inheritence:
$M, s \models I_T\varphi$ if $\varphi \in$ T and T $\prec$ T$'$ and $M, s \models I_{T'}\varphi$.

A more constraining definition would be to impose that interesting formulas belong to all the current topics of interest extensions. We can easily see that this definition would not be sensible because in many cases the intersection of all the current topics is an empty set.

Comments: in the above formalization, Iφ intuitively says that φ is interesting if φ is related to an interesting topic. However, in practice, formulas like: p $\wedge$ p, or: p $\wedge \neg$p, are interesting for no user. Hence, we will need to refine the definition of Iφ by using logical criteria: for example, removing Iφ if φ is a tautology or a contradiction, or if φ is not minimal in some sense; or by using pragmatic criteria: for example, removing formulas which are not in some normal form which is more easy to understand for users.

4.2 Ordering Interesting Formulas

The set of interesting formulas generated by the topics of interest method may be too large, and it can be useful to have criteria to order formulas in function of their interest.

This allows to provide the users with the most interesting formulas in a first step. In further steps, if the user wants to acquire more information, he can interactively request the formulas of lower interest. Here we consider several criteria to order formulas.

4.2.1 Syntactic Criteria

We call syntactic criteria, criteria which are defined in function of structural properties, independently of an application domain. The following criteria seem to be natural.

(i) If formula F1 can be fully decomposed into subformulas which are primitive propositions belonging to a topic of interest T1, and if that property does not hold for formula F2, then F1 is said to be more interesting than F2. The intuition is that formula F1 is preferred to formula F2 because it is "fully" relevant to T1.

(ii) Let T1 and T2 be two topics of interest, such that T1 $\prec$ T2, i.e. T1 is more specific than T2. Let F1 be a formula in the extension of T1, and F2 a formula in the extension of T2. If F2 does not belong to the extension of T1, then F1 is more interesting than F2. The intuition is that the more specific is the interesting topic to which a formula belongs, the more interesting is this formula.

(iii) Let F1 and F2 be two formulas. Let n1 (respectively n2) be the number of topics of interest to which F1 (resp. F2) belongs. Then formula F1 is more interesting than formula F2 if n1 > n2. The intuition is that the more important is the number of topics of interest to which the formula belongs, the more interesting is this formula.

4.2.2 Semantic Criteria

Ordering criteria can also be based on the application domain. For example in the user representation, we can define a partial order on the topics which reflects the user's preferences.

A simple ordering criterion can be defined as follows : formula F1 is more interesting than formula F2, if F1 belongs to a topic T1, and F2 belongs to a topic T2, and T1 is greater than T2, according to the given partial order. Though this definition seems to be intuitive, it is in fact confusing because formulas can belong to several topics. For example, it may be the case that F1 also belongs to T'1, F2 also belongs to T'2, and T'1 is lower than T'2. In such a case it is no longer clear which of the two formulas should be preferred.

In fact, the partial order on the topics can be viewed as a sort of preference, as defined by Shoham in [9]. The problem of combining preferences is still extensively investigated in other areas, and it is well known that it is not a trivial issue to define intuitive composition rules between preferences. That will also need further investigations.

5 Conclusion

We have recalled at the begining three possible methods which can be implemented in an intelligent system to help users to retrieve information. Then we focused on the method based on the topics of interest. The main contribution of this paper is to propose a first attempt to formalize the notions of topic, topic of interest and interesting formula, in a variant of the Epistemic logic, which takes inspiration from the logic of General Awareness [6]. Issues requiring more investigations have been explicitly mentioned in the paper. Another important issue will be to define a Proof Theory associated to the Model Theory. The Model Theory we presented, gives a precise definition for the new concepts, but a Proof Theory is needed for computational objectives. We think the concept of topic can have many applications for Intelligent Information Retrieval in its broad sense, because it gives a more abstract description of stored information than predicates do, and because terms used for topic definitions come from natural language and are easier to understand by any user. Possible applications are, for example, homogeneous description of distributed databases which have been designed independently. Another application is to provide a uniform description of multimedia database contents. Indeed, topics can be used as well to describe document contents or pictures, and they can be viewed as a sofisticated extension of the concepts of keywords and thesaurus, combined with automated reasoning techniques.

Thanks: This work has been partially supported by the CEC, in the context of the Basic Research Action MEDLAR.

References

[1] J. F. Allen. Speech acts. In S. C. Shapiro, editor, *Encyclopedia of Artificial Intelligence*, volume 2, pages 1062–1065. Interscience, 1987.

[2] J.M. Boi, E. Innocente, A. Rauzy, and P. Siegel. Production fields : A new approach to deduction problems and two algorithms for propositional calculus. In *To appear*, 1991.

[3] B. F. Chellas. *Modal Logic An introduction.* Cambridge University Press, 1988.

[4] P.R. Cohen, J. Morgan, and M.Pollack. *Intentions in Communication.* The MIT Press, 1990.

[5] F. Cuppens and R. Demolombe. Cooperative Answering: a methodology to provide intelligent access to Databases. In *Proc. of 2d Int. Conf. on Expert Database Systems*, Tysons Corner, Virginia, 1988.

[6] R. Fagin and J. Halpern. Belief, awareness and limited reasoning. *Artificial Intelligence*, 34:39–76, 1988.

[7] M.P. Georgeff and A.N. Rao. Modeling Rational Agents within a BDI Architecture. In *Proc. 2nd Int. Conf. on Knowledge Representation and Reasoning*. Morgan Kaufmann, 1991.

[8] C. Seguin. *De l'Action à l'Intention: Vers une Caractérisation Formelle des Agents.* PhD thesis, Université Paul Sabatier, Toulouse, 1992.

[9] Y. Shoham. *Reasoning about change.* The MIT Press, 1988.

Personal Computers and Intelligent Systems / F.H. Vogt (Editor)
Information Processing 92, Volume III
Elsevier Science Publishers B.V. (North-Holland)

Computer-Aided Drug Design: A Neural Network Approach

A. J. Harget[a] and N. Bodor[b]

[a]Department of Computer Science and Applied Mathematics, Aston University, Birmingham, B4 7ET, U.K.

[b]Center for Drug Design and Delivery, College of Pharmacy, J. H. M. Health Center, University of Florida, Gainesville, Florida 32610

Abstract

Artificial neural networks have received considerable attention in recent years as their particular properties have come to be recognised, especially their ability to learn and tolerance to noise. In this paper, we describe how some of the properties of neural networks can be used to assist the medicinal chemist in the design of drugs. Specifically, the back propagation neural network has been used to determine the partition coefficient and aqueous solubility of a number of organic compounds. The partition coefficient and aqueous solubility were chosen since they are known to correlate well with biological activity. The results obtained show that the neural network after training can be used to determine the partition coefficient and solubility of a series of unknown compounds to an accuracy comparable to the experimental error.

Using the partition coefficient data we have conducted an extended series of experiments into the effect that network parameters have on performance. The results show that performance of the neural network can be significantly affected by the choice of network parameters.

In conclusion, we propose a system for predicting pharmacological activity incorporating an expert system and multiple neural networks and describe the benefits that such a system may offer.

Keyword Codes : I.2.1; I.5.4
Keywords: Artificial Intelligence, Applications and Expert Systems; Pattern Recognition Applications

1. INTRODUCTION

A variety of computational techniques have been used by the medicinal chemist to determine the pharmacological activity of an organic compound. The techniques have become increasingly sophisticated and their utility to the medicinal chemist demonstrated in this laboratory and elsewhere [1], [2]. As part of our ongoing study to develop computer programs which can give assistance to the medicinal chemist we have investigated the performance of the relatively new technique of neural networks. The studies conducted in this laboratory show that neural networks have the potential to become an important addition to the computational repertoire available to the chemist.

Neural computing offers exciting new techniques that allow computers to be trained to recognise patterns in data of high dimensionality. Unlike conventional computers, neural networks have a high degree of parallelism in their structure and in the way they process information. In addition, they also have a number of important distinguishing features such as the ability to learn, a resistance to noise and a high degree of fault tolerance. The worth of neural networks has already been demonstrated in applications as diverse as text-to-speech conversion [3], natural language processing [4] and the analysis of sonar data [5]. Given this variety of application a study has been conducted in this laboratory to determine the scope and performance of neural networks applied to chemical problems. As part of this study we now describe a neural network approach to the estimation of the partition coefficient and aqueous solubility of organic compounds. The partition coefficient of a compound is well-known to be a good predictor of drug activity, since it determines the delivery of a drug, its transport and distribution to the active site. The aqueous solubility of a compound is also of considerable importance to the drug designer since it is an important determinant in drug delivery and the transport and distribution of a drug. Although both of these properties can be easily determined experimentally it is not always appropriate to do so and is clearly impossible for compounds which have not been synthesised. Thus a theoretical approach which can give a good estimation of these properties will be of considerable benefit to the drug designer since it would allow promising candidates for a drug to be identified. The elimination of large number of unsuitable candidates would provide considerable savings in time and resources, which could be directed to the synthesis and testing of potentially more promising candidates.

In this study we have used a neural network to determine the partition coefficient and aqueous solubility of a compound from calculated values of selected properties of the compound. Comparison is made with the results obtained using a regression analysis approach. In addition, an extended study has been made using the partition coefficient data into the effect of changing various parameters of the neural network on its performance. The results of this study are given together with our conclusions. Finally we propose a system containing an expert system combined with several neural network knowledge bases to provide assistance to the medicinal chemist in the drug design process. The likely merits of this integrated approach are discussed.

2. THEORY OF NEURAL NETWORKS

Several neural network topologies and training methods have been described in the literature. In this study we have used the back propagation algorithm [6] which is currently the most popular neural network approach, and the one found to be the most effective for the majority of applications. A description of the approach taken in our studies has been given elsewhere [7].

A computer program was designed for a neural network using the backpropagation algorithm and implemented in Pascal. The program allows an arbitrary number of hidden layers, and units within each layer, to be defined and incorporates both a training and predictive capability.

3. RESULTS AND DISCUSSION

The performance of a neural network depends upon many factors, for example, the number of patterns in the training set, the choice of network parameters, the number of hidden units and the degree of homology between the training and prediction sets. It is not possible to carry out an exhaustive study of all these factors since the computational time required to achieve this would be excessive. Instead, we have investigated the effect on neural network performance of varying some of the parameters and the results are now described. For the studies conducted here we have used the partition coefficient data of Bodor et al [8] where the training set was composed of 302 compounds consisting of a wide range of organic molecules including hydrocarbons, halohydrocarbons, substituted benzenes, polynuclear aromatics, ethers, alcohols, aldehydes, ketones, esters, nitriles, amines, nitro compounds and organosulfur compounds. Using the semi-empirical AM1 method [9] molecular properties were calculated for each compound and included the dipole moment, charges, the molecular surface area, volume and ovality. It was found that the partition coefficient could be described by the 17 molecular properties described in Table 1.

Table 1
Selected properties of the organic compounds

Parameter	Definition
D	The calculated dipole movement
Ialkane	The indicator variable for alkanes
QN4	The square of QN2
QN2	The square of QN
QN	The square root of the sum of the squared charges on nitrogen atoms
QO4	The square of QO2
QO2	The square of QO
QO	The square root of the sum of the squared charges on oxygen atoms
QON	The sum of absolute values of atomic charges on nitrogen and oxygen atoms
MW	The molecular weight
S2	The square of the molecular surface
S	Molecular surface
O	The ovality of the molecule
O2	The square of the ovality
nc	The number of carbon atoms
ABSHQ	The sum of the absolute values of atomic charges on each atom
O4	The fourth power of the ovality

The experimental values for the partition coefficients were determined under identical conditions, namely, at atmospheric pressure and a temperature of 25 degC. The partition coefficients used in this study were all determined in the 1-octanol water system because such values appear to give the best correlation with biological activity.

The network architecture therefore consisted of 17 input neurons, a specified number of hidden units and 1 output neuron. The calculated molecular properties and the experimental partition coefficients were all normalised to the range 0.0 to 1.0. After training the neural network was tested on its ability to predict the partition coefficient of an unknown set of organic compounds. For this study the unknown set consisted of 21 compounds which had known experimental values but were not members of the training set. A performance comparison was made with the results obtained using a regression analysis approach on an identical set of data.

3.1 Determining the number of hidden units

The existence of hidden units allows the network to develop complex feature detectors for the training set being presented. If a network contains too few hidden units then it may not be capable of extracting all the pertinent features in the training data. With too many hidden units the network will tend to 'overfit' the data with a model that is accurate on the training examples, but does not properly generalise to any new inputs. In an attempt to optimise the performance we varied the number of neurons in the hidden layer since it has been shown that this has a significant effect on performance. For each number of hidden units a minimum of 30 training sessions was conducted and for each training session the neural network was initialised to a different set of weights. Training continued until the generalisation performance of the neural network began to degrade; this took typically 30,000 epochs, where an epoch is designated as an entire pass through the training set which in this case is equivalent to 302 pattern presentations.

For each architecture the mean standard deviation obtained over the training sessions was calculated for both the training and prediction sets together with the variance for the mean standard deviation. The results obtained are summarised in Table 2 and show clearly that a

Table 2
The influence on neural network performance of the number of hidden units

Number of hidden units	Training set performance		Prediction set performance	
	Std. deviation	Variance	Std. deviation	Variance
2	0.372	0.00004	0.646	0.00063
3	0.278	0.00077	0.528	0.01275
4	0.281	0.00151	0.597	0.02692
5	0.249	0.00077	0.647	0.01891

network consisting of a hidden layer of 3 units gave the best performance for generalisation. Consequently this architecture was taken for all subsequent training and testing sessions. A typical set of results for the training set gave a standard deviation of 0.26 between the experimental and calculated results, which is somewhat similar to the experimental error. This is to be compared with a standard deviation of 0.31 calculated by the regression analysis approach. Consideration of the individual compounds of the training set shows that the neural network approach gives a calculated value for the partition coefficient which is superior to the regression analysis in 171 of the 302 compounds [10].

The performance of the trained neural network was tested on its ability to predict the partition coefficient of an unknown set of organic compounds. All the members of the prediction set had known experimental values but were not members of the original training set. A typical set of results is shown in Table 3 together with the results obtained from the regression analysis approach. The standard deviation for the neural network was 0.38 which is comparable to that given by regression analysis. Overall the predicted results are very satisfactory given that some members of the prediction set were quite unrelated in combined structure and substituent to the training set, and that a certain experimental error is attached to the data.

Table 3
Predicted results for logP using neural networks and regression analysis

		Exp.	NNa	RAb	Ref
1	Testosterone	3.31	3.06	3.63	8
2	Prednisone	1.46	1.81	1.95	8
3	Penicillin	1.83	2.17	1.91	8
4	Phenytoin	2.47	1.95	2.48	8
5	Triamcinolone	1.03	1.24	1.59	12
6	Dexamethasone	1.99	1.91	1.90	12
7	Betamethasone	1.94	1.92	1.96	12
8	P-cresol	1.96	1.81	1.70	12
9	2,4,4-PCB	5.62	5.54	5.52	13
10	2,5-PCB	5.16	5.01	5.14	14
11	2,6-PCB	4.93	5.05	5.12	14
12	2,4,6-PCB	5.47	5.49	5.55	14
13	Deoxycorticosterone	2.90	2.72	3.17	12
14	Cortisone	1.42	1.54	2.07	12
15	3-chlorophenyl acetic acid	2.09	2.61	2.45	11

a Estimation of logP using neural networks b Estimation of logP using regression analysis

A similar study was also undertaken into the estimation of aqueous solubilities using the data described by Bodor et al [15]. Here the training set consisted of 331 compounds described by 17 parameters, which were similar to the parameters taken for the partition coefficient study. For this study the neural network gave a standard deviation of 0.22 for the training set which is to be compared with a value of 0.34 obtained from the regression analysis approach. On an unknown prediction set the neural network gave a standard deviation of 0.37 against 0.36 for that of the regression analysis. Thus the success of the neural network approach and its utility to the medicinal chemist has been confirmed by two separate studies.

3.2 Choice of network parameters

A study was made on the effect of neural network performance of varying some of the network parameters. It is not possible to carry out an exhaustive study of all the parameters that could be varied because of the inordinate amount of computation time that this would require. Instead we chose to study the effect on network performance of varying the initial weights, of adding random noise to the input data, of relaxing the error condition and finally a combination of the latter two. The results obtained are summarised in Table 4.

In varying the initial weights we chose to vary the range of weight between 0.0 and 1.0, -1 to -2 and +1 to +2, -1 to +1, -0.3 to +0.3, and for the weights and biases to the hidden units to be zeroed and the weights and biases from the hidden units to the output units set to a random number in the range 0 to +1. For each study we executed 30 different training

Table 4
Choice of network parameters- Effect on performance

Expt	Training set		Prediction set	
	Std. deviation	Variance	Std. deviation	Variance
A	0.278	0.00077	0.528	0.01275
B	0.279	0.00206	0.533	0.01248
C	0.277	0.04289	0.518	0.00857
D	0.296	0.00270	0.547	0.01182
E	0.279	0.00139	0.547	0.01023
F	0.272	0.00038	0.523	0.01094
G	0.300	0.00111	0.605	0.01467
H	0.263	0.00035	0.480	0.00742
I	0.283	0.00035	0.491	0.00742
J	0.250	0.00042	0.404	0.00921

A - initial weights in the range 0 to 1
B - initial weights in the range -1 to +1
C - initial weights in the range -0.3 to +0.3
D - initial weights in the range -2 to -1 and +1 to +2
E - weights and biases to hidden units set to zero, weights and biases for output units set to the range 0 to +1
F - 5% noise added to input data of training set
G - 10% noise added to input data of training set
H - weights not changed if error difference between calculated and observed results is less than 5%
I - 5% noise added to input training data and weights unchanged if difference between calculated and observed values is less than 5%
J - 3% noise added to input training data and weights unchanged if difference between calculated and observed values is less than 3%

sessions and for each session a different set of starting weights was defined by varying the seed to the random number generator. The results show that for the conditions studied the performance of the neural network is essentially invariant to the initial conditions taken, there being little significant statistical variation between the results. Thus for the subsequent studies reported here we took the initial weights to be in the range 0.0 to 1.0. It has been reported elsewhere [16] that adding noise to the input data improves the generalisation performance of a neural network. We chose to study this by adding 5% and 10% random noise to the input data. The results in Table 4 show that adding 5% noise to the input data has little effect on performance but that when 10% noise is added the performance degrades markedly. To test the relaxation of the error condition during training we determined that if the error between the calculated and observed results for a pattern was less than 5% then the learning algorithm would not be invoked and the weights therefore not changed. The results obtained are somewhat similar to those found for the noise study. Finally, we decided to consider the effect on performance of combining both the noise and error condition for factors of 3% and 5%. The results obtained in Table 4 show clearly that a significant improvement in performance was obtained for the 3% case.

Neural networks attempt to follow every fold and dimple in the decision surface Although this is a desirable quality it may lead in certain cases to a degradation in generalisation performance particularly when there is considerable experimental error attached to the data as in this study. By relaxing the error condition and adding noise we have in effect 'flattened out' the decision surface and thus reduced the significance of individual patterns. The surface obtained is thus more likely to be a true reflection of the general decision surface and hence be capable of providing better generalisation results.

4. AN INTEGRATED SYSTEM FOR COMPUTER-AIDED DRUG DESIGN

The object of the studies described here is to develop a system containing an expert system integrated with a series of neural network 'knowledge bases' each describing some biological activity. Expert systems, in contrast to neural networks, have the advantage that they can provide an explanation of their decision-making process, but have the disadvantage that they undergo severe degradation at the boundaries of the knowledge base. Neural networks, on the other hand, are robust and can operate outside the boundaries of the limits defined by the training set. Neural networks excel at classifying problems where 'fuzzy' pattern recognition of data representations and relationships is required. Thus by combining expert systems and neural networks we can avoid many of the weaknesses inherent in each method whilst capitalising on their unique strengths.

The system we envisage contains an expert system and several neural network knowledge bases each describing some important biological determinant. This system differs from the earlier studies of using neural networks as expert systems [17], [18], where knowledge was acquired through learning from the training data. In our system the neural networks will be one of a number of contributing knowledge sources. When a neural network finishes processing then its results appear on a 'blackboard' [19] where they can be accessed by the expert system. Using the blackboard concept one knowledge source can relay information to another or to all and thus improve communication and the quality of the solution.

The knowledge base in the system proposed here consists of 3 sub-knowledge bases: a fact base which describes the current state of the consultation, a set of neural network knowledge bases and finally the traditional rule base composed of rules of the form:

IF C THEN A

where the usual semantics hold, namely, that if condition C is true then action part A can be performed. When the inference engine encounters a rule which contains data within the condition part of the rule that only a neural network can supply then the blackboard will be accessed to read the result. In the absence of a value the corresponding neural network will be invoked. If during the inference process there is substantial evidence that the neural network has incorrectly classified a compound then retraining of the network will be requested. Detection of misclassification could be deduced automatically or by human intervention.

We are currently moving towards this system by building up the neural network knowledge bases which will be accessed by the expert system for candidate structures described by the medicinal chemist. In this paper we have shown that the neural network approach can give useful results on the estimation of partition coefficients and aqueous solubility which are important determinants to biological activity. Further neural network knowledge bases need to be defined before they can be combined with an expert system to provide an integrated system capable of contributing to the drug design process. We are currently in the process of constructing further neural network knowledge bases.

5. CONCLUSION

The utility of the neural network to the medicinal chemist has been demonstrated in studies on two important biological determinants, namely the partition coefficient and aqueous solubility. Our study shows that both the partition coefficient and aqueous solubility of an organic compound can be calculated by the neural network to an accuracy comparable to the experimental error. Further studies have shown the importance of the architecture and training conditions on neural network performance, and lead us to the general conclusion that when neural networks are applied to data in which the experimental error is significant then some relaxation of the error condition combined with the addition of random noise to the input data will improve the generalisation capability of the neural network.

The results obtained clearly demonstrate the potential of neural networks to the prediction of pharmacological activity and confirm our belief that neural networks integrated with expert systems will provide a powerful system for the medicinal chemist involved in computer-aided drug design.

6. REFERENCES

1. Bodor,N.; Harget, A.J.; Phillips, E.W. J. Am. Chem. Soc. 1983, 26, 318.
2. Martin, Y.C. Quantitative Drug Design, Medicinal Research Series. Marcel Dekker, New York. 1978, vol 8.
3. Sejnowski,T.; Rosenberg, C. Complex Systems. 1987, 1, 145.
4. Allen, R. Proc. of the IEEE First Internat. Conf. on Neural Networks. 1987, 2, 335.
5. Gorman, R. P.; Sejnoswki, T. Neural Networks 1988, 1, 75.
6. Rumelhart, D.E.; McClelland, J.L. Parallel Distributed Processing: Explorations in the Microstructure of Cognition. Bradford Books, MIT Press 1986.
7. Bodor, N.; Harget, A. J.; Huang, M.J. J. Am. Chem. Soc. 1991, 113(25), 9480.
8. Bodor, N.; Gabanyi, Z.; Wong, C.-K. J. Am. Chem. Soc. 1989, 111, 3783; Bodor, N.; Huang, M.-J. J. Pharm.Sci. In press.
9. Program AMPAC, Dewar Group, 1986.
10. A copy of the results described in this paper is available on request from the authors.
11. Kamlet, M. J.; Doherty, R.M.; Abraham, M.H.; Marcus, Y.; Taft, R.W. J.Phys. Chem. 1988, 92, 5244.
12. Valvani, S.C.; Yalkowsky, S.H. In "Solubility and Partitioning in Drug Design: Physical Chemical Properties of Drug"; Yalkowsky, S.H.; Sinkula, A.A.; Valvani. C.C. Eds.; Marcel Dekker, Inc.: New York and Basel, 1980, pp. 201 - 229.
13. Chiou, C.T.; Portor, P.E.; Schmedding, D.W. Environ. Sci. Technol. 1983, 17, 227.
14. Miller, M.M.; Wasik, S.P.; Huang, G.L.; Shiu, W.Y.; Mackay, D. Environ. Sci. Technol. 1985, 19, 522.
15. Bodor, N.; Huang, M.-J. submitted for publication.
16. Elman, J.L.; Zipser, D. J. Acoustical Society of America. 1988, 83(4), 1615.
17. Gallant, S.I. CACM 1988, 31, 152.
18. Dutta, S.; Shekhar, S. IEEE International Conference on Neural Networks, San Diego, 1988, 443.
19. Erman, L.D.; Hayes-Roth, F.; Lesser, V.R.; Reddy, R.D. ACM Computing Surveys 1980, 12(2).

Personal Computers and Intelligent Systems / F.H. Vogt (Editor)
Information Processing 92, Volume III
Elsevier Science Publishers B.V. (North-Holland)

Decision Support in Non-Conservative Domains: Generalization with Neural Networks

Soumitra Dutta[a], Shashi Shekhar[b] and W.Y. Wong[b]

[a]Technology Management Area, INSEAD, Fontainebleau Cedex, France 77305

[b]Department of Computer Science, University of Minnesota, Minneapolis, MN 55455, USA

Abstract
This paper explores the use of neural networks (NNs) for providing decision support by generalization in non-conservative/unstructured domains. The results of two different experiments are reported. The first experiment is a controlled study of the ability of NNs to generalize simple, continuous functions. The other experiment explores the utilization of NNs for decision support by generalization in the real world domain of the assignment of corporate bond ratings. Our results indicate that NNs have the potential to provide adequate decision support in non-conservative/unstructured domains.

Keyword Codes: I.2.0; I.5.0.
Keywords: Artificial Intelligence, General; Pattern Recognition, General.

1. Introduction

This section describes the problem types solved by NNs, and shows how NNs can enhance the model base of a decision support system (DSS).

1.1 Problem Types Solved by Neural Networks

Neural network applications can be classified into two broad categories: *recognition* problems and *generalization* problems. In the recognition problem, (input, output_label) pairs (I_1, O_1), $(I_2, O_2), \ldots, (I_n, O_n)$, are used for training the NN, and the trained NN is tested with the input I_j $(1 \leq i \leq n)$ corrupted by noise. The trained NN is expected to reproduce the output O_j corresponding to I_j, in spite of the presence of noise. Applications of NNs to domains such as speech recognition [9] and pattern recognition [4] are examples of recognition problem solving.

A variant of the recognition problem is the *generalization* problem, in which the trained NN is tested with input I_{n+1}, which is distinct from the inputs $I_1, I_2, \ldots, I_n$ used for training the NN. The NN is expected to correctly predict the output O_{n+1} for the (previously unseen) input I_{n+1} from the model of the domain it has learned from the training input-output pairs. Typical applications of NNs for generalization problems include the assignment of corporate bond ratings [3,5] and economic prediction [18]. NNs used for generalization problem solving have also been termed as *expert networks* [1] as they are able to respond to unseen inputs, and thus can be considered as being able to display some "expertise" about the problem domain.

Non-conservative domains lack a well defined domain model. It is difficult to apply conventional mathematical techniques in non-conservative domains as most mathematical models require a parametric formulation of the domain. Erroneous assumptions about the underlying distributions in formulating a parametric model distorts the results of the models. Rule-based systems also cannot be built as they require expert (deep) knowledge about the domain. It is interesting to explore the use of NNs in such domains because they are non-parametric and make weaker assumptions about the shapes of the underlying distributions than traditional statistical classifiers [10]. They are thus more robust in the face of non-linear processes, non-Gaussian behavior, and noise. Many domain models change with time. The adaptive nature of NNs permits them to respond to and adapt with changes in the external world state (a feature lacking in most conventional techniques). NNs also do not require detailed rules about domain behaviors as they are trained by presenting examples of input-output pairs. More details about NNs can be found from references [6,10,14].

1.2 Decision Support Systems and Neural Networks

Models in a decision support system (DSS) [17] are usually either mathematical or heuristic in nature. DSSs typically have ignored (non-conservative) domains lacking a domain model because it is difficult to build mathematical and heuristic models for such a domain. NNs can play an important role in augmenting the range of applicable domains for DSSs. As mentioned above, the ability of NNs to learn the domain model autonomously from a set of training examples and then generalize from it makes them potentially useful for non-conservative domains. NNs thus represent a different modelling approach for DSSs.

2. Generalization in a Controlled Experiment

This section describes a controlled study of the generalization abilities of back-propagation networks in domains represented by smooth continuous functions. More details on this experiment are given in reference [3].

2.1 Generation of Learning and Testing Data

Four different domains were considered in this study: linear, quadratic, logarithmic and trigonometric. The data sets were derived from the four functions shown analytically in Table 1. To study the effects of noise, four noise levels of 0%, 2%, 5%, and 10% were added to $f_i(x,y)$. The random noise is assumed to be a uniform distribution with zero mean, and constant variance. Each data set consists of 225 input pairs of (x,y) values which are generated from a rectangular grid with 15 distinct values each for x and y. Each data set of 225 points is grouped randomly into three sets: 125 points for the learning sample, and 50 each for the testing and overfit-testing samples.

Table 1
Functions used for data synthesis

Function	Valid Input Ranges	Type of Domain
$f_1(x,y) = x + 2y + 3$	$10 \le x,y \le 150$	linear
$f_2(x,y) = 0.5x^2 + 0.2y^2 + 9.0$	$10 \le x,y \le 150$	quadratic
$f_3(x,y) = 3\log(x) + \log(y) + 2.0$	$10 \le x,y \le 150$	logarithmic
$f_4(x,y) = 2\sin(x) + \cos(y) + 4.0$	$40 \le x,y \le 320$	trigonometric

2.2 Network Architectures

Three different feed-forward network architectures were considered: 2X2X1, 2X2X2X1, and 2X6X6X1, where the leftmost and rightmost numbers give the number of nodes in the input and output layers respectively, and the intermediate numbers specify the number of nodes in the hidden layers. The learning algorithm used was Back propagation with the Generalized Delta rule [13]. The network was trained in the epoch mode, i.e., weights on the connections of the network were changed only after each sweep through the patterns in the learning sample. All the NNs (for all data sets) terminated upon reaching 50,000 epochs. The trained networks (after 50,000 epochs) were applied to the testing samples to determine their generalization capabilities.

2.3 Performance Evaluation by Numeric Metrics

The numeric metric chosen is the mean absolute percent error (MAPE) per pattern, which is defined for both the learning and testing samples as:

$$\text{MAPE} = \frac{1}{\text{no\_of\_patterns}} \sum_{\text{all\_patterns}} \frac{|\text{Actual\_output} - \text{Target\_output}|}{\text{Target\_output}} * 100\%$$

As the input patterns are corrupted by varying degrees of noise, a more accurate indicator of network performance is the noise adjusted MAPE (NAMAPE), defined as:

NAMAPE = MAPE - Average noise level

NAMAPE discounts the contribution of noise to the MAPE value. A value of NAMAPE close to 0 shows good generalization capabilities. A large positive value of NAMAPE points to poor generalization capabilities and a large negative NAMAPE value indicates the presence of overfitting. Tables 2 and 3 summarize the results of the application of the numeric metric for the learning and testing phases respectively. Several runs of the different network configurations was made for the various noise levels. For each of the four different domains, the best, worst and average NAMAPE values are listed for the different network configurations and for a regression oracle. NAMAPE for the regression oracle characterizes the mean noise in the data. For zero mean noise, it should evaluate to zero. The apriori functional forms chosen for the regression models are based on the appropriate domain forms (e.g., sin(x) and cos(y) are used for the trignometric domain).

Table 2
NAMAPE values for the learning phase

Domain Form	2X2X1 NN	2X2X2X1 NN	2X6X6X1 NN	Regression Oracle
Linear NAMAPE				
Best	0.16	0.05	0.11	0.00
Worst	1.41	1.49	0.82	0.12
Average	0.60	0.63	0.37	0.04
Quadratic NAMAPE				
Best	0.75	1.39	0.64	0.00
Worst	12.27	3.89	4.09	0.48
Average	5.87	2.22	1.97	0.19
Log. NAMAPE				
Best	0.19	-0.01	-0.01	0.00
Worst	1.48	1.14	0.30	0.06
Average	0.63	0.36	-0.01	0.02
Trig. NAMAPE				
Best	8.55	3.67	0.12	0.00
Worst	13.81	10.67	2.15	0.02
Average	11.26	7.33	0.94	-0.01

2.4 Interpretation of Results

The following preliminary observations can be made about the results of this experiment:

- The NN model can learn the domain functions very well for the linear, quadratic and logarithmic domains, and reasonably well for the trigonometric domain.
- There is a improvement in the performance of the NN with increasing network size, specially for the trignometric domain.
- The performances of the regression models were not significantly better than the best comparable NN performance. Note that the regression models had an advantage over the NN models as they were trained using the known functional form (with unknown coefficients) of the corresponding domain.
- Small amounts of noise helped the generalization abilities of NNs. It was observed that the NAMAPE values generally decreased with increasing levels of noise (upto 5%).
- A relatively small amount of overfit was observed in our experiments. This is probably because the size of the networks were deliberately chosen to be small and the domains under consideration are relatively simple continuous functions.

Table 3
NAMAPE values for the testing phase

Domain Form	2X2X1 NN	2X2X2X1 NN	2X6X6X1 NN	Regression Oracle
Linear NAMAPE				
Best	-0.03	0.11	0.00	0.00
Worst	0.84	0.91	-0.55	-0.52
Average	0.12	0.12	-0.06	-0.22
Quadratic NAMAPE				
Best	0.00	0.08	-0.21	0.00
Worst	5.32	2.15	2.05	-0.63
Average	2.25	0.84	0.75	-0.26
Log. NAMAPE				
Best	-0.01	-0.07	0.00	0.00
Worst	1.34	1.05	-0.41	-0.47
Average	0.53	0.25	-0.06	-0.20
Trig. NAMAPE				
Best	9.62	4.10	0.26	0.00
Worst	14.75	11.41	1.78	-0.52
Average	12.12	7.32	1.01	-0.22

3. Corporate Bond Rating

This section describes our experiment in generalization for the real-world problem of assigning corporate bond ratings. These results were first reported in reference [2], and are interesting in light of the experiment described in section 2. The main results are summarized below.

3.1 Introduction and Prior Research

The default risks of the most actively traded bonds are rated by various independent organizations such as S&P and Moody's. To evaluate a bond's potential for default, rating agencies rely upon a committee analysis of the issuer's ability to repay, willingness to repay, and protective provisions for an issue. It is not known what model, if any, do these rating agencies use for rating the various bond issues.

Many complex regression models have been proposed in the literature [7,11,12] for the problem of corporate bond rating. However, they all have acheived a prediction accuracy of about 60% to 65%. Dutta and Shekhar [2], Surkan and Singleton [15], Garavaglia [5] and Utans and Moody [16] have used NNs for the task of bond rating. The work of Dutta and

Shekhar [2] was the first application of NNs to bond rating and is described below in this section. Surkan and Singleton [15] observed that NNs outperformed discriminant analysis on the same data. Garavaglia [5] used the counter-propagation NN for bond rating. Her results indicate that while NNs gave poor results (maximum accuracy 55%) for predicting any one particular bond rating, the accuracy of NNs increased substantially (maximum accuracy of 92%) if the the problem was simplified to detecting three broad classes of bonds (investment, speculative and poor quality). Utans and Moody [16] conducted experiments in the domain of bond rating to select appropriate NN architectures. They used 196 companies and found a maximum accuracy of prediction of 28% for the prediction of any one rating. The success rate increased to 67% for errors of one or less rating.

3.2 Experimental Design

Based on the results of prior researchers in bond rating, we selected ten financial variables for predicting bond ratings (Table 4). Values of the necessary input variables were collected from the April 1986 issues of the Valueline Index and the S&P Bond Guide. Bond issues of forty seven companies were selected at random. Thirty companies were used as the learning sample, i.e., to train the neural network (learn the weights on the different connections) and obtain the regression coefficients. The rest seventeen companies were used to test the neural network and the regression performance. All selected bonds had approximately the same maturity date (1998 - 2003). All variable values were scaled to lie in the range [0,1].

Table 4
Financial Variables Used to Predict Bond Ratings

Var #	Definition	Var #	Definition
1	Liability/(Cash + Assets)	2	(Total funded debt)/(net property)
3	Sales/Net worth	4	Profit/Sales
5	Financial strength of company as given in the Valueline Index	6	Number of times available earnings cover fixed charges
7	Past 5 year revenue growth rate	8	Next 5 year projected revenue growth rate
9	Working capital/Sales	10	Subjective prospects of company

For the purposes of our experiment, the symbolic ratings of bonds were converted into numerical values (Table 5). For enhancing discrimination in the output, we mapped similar ratings (e.g., AA+, AA and AA-) onto the same numerical value (e.g., 0.9).

Table 5
Conversion of Bond Ratings to Numerical Values

Bond Rating	Numerical Value	Bond Rating	Numerical Value
AAA	0.95	BBB+, BBB, BBB-	0.5
AA+, AA, AA-	0.9	BB+, BB, BB-	0.35
A+, A, A-	0.7	B+, B, B-	0.25

Five different feed-forward networks were used in this experiment: 6X1, 6X3X1, 10X1, 10X3X1, and 10X4X1. For the first two networks, only the first 6 variables in Table 4 were used as inputs. The back-propagation algorithm [13] was again used for learning. The network was trained in the epoch mode, and the termination condition was set to be 50,000 epochs.

3.3 Interpretation of Results

The models were expected to recognize if a given bond belongs to class of all bonds with AA rating. Table 6 condenses the results of the learning phase and Table 7 summarizes the results of the testing phase. The % entries in Tables 6 and 7 represent the % of correctness of prediction of the two models (regression and NN). We also list the absolute error as tot_sq_err for each model to give an idea of the goodness of fit by various models. The tot_sq_err gives the sum of the squares of the errors in prediction in all the cases.

The following observations can be made from the results of this experiment:

- NNs consistently outperform the regression model in predicting bond ratings from the given set of financial ratios. Both in the training and learning samples, the total squared error for (linear) regression analysis is about an order of magnitude higher than that for NNs .
- Comparing the performance of 2 and 3 layered NNs, we observe that the performance of 3 layered NNs is better during the learning phase. But surprisingly, the performance of 2 layered NNs is superior during the testing phase. This is possibly due to "over-fitting" to data while using 3 layered NNs.
- The testing accuracy is generally higher while considering 10 variables as opposed to 6 variables. This indicates the value of choosing a complete input feature space.
- It was observed that the NN models usually generated errors of a single rating category. In contrast, regression models usually generated errors of two or more rating categories.

Table 6
Results from the learning Phase

Number of Variables	Neural Network 2-layered	3-layered	Regression
6	80% tot_sq_err = 0.236	80% tot_sq_err = 0.175	63.33% tot_sq_err = 1.107
10	80% tot_sq_err = 0.224	92.4% tot_sq_err = 0.054	66.7% tot_sq_err = 0.924

Table 7
Results from the testing Phase

Number of Variables	Neural Network 2-layered	3-layered	Regression
6	82.4% tot_sq_err = 0.198	76.5% tot_sq_err = 0.194	64.7% tot_sq_err = 1.528
10	88.3% tot_sq_err = 0.164	82.4% tot_sq_err = 0.228	64.7% tot_sq_err = 1.643

4. CONCLUSION

Mathematical model demands a good understanding of the underlying domain model. Heuristic rule-based systems also require a fair knowledge about the relevant domain model (which is usually acquired incrementally during knowledge engineering). Both these modelling techniques are not very applicable for non-conservative domains where knowledge about the underlying domain model is poor, and knowledge engineering is difficult. NNs represent an alternative modelling technique which is applicable to problem solving and modelling in non-conservative domains. NNs autonomously learn the domain model from examples and do not require the a priori specification of the model.

Most successful NNs applications have been reported for recognition problems [4,9]. Recently there has been an increased emphasis on the application of NNs for generalization problems [1,2,5,8,18], and the findings in the literature are mixed. This paper has described the use of NNs for generalization in two different non-conservative domains: an artificially simulated controlled setting, and the real world domain of corporate bond rating. Our results from the controlled experiment indicates that NNs have the potential to generalize effectively in domains with simple continuous models. The performance of NNs for corporate bond rating is impressive, but one must keep in mind the limitations of the experimental design. It is quite likely that the performance accuracy of NNs for bond ratings in our experiments is optimistic. However, it is useful to note that both our results and those of Garavaglia [5] indicate that NNs can play an important role in predicting bond ratings if the problem is suitably posed (in this case, as the determination of three broad bond categories as opposed to distinguishing between individual categories). The research presented in this paper is described in more detail in [3].

REFERENCES

1. Caudill, M., Using Neural networks: Making an Expert Network, AI Expert, pp. 41-45, July 1990.
2. Dutta, S. and S. Shekhar, Bond-Rating: A Non-conservative application of neural networks, in the Proc. of the IEEE Int'l Conference on Neural Networks, July 1988.
3. Dutta, S., S. Shekhar, and W.Y. Wong, Decision Support in Non-Conservative Domains: Generalization with Neural Networks, forthcoming Decision Support Systems, North Holland, 1992.
4. Fukushima, K., A neural network for visual pattern recognition, IEEE Computer, pp. 65-75, March 1988.
5. Garavaglia, S., An application of a Counter-Propagation neural network: Simulating the Standard & Poor's corporate bond rating system, in the Proc. of the 1st Int'l Conf. on Artificial Intelligence Appl. on Wall Street, pp. 278-287, 1991.
6. Hertz, J., A. Krogh and R.G. Palmer, Introduction to the theory of neural computing, Addison Wesley, 1991.
7. Horrigan, J.O., The Determination of Long Term Credit Standing with Financial Ratios, Empirical Research in Accounting: Selected Studies, Journal of Accounting Research, 1966.
8. Irani, A., J.P. Matts, J.M. Long and J.R. Slagle, Using artificial neural nets for statistical discovery: Observations after using back-propagation, expert systems, and multiple-linear regression on clinical trial data, Univ. of Minn. Technical Report, 1989.
9. Kohonen, T., The "neural" phonetic typewriter, IEEE Comp., pp. 11-22, March 1988.
10. Lippman, R.P., An Introduction to Computing with Neural networks, IEEE ASSP Magazine, pp. 4-22, April 1987.
11. Pinches, G.E. and K.A.Mingo, A Multivariate Analysis of Industrial Bond Ratings", Journal of Finance, March 1977.
12. Pogue, T.E. and R.M.Soklofsky, What is in a Bond Rating?, Journal of Financial and Quantitative Analysis, June 1969.
13. Rumelhart, D.E., G.E. Hinton, and R.J. Williams, Learning Representations by Back-Propagation Errors, Nature, Vol. 323, pp. 533-536, 1986.
14. Rumelhart, D.E., and J. McClelland (Eds.), Parallel Distributed Processing: Explorations in the Microstructure of Cognition, MIT Press, Vols. 1-2, Cambridge, MA, 1986.
15. Surkan and Singleton, Neural networks for bond rating improved by multiple hidden layers, in the Proceedings of the IEEE International Conference on Neural Networks, San Diego, IEEE Computer Society Press, 1990.
16. Utans, J. and J. Moody, Selecting neural network architectures via the Prediction Risk: Application to Corporate Bond Rating Prediction, in the Proceedings of the 1st International Conference on Artificial Intelligence Applications on Wall Street, pp. 35-41, IEEE Computer Society Press, 1991.
17. Watson, H.J. and R.H. Sprague, Jr., The Components of an Architecture for DSS, in Decision Support Systems (R.H. Sprague & H.J. Watson, Eds.), pp. 107-117, Prentice Hall, 1989.
18. White, H., Economic prediction using neural networks: The case of IBM Daily stock returns, in the Proceedings of the IEEE International Conference on Neural Networks, San Diego, July 1988.

Personal Computers and Intelligent Systems / F.H. Vogt (Editor)
Information Processing 92, Volume III
Elsevier Science Publishers B.V. (North-Holland)

The user interface in expert systems for real-time process control: The MIP system experience [†]

C. Aguirre, E. de Pablo, J.L. Zaccagnini, and X. Alamán

Instituto de Ingeniería del Conocimiento, UAM Cantoblanco,
Modulo C-XVI, planta 4, 28049 MADRID, SPAIN.

Abstract

The development of ergonomic user interfaces is specially relevant for real-time process control applications because of the stressful conditions in which industrial plant operators have to take decisions. This paper shows the development process and the results obtained during the development of the user interface of the MIP system. MIP is a a successful real-time expert system developed at the Instituto de Ingenieria del Conocimiento (Knowledge Engineering Institute at Madrid), an university institution devoted to the transferring of technology to industry. MIP is deployed and in current use since March 1991 in an plant of REPSOL QUIMICA, S.A. at Tarragona (Spain), with a reported success both from the technical and the economical point of view.

Keyword Codes: H.1.2; H.5.2; I.2.1
Keywords: User/Machine Systems; User Interfaces; Artificial Intelligence, Applications and Expert Systems

1. INTRODUCTION

During the last years the development of high quality user interfaces that assure an effective and ergonomic use of knowledge-based systems (KBS) is receiving special attention. A great effort is put in creating environments that truly facilitate the human-machine communication (see Baecker and Buxton, 1987; Gilmore and Gertman, 1989; Hancock and Chignel, 1989; Maddix, 1990).

This subject is especially important when integrating KBS in industrial environments with the purpose of assisting (in real-time) to decision procedures related with the control of industrial processes. The actual state of the art in process automation is based on the introduction of sophisticated automatic mechanisms to decrease the need of human intervention. The automated control systems currently used have

[†] This project has been partially supported by the PEIN II program of the Spanish Ministry of Industry, Commerce and Turism.

achieved important results in this area, from the simplest feedback loop to the most complex computer-based control application. However, the elusive nature of many industrial processes together with their variability and continuous change, have made the supervision by human operators unavoidable. The job of the operator is to look after the automated control system and to certify the correct optimization of all the parameters, as well as to be prepared to check, and in extreme circumstances to substitute, the automated control system in case of malfunction.

Specific methodologies for designing user interfaces for KBS's that work in industrial environments have been developed with the objective of optimizing man-machine interaction, and therefore improving the effectiveness in performing these supervision tasks (see Waern, 1989; Gilmore and Gertman, 1989; Bodker, 1991). Some common conclusions are that an user interface for industrial environments has to be designed taking into account the ergonomical aspects and the user psychology as part of the specifications that the main application has to accomplish, that the user interface has to be constantly evaluated in its different developing stages, not only by the designers but also by the future users, that it has to be highly efficient (presenting a quick feedback to operator interaction), it has to be easy to use, and it has to be capable of integrating information from disparate sources.

In this paper we present the the user interface of the MIP Real-Time Expert System, that has been designed taking into account all these considerations, but that has additionally played an especial role during the development of the whole system, being a central element for the "maquette based" methodology of KBS development (see Alaman and others 1992c).

2. INTELLIGENT PROCESS MONITORING (MIP)

The main goal of the MIP Expert System is to assist in controlling a petrochemical reactor in a refinery plant in Tarragona, Spain. It supplies information and recommendations in real-time that help to diagnose and to take decisions concerning the control of the plant. These recommendations mainly address two issues: efficiency supervisory control, that consists in optimizing parameters with the aim of improving the overall productivity of the process, and stability supervisory control, that deals with diagnosing would-be problems before they actually occur, describing their causes and indicating possible actions to be taken.

Usually the operator is consulting the user interface main screen representing the chart of the plant, where many actual values of significant variables are shown. The information in this screen is displayed using color codes, to differentiate measured sensors, measured effectors, simulated variables, variables from the mass spectrometer analysis, etc. In addition the operator has continuously available the main diagnostic messages from the Expert System at the bottom lines of each screen. These messages focus the operator attention to the most important problems in each moment (see Figure 3). A special message screen may be consulted to obtain suggestions about how to solve these problems. Some other information is available to the operator to complement and to facilitate the diagnosis, such as data log screens, complete analysis screens, etc. All the navigation is done using either the mouse or the keyboard. Any screen can be easily selected from any other screen,

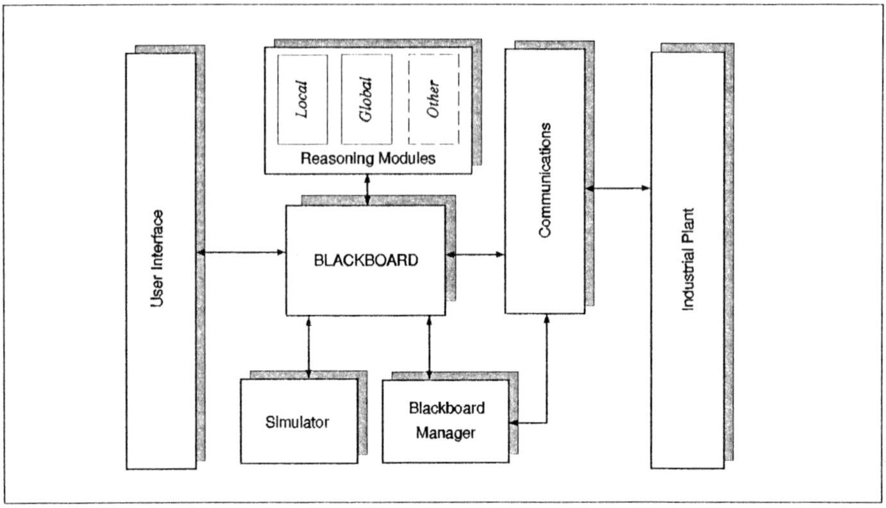

Figure 1. MIP architecture

avoiding the need of complex navigational mental models. As an user requirement, no window sizing, dragging, or overlapping is allowed. Many of these facilities, so helpful for the developer, may result in problems when collective use of the system is expected. An example of data log screen with expert system messages is shown in Figure 2.

The MIP system is designed using a blackboard based architecture (see Engelmore and Morgan, 1988). The main characteristic of the Blackboard (see Figure 1) is that any module in the system uses this data structure to communicate with any other module. The Blackboard has its own mechanisms to certify the consistency and validity of the data it contains, being the only centralized knowledge representation in the system. This blackboard architecture enables the integration of several different technologies in a cooperative framework. In the MIP system these technologies are numerical calculus (a simulator of the plant), rule-base technology (a heuristics-based expert module) and the user interface. The modularity inherent to blackboard architectures has made the development of the user interface highly independent from the development of the rest of the modules. The maquette methodology, described in the next section, has emerged as a natural development strategy under these conditions.

MIP is deployed and in current use since March 1991 in an acrylonitrile plant of REPSOL QUIMICA, S.A. at Tarragona (Spain). The system runs under OS/2 on an IBM PS/2[1] model 80, with 16MB RAM, 300 MB hard disk, math coprocessor, one additional RS232 communication card, and 8514 monitor (768 * 1024 pixel, 256 colors). The system has been enthusiastically received by operators and process engineers, and an estimated 1% improvement in productivity is being obtained. A more detailed description of the MIP project can be found in Alaman and others (1992a; 1992b).

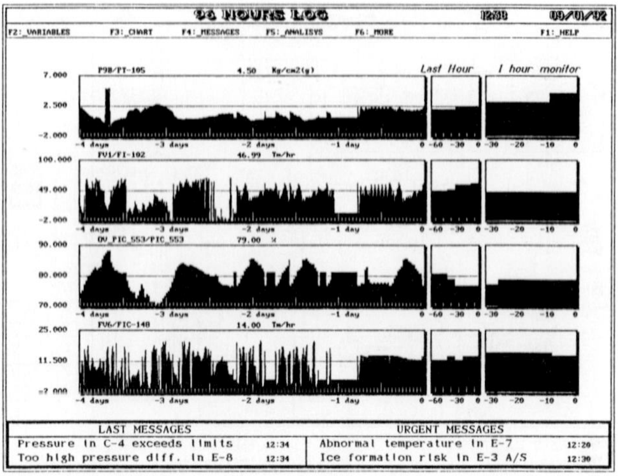

Figure 2. Final user interface (data log screen).

3. DEVELOPMENT ISSUES IN THE MIP USER INTERFACE

The main objective during the development of the user interface for the MIP project was to complement and to facilitate the control of the system, empowering person-machine dialogue by means of graphics and images. The methodological approach was to implement the user interface incrementally and in parallel with the other modules of the system (see Figure 1). In each stage of development of the MIP system some modules were deployed, with their corresponding part of the user interface. This follows the "maquette-based" approach to development of knowledge-based systems (see Zaccagnini and Alarcon, 1991; Alamán and others 1992c). This approach proposes two stages. The first stage is application maquetting, using a higher-level tool that allows to optimize the definition of the specifications and the ergonomic aspects. In the second stage the definitive version of the user interface is built using tools that optimize other aspects of the system, as for example runtime efficiency.

3.1. First stage: the maquette

The maquette is a toy-model of the real application that is deployed at the user environment at a very early stage of the development. Note that the maquette approach is very different from the usual "rapid-prototyping" approach in the sense that the former covers the whole final system look, although with no expert knowledge behind it. In the MIP project the maquette was installed at the plant after the

[1] PS/2, OS/2, The Integrated Reasoning Shell, and AVC are trade marks of IBM Corporation.

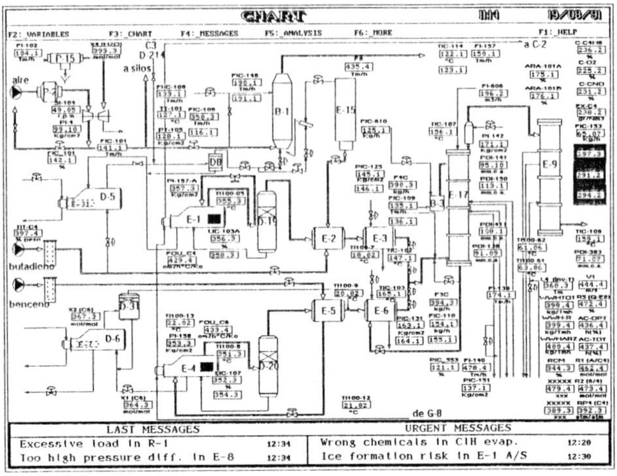

Figure 3. Final user interface (main screen).

first three months of development. The maquette was a model of the desired user interface implemented by means of an hypermedia tool (AVC)[1]. This deployment of an early version of the user interface at the real user environment not only had impact in user interface design issues, but what is more important, it influenced general aspects of the whole application. Some of the advantages of this maquette approach were:

- There was an early interaction with the real user environment. Constraints in this environment were faced right from the beginning, allowing the design of realistic approaches to the existing problems. Examples of such constraints are the shortage of physical space to install the system, the working habits of the users, the noisy or stressful environment, and the user acceptance of the new system. A common mistake is to delay the solution of this kind of constraints to the end of the project.
- There was an early interaction with the data environment. Automatic data acquisition procedures are essential, specially for real-time expert systems. Learning the constraints in this area has a huge impact in the design of the final system.
- The maquette was used as a common reference for experts and knowledge engineers to discuss about the final goals of the system. The communication between experts and knowledge engineers was notably improved.
- The maquette was used to define end-user characteristics and to subsequently design the final user interface. This guaranteed user acceptance of the final system.
- In addition, the early installation of the maquette at the user environment gave to the users, experts and management an impression of progress that encouraged their involvement in the project, being this an essential factor for the success of any innovative application.

Summarizing, the early deployment of an initial version of the user interface into the real user environment enabled to face the solution of a set of problems that, if delayed to a posterior phase of the project, would have probably invalidated the whole system. This is specially true in the case of knowledge-based applications, where the interaction with the user and environment is of a very special nature.

3.2. Second stage: the final interface

The development of the final user interface was carried out in parallel with the development of the maquette. It was coded in C language for efficiency reasons. A set of tools for translating from the AVC specifications to C language were developed, that allowed to build the final user interface module with an effort of less than 3 person/month.

The final result was an user interface connected to a real-time expert system that is deployed since March 1991 in an acrilonitrile plant of REPSOL QUIMICA,S.A. at Tarragona (Spain). The conclusive interface, obtained from the first maquetting, was deployed in May 1991.

Some characteristics of the final user interface are:

- Graphic information on the plant chart, integrating selection buttons that correspond to 85 selected variables, over a total of 460 available variables in the application (see Figure 3).
- Information from the expert system is always present in the form of messages at the bottom lines of all the screens. These messages are described and commented under user requirement.
- The speed of change from one screen any other screen is less than 2 seconds.
- The actualization of the data on the screens is made automatically by means of inner semaphores depending on the system cycle.
- Indistinct handling of the user interface by means of either the mouse or the keyboard, being possible to select objects in three different ways. This assures quick and intuitive operation.
- The information that the user requires is grouped in logically coherent groups that do not always coincide with the process representation structure in the computer system.
- No window sizing or dragging allowed. This criteria responds to the collective use of the system. The information is presented in an unique format facilitating the occasional user a quick localization of any desired item.
- To facilitate the comprehension of the interface, a limited number of screens is used, in a manner such that the mental representation that the user has to maintain with respect to the system is as simple as possible.

4. CONCLUSIONS

The user interface development has been proposed in our approach as a central element in the development of knowledge-based systems. It contributes to the success of such systems not only because of its specific role as interface for man-machine communication, but also as a tool to facilitate several elusive issues such as knowledge acquisition, user motivation and early problem identification. Additionally, the early installation of a maquette of the user interface enables the ergonomic design of the man-machine interaction from a grounded and realistic point of view.

This approach has been generalized in the frame of a complete methodology for development of knowledge-based applications, based on the concept of maquette, that is being used in several projects at the IIC (Instituto de Ingeniería del Conocimiento).

We would like to thank Guzman Garcia Tornero, Ramón Nieto, Graciano Ruiz and Juan Romero for their participation in the MIP project. We would like also to thank Juan Antonio Aguilar, Jose Dorronsoro, Guillermo Fernandez, Vicente Lopez, Rafael Muñoz, Sesh Murthy, Soledad Romero, and Pedro Serrahima for their involvement in the development of the MIP project. We want also to mention Idoia Alarcon and Guillermo Alonso because of their contribution to the maquette methodology.

5. REFERENCES

Alaman, X., S. Romero, C. Aguirre, P. Serrahima, R. Muñoz, V. Lopez, J. Dorronsoro and E. de Pablo (1992). "MIP: A Real-Time Expert System", *8th. Conference on Artificial Intelligence for Applications (CAIA'92)*, Monterey, California.

Alaman, X., S. Romero, C. Aguirre, P. Serrahima, R. Muñoz, V. Lopez, J. Dorronsoro and E. de Pablo (1992b). "Knowledge-Based Systems for Real-Time Process Control: The MIP Project", *1992 IFAC/IFIP/IMACS International Symposium on A.I. in Real-Time Control*, Delft, The Netherlands, June 1992.

Alaman, X., I. Alarcón, E. de Pablo and J.L. Zaccagnini (1992c). "The Maquette-based Methodology Applied to Real-Time Knowledge-Based Systems", *10th European Conference on Artificial Intelligence (ECAI'92)*, Vienna, Austria, Aug. 1992.

Baecker, R.M., and W.A.S. Buxton (1987). *Readings in Human-Computer Interaction.* Morgan Kaufman Pub.Inc. CA. U.S.A.

Bodker, S.(1991) *Through the Interface.* L.E.A. N.J. U.S.A.

Engelmore, R., and T. Morgan (1988). *Blackboard Systems*, Addison-Wesley, New-York.

Gilmore, W.E., D.I. Gertman, and H.S. Blackman (1989) *User-Computer Interface in Process Control.* Academic Press. C.A. U.S.A.

Hancock, P.A., and M.H. Chignell (Eds.)(1989) *Intelligent Interfaces.* North-Holland/Elsevier, The Netherlands

Maddix, F.(1990) *Human-Computer Interaction*, Ellis Horwood Chichester U.K.

Waern, Y.(1989) *Cognitive aspects of Computer Supported Tasks*, John Wiley & Sons Ltd. U.K.

Wickens, C.D., and A. Kramer (1985). *Egineering Psychology. Ann. Rev. Psychol. vol:36*, 307-348.

Zaccagnini, J.L. and M.I. Alarcon (1991). "Metodologia para S.B.C.: La Estrategia de Desarrollo Basada en Maqueta", *Spanish National Conference on Artificial Intelligence (AEPIA-91)*, Madrid, October 1991.

Personal Computers and Intelligent Systems / F.H. Vogt (Editor)
Information Processing 92, Volume III
Elsevier Science Publishers B.V. (North-Holland)

An application of case-based reasoning for fault restoration support in electric power systems

Kenzo Okuda[a] and Katsuhiro Yamazaki[b]

[a]Dept. of Information Science, Faculty of Engineering, Utsunomiya University, Utsunomiya 321, Japan

[b]Dept. of Computer Science and Systems Engineering, Faculty of Science and Engineering, Ritsumeikan University, Kita-ku, Kyoto 603, Japan

Abstract

This paper describes methods of quickly and precisely generating restoration plans using case-based reasoning for a wide range of power failures in electric power systems. The proper restoration plans, based on experiences of veteran experts, are given as cases that are indexed by outage system, power failure area, shutdown equipment, and fault point. Similar cases are adapted to failures by restoration using sound power sources, load switching, and transfer of loads to other restoration plans. The simulation results showed that an optimum solution is obtained for each failure, and the processing time is shortened to one third or one fifth compared with an approach using exhaustive searching for solutions. Moreover, there is an optimum number of cases that should be registered into the case base.

Keyword Codes: I.2.0; I.2.1; I.2.6
Keywords: Artificial Intelligence, General; Applications and Expert Systems; Learning

1. INTRODUCTION

Power failures in electric power systems should be quickly and carefully dealt with because of their disruptive effects on daily life. While most failures are automatically restored by protection systems, failures which extend over a large area, such as those in substations, are left to operators' actions. Operators are required to follow complex restoration procedures and make accurate evaluations of the situation. Case-based reasoning which directly utilizes past cases to quickly solve a new problem has been receiving widespread attention in the past few years[1-2]. The advantages of case-based reasoning are performance enhancements according to easiness of knowledge acquisition, and high reliability of solutions[3].

In this research, first we prepared cases that are proper restoration plans based on the experiences of veteran operators dealing with power failures in electric power systems. We wanted to get quick and precise generation of a restoration plan by searching for the most similar case to the new failure and modifying it to fit the failure. The system not only utilizes existing similar cases, but also enhances the applicability of cases by learning. The main parts of the system are the generation part of the restoration plans by case-based reasoning and the general restoration logic part. The system generates restoration plans using the former when the similar case exists, otherwise the latter part is used. Secondly, we clarified the effectiveness of case-based reasoning by minutely simulating many faults in a real-scale model system. From this, the method for constructing the case base, that for searching, evaluating and adapting the most similar case, and the method for refining the case base, along with their experimental results[4-6] were described.

2. FAULT RESTORATION SUPPORT IN ELECTRIC POWER SYSTEMS

2.1. Definition of the problem

The target systems are 60KV (secondary) power systems containing multiple substations, which are under the supervision of one branch office of a power company. The secondary network of each substation is radially composed, and no subsystem operates in parallel. The fault points are high-tension buses and transformer banks of each substation which experience large effects from faults. Transformer banks are also a concern during equipment shutdown for inspection and maintenance, which influence the system conditions before a failure occurs.

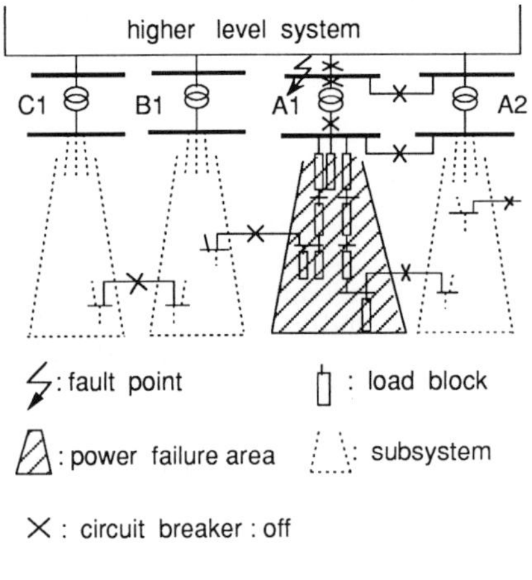

Figure 1. Diagram of a secondary electric network .

The fundamental principles for generating restoration plans are minimization of the failed power, shortening the failure time and generation of optimum restoration plans. The decision criteria for optimum restoration plans are to have the smallest number of operating circuit breakers and of power sources for restoration. The basic procedure for generating restoration plans is described using Figure 1. We assume that a permanent fault occurs at the high tension bus of subsystem A1 so that the diagonal line part is in the power failure area.

(a) Restoration from a sound bus A2 of the same substation.

(b) Restoration from a directly neighboring subsystem B1.

(c) Restoration by load switching.

If the power failure still remains, then part of the loads in subsystems

B1 and A2 are switched to another subsystem C1 and so on that neighbors them, and the transmissible power from B1 and A2 is increased to A1.

The case base of this problem is composed of the circumstances of the failure and a plan for restoring the resulting power failure. Generation of the restoration plan is done by selecting available power sources for the power failure area, fixing the restoration range for each power source, and determining the operating sequence of the circuit breakers.

2.2. Expression of the cases

Restoration plans are composed of the following several frames.

(a) The frame of a total restoration plan

This frame is composed of an outage system, shutdown equipment, fault point, power failure area, power failure load, restoration sources, and restoration plan. These are used to search for one restoration plan.

(b) The frame of a restoration source

This frame is composed of a power source name, power source system, transmissible power of the restoration source, and load switching.

(c) The frame of a restoration plan

This frame shows the contents of a restoration plan by one power source and is composed of power source name, a list of restored components, total restoration load and the next candidate. The total restoration plan is composed of multiple frames of the restoration plan. The next candidate slot points to the frame of the restoration plan that can be used to restore part of the restored components. The solution for the case when restoration source capacity is short is registered in this frame.

(d) The frame of load switching

This frame is composed of a system name, shutdown equipment, increased power, target system for restoration, restoration source, restoration plan and the next candidate in the load switching plan. Figure 2 shows an example of case frame representation. The total restoration plan T1 is composed of restoration plans P1, P2 and P3 which are restored by power sources S1, S2 and S3, respectively. S1 has C1 as a load switching plan. Since the load to be restored is 96MW and the transmissible power of S1 is 41MW, C1 switches an 82MW load using source S5 so that the transmissible power of S1 increases to 123MW. The system computes restoration plans for the failures of all banks and one bank of substation transformers in each subsystem, provided that one transformer bank is stopped in each substation. The load level is assumed to be heavy, i.e. 85% of the peak load in a year. The selection criteria for a case to be registered in the case base were described in section 2.1. Thus, the system classifies the restoration plans obtained by exhaustively generating solutions into each restoration source, and then selects cases that include optimum solutions for each failure.

2.3. Retrieval, evaluation and adaptation of cases

(1) Case retrieval

The system retrieves the most relevant cases for a problem. Indexing of the cases involves the failed system, power failure area, shutdown equipment, and the fault point in that order from high to low priority.

(2) Case evaluation

The system clarifies the difference between the power failure area of the

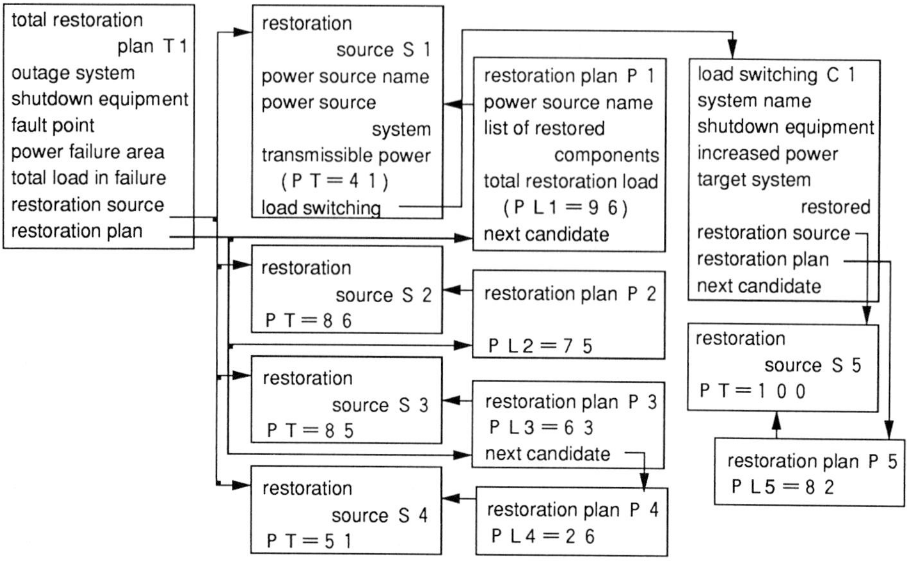

(a) Construction of case-frames

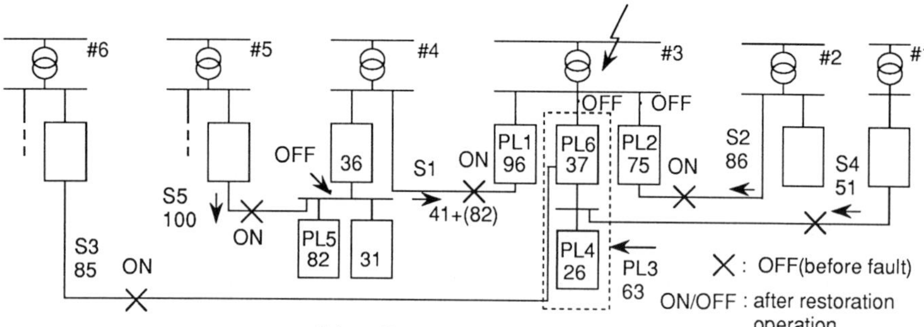

(b) System diagram

Figure 2. Frame representation of a case.

case and that of the given problem. Then, it stores the power failure area into a list of restored components.

(3) Case adaptation

If the power source capacity in each frame of the restoration plan is short of the total load to be restored, the system adapts the case to the problem using the following steps(a)-(c).

(a) Adaptation by load switching

As shown for S1 of Figure 2, the case is adapted using a load switching plan pointed by the load switching slot in a frame of the restoration source.

(b) Adaptation by the next candidate in a restoration plan

As shown for P3, a frame is adapted in the restoration plan as pointed by the next candidate slot in the referred to frame of the restoration plan.

(c) Transfer loads to other frame of a restoration plan

Part or all of the restored components that lack the power source capacity are transferred to a list of restored components of another frame of the restoration plan which has sufficient transmissible power. Thus, while (a) and (b) generate restoration plans based on retrieved cases, (c) generates a slightly different restoration plan. Finally, the system generates a sequence of circuit breakers which should be made and broken.

2.4. Refinement method of the case base

Assume that a restoration plan for power failures is described as iCjR, i.e. the number of load switching is i and the number of restoration sources is j. As the load decreases, i,j monotonously decrease to 0,1, respectively, so that the cost of restoration operations decreases. The learning process of restoration patterns for some failure conditions when the load conditions of a system change is conceptually shown in Figure 3. Figure 3(a) shows the initial stage of constructing the case base, and just a restoration plan of 1C3R is registered. Figure 3(b) shows examples of learning processes for several load conditions. The mark ↓ indicates a plan using a fewer number of power sources for a newly learned problem. Figure 3(c) shows a matured stage of learning, and the bold lines indicate the application range of the plan.

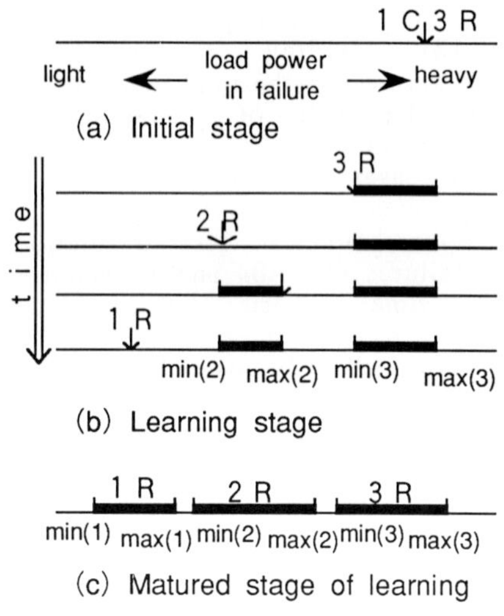

Figure 3. Learning process of restoration patterns .

3. EXPERIMENTAL RESULTS AND DISCUSSION

3.1. Experimental conditions

The target secondary system is real-scale, and composed of ten subsystems each of which has 1 to 10 load blocks. The standard load conditions of the system are assumed to be 85% of the peak load in an expected power flow diagram during August. The program is written in K-Prolog on a Sony workstation NEWS 821.

3.2. Constructing the case base and case-based reasoning

According to the selection criteria of cases described in section 2.2, the total number of cases registered in the case base is 24, and each subsystem has 1 to 6 cases.

Table 1 Effect of the number of cases on restorative plan generation

number of cases	10/1				24/4				26/6		32/12		optimum solution		
fault no.	re	ex	cb	pt	re	ex	cb	pt	re	ex	re	ex	ex	cb	pt
4A01	0.8	4.5	3	2R	1.9	5.7	3	2R	2.0	5.8	2.4	6.2	17.0	3	2R
4A02	0.8	32.6	9	1C3R	2.0	7.3	9	3R	2.3	7.5	2.5	7.8	7669.8	9	3R
4A03	0.8	37.7	7	1C3R	1.9	14.6	5	1C2R	2.0	15.8	2.3	16.2	64.0	5	1C2R
4A04	0.8	54.6	9	2C3R	2.0	52.8	9	2C3R	2.1	21.6	2.4	22.1	112.7	9	2C3R
4A05	0.8	4.4	3	2R	2.0	5.7	3	2R	2.4	6.1	2.4	6.3	16.9	3	2R
4A06	0.9	4.7	3	2R	2.0	5.8	3	2R	2.3	6.1	2.3	6.4	16.9	3	2R
4A07	0.8	4.5	3	2R	2.0	5.8	3	2R	2.3	6.1	2.4	6.9	13.7	3	2R
4A08	0.8	68.9	9	2C3R	2.0	66.4	9	2C3R	2.0	21.4	2.4	21.5	128.1	9	2C3R
4A09	0.8	9.9	5	3R	1.9	6.6	5	3R	2.0	6.8	2.4	7.3	33.5	5	3R
4A10	0.8	10.0	5	3R	2.1	6.8	5	3R	2.3	7.1	2.4	7.2	33.4	5	3R
4A11	0.8	9.9	5	3R	2.0	6.8	5	3R	2.3	7.1	2.4	7.3	24.1	5	3R
4A12	0.9	4.4	3	2R	2.1	5.8	3	2R	2.4	6.1	2.4	6.2	16.8	3	2R

number of cases : total number of cases / number of cases in subsystem no.4 ,
re : retrieval time of cases (s) ,ex : excution time including retrieval (s) ,
cb : number of circuit breaker operation , pt : restoration pattern

The numbers of each frame are 24 for the total restoration plans, 149 for the restoration sources, 77 for the restoration plans, and 22 for load switching plans. The example is a power failure in subsystem 4 which has four load blocks and four neighboring systems. Table 1 shows the number of cases registered in the case base, the retrieval time of relevant cases, and the execution time for getting restoration plans toward twelve power failures. They are composed of no equipment shutdown, i.e. all transformers in each subsystem work (4A01), and there is an equipment shutdown in each subsystem except subsystem 4 (4A02-12). According to the results, the system gets restoration plans for all failures even when the total number of cases is 10 where each subsystem has one case. Here many of the restoration plans are obtained by the adaption method (c) in section 2.3. If the total number of the cases is 24, i.e. the number of cases for subsystem 4 is four, the execution time for getting the restoration plans becomes shorter on the whole. This is because the restoration plans are obtained by less adaptation using methods (a) and (b). Since the two failures of 4A04 and 08 require complex restoration operations, the execution time is shortened to less than 40% by registering them in the case base.

Compared with the occasion when the cases for all 12 power failures in this subsystem are registered in the case base, and the total number of cases is 32, the retrieval time is increased about 20% so that the execution time to get the restoration plans is increased. If the number of cases for failures in all subsystems increases, the total number of cases rapidly increases so that the retrieval time increases even further. Thus, an optimum number exists in the total number of cases that should be registered if the execution time is important, such as in restoration operations for power failures.

We compare the execution time between case-based reasoning and the exhaustive generation of restoration plans using Table 1. Since the latter selects an optimum solution based on the criteria from restoration plans obtained by exhaustive searching, the time for getting all solutions is shown in the optimum solution column. The results show that the execution time of case-based reasoning is shortened to one third or one fifth of that for exhaustive searching, and the solutions are equal to the optimum ones.

3.3. Refinement of the cases

We investigated the situation for generating restoration plans, uniformly changing the load level of the system from 85% to 50% at 5% intervals. Both the number of power sources for restoration and the number of circuit breaker operations gradually decrease if the load level decreases in all failures. Thus, the refinement of cases can generate detailed optimum restoration patterns according to the change of load conditions which is one important system condition, without increasing the total number of cases registered. Furthermore, we can shorten the processing time through the learning process of the cases.

4. CONCLUSION

This paper described the construction of the case base, retrieval, evaluation and adaptation of cases, and their refinement based on changes of load levels. Case-based reasoning was successfully applied to the generation of fault restoration plans in electric power systems. Furthermore, the key issues in constructing and refining the case bases were identified. We believe that this knowledge can be applied not only for generating fault restoration plans in electric power systems, but in a wide range of application fields.

ACKNOWLEDGEMENTS

We thank Mr.Hiroyoshi Watanabe and Mr.Kazumitsu Nakagawa for their invaluable assistance in system development and simulation.

REFERENCES

[1] Ashley, K.D. and Rissland, E.L., A Case-Based Approach to Modeling Legal Expertise, IEEE EXPERT, Fall (1988)70.
[2] CASE-BASED REASONING from DARPA: Machine Learning Program Plan, DARPA Case-Based Reasoning Workshop(1989)1.
[3] Okuda, K. and Yamazaki, K., Case-based Reasoning and Its Applications, Journal of IPS Japan,31, 2 (1990) 244.
[4] Okuda, K., Watanabe, H., Yamazaki, K. and Baba, T., Fault Restoration Operation Scheme in Secondary Power Systems using Case-based Reasoning, Trans. IEE Japan, 108-B,12 (1988) 553.
[5] Okuda, K., Nakagawa, K. and Yamazaki, K., Construction Method of Case-Base for Fault Restoration Support System in Secondary Power Systems, ibid., 111-B,3 (1991) 259.
[6] Okuda, K. and Yamazaki, K., Construction and Refinement Method of Case-Base for Fault Restoration Support in Secondary Power Systems, IPSJ SIG Reports, 91-AI-75-6 (1991) 49.

Personal Computers and Intelligent Systems / F.H. Vogt (Editor)
Information Processing 92, Volume III
Elsevier Science Publishers B.V. (North-Holland)

Knowledge Based Systems and Process Simplification

Scott A. Hatfield (shatf.wbst845e@xerox.com)

Xerox Knowledge Based Systems Competency Center
Webster, New York, USA 14580

Abstract

A key capability of knowledge based systems, the ability to enable radical business process simplification, is discussed. Two applications are described to highlight what is meant by business process simplification and to compare the pre- and post-implementation processes as well as to illustrate the benefit to industry for the next decade. An emphasis is placed on how intelligent systems can act as agents to transform a business operation and why thinking of knowledge based systems in this way might yield better success with the technology.

Keyword Codes: I.2.1
Keywords: Artificial Intelligence, Applications and Expert Systems

1. INTRODUCTION

For most of the history of knowledge based systems, practitioners have struggled to effectively market and position the field to industry. In this paper, I will demonstrate a unique capability of knowledge based systems - to effectively support and enable radical business process simplification. I will highlight two applications developed at Xerox and use them to define what is meant by process simplification. Finally, I will propose that identifying appropriate application domains which feature process simplification is a key element of success in using intelligent or knowledge based systems.

2. ORIGINS OF THE APPROACH

In 1988, Xerox Corporation chartered the Knowledge Based Systems Competency Center (KBSCC). The mission given this group involved the development and deployment of production quality knowledge based systems for internal use. These systems were intended to address key internal business issues.

Based on that mission and strong executive sponsorship, the KBSCC set out to build systems of strategic importance to the Company. Without focused consideration of process simplification, the KBSCC identified a number of large, critical domains and began development. While we originally thought of these applications as "strategic", we came to understand that the process of developing knowledge based systems in these areas also brought about process reengineering. The end results were exactly what the executives hoped for and have resulted in dramatically optimized processes and systems for performing a number of critical business functions. The next two sections describe two of the applications in detail.

3. CASE STUDY - DESIGN, MANUFACTURABILITY, AND COST MODELS

As with many companies in the 1980's, Xerox was looking for ways to reduce the cost of its manufactured goods. Cost reduction was one of three Corporate priorities and received a great deal of attention in the face of Japanese competition that priced competitive products for what it cost Xerox to manufacture them. One identified cause of high manufacturing cost was the inability to accurately predict the future manufacturing cost early in the design phase of product development when changes could be made inexpensively. Long design cycles, functional handoffs, and multinational manufacturing all led to inaccurate estimates. The paradigm where Designers design and then "throw the design over the wall" to Manufacturing was understood to be suboptimal. A number of non-systems techniques were implemented such as early supplier involvement, colocation of teams, "Design for Assembly" and "Design for Manufacturability". Each of these approaches raised the awareness of Designers and many improvements have been seen, especially in critical, high cost parts. The process used from the 1970's into the 80's is depicted in Figure 1.

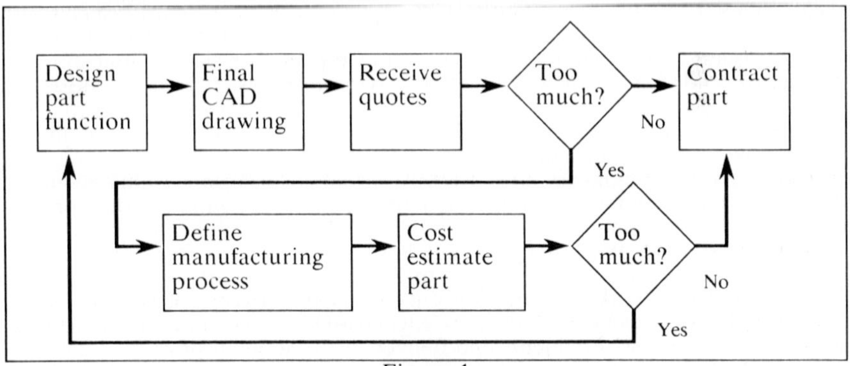

Figure 1

An additional historical solution was to create a group of Cost Engineers who were colocated with the various product design teams and served to review designs and forecast part costs. Such an organization still led to a compartmentalized, sequential process. The design was conceived, specified, and toleranced in such a way as to provide a certain function. Once the Engineer believed that the part would "work", he handed the design off to a Designer who would enter the part into a CAD system. Finally, for most parts the design was sent to a Cost Engineer only on its way to Manufacturing or to be quoted by an external supplier. The Cost Engineer would draw on a large number of years of manufacturing experience, refer to several purchasing databases to get contracted rates for materials and processes, and return a cost back to the design team. If the part cost was below or near the allocated part budget, the design team would submit the part for build authorization and consider the job complete. Only if the part was too expensive would a detailed study of the part's design and manufacturing process be undertaken. One can immediately see several disadvantages to this process, among them:

- There were multiple hand-off's included in the process, up to 6 participants.

- Cost knowledge was partitioned away from the primary users, the Engineer and the Designer. Without understanding the cost drivers, it was impossible to learn how to reduce the cost of products.
- No optimization was performed, simply cost target achievement.
- Rework to meet cost targets involved extremely long cycle times.
- Large variations were possible between Cost Engineers.
- Training was given in cost reduction principles but tools for determining actual costs were unavailable.

In the Spring of 1990, Xerox initiated the construction of the Design, Manufacturability, and Cost Models System (DMCM). Intended as a tool to directly support Designers and Engineers, the system aids in developing cost estimates for individual components designed using a number of commodities such as plastics, sheet metal, and electronics. The system contains knowledge about how a part will be manufactured. It knows about material specifications, process specifications, and how to cost them using Xerox's central purchasing databases. DMCM knows about dimensions and geometry and, with a user's help, can read a CAD description of the part. The system can consider many more aspects more accurately than a human ever could, or would. It considers factors such as economic trends, duties and tariffs, currency impacts, operator fatigue, tooling costs, setup and teardown costs, alternative materials, finishes, tools, and manufacturing processes. Finally, the system supports what-if reasoning to review alternatives and will make recommendations to reduce the cost of a part, showing precisely how much money can be saved with each change.

Designers and Engineers now use this system to feed cost estimates into the design budgeting system and perform proactive cost estimation and reduction. The new process flow is demonstrated in Figure 2. Process simplification has occurred in a number of ways: process cycletimes have been reduced from months to an afternoon, handoffs have been reduced to zero until the part is quoted, and the number of parts being redesigned is reduced. While other cost reducing design techniques remain beneficial, the knowledge based system additionally leverages the expertise of the Cost Engineers and delivers it to the point of need.

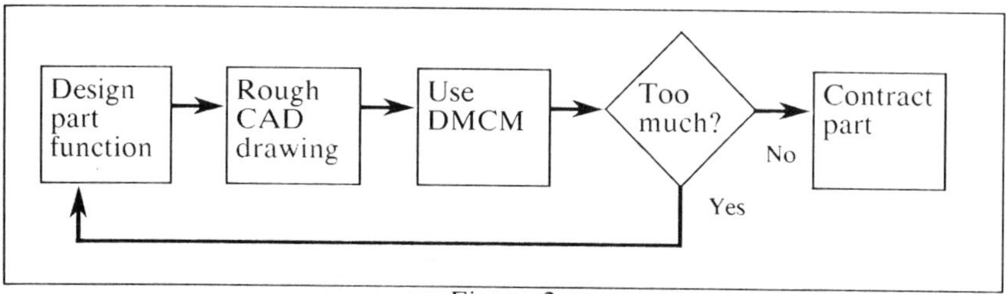

Figure 2

The net result to Xerox, when all commodities (optics, turnings, circuit boards, etc.) are available will be a cost of goods reduction in the tens of millions of dollars every year. Figure 3 contains the screen that is returned, showing the material and processes required to manufacture a sample part.

Perhaps the greatest benefit over time is that the modified business process enables people to learn about costing. The Designers and Engineers are now directly aware of the impact that various design parameters will have on part costs. The availability of this information will drive down parts cost as no other mechanism could have.

```
                    MANUFACTURING PROCESS INFORMATION

     Design: NOBLE86                                  Revision: A
     User:   DMAST                                    Program:  DEMO1

               -------------------- MATERIAL USAGE --------------------
Spec     Description                        Amount   Unit     Rate     Cost $US
46-0311  Full Skid Load                        1.3    DM3      .06        .08
46-0200  Plastic Bag                           1.1    EA       .032       .04
50-0506  Paint                                 8.93   DM2      .0032      .03
46-5006  Misc Hardware                         1      EA      8.0        8.00

                -------------------- PROCESS STEPS --------------------
Seq  Spec     Description                         Minutes  Rate     Cost $US
10   PBB020   Press Op 2                              .15  .4551    .07
20   PBB020   Press Op 1                              .11  .4551    .05
30   WLD020   Multi-Hole Tap                          .50  .4856    .2449
30   WLB010   Single-Hole Tap                         .27  .4317    .1145
40   PCA010   Spotwelds                              1.41  .695     .9774
50   PHA020   Degreasing                              .13  .5476    .0731

        Char Mode: Replace   Page 1                   Count: *0
```

Figure 3

4. CASE STUDY - XEROX TERRITORY CONFIGURATOR

A second application involves the domain of sales support tools. Xerox utilizes a direct sales force in most of the countries in which it operates. This sales force numbers in the tens of thousands. On an annual basis, Sales Managers must reallocate sales territories among the many Sales Representatives. The steps of the process that we found are listed in Table 1.

Person	Activity	Duration
Commissions Administrator	Request Master Customer List	1 week
Administrator	Obtain district Establishment List (non-customers)	1 week
Commissions Administrator	Obtain current assignments from district sources	3 days
Sales Managers	Translate materials into meeting documents	2 weeks
Sales Managers	Create vertical territories (e.g. automotive or pharmaceutical)	1-2 weeks / round
Sales Managers	Create vertical territory reports	2 days
Sales Managers	Create geographic territories (by postal code)	1-2 weeks / round
Sales Managers	Create geographic reports	2 days
Sales Managers	Create budgets and quotas	2 days
Sales Managers	Create Change Requests to update database	3 days
Administrator	Key changes	4 days
Administrator	Generate new reports and communicate to teams	2 days

Table 1

Some of the key observations about this process include:

- There were no automated tools available. This lead to a process which could take multiple months to execute.
- The process was prone to a great deal of error as establishments were left uncovered or duplicated. Such establishments would not be called on and were therefore unlikely to generate revenue for the year.
- There was a significant level of dissatisfaction on the part of the sales force, each of whom felt that his territory assignment was inferior to what others had received.
- The assignment process took sales management away from the field during a time of year when they should be closing deals for the end of the fiscal year.
- Geographic compactness (to decrease wasted travel time) was infrequently considered due to a complete lack of automation.
- The process was based on so few facts as to usually degenerate into bad feelings and poor allocations; there was no process capability to perform configuration well.

Into this environment we have introduced the Xerox Territory Configurator (XTC). Conceptually, the tool is very simple. It is a knowledge based system that brings together four key elements:

- A mapping database that includes postal code boundaries in latitude and longitude measures
- An establishment database that includes all prospects, customers, industry codes, number of employees, and geographic location
- A state-of-the-art graphical user interface that allows direct manipulation of assignments and gives immediate feedback to the user
- A knowledgebase that includes knowledge about customer potential, industries, types of Sales Representatives, and the configuration process itself

Each modification is reflected in changes to graphs, tables, and warnings as the configuration is optimized from multiple perspectives.

With this tool, sales management teams are able to configure sales territories with assistance in a fraction of the time formerly required, based on facts. The process has been simplified to the point where it can't even be diagramed. A team gathers around a display, moves establishments into vertical markets, moves zip codes into geographic territories and adjusts them with intelligent assistance from the system until they are equitable. The total time requirement has been reduced to little more than a day. All data feeds in and out of the system are automatic.

Some of the direct benefits associated with this approach include:

- Fewer establishments are left uncovered each year, resulting in increased revenue.
- Optimized territories have resulted in decreased local mileage costs as well as allowing Sales Representatives to make more sales calls per day.
- Data entry has been eliminated.
- Sales force attrition is reduced as a result of increased job satisfaction.
- The system considers the relationship that develops between salesmen and customers and disrupts as few as possible in the reconfiguration process.
- Industry oriented assignments are easier to define and manage and result in improved sales efficiency.

As with the DMCM system, XTC enables a new user community to manage a task that was unmanageable without a knowledge based system. The Sales

Managers have become much more sophisticated about territory management because they now have the data that they need and the time with which to manage the process.

The XTC system has been used today by multiple Xerox divisions to configure territories as broad as the U.S. national market. By simply changing databases and acquiring new mapping data we are able to use the same process and tool in multiple countries.

5. PROCESS SIMPLIFICATION

Both DMCM and XTC demonstrate the concept of using knowledge based systems to enable process simplification. Both applications make possible radically simpler and more efficient business processes than could be performed without the benefit of knowledge based systems technology.

As simplification initiatives the applications can claim significant measurable benefits. Functional Xerox management, Sales Operations and Cost Engineering respectively, have readily endorsed the applications and served as their sponsors. It is unlikely that they would have expressed the degree of support for anything less than the order of magnitude process improvements delivered.

Given the two experiences described above, it seems appropriate to consider process simplification when selecting applications of knowledge based systems technology. It seems likely that both of the following are true:

1) Knowledge based systems technology can be more successfully applied in process change situations.
2) Radical process transformations may call for knowledge based systems technology.

I believe the first point to be supported by considering some of the key guidelines that successful industrial AI practitioners have identified.

- Process simplification applications can be readily justified through measurable benefits. Process simplifications usually decrease paper flows, calendar time, personnel requirements, cost, or some other readily measurable, tangible metric. This enhances the ability to develop and maintain management sponsorship and funding.
- Process simplification applications may not need to be technically sophisticated; they derive their major benefit from the new process itself. In many cases, the use of fairly routine knowledge modeling and inferencing techniques will suffice to enable the new process. The XTC application uses fairly traditional search techniques (conventional depth-first plus some genetic algorithms) to perform most of its processing. DMCM uses rule-based programming to encode the knowledge of costing and manufacturing experts. This reduces project risk.
- Process simplification projects get a team intimately involved in the expert and user communities. To build systems, the team must understand what is done today, how it is done, what systems are used, and what documents are created. Such understanding builds credibility with functional participants and promotes understanding of the problem. Such an engagement helps to ensure that cooperation is maintained between the application developers and end users.
- Process simplification applications must interface with existing peripheral information systems. XTC and DMCM read mapping data, establishment databases, and contracted cost data. In turn, they feed assignment databases and product development cost tracking systems. By

acknowledging and designing for these connections, the final system will be a integral part of a process.
- Process simplification approaches can yield the order of magnitude improvement that can excite and galvanize action to build such systems.

The second point, that radical process transformations may call for knowledge based systems has also been demonstrated. To simplify the costing process, a knowledge based system was required to capture and deliver the knowledge to the point of need. It is such behavior that defines an intelligent or knowledge based application. If we had delivered a costing database or a marketing database alone, the users would still not have had the expertise to move to a new process. Such applications seem to be the most promising potential uses of knowledge based systems technology.

Based on these considerations, applications with a strong process reengineering flavor should be more likely to succeed and deliver real benefits. If a number of such applications are developed, an organization can experience significant beneficial change. Such successes with the technology will enable businesses to meet the challenges of the 1990's.

6. ACKNOWLEDGEMENTS

I would like to acknowledge the two Project Managers who designed, constructed, and launched the two applications described here, Tilak Dissanayake for XTC and Norman Crowfoot for DMCM. In addition, I would acknowledge the dozens of members of the development teams and each of the many Xerox organizations that have contributed to the success of these applications.

7. REFERENCES

1 John Seely Brown, "High Performance Work Systems for the 1990's", in Benchmark, pp. 8-11, Fall 1989.

2 Crowfoot, Hatfield, and Swank, "The Design, Manufacturability, and Cost Models Application", Proceedings of the Innovative Applications of Artificial Intelligence, AAAI Press, 1992.

3 C. Dym, "Issues in the Design and Implementation of Expert Systems", AI EDAM, Vol. 1 No. 1, pp. 37-46.

4 David P. Hanna, Designing Organizations for High Performance, Addison-Wesley, 1988.

5 Scott A. Hatfield and Norman C. Crowfoot, "Knowledge Based Systems in Cost Estimating and Design" in Proceedings of Autofact 1990, Society of Manufacturing Engineers.

6 S. P. Robbins, Organization Theory: Structure, Design, and Applications, Prentice Hall, 1990.

7 R. Rothwell and T. G. Whiston, "Design, Innovation, and Corporate Integration", R&D Management, Vol. 20 No. 3, July 1990, pp.193-201.

8 Edgar H. Shein, Process Consultation Volume II, Addison-Wesley, 1987.

SYMPOSIUM:
COOPERATIVE RESEARCH PROGRAMS

Symposium Organizer:

B. Oakley
Logica Cambridge Ltd., London, UK

Personal Computers and Intelligent Systems / F.H. Vogt (Editor)
Information Processing 92, Volume III
Elsevier Science Publishers B.V. (North-Holland)

RESEARCH AND DEVELOPMENT PROGRAMS IN INFORMATICS: AN AUSTRALIAN PERSPECTIVE

Dr. John F. O'Callaghan
Chief, CSIRO Division of Information Technology

SUMMARY

Australian Research and Development (R&D) in Informatics is currently characterised by the following:

- strong public sector strategic R&D in government research organisations and academic institutions,
- a dramatic increase in R&D within the industrial sector, mainly due to recent Government incentives,
- an increase in the mechanisms for linking the public and private sector R&D activities for the national benefit.

Recent assessments of the potential benefits of Australian R&D have been made within a framework development by CSIRO. The assessment indicates that overall the potential benefits for Australia from R&D in Informatics is not as high as R&D in such sectors as mineral exploration and mining, environment, animal production and primary products, plant production and primary products and health.

There are nevertheless areas of R&D in Informatics where Australia can benefit substantially and be a significant player in the Asia-Pacific region. These areas include quality software and systems engineering and telecommunications services, and are being driven strongly by the changing nature and structure of the Australian-based industries in the Software and Services and the Telecommunications sectors.

The potential benefits derived by successfully utilizing Informatics products and services in other industry sectors, particularly mineral exploration and mining, environmental management, manufacturing and the services industries is being increasingly recognised.

As a result, many of the Government's funding schemes and recent initiatives have been oriented towards deriving the potential benefits from R&D in Informatics for these other industry sectors.

The Industry Research and Development grants in Information and Communications Technologies for example have given more emphasis to the commercialisation of the results of the research.

The recent Government initiatives include the Cooperative Research Centres scheme which is establishing 50 science and technology centres, linking end-users, industry and public sector research groups. Centres already announced in the area of Informatics include those on Intelligent Decision Systems, Optical Fibre and Photonic Technology, Robust and Adaptive Control, Signal Processing and Distributed Systems Technology.

Other initiatives include a Collaborative Grants scheme to promote collaborative R&D between industry and academic institutions and the formation of the Australian Computing and Communications Institute, a major industry-based R&D consortia.

The importance of computing and communications infrastructure in supporting R&D in Informatics has been given more emphasis recently. Special governments grants have been given to academic institutions for high-performance computing, especially for parallel architecture systems. In addition, the Australian Vice-Chancellors Committee and the CSIRO have established AARNet, the Australian Academic and Research Network, for communications services within the research community and industrial affiliates. A recommendation has been made to establish a high-speed network, with wide bandwidth international connexions, to support R&D in Informatics across the academic, government and industry sectors.

Initiatives are also being taken to increase the skills base in Informatics, following reviews of the educational and training requirements of the Australian Informatics industry and a review of the discipline of Computing in Australian academic institutions.

Personal Computers and Intelligent Systems / F.H. Vogt (Editor)
Information Processing 92, Volume III
Elsevier Science Publishers B.V. (North-Holland)

COLLABORATIVE RESEARCH PROGRAMS IN CANADA

Vince Thomson, PhD

Institute for Information Technology
National Research Council of Canada

ABSTRACT

Collaborative research programs sponsored by Canadian governments have become very prevalent in the last decade. Governments at all levels have used partnering as a policy tool to improve industrial competitiveness and to attract and retain industries within their jurisdictions. Research partnering is seen by industry as a strategy to improve competitiveness by sharing technology development, where the measure of success is economically beneficial exploitation of technology.

Canadian programs range from the creation of Centres of Excellence at universities to develop technology in key areas and to train students, to the formation of industrial consortia in many technology specific domains. Many provincial and local governments sponsor technology institutes at universities to develop university-industry linkages and to create environments conducive to strengthening high technology companies in their area. Examples of several types of programs are given, and strengths and weaknesses of programs discussed.

In Canada the majority of funding for research partnering programs is being contributed by governments. This is viewed by taxpayers, participants and governments as a role of government in order to help offset the technical risk on the part of companies participating in precompetitive R&D and to fulfil government's responsibility in the domain of university education.

The various players: universities, research organizations and industry, are just becoming familiar with working together. There will continue to be adjustments in the relative roles of these performers in order to further improve the benefits of collaborative research programs. Overall, the future should see many more collaborative research activities in Canada and more than likely some new, innovative programs.

INTRODUCTION

Collaborative research projects on a one-on-one basis between many types of organizations have been done for a long time. This is especially true of research and development (R&D) partnerships between companies. Recently, collaborative research has become more and more a way of doing business for industry and a tool of industrial policy used by governments which try to improve the competitiveness of the economies within their jurisdictions.

As the focus of commercial activity has moved from local to national to international, industry has used various strategies to be competitive. One strategy that has emerged is the use of partnerships for precompetitive or preproprietary technology development. This is a relatively new phenomenon which is different than partnering for marketing, strategic or organizational goals. In addition, as one of the strategies of governments to attract and retain industries within their jurisdictions and to improve local industrial competitiveness, governments have added new policies for technology development. One of these policy directions has been the fostering of R&D partnerships. Thus, there are two driving forces for the promotion of R&D collaboration, the international competitiveness of industry and the policy of government; the two are predominantly complementary.

Today, partnering at all levels is seen as a necessity to improve the ability of companies to compete. Research partnering is a specific strategy which has been adopted by a large number of OECD governments to improve industrial competitiveness. Canadian governments at all levels (national, provincial and municipal) have considered policies for promoting R&D partnerships. Certainly the national government, most provincial governments, and a few local or municipal governments have put policies and programs in place within the last 10 years. A discussion of some of the general reasons for having such programs follows. In addition, a description of some of the collaborative research partnerships and programs, as well as some observations of the present strengths and weaknesses of the programs are given.

CANADIAN POLICY/PROGRAM GOALS

In Canada, the main reasons for the promotion of collaborative R&D programs are the acceleration of technology creation and dissemination, the training of scientists and engineers, and the development of partnerships. Collaborative programs specifically target the formation of linkages among universities, research organizations and industry, the formation of strategic alliances among companies, and the promotion of 'critical' technologies.

Most of these programs have also had the effect of diversifying funding for research, i.e. providing new mechanisms for funding, and providing funding for new types of programs. This has resulted in several new programs (some of which are described below) and better linkages between universities, research organizations and industry. The types of collaborative research programs have been highly varied, such as: Centres of Excellence, targeted programs, industrial chairs, and consortia. Research organizations have not been targeted by specific programs, but have generally participated in most of the university and industry formed projects, as well as initiating some of their own. Regional governments have promoted collaborative programs, viewing them as an additional tool for attracting industry to their region.

Themes for collaborative research programs are the same everywhere: access to technology, access to trained labour, and access to government funding for risk reduction. The underlying premise is that collaborative research programs will enhance benefits for industry for the benefit of society at large.

Large, collaborative, multinational programs were first initiated and operated by the European Community, such programs as: ESPRIT, RACE, EUREKA, etc. More recently, global collaborative research programs have been conceived: the Human Frontiers Science Program (HFSP), which does research in biological science, and the Intelligent Manufacturing Systems (IMS), which is aimed at research in advanced manufacturing.

CANADIAN NATIONAL PROGRAMS

Networks of Centres of Excellence

The Networks of Centres of Excellence Program was started in 1988 as a means to fund university-industry collaborative research. The Networks are groups of scientists from many universities, usually geographically distant, who pool expertise in partnership with some companies to do cooperative research in a targeted area. The number of Centres by research area is: biotechnology: 3, medical: 4, science: 3, engineering: 5.

Objectives:

1) to stimulate the production of leading edge fundamental and long term applied research;
2) to develop and retain world class Canadian scientists and engineers;
3) to integrate Canadian research and technology development efforts into national networks;
4) to develop strong industry-university partnerships in order to accelerate the diffusion of advanced technological knowledge to industry.

Funding:

The Canadian government is providing $240M over 5 years. Industry also participates in a few projects with in kind contributions. Infrastructure costs are contributed by universities.

Performance criteria:

excellence of science and of people,
linkages and networking,
relevance to industrial competitiveness,
management capability.

Examples:

CITR	Canadian Institute for Telecommunications Research
IRIS	Institute for Robotics and Intelligent Systems
ULSI	Microelectronic Devices, Circuits and Systems for ULSI

A detailed example of one of the Centres is given below.

Institute for Robotics and Intelligent Systems (IRIS)

The Institute for Robotics and Intelligent Systems (IRIS) is one of the 15 Research Networks selected by the Canadian government under the Networks of Centres of Excellence Program. It is focused on the use of intelligent systems in order to improve the competitiveness of Canadian industry whether the technology is expert systems to control increasingly complex manufacturing processes, or intelligent robotic devices employed in difficult or hazardous environments. The research program of IRIS includes 22 projects at 18 Canadian universities and over 120 research professors.

Objectives:

1) to improve the networking among researchers within IRIS;
2) to create technology in intelligent systems for transfer and diffusion to improve the competitiveness of industry;
3) to train and develop world class researchers.

Funding:

IRIS has a budget of $23.8M over the next four years to fund its programs; as mentioned above, this money comes from the Canadian government as part of the Networks of Centres of Excellence Program. PRECARN, an industrial consortium (described below), provides professional management.

Program:

IRIS has a research program in three areas:

Computational Perception
visual & auditory perception, vision systems for navigation, sensory processing architectures;
Knowledge Based Systems
interfaces, design/management of information systems, reasoning systems, constraint logic programming;
Intelligent Robotic Systems
telerobotics, planning/simulation/control, dynamical design and control.

Strategic Technologies Program

The Canadian government department of Industry, Science and Technology has a program aimed at promoting alliances for technology development, called the Strategic Technologies Program. This program is part of an overall effort to assist in improving Canadian industry in the three 'strategic' technologies of biotechnology, materials, and information technology. There are not many formal restrictions to participation in the program, other than it is aimed at promoting long term partnering for technology development leading to commercial exploitation. The program funds several industrial consortia, one of which, PRECARN, is described below.

PROVINCIAL PROGRAMS

Ontario Centres of Excellence

Started in 1987, the Ontario Centres of Excellence Program networks leading scientists from Ontario universities in seven Centres in the areas of lasers and lightwaves, space and terrestrial science, manufacturing technology, groundwater research, new materials, telecommunications, and information technology.

Objectives:

1) to stimulate advanced research;
2) to train and develop world class researchers;
3) to encourage the transfer and diffusion of technology to industry.

Funding:

The province of Ontario contributes about $40M/yr to the seven Centres. Industry contributions are about $2.5M or about 5% of the total funding for all the Centres.

Examples:

ITRC	Information Technology Research Centre
TRIO	Telecommunications Research Institute of Ontario

The following provides some details on one of the Centres.

Information Technology Research Centre (ITRC)

ITRC is one of the seven Ontario Centres of Excellence. It is a university based, distributed research institute that promotes fundamental and applied research in information technology and effectively transfers the results of the research program to Ontario industry. It operates at the following universities: University of Toronto, University of Waterloo, Queen's University, and University of Western Ontario.

Funding:
ITRC's budget for 1991 was $7.5M with almost all of this being contributed by the Ontario government.

Program:
Artificial Intelligence, Cognitive Science and Intelligent Control,
Computer Networks and Communications,
Mathematics of Computation,
Microelectronics,
Software Systems and Graphics.

Two further examples of centres for the promotion of collaborative research in other provinces are given below.

British Columbia Advanced Systems Institute

The British Columbia Advanced Systems Institute is an organization which promotes and facilitates collaborative research between British Columbia industry and British Columbia's three universities: University of British Columbia, Simon Fraser University and University of Victoria. It maintains no research facilities, but organizes research projects between its members and local universities.

Objectives:
1) to promote research in the fields of computer science, microelectronics, artificial intelligence and robotics;
2) to encourage and facilitate research which will enhance the application of computing to British Columbia industries.

Funding:
The Institute had an initial budget of $8M over 5 years from the Canadian and British Columbia governments.

Program:
Support for 12 industrial chairs at the three British Columbia universities,
Scholarships for graduate students,
Support of university-industry research projects,
Support for workshops to encourage university-industry interaction.

Centre de Recherche Informatique de Montréal (CRIM)

CRIM is a not-for-profit corporation which brings industrial members together with seven Quebec universities: Concordia University, École Polytechnique de Montréal, McGill University, Université de Montréal, Université de Sherbrooke, Université du Québec à Montréal, Université Laval. CRIM is a research Institute with 70 employees which is involved in long term, precompetitive and contract research.

Objectives:

1) to promote and conduct R&D in areas of mutual interest to its members;
2) to assist in the dissemination and transfer of knowledge and to encourage its use to benefit Quebec's economy;
3) to help train a qualified work force, especially at the doctorate level.

Funding:

The Quebec government contributed 53% of CRIM's 1991 budget of $6.9M.

Research Projects:

reduction in pitch deposits in paper making,
creation of an environment for developing human-computer interfaces,
flight simulation,
telecommunications network management,
speech recognition,
expert system for weather forecasting,
software engineering.

MUNICIPAL PROGRAMS

There are a few programs which are supported by municipalities. These programs are seen as a mechanism for attracting and promoting high technology organizations (companies, research organizations, universities, colleges) in a local region. One such program is described below.

Ottawa-Carleton Research Institute (OCRI)

The Ottawa-Carleton Research Institute is a consortium of post-secondary academic institutions, government and industry building on the high technology excellence in the region of Ottawa-Carleton. OCRI does not do any research itself, but actively promotes and organizes research activities in the region. It works to bring industry and government support to research activities at the three universities and two colleges in the Ottawa-Carleton area. It also works to set up specific large projects in conjunction with consortia and the Centres of Excellence which have a base in its area.

Objectives:

1) increase interaction among people from educational institutions, government and industry to enhance the effectiveness of R&D in the region of Ottawa-Carleton;
2) increase the resources available for R&D within the region;
3) promote the development of the region in the high technology sector.

Funding:

OCRI had a 1991 budget of about $1M with about $850K contributed by industry and $150K by the region of Ottawa-Carleton.

Programs:

Organizing, operating and promoting industrial consortia: SSOC, SIMCON, etc;
Promoting activities with Centres of Excellence: TRIO, ITRC, CITR;
Organizing and operating conferences;
Providing information services for various research organizations, projects and activities;
Organizing funding for industrial chairs at universities;
Organizing support for cooperative research programs and projects.

INDUSTRIAL RESEARCH CONSORTIA

In general, industrial research consortia have a narrow program focus, and in addition to industrial members include participation by universities and research organizations. Due to the narrow focus and emphasis on directed, applied research, projects tend to be easier to manage, and the industrial benefits are more easily identifiable. There are many examples of formal industrial consortia in Canada. A few are:

ATHENA	(advanced audio speaker design)
FORMTECH	(advanced engineering for metal stamping)
PRECARN	PRECompetitive Applied Research Network (AI and robotics)
PROGERT	Projet de Recherche pour l'Observation et la Gestion des Ressources Terrestres
SIMCON	Software for Integrated Manufacturing CONsortium
SMC	Strategic Microelectronics Consortium
SSOC	Solid State Optoelectronics Consortium
Vision 2000	(advanced personal communications)
VOLVOX	(large scale environmental management)

A detailed description of one of these consortia is given below.

<u>PRECompetitive Applied Research Network (PRECARN)</u>

Established in 1987, PRECARN is an industrial consortium which has developed an innovative model of cooperation between corporations, governments and universities to foster precompetitive research into artificial intelligence and robotics.

Objective:

1) to encourage industry to work collaboratively on long term research projects;
2) to form an effective linkage between Canadian companies, government laboratories and universities;
3) to convince both national and provincial governments of the importance of supporting long term research initiatives in which Canadian industries are collaborating;
4) to demonstrate to Canadian companies, regardless of size, that they can no longer afford to undertake all important research projects on their own.

Funding:

PRECARN has a research program with a proposed budget of $76M over 5 years (92-96). This would be roughly funded at 40% PRECARN members, 46% Canadian government and 14% provincial governments. Members provide some general funding, but major funding by members for projects comes from members participating in projects.

Major projects:
- Advanced Process Analysis and Control System (APACS)
- Intelligent Graphics Interface (IGI)
- Autonomous Robot for a Known Environment (ARK)
- Telerobotics Development System (TDS)
- Knowledge Aided Design (KAD)
- Mining Automation Plan (MAP)
- Control of Robots for Future Applications (CORFFA).

DISCUSSION

It is difficult to determine if there are universally applicable conclusions that can be drawn from the various types of collaborative research activities that have been described since the programs and experiences of the many examples of research partnerships are quite varied, and the environment in which they are fostered is peculiar to Canada. However, a discussion follows which gives some observations.

Industrial Research Consortia

It has been recently accepted and promoted in the world economic community that access to and development of technology is a significant factor for economic competitiveness. Research partnerships offer this type of access with the benefits of synergy, leverage, and risk sharing among partners. Industrial consortia for precompetitive research provide a good vehicle for access to technology and many have been formed in the last decade within Canada.

These partnerships are obviously led by industry, although not always organized by industry. They tend to be highly focussed with the emphasis on technology development, sharing and marketability. The measure of success is economically beneficial exploitation of technology. Research programs are organized with commercial benefits as a specific target, as opposed to just one of many program outcomes. Project management is very professional and tends to be in an 'industrial' style.

In terms of the role of government, this is in two areas: funding and regulation. Governments at all levels, but predominantly the national and provincial governments give grants and tax advantages to research consortia. In some cases the national and provincial governments contribute to the same consortia, and there is an agreed upon 'stacking rule', whereby the total contribution by all governments cannot exceed 75%. Sometimes when a consortium is organized within a single province, there tends to be a restriction of participation to organizations within that province. This tends to develop a dichotomy: the desire to develop technical capabilities within a region is pitted against the probability of success due to lack of appropriate capabilities (technical, logistic and market) of the partners at the outset.

One area that needs some attention is that of government regulation, especially, the coherency of regulation in domains such as: legal, tax, R&D definition, intellectual property, and funding. Since regulations in specific government policy domains existed before the concept of research partnerships had been developed, regulations for research partnerships tend to be an ad hoc patchwork where certain existing regulations appear to be at cross purposes to the intention of new policies. Regulations need to be simplified and systematically integrated so that a coherent message is given to industry and other consortia participants about the goals and benefits of research partnerships.

Industrial research consortia in Canada have tended to develop around new technologies, and while there are no limitations to the topics chosen for consortia, both topics and participants are generally in high technology areas. There is a need to have a much broader participation by industry both in the sense of having research consortia in traditional technologies: steel, equipment, manufacturing, etc, and in the sense of having more non-high technology companies participating.

University Centres of Excellence (all levels)

The purpose of the University Centres of Excellence Programs in Canada has been to develop research activities at universities which have focus and critical mass. The implementation of this type of program is complex due to the large geographical distribution of universities in Canada and the rivalry between them. Thus, the concept of networks was developed. This has been a 'carrot' approach to promoting cooperation among university scientists. The network approach also reduces the need to invest in new infrastructure by building upon existing capabilities, so that funding can be incremental.

In general, the Centres of Excellence Programs have been successful. University-industry linkages have increased. There has been more funding and more diversified funding for universities, i.e. researchers can apply to more than one program for funding. Besides applying for research operating grants from granting councils, researchers can also apply to be part of both the national and provincial Centres of Excellence Programs. Funding for the national Networks of Centres of Excellence Program comes from the three national granting councils: the National Science and Engineering Research Council (NSERC), the Medical Research Council (MRC), and the Social Sciences and Humanities Research Council (SSHRC). Funding for provincial Centres of Excellence comes from provincial governments.

The Centres of Excellence tend to be in new technical areas and this overcomes the 'traditional' or historical pattern of funding within granting councils. One problem has been the development of 'star' performers who receive funding from many different programs. This tends to distort the overall distribution of funds to a few individuals; as well, the best researchers tend to become more managers than scientists.

Another feature of the University Centres of Excellence Programs has been the funnelling of students into targeted areas. Since the targeted areas are the ones which attract professors and have more funds associated with them, more graduate students participate in these targeted areas. As well, due to industry participation, work in the Centres of Excellence is seen by students as more promising for finding a job upon graduation. It is clear that this is a very significant outcome of the organization of the Centres of Excellence Programs; it is unclear whether the ramifications are positive or negative in attempting to have an appropriate distribution of educated graduates from universities.

The main reason for industrial participation in these programs seems to be access to students for hiring upon graduation. In fact, most University Centres of Excellence publish a list of graduate students with research profiles and times of graduation. This focus on technology transfer through education/hiring of students, while successful, has led to some frustration on the part of consortia organizers, participants and industry. The frustration is that the initial expectation of benefits of technology creation and transfer to industry through the performance of research projects has not been totally realized.

There are also the issues of applied versus basic research, and serendipity versus directed research. The initial intention of the Centres of Excellence was to get closer links between universities and industry. To a great degree this has been accomplished, but not to the desired level. Some technical areas have been more attractive to industry than others. In addition, the scientific areas, which were initially chosen, were chosen with more regard to scientific excellence than industrial interest. Also within academia, the Centres of Excellence Programs are viewed as alternative sources of funding for academic research interests. However, to develop a better emphasis towards industrial benefits, program organizers are trying to have more university-industry interaction, more industry participation, and more technology transfer. In the future, this will probably mean changing the balance of the research programs towards more applied research and more industry directed research. This can be accomplished by having the availability of funds tied directly to industrial participation as is the case with industrial research chairs funded by NSERC.

Provincial Organizations

Provincial governments are looking to technology development programs as tools for industrial policy. These governments use a wide range of programs; many are similar to the national government programs.

The British Columbia Advanced Systems Institute (BC ASI) and the Centre de Recherche Informatique de Montréal (CRIM) are both successful, but in direct contrast. They both develop university-industry linkages, promote collaborative research, and have similar objectives. However, one is an institute with its own research staff (CRIM), and the other has no research staff, but only promotes collaboration and research projects (BC ASI).

Although provincial programs have been successful, one policy could be counterproductive in that partnering policies are presently restricted to 'local' industrial development and participation. This is occurring at the same time as industry is moving towards international technology acquisition and partnering. Provincial governments, and indeed national governments, will have to reconcile how to foster and fund research programs to support local industries, but which must draw on participation from organizations outside their jurisdictions.

Municipal Organizations

The one example described was the Ottawa-Carleton Research Institute (OCRI). It has been very successful at promoting research activities in its region, at developing linkages among the various players: technology companies, research organizations, and universities, and at information dissemination for the purposes of education and communication. Although its mandate is the promotion of activities based in the Ottawa-Carleton region, a great deal of its success has been its willingness and drive to have connections to programs on a provincial and national basis.

The success of OCRI has been highly dependent on:
i) the environment of receptiveness in the Ottawa-Carleton community to collaborative activities; and
ii) having a manager in place who brings energy and vision to partnering which is well aligned with program objectives.

The latter is true at all levels of organizing partnering, but especially true at the local level. Forming linkages is a people activity.

Intellectual Property

Intellectual property rights are a very complicated and difficult issue. The topic will only be discussed in a general way.

Universities throughout Canada have many different policies for the treatment of intellectual property, but there are two major thrusts to the policies: i) the scientist is given rights to ownership and potential exploitation; ii) there is some division of ownership between the university and the scientist. This is true with work done under the different University Centres of Excellence Programs.

Within research consortia there are usually clear intellectual property rights. The definition and distribution of these rights is as numerous as the number of consortia. In general, however, rights are distributed in such a way as to allow for rapid technology exploitation and product development.

In Conclusion

Research consortia are one of the best vehicles for improving the development of technology for industrial exploitation. They provide a venue for bridging the gap between the long term outlook of universities and other research organizations, and the short term outlook of industry in order to work on focussed, industry oriented research where the output is technology for products or processes. Partnering also provides a vehicle for bringing focus and critical mass to desired research activities, especially in the university community. The future promises to see more and more consortia activities formed both at the national and international levels.

Personal Computers and Intelligent Systems / F.H. Vogt (Editor)
Information Processing 92, Volume III
Elsevier Science Publishers B.V. (North-Holland)

National and International R&D Programmes in Informatics Cooperative R&D Programmes - An Overview

Brian Oakley, Logica UK

The concept of cooperation in R&D goes back a long way. Industrial Research emerged as a recognised and separate activity in the second half of the nineteenth century, first in the industrial dye-stuff industry of Germany and then in the wider chemical industry for explosives, etc. Most of the new industries saw the seed corn of research as at the heart of their industrial prospects, with the electrical generation industry leading the way, followed by the radio industry who had no choice but to build on research if they were to create products that would generate a market for an activity totally new to man. This industrial work was usually closely linked to certain distinguished figures in the academic world. In the UK, names like Davies, Faraday and Kelvin managed to combine an academic research career with consultancy on problems with very direct industrial relevance. So cooperative research between the academic world and industry has a very honourable past. But cooperation in R&D between firms is a phenomenon of the twentieth century.

In the UK this first started under the stress of the 1914-1918 Great War. It was discovered that the UK was almost totally dependent upon German industry for its optical components - and German products were now cut off from the UK market. This led a committee of enquiry to recommend that industrial research associations should be set up, to help to develop advanced technology for certain industries - indeed, to help to develop advanced technology for certain industries. The Government of the day agreed to provide half the cost of these Research Associations for a strictly limited period. Such funding was extended for rather longer than intended and indeed some Government funding is provided for work in the "RAs" to this day. At the peak there were some 58 RAs, ranging from brush manufacture through to the iron and steel industry, from spring design to welding. In Germany the Fraunhofer Institutes perform a somewhat similar function and date from much the same period.

Such cooperative industrial research was largely based on co-located work centred round an institute, where the outcome of the work was largely shared by the member firms. In modern times it is the Japanese who have established a somewhat different pattern for cooperative industrial research. With the notable exception of the few Ivy League State Universities, relatively little research is, or was until recently, carried out in the Japanese Universities. To compensate the large Zaibatues developed strong industrial research teams. In fields where these firms were not strong, for example integrated circuits and supercomputers, MITI started to run cooperative research programmes. Though they sometimes relied upon staff seconded from the participating firms to some central laboratory - eg ETL, ICOT - they also brought together work that was being stimulated in the research laboratories of the firms.

This way of organising cooperative research began to be copied in the Western world early in the 1980s. The publicity for the launch of the Japanese so-called "Fifth Generation" programme spawned a rash of vaguely similar programmes in many countries. The Alvey programme in the UK and the ESPRIT programme in the European Community were very similar in nature, rejecting the concept of a central laboratory, but linking industrial and academic research teams in a set of loosely coupled projects. Even in the USA cooperative research began to flourish, even though this required a change in the Anti-Trust laws. Perhaps the most famous scheme in the USA was the creation of the Microelectronics Computing Corporation, which relied on the central laboratory model. Some trace of cooperative research could be found in some of the DARPA programmes.

It is obvious why cooperative research is seen to be attractive, when an industry needs to jack up its competence in a hurry, and pre-competitive (whatever that means) research is desirable to share scarce resources of expert manpower and equipment. However, there is a price to pay in the overhead of cooperation. For some of the programmes, like ESPRIT, this is far from trivial. And at least for the central laboratory model, the problems of exploitation of research are made even more acute if the work is not close to the exploitation team. This paper, and indeed the whole "National & International R&D Programmes" stream will examine the pros and cons of cooperative research to try to establish what the balance of advantage is, and how a firm can get the most out of participating in such programmes.

Personal Computers and Intelligent Systems / F.H. Vogt (Editor)
Information Processing 92, Volume III
Elsevier Science Publishers B.V. (North-Holland)

THE SWEDISH NATIONAL IT-PROGRAMME

Dan Andrée
Swedish Board for Industrial Development of Information Technology
Järntorget 84, 2tr, 103 33 Stockholm, Sweden

The Swedish National IT-Programme consits of a number of initiatives spread out in time from 1984 to 1992. The two largest elements have been the Microelectronics Programme (1984 - 1988) and the Industrial IT-Programme (1987 - 1992). Other activities have been goal oriented research, demonstrations, awareness campaigns etc.

This paper will mainly deal with the Industrial IT-Programme which was set up in 1987 to "sustain an internationally competitive capability in selected key areas and thereby maintain a base from which to take advantage of the technological development in other fields in the rest of the world".

This paper will cover experiences from running the programme, results of the evaluation, comparison with other programmes (Alvey & Esprit) and some future directions of Swedish IT-policy.

In order to carry out the programme a Board was set up with representatives from government and industry. A small secretariat was also established to administrate the programme. This was the first time industry was directly involved in the decisionmaking process.

A totoal of 495 million Swedish Crowns (≈ 67 MECU) of government funds were allocated and industry was supposed to contribute the same amount. The government funds came from three sources; the Department of Industry, the Department of Defence och Swedish Telecom.

More than 100 projects have been approved in six different IT-areas (Micro- and Optossystem Technologies, Software and Knowledge Based Systems, Tools for Manufacturing Systems, Telecommunications and Standards, Information Processing Systems, Data Security). Further, around 130 organisations have been involved in the projects. Most of the work in the projects has been carried out by industry (≈ 60 %) but a substantial part (≈ 27 %) has been carried out by research institutes in the role of subcontractors. Universities are involved on a smaller scale (≈ 6 %) which is natural given that institutes are often a link between industry and the universities.

Most of the funds were allocated during the three first years. The projects will normally run for three years. The last project will finish by the end of 1993 and the Board has put forward suggestion for further support in some areas.

A numer of dissemination activities, demonstrations projects etc. have been initiated in the two last years. Four major national conferences have been held as well as 10 - 12 more specialised conferences. When the programme started it was not foreseen that these activities would be on such a large scale.

For every project the Board has appointed a monitoring officer, usually from a government agency. For each of the six technical areas a number of Area Co-ordinators have been appointed to assist the Board in selecting projects, co-ordinating projects etc.

A mid-term and a final evaluation have been carried out and the final report will be published in the spring of 1992. In the midterm evaluation it was pointed out that it is important for every country to have a national programme in order to be accepted as part of the "European club". It was regarded as a good thing that industry had taken part in drawing up the strategy.

As part of the programme the Board has also supported Swedish participation in RACE (1988 - 1990) and EUREKA (mainly the Prometheus project). From 1990 the government has increased funds for participation in the ECs framework programme ($\approx$ 18 MECU for 1991/92). When the EEA-agreement between the EC and EFTA is signed our participation is expected to increase. This will also affect our national activities.

Three committée (IT2000), with representatives from industry and government, were set up by the government in 1991 to make suggestions on future IT-policy concentrating on "large companies' needs", "users' needs" and "SME's needs". A report was published in the autumn of 1991 and will, together with experiences from the IT-programme, provide input for the government's Research Bill which will be presented early in 1993.

SYMPOSIUM: ENCOURAGING ACADEMIC/PRACTITIONER COLLABORATION

Symposium Organizer:

B. Glasson
Curtin Univ. Perth, Australia

Personal Computers and Intelligent Systems / F.H. Vogt (Editor)
Information Processing 92, Volume III
Elsevier Science Publishers B.V. (North-Holland)

Academic-Industry collaboration: Towards a pro-active IFIP role

Bernard Glasson

School of Information Systems, Curtin University of Technology, Kent Street, Bentley 6102, Western Australia

Abstract
There is reason for concern with the imbalance between academics and practitioners at IFIP events. In general academics dominate the working group membership; they dominate working conference committees; they are in the majority when it comes to working conference contributions; and they attend working conferences in far greater number than do practitioners. While this situation has its exceptions, the pattern is sufficiently consistent across all IFIP working groups to give cause for concern. Concern that led to today's symposium entitled "Encouraging academic-industry collaboration". This paper gives some background to the problem; it gives pragmatic and professional reasons as to its significance for the IFIP community; and it proposes changes to IFIP's way of work to redress the problem without losing the reputation for research excellence IFIP enjoys.

Keyword Codes: K.7.0
Keywords: The Computing Profession (General)

INTRODUCTION

Today's symposium on encouraging academic-industry collaboration grew out of a concern first raised publicly in 1989 at the IFIP WG 8.2 working conference. Given the conference theme, organisers were surprised that only 4 of some 64 attendees were industry-based "practitioners" as opposed to university-based academics. They were also concerned enough to arrange a panel addressing the question "How might practitioners be encouraged to participate in IFIP WG 8.2 working conferences?" for their next working conference. In organising that panel, it became obvious the problem went beyond WG8.2 and even beyond TC8. Anecdotal evidence indicated many IFIP activities failed to attract or retain practitioners. It also became obvious the solutions being offered to address the problem within WG 8.2 apply to any working group. These observations led in turn to today's symposium entitled "Encouraging academic-industry collaboration". The symposium's aim is to explore ways IFIP can increase industry involvement in its activities without losing the academics' support.

I would like to introduce the symposium by making a case for a more proactive role for IFIP in bringing this collaboration about and to suggest ways that might happen. Why? - because if IFIP is to survive as a leader in informatics research, development, application, dissemination and exchange, it must take positive steps to get practitioners involved in its activities. IFIP seems to be dominated by the developers of novel theory. IFIP also needs to attract those capable of implementing or applying those same theories in sufficient number to expedite technology transfer. In short, IFIP needs a better balance between university-based academics and industry-based practitioners participating in its events. It can do this by making two changes to the way that it works - one administrative and one more fundamental. The administrative change concerns the way we run our events. The more fundamental change is to the way we undertake our research.

1. THE CONCERN

There is concern within the IFIP community at the lack of practitioner involvement in its activities. This lack of industry participation in IFIP is a problem for reasons that will be explained shortly. In an attempt to obtain some feel for the extent of the problem, a brief, informal, survey on membership profiles was sent to all IFIP working group secretaries in March 1992. Attachments 1 and 2 contain the survey questions and the resultant replies. The academic in me wants quickly to highlight the imprecise nature of the survey - the inadequate definition of terms, the imprecise measures, the subjective nature of the replies, and the reliance on the views of one observer. However, the practitioner in me wants to point out that the results give at least some indication beyond the anecdotal as to the likely situation. Suffice it to say the replies support the anecdotal evidence. That is, in general, academics dominate IFIP committee and working group membership; academics dominate when it comes to working conference contributions; and academics form the majority of working conference attendees.

Something must be fundamentally wrong with the way we organise our research activities if we cannot get an appropriate balance of academic and practitioner involvement in them. Most IFIP working groups are not attracting practitioners to working conferences in sufficient numbers to ensure an appropriate participation balance. Further, those few practitioners we do attract to these conferences lose interest after one or two experiences of them. This lack of balance should concern all who do participate for two reasons - one pragmatic and one professional.

2. NEED FOR BALANCED PARTICIPATION

The pragmatic reason is that unless a working group achieves this balance, it could stand accused of operating outside of its charter. Case proven the group could be disbanded. IFIP exists on the support provided by its member associations. The member association membership is dominated by practitioners. The executive committees and boards of those member associations are always looking for ways of containing or cutting costs. At budget time, activities seen by members as having little relevance are constantly under attack. In the long term, unless the practitioner members of the informatics profession see IFIP as serving some real purpose it will lose member association support.

The professional reason relates to our research. We do our research to influence practice. Practice is a source of real problems. Practitioners, acting as critics, can ensure that our research is relevant and its results clearly communicated. Therefore as long as we continue to use the working conference as our principal method of work, we must attract an appropriate balance of research oriented academics and inquisitive practitioners to them. IFIP uses the working conference to promote science and technology by stimulating research, development (my emphasis) and the application (my emphasis) of information processing in science and human activity; and furthering the dissemination and exchange (again my emphasis) about the subject [1]. The aspects of research work emphasised demand we involve business and industry in our research work.

Therefore for pragmatic and professional reasons, we must make every effort to increase the level of practitioner involvement in IFIP sponsored research work. We need to make our working conferences more attractive to inquistive practitioners. Not all practitioners, but those thinking practitioners involved in research and development, strategic planning, product development, human resource development and the like. Those who will implement the new theories or develop products based on them. We need to attract this kind of person without losing the academics. IFIP should be rightly proud of its scholarly output generated, in the main, through its academic contributors' efforts. We do not want to lose them. However, as Gordon Davis says, "...There should always be an objective (in our research work) of making a connection to practice, encouraging a dialogue between researchers and practitioners, and transforming research results to practical use" [2]. While Davis was speaking of TC8, what he says applies to all working groups. We do not want to lose the academics, we need to increase practitioner participation numbers - albeit of the right type - to ensure a proper dialogue between the two.

Two things are needed to achieve a better participation balance between academics and inquistive practitioners in IFIP. First, the research we do must be relevant and the best way to be sure of that is to collaborate with industry. Second, we need to give much more attention to the way we organise out principal method of work namely the working conference. The paper will deal with the second issue first. The collaborative research issue will be discussed briefly when the four panel members are introduced. It will be their task to take us through a number of successful collaborative research scenarios that might be emulated within the context of IFIP.

3. Working Conference Organization

3.1 Introduction

IFIP uses the working conference as its main method of work. An IFIP working conference, for those who have not participated in one is

> "(a) general category for events within a particular subject area organized by a TC or WG for professional purpose, a restricted and small (usually less than 100) attendance, with refereed contributions intended for publication as preprints or proceedings." [3]

The investigation into the low level of practitioner participation in WG 8.2 working conferences resulted in two pieces of work which are relevant here. The first was a pilot study into academic and practitioner participation in IFIP related conferences. It indicated some interesting similarities and differences between the two groups [4]. While only a pilot study, it indicated differences in the expectations academics and practitioners have of a conference that warrant further investigation. The second piece of work came out of the WG 8.2 panel referred to earlier. The panel session aim was to find ways of correcting the perceived participation imbalance in WG 8.2 working conferences. After some initial input from the panel speakers, a modified nominal group technique was used to solicit the views of the 30 or so people who attended that conference session. The resultant summary paper contains some 90 suggestions as to how WG 8.2 might improve its participation balance [5].

For our purposes today I will elaborate on a small subset of those suggestions. The suggestions chosen could apply to any working group keen to increase the level of practitioner involvement in its activities without losing the academics. The suggestions relate to the group's membership; collaborative research; the way a group chooses its conference theme; the choice of activity format; the working conference format; some program committee matters; and some organisation committee matters.

3.2 Working Group Membership

We will not improve the participant balance in our working conferences until we correct the imbalance between practitioners and academics in IFIP working groups and committees. Unless there is an appropriate balance between academics and practitioners in WG membership, on executive committees, and, in particular, on conference committees, it will be extremely difficult to get an appropriate participation balance at WG events.

This balance could be achieved constitutionally (eg by making a person's active involvement in their national IFIP affiliated member society a condition of WG membership); or by taking steps to foster closer industry links (eg through collaborative, industry-based, research); or encouraging WG members and friends personally to invite appropriate practitioners to contribute to the group's activities.

3.3 Collaborative Research

A working conference paper is usually an end-product of research. If we are to encourage practitioner participation in IFIP events, then we ought start by looking for ways of encouraging collaborative, industry-based, research, before the conference. IFIP could negotiate with new funding groups to provide outlets for research and development (eg ESPRIT); it could encourage industry-based case studies to test out previously reported theories or theoretic assumptions; it could provide a link between academic and industrial researchers via, say, an expertise data base; it could lobby to have international e-mail links extended to include industry-based research and development groups; it could encourage TC's or WG's to include a "computing practice" section in newsletters; it could use the TC national representatives to connect into member societies (eg for marketing, organisational support, reporting, research topic identification); and it ask practitioners (and inactive "friends") why they have lost interest in a WG activities.

Having addressed the fundamental issues of membership balance and appropriate research, a WG should next focus on the events that it runs.

3.4 Theme (Problem, Opportunity) Identification

The conference theme is important to both academics and practitioners. There are several ways a WG could identify relevant conference themes including - initiating joint academic-industry "problem identification" dialogues (eg through industry associations); undertaking formal research, or commissioning sponsored market research, to identify real problems of mutual interest to academics and practitioners; identifying the range of research problems or opportunities facing practitioners (within the WG's terms of reference) before the event theme is chosen; establishing practitioner advisory or sponsorship boards to help identify themes relevant to practitioners that warrant research effort; and seeking input from the local member association in the country and city hosting future working conferences.

3.5 Activity Determination

IFIP uses a variety of formats to achieve its aims. Perhaps IFIP relies too much on the working conference format academics prefer. Where the ratio of academics to practitioners is too high, this acts as a disincentive for practitioners to attend. Open conferences attract more practitioners than do working conferences. We could use the open conference format more frequently. Again joint events with one or other of IFIP's member societies or SIG's (Special Interest Groups) provide a broader base from which to attract practitioners. It seems WG's decide to hold a working conference and then look for a theme. Why not identify a topical theme or issue first, and then decide the form of activity most appropriate to address it.

However, if working conferences remain the principal method of work, then perhaps we could look to ways of making them more attractive to practitioners

3.6 Working Conference Format

IFIP favours the working conference format. Even within that format a WG can choose to run its conference in a variety of ways namely by - running some separate parallel practitioner and academic streams; having two distinct sets of papers, one practitioner or outcome oriented and one academic or research oriented; having two discussants for each session, one addressing research issues and one addressing practitioner outcomes; inviting practitioners to give presentations or contribute to panels without having to write a paper; having pre-conference practitioner oriented workshops; arranging an exhibition of selected types of technology related to the WG terms of reference; arranging pre-conference tutorials for participants who may not be fully familiar with prior, seminal, work in the particular field; or arranging a pre or post event "researcher only" workshop to help retain the academics' interest.

The simplest way to get an appropriate format is to have an appropriate balance of academics and practitioners on all conference committees.

3.7 Program Committee Matters

A program committee influences the event's technical content through its paper reviewing policy and procedures; its "call for papers" publicity; and its preprints and proceedings editorial policy. The technical content will have a significant bearing on the attendee mix. In trying to attract more practitioners, the program committee must realise practitioner involvement changes the nature of the conference. Practitioners, and their employers, are put off by too high a level of abstraction; by treatments being too theoretical or rigourous rather than pragmatic and rooted in concrete cases. There is a need to recognise (and counter) the disincentives for professionals and their employers. However, in doing so, there is a real danger of introducing disincentives for academics. The challenge is to find a balance.

In trying to find this balance the program committee should consider - encouraging academic-practitioner "team" input; encouraging "success story" reports on joint industry-university projects; encouraging joint academic-practitioner authorship a submissions for some (all) papers at all (some) conferences or selected sessions of same; having an extended abstracts section where papers need be no more than 3 or 4 pages long; having special reviewing standards for practitioner papers (eg practitioners could present a problem which could form the basis for workshop discussion); including practitioners on the reviewing panel; requiring each paper to contain a concluding section entitled "implications for practice" (or similar) wherein the value of the research to practice (eg opportunities for productivity improvements) is clearly spelled out; suggesting (insisting) papers clearly separate the discussion of the research outcome and discussion of the research method to highlight the paper's main contribution (eg by insisting one or the other be covered in an appendix or attachment); agreeing, and advertising, three levels of reviewing rigour for papers - the highest level being for papers intended for presentation and publication in both the preprints and the proceedings, the next level for those to be presented and published in the preprints only, and the least rigourous level being for papers that will be presented, perhaps accompanied by a handout, but not published as part of the conference preprints or proceedings; running an industry-sponsored competition for the best research paper from an industry perspective; highlighting the program committee's liberal reviewing policy; explicitly stating that research papers addressing practical problems will be preferred; highlighting aspects of the conference directed at practitioners (eg invited practitioner speakers, associated exhibition, professional development "credits"); and placing the calls for contribution in practitioner newsletters and journals, particularly those of member societies.

Events could include a (near to) closing session for papers focussing on future research issues, problems or opportunities. This would provide a more formal way of identifying topics and themes for the future WG events.

3.8 Organising Committee Matters

The organising committee is responsible for conducting the conference. This involves marketing the event to potential participants; arranging the venue; administering the event; and stage managing the presentations. The organising committee will also need to recognise (and counter) the disincentives for professionals and their employers (eg event price too low) without turning off the academics. When it comes to marketing research conferences, opinion seems to be that the best way to attract practitioners is by personal invitation, a view supported by the respondents to the membership profile survey (see Attachment 2 Question 4).

IFIP should encourage TC's and WG's to call for expressions of interest from IFIP's member societies in all countries to host events and to provide the bulk of the organisation committee resources. Having the local member association host an IFIP event will increase practitioner participation, if only those from the local area.

Finally IFIP should formally evaluate every event. The evaluation should cover both those who attended the event and those on the event mailing list who did not.

4. CONCLUSION

If IFIP believes it has something to contribute to our world, it needs to monitor four things - the methods used by its researchers, to be sure the work is effective, efficient and valid; the TC and WG research focus, to be sure the work is relevant; its methods of collegiate communication, to be sure communication includes all parties concerned with IFIP's research activity; and the way it publicises its research findings, to reach the widest possible audience expeditiously and to attract new members to our groups. To achieve those last three things IFIP must take steps to involve practitioners in its activities to a far greater extent than has happened in the past.

For nearly three decades IFIP has been a leader in informatics research. If individuals want to research under the IFIP umbrella, using the infrastructure IFIP provides, then they should take note of its aims and methods. IFIP aims to promote science and technology by stimulating research, development and the application of information processing in science and human activity; and furthering the dissemination and exchange about the subject. The aspects of IFIP's research work I have emphasised by underlining demand that we involve business and industry in our research work.

We must get more practitioners actively involved in our IFIP work. For this to happen, we must change the way IFIP works in two ways - one administrative and one more fundamental. Administratively, we can make IFIP events more attractive to practitioners by implementing some of the many suggestions made here. More fundamentally we can bring in to the IFIP community practitioners of the right kind by involving them in our research.

IFIP must take a more pro-active role in fostering academic-industry research collaboration. Increased collaboration will accelerate the transfer of informatics technology from research to practice. In the panel that follows we will discuss how this collaboration can be brought about. The panelists will share their considerable and diverse experience of successful academic-industry research collaboration schemes in various parts of the world. My hope is the IFIP community will react to what they say by capitalising on, or emulating, which ever scheme or schemes are appropriate. By encouraging collaborative research, IFIP will attract and secure the level of industry involvement it needs to ensure its long term survival in the form its founders envisaged.

REFERENCES

1 IFIP Information Bulletin No 22, March 1990, p 3.

2 Davis, G.B. Report from the chairman on strategic planning by IFIP Technical Committee 8 (Information Systems), News/8 IFIP TC8 Newsletter/12, July 1990 page 3.

3 WG Chairman Handbook, IFIP Secretariat, 24 May, 1992 page 5.

4 Chin, K.L., Pervan, G.P. and Glasson, B.C., A preliminary analysis of organisational factors potentially impacting participation patterns in IFIP related conferences, School of Informations Systems, Curtin University, Western Australia, working paper, August 1990.

5 Glasson, B.C., How might practitioners be encouraged to participate in IFIP WG 8.2 Working Conferences? - Some suggestions, in Nissen, H-E, Klein, H.K., and Hirschheim, R. (eds) Information Systems Research: Contemporary Approaches and Emergent Traditions, Amsterdam, North-Holland, 1991, pp 703-714

Survey Questions Attachment 1

Preamble:

If we consider "researchers" to be working group members and friends whose primary affiliation is a university or research institute and if we consider the members and friends who are not affiliated with universities or research institutes to be "practitioners";

Questions:

1. In your judgement, based on their reported affiliation, what proportion of your working group could be classed as "researchers" and what proportion could be classed as "practitioners"?

   Researchers
   Practitioners

   100%

   (if you prefer you could send me your membership mailing list and I will do an analysis here).

2. Can you give brief particulars of the last working conference held by your working group which was, in your judgement, representative of your WG's activities:

   Title:
   Place/Date:
   First Named Editor
   of the Proceedings:

3. In your judgement, what proportion of the attendees at that working conference could be classed as "researchers" and what proportion could be classed as "practitioners"?

   Researchers
   Practitioners

   100%

   (again if you prefer you could send me a copy of the attendees name and address list and I will do an analysis here).

4. Does your working group take any positive steps to encourage practitioner (industry?) involvement in your events and activities?

   YES or NO

Survey Replies Attachment 2

Caution: The results are based on one person's analysis of the reported affiliation of that working groups members and friends. Many respondents commented of the difficulty of distinguishing between "researchers" and "practitioners" based on the simplistic distinction they were asked to use. Therefore the results reported here should only be taken as an indication of the true situation - not a measure of it.

1. Working Group Membership

81 - 100%	"researchers"	14	Could not distinguish	2
61 - 80	"researchers"	7	Non returns	29
41 - 60	"researchers"	3		
21 - 40	"researchers"	2		
0 - 20	"researchers"	3	Total	60

2. Proceedings Details

A cursory examination of a small sample of the cited publications indicated the working conference contribution pattern, as evidenced by the affiliation of authors, was consistent with the working group membership pattern as shown in 1 above.

3. Working Conference Attendance Pattern

81 - 100%	"researchers"	4	N/A New working group	4
61 - 80	"researchers"	6	No response	10
41 - 60	"researchers"	5	Non returns	29
21 - 40	"researchers"	2		
0 - 20	"researchers"	0	Total	60

4. Encouraging Industry Involvement

Respondents were asked if their WG took positive steps to encourage practitioner involvement

Yes	16
No	7
Not yet (new group)	2
No response	6
Non-returns	29
Total	60

Of those who elaborated, or who responded further when asked, the majority relied on personal invitations to attract appropriate practitioners to their events

Personal Computers and Intelligent Systems / F.H. Vogt (Editor)
Information Processing 92, Volume III
Elsevier Science Publishers B.V. (North-Holland)

Academic-Industry collaboration: Some Success Stories and Experiences in Australia

Megan Alexander

Expertise Australia Pty Limited, Cornelius Court, 147A King Street, Sydney, N.S.W. 2000, Australia

Abstract

From a period with relatively low industrial research and development, and little collaboration between the public and private sector researchers, there has been a significant growth in industrial R&D in Australia in the 1980's. Private sector R&D, with a particularly high growth rate in software, has developed as a firm outcome of government policies and funding programs.

Key opportunities have been determined in the telecommunications and software areas, and these are targeted by government programs of funding for strategic research. The grants schemes have been expanded and now encourage market/product oriented research with expectations of firm commercial outcomes for the benefit of Australia. All encourage collaborative research, between the public and private sector, and are moving to address the issue of commercialisation. These linkages are crucial, and are leading to multidiciplinary research and development teams.

Some examples of collaboration are addressed in the telecommunications area, and conclusions drawn regarding the motivational and business issues which must be faced for a successful research, development and commercialisation outcome.

Keyword Codes: C.2.0; K.5.2; K.6.1
Keyword: Computer-Communications Networks, General; Legal Aspects of Computing, Governmental Issues; Management of Computing and Information Systems, Project and People Management

1. Directions in Research in Australia

Expenditure on the Australian public research system is comparable in size (as a proportion of GDP) with that of other industrialised nations. The major performers of R&D are universities, Commonwealth Government research organisations such as the Commonwealth Scientific and Industrial Research Organisation (CSIRO) and State Government research arms. The private sector contribution is considerably smaller but is growing largely as a result of policy initiatives of the government to create special industry research grants and the 150% R&D Taxation Concession.

Recent studies by the Department of Industry Technology and Commerce (DITAC) and the Australian Science and Technology Council (ASTEC) discuss the weakness of Australian industrial R&D effort in comparison with OECD countries and a number of major initiatives have been recently announced by the Government to improve the productivity of the research system. As a result, the Australian higher education research system is increasingly oriented to economic and commercial concerns and this new focus has several implications for the role of academic researchers.

Within this context, research policy in Australia has undergone considerable changes. Some of these changes include provisions for special funding mechanisms; declaration of directed research programs; creation of post graduate training packages and the provision of incentives and grants for industries. Amongst these, measures to improve linkages among industry, university and other public sector institutions constitute the driving force of government policy.

2. Australia's Information Technology and Telecommunications Industry

Australia is a major user of Information Technology and Telecommunications goods and services. The domestic IT is industry is worth $10 billion, and growing at a rate of 7% per annum. Telecommunications services are worth $11 billion, growing at 12% per annum. Putting these figures into the context of our national economy, this represents 6.5% of GDP in 1990, growing to 12.5% by the year 2000, three quarters of the size of the manufacturing sector.

Current figures show total exports of $1.68 billion, total imports $4.76 billion, with the trade imbalance reducing as a result of strong emphasis on sustainable product and services development for the global market through government policy and industry internationalisation.

Our relative strengths in IT&T are particularly evident in the areas of computer software and services and telecommunications services, where the figures are nearly balanced and Australia is particularly competitive.

Computer software and services exports are $359 million, imports $370 million.

Telecommunications services exports are $463 million and imports $568 million. In each of these areas there is significant Australian ownership and control of the intellectual property. In computer software and services, six of the top ten companies are Australian, bringing in 61% of that sector's revenues, a figure of $889 million. In telecommunications services the revenue is mainly earned by TELECOM and OTC, now known as AOTC.

We have a significant trade deficit in computer and telecommunications equipment exports. Though exports have grown from $491 million in 1987/88 to over $1 billion in 1991/92, the deficit is still $3 billion.

3. The Key Opportunities - Telecommunications and Software

Australia has determined that the area of telecommunications provides a key opportunity for indigenous development and export growth. It is entering a period of rapid change, taking into account such factors as high capacity channels, radio-based communications, data communications and extensive and widespread deregulation.

Therefore in examples to be presented today of successful academic/industry collaboration, I will refer to case studies in this area. Our R&D potential in this area is high, with rapid improvements in performance occurring and a number of international success stories.

We also have a number of success stories in the international arena in the area of software and services, but these are more likely to be the result of industry research, or collaboration with major advanced user organisations in the areas such as applications, development tools and some systems and network management software.

4. Funding for Research in Australia

Funding for Research in Australia comes from a number of sources.

Total Commonwealth Government expenditure on programs for science and innovation is around $2.5 billion per annum. The schemes with which I am directly involved comprise the bulk of the item Industry R&D and Incentives which total around $360 million.

A significant area of funding and support is to major government research organisations, the Commonwealth Scientific and Industrial Research Organization (CSIRO) and Defence Science and Technology Organisation (DSTO). The CSIRO's main role is to carry out strategic research which can be applied by Australian industry or government for the well being of the Australian people. It is a significant national resource in terms of research capabilities and particularly given the CSIRO objective of obtaining 30% of its funding through outside sources represents an opportunity for industry to source technology or to undertake collaborative ventures or contract research.

Funding through the Australian Research Council (ARC) of higher education R&D is essentially provided to the university system to support R&D with the ARC providing directional support including centres of research excellence. There is also a significant amount of funding going into rural R&D and also into the medical field which is of relevance to industry.

One area worth specific mention is the Government's relatively new Cooperative Research Centres Program, which is being addressed in a session tomorrow. The Cooperative Research Centres Program was launched in May 1990 with funding rising to $100m per annum by 1995 to support up to 50 centres. The program is aimed at developing concentrated centres for long term high quality research projects and to strengthen links between researcher and industry.

The Research Centres have a strong industry presence and it is worth noting that industry contributions to the centres are eligible for the 150% tax concession.

Expenditure within the Industry Technology and Commerce portfolio is primarily aimed at industrial research and development or related activities. Some specific schemes worth briefly noting are the:

- the computer bounty which provides assistance for the production of computer hardware, certain assemblies and electronic microcircuit printers circuit boards, systems design and systems software;
- the factor F pharmaceutical industry development program which provides higher prices for some products in return for commitment by individual manufacturers to undertake increased activity in Australia including new investment production research and development;
- the National Industry Extension Service (NIES) which is a joint Commonwealth State program to provide extension services to small to medium sized firms to increase their internal efficiency and international competitiveness. This is a technology and best practices diffusion program;
- the Australian Space Office which aims to encourage local industry involvement in space research and development and to promote to commercially viable industries based on space technologies.

The Government has introduced a number of schemes which are administered through the Industry Research and Development Board aimed at making Australian companies more innovative and internationally competitive by increasing the level of research and development and changing the culture in these organisations. Introduction of these schemes from 1985 onwards was spurred on by the low level of research and development being undertaken by Australian industry both historically and by international comparison, together with concern over management appreciation of the strategic role of R&D.

150% R&D Tax Concession

This program has operated from 1 July 1985 and will continue at the 150% rate until 30 June 1993. From this time it will reduce to 125% indefinitely. At current corporate tax rates the concession provides an incentive of 19.5 cents in the dollar for research and development bringing the total cost to the company to around 40 cents in the dollar. The concession is an entitlement and all companies need to do to be eligible is register annually and then submit claims with their tax returns. The estimated cost to revenue of the scheme is over $250 million annually. The scheme is administered jointly by the Australian Taxation Office and DITAC. DITAC through the IR&D Board is responsible for determining eligible R&D activities and exploitation.

Eligible companies are:

- those incorporated in Australia or public trading trusts.

Eligible activities are:

- R&D activities which involve a systematic, investigative or experimental approach;
- activities involving innovation or technical risk;
- activities carried on in Australia;
- activities with the purpose of:
    - acquiring new knowledge
    - creating new or improved materials, products, devices, processes or services.

The results of R&D activity claimed under the concession must be exploited to the benefit of the Australian economy and on normal commercial terms. R&D may be either carried out in house or contracted out to other parties such as CSIRO or universities. In this case the person paying for the R&D is entitled to make the claim. Eligible expenditure includes:

- expenditure on plant;
- expenditure on technology acquisition;
- other expenditure such as salaries, administrative costs and overheads directly associated with the R&D; and
- contract work.

There is a phasing in of the concession which means that companies need to spend at least $50,000 per annum on R&D to be eligible for the full benefit. There is also provision for joint registration or syndication which is aimed at encouraging investment in large and risky projects.

Discretionary Grants Scheme

This is one of several R&D support schemes operating under the general heading of Grants for Industry Research and Development (GIRD).

The Discretionary Grants Scheme is targeted at supporting R&D projects in companies unable to benefit from the tax concession scheme.

Project proposals are considered by a committee of the Industry Research and Development Board. About 45% of proposals are successful.

The relative merit of project proposals covers three main fields:

- the apparent commercial opportunity offered by the R&D, including ways in which the applicant company will move to commercialise outcomes;
- the financial strengths of the company, e.g. ability to support its part of project costs and capacity to finance commercialisation stages;
- the technical merit of the proposal.

Grants are for up to 50% of project costs. Projects may be up to three years duration. Payments are made in advance, on the basis of progress reports from companies.

Since the scheme started in 1986, 373 projects have been supported at a cost to the Commonwealth of $108 million. Currently, grants amount to about $18 million per annum and there is a portfolio of 120 active projects.

Generic (Strategic) Technology Scheme

This scheme promotes the development of particular enabling technologies which have widespread and pervasive application across industry.

Areas receiving support are:

- biotechnology;
- communications technology;
- information technology;
- manufacturing and materials technology;
- environmental technology.

These schemes are based on support for strategic R&D rather than product-specific research. IT&T based research in the other strategic areas is also possible and likely to receive grant support, reflecting the pervasiveness of our IT&T technologies.

Projects must involve at least one commercial partner and one public sector research body, although it is quite possible to involve more partners in a project consortium.

Support is provided for up to a maximum of 90% of project costs, depending on the degree to which the participating parties can reasonably expect to derive the economic benefits of successfully commercialising the R&D outcomes. Thus, high technical risk projects where the partners would have difficulty capturing the full benefits of the work would attract relatively high levels of subsidisation, relative to other projects where the commercial benefits could be captured by the parties involved.

The relative merit of applications takes account of following objectives for the scheme:

- encouraging clever collaboration between research institutions and industry;
- developing significant enabling technologies;
- the project would not proceed satisfactorily without grant assistance;
- there is strong commercial potential for the R&D outcomes;
- there is demonstrated commitment from a commercial enterprise to exploit the results.

Also considered are:

- the scientific or technical merit of the project;
- the quality of research to be undertaken;
- the ability of the researchers to undertake the project successfully;
- the extent of industry commitment;
- likelihood of achieving a commercially exploitable process, product or system;
- magnitude and pervasiveness of benefits;
- the degree of proposed dissemination of results.

The Generic (Strategic) Technologies Scheme it the second major plank of the government's GIRD scheme, alongside the Discretionary Grants Scheme. It attracts funding support of about $16 million per annum.

Recent changes have been made to improve the relevance of the Generic (Strategic) Scheme to address current issues. This has resulted in the introduction of Environmental Technology as a new Strategic Technology category and to reconfigure the former New Materials category to also include Manufacturing Technology.

National Procurement Development Program (NPDP)

This scheme developed from a report on government policy in the mid-80's. This report (the Inglis Report) found that government markets were important in a range of technology-related product areas - typically government agencies demand leading edge products, services and systems. However, their buying behaviour was very risk averse in terms of a willingness to work with relatively small or unproven suppliers, regardless of the merits of the product in question.

The NPDP scheme started in 1987. It supports projects aimed at primarily trialing and demonstrating new products, services or systems, initially in government markets - but with application in wider domestic and world markets. Government agencies and companies work together on the project, with the government partner typically acting as test bed for product development, trialing and demonstration.

To date 89 projects have been supported involving Commonwealth outlays of $24 million. $7.4 million is available for commitment in 1991/92. Grants are provided for up to 50% of project costs.

NPDP is an area where the Commonwealth and State Governments are working together - there is some financial support, plus "in kind" support in marketing the scheme, flowing from most State Governments.

The NPDP has some specific characteristics which may point the way for innovation support programs in the future:

- it emphasises support to the "early commercialisation" phases of innovation - after R&D but before gearing up for full-scale commercial production;
- it seeks to establish a close relationship between supplier and potential user of a product or service thus enhancing opportunities for the product to be relevant to user needs;
- it alerts major users in government markets (Commonwealth, State, Local) of the potential available in Australian suppliers of products and services;
- by undergoing a trialing phase in this way, the suppliers can enhance their credibility both for government markets and in wider commercial markets.

Advanced Manufacturing Technology Development Program (AMTDP)

This program commenced this financial year:

- it was announced in Government's 12 March 1992 Industry Statement
- $5 million is available for commitment over each of four financial years.
- AMTDP it modelled on NPDP. It brings together private sector suppliers and users of advanced manufacturing technology.

The justification for the AMTDP is:

- Australian industry is poor at utilising AMT applications and thus is less likely to be competitive in cost productivity or quality terms, relative to international competitors;
- Australian suppliers of AMT are very inventive but are typically only small

companies with little credibility.

The scheme aims to influence the use of AMT in Australian industry and to establish the credibility of Australian suppliers, both in terms of excellence of technology and reliability as suppliers.

National Teaching Company Scheme (NTCS)

This scheme has been operating since about 1985. It aims to encourage long term relationships between tertiary education institutions or research agencies and companies. This is achieved by providing support of up to $50,000 over two years toward the cost of employing and supervising graduates to work on projects which will improve company performance.

The normal distribution of the grant is:

. salary subsidy	$34,000
. contribution to salary overheads	$ 6,000
. payment to institute for oversighting/use of facilities	$10,000

Current expenditure on the scheme is about $2 million annually, with about 90 active projects at any one time.

In summary, the suite of programs described involve Commonwealth expenditure or revenue forgone totalling about $308 million per annum. This is made up of

. 150% tax scheme (revenue forgone)	$260 million
. Discretionary Grants Scheme	$ 18 million
. Generic (Strategic) Technologies Scheme	$ 16 million
. National Procurement Development Program	$ 7 million
. Advanced Manufacturing Technology Development	$ 5 million
. National Teaching Company Scheme	$ 2 million

The Government's Partnerships for Development Program is also an important initiative in terms of encouraging the subsidiaries of overseas companies to undertake more research and technology activities in Australia. It has proved an important step in helping Australia to capture more of the benefits arising from the increasingly integrated nature of international research and technology activities.

As indicated, a great deal of consideration is currently going into the question of the role of government in innovation, broadly defined. Some of the relatively new support schemes, eg NPDP and AMTDP, target the "post R&D" elements of innovation, at least partially. Such models may be pointers for the way the government will address the national issue of managing R&D.

6. The Importance of Linkages

In a recent study of Communications Technology Research in Australian Tertiary Education Institutions, external funds are very dominant, and a number of major sources of external funding were identified. Commonwealth Government direct funding sources (44%) closely followed by the combination of Australian Telecommunications carriers (Telecom, OTC and AUSSAT) and Australian companies (together a total 40%). Overseas carriers and industry funding is also substantial (13% of which 97.5% is from private overseas companies). State Governments provide only 3% of external funding.

If we return specifically to the Generic (Strategic) Grants schemes which aim at research collaboration, there is no shortage of good grant applications, only a limited number of which can be funded from a limited budget. Both technical success and the likelihood of long term commercial benefit for the good of the nation must be considered. The commercial partner brings the knowledge of the market, the distribution channels, and the capacities to commercialise the outcomes of the research. The public sector researcher partners have excellent knowledge of leading edge technology developments around the world. It is essential for a firm to possess a good knowledge of relevant public sector R&D capacity to tap into sources of knowledge about technology development. Firms are encouraged to approach researchers they know and initiate collaborative R&D projects that may include applying for generic technology grants.

The Research Centre Program of the Australian Research Council (ARC) has contributed to a rapid change from the traditional discipline bound research to multidisciplinary research systems at universities. This program was set up to strengthen university research capacity and to forge links between researchers in the public sector institutions such as universities and private sector industries. The Research Centres Program launched in 1982 provides a new research focus in higher education institutions. The scale of competitive funding to the Research Centres Program has grown considerably with the introduction of the CRC program. Rapid growth of research centres in academic institutions has given a new orientation to academic research by shifting the focus from traditional "knowledge base" development activity to encompass research with a more commercial orientation.

We have also found another linkage in that the Generic Technology Grants function as a platform for research areas that are presented in Cooperative Research Centre (CRC) Program. It must be noted by policy makers though that limits to the growth of innovative ideas exist. Frontier ideas which can be presented to a major granting scheme may be limited by :

- the narrow band of possible research and innovation (in the case of CRC's the merging boundary between strategic basic research and applied and experimental development activity);
- the capacity of industry to absorb major innovations (In Australia, the

relatively small manufacturing base may be a limiting factor);
- the scale of competitive grants (needs to be developed according to the composition of private sector industry capacity rather than academic research capacity).

The impact of research concentration at the commercial end or research activity is bound to exert major structural changes to University charters with some institutions becoming more research oriented whereas other retain a stronger role as scholastic and learning institutions. The purpose for conducting research is not clearly addressed in a number of universities and presently the driving force is to secure a substantial slice of external funding available for research.

7. Some Success Stories

Video Communications Research Team

Telecom Research Laboratories (TRL) is involved in a joint project with Siemens Australia, Monash University and the Australian Defence Forces Academy (ADFA) to develop a multi-service communications system which will enable the use of a single screen for a variety of image services, such as colour facsimile, television, video conferencing, video-phones and digital high definition television. The project received Generic Grant support. After a little over twelve months intensive research, the Universal Video Codec project team developed a dramatic reduction of the bit rate penalty paid when separating video signals into layers. The team found that in doing the layering, a lot of extra information had to be sent across the network. There has been a penalty of up to 50 per cent paid in the amount of information to be sent. The team has developed a method to reduce this to less than 10 per cent.

The commercial reality of the success of the project is reflected in the solution of the perennial "chicken and egg problem". To quote a team member, "For instance, if service providers wanted to broadcast in 3-D television, they would find it difficult to attract advertising revenue to their new service, because there are no customers who could pick up the service on their televisions. However, no one would want to but a 3-D television as long as no service provider broadcasts this service. The system currently under development by the project group puts an end to these problems."

Mobile Satellite Systems

This project has a consortium of British Aerospace, University of South Australia and the University of Sydney. It successfully applied for a Generic Grant. It has developed innovative hardware and software for mobile satellite systems, and influenced standards for satellite protocols. It has resulted in its first commercial mobile terminals to be Australian-made, the award of multi-million dollar contracts for network base stations, and a future for Australian manufactured terminals for domestic and international markets in the multi-million dollar range. It has enabled the Australian Mobile Satellite Equipment Consortium to be formed.

Many cases of research and commercial success as a result of industry/public sector research collaboration are commercially sensitive, and not detailed publicly.

8. Conclusion

From an industry viewpoint, the main issue of success of research relates to the commercial success in the global market place, in a timely way, within internationally accepted standards, and with appropriate protection and control of the intellectual property and the resultant products and services.

There has been a realisation of the tremendous technological capabilities of the public sector researchers, tempered by the hard facts and figures of the costs to commercialise and market the product. There has been a realisation of the conflicting motivations of the public and private sectors in obtaining funds and undertaking research. The immediate and career/commercial needs of both parties must be recognised and accommodated.

The greatest opportunities for mutual success arise when the collaborative venture is set up at the beginning of a research project, and issues of project management and control, sensitivity of public release of the core technology findings, ownership and application of the intellectual property, and a true realisation of the cost and urgency of getting an idea to market, and to a profitable stage of the product life cycle.

Early, cautious collaborations from the commercial partners frequently turn to active pursuit of the technology as a significant new business area. Further, an earlier collaboration leads to greater teamwork between the two organisations, and subsequent contracts for commissioned research from the commercial partner for core/key areas of their new product developments. The public researcher learns first hand the true cost of commercialising a product, often 90% of the total project cost, and the further costs in establishing and sustaining a market share.

One can see during the 1980's a progression away from pure research to research applied to the market place, industry driven, firmly supported by evolving government policies and set in the context of international collaborative programs. We believe that this approach offers significant benefits for the both public sector researcher and industry, and look forward to continued success for all of us.

Personal Computers and Intelligent Systems / F.H. Vogt (Editor)
Information Processing 92, Volume III
Elsevier Science Publishers B.V. (North-Holland)

Encouraging Acdemic-Industry Collaboration: Industry - University Interaction in the US

A Nico Haberman

National Science Foundation, 1800 G Street N.W., Washington DC 20550, USA

Abstract

The interaction between industry and universities in the US is generally speaking lively and healthy. It takes many forms ranging from equipment donations to joint projects. The US government is not controlling or managing this interaction, but plays the role of a catalyst in several important instances.

In my position of department head and later dean of the School of Computer Science at Carnegie Mellon University I had the privilege of being involved in a number of fruitful interactions with industrial partners. The first I want to mention is the joint project with IBM in the early eighties which involved building a campus-wide network with a capacity of more than 10,000 connections, two orders of magnitude larger than what was available at that time. The project resulted in a heavily used network, useful software development and tech transfer to IBM.

The second example of a fruitful collaboration is project Athena, a project in which MIT, IBM and DEC worked together. It resulted in the X-window system which is now a universal interface on many types of workstations.

The field of computer science has a tradition of close university-industry interaction in both hardware and software research and development. A particularly interesting and successful interaction is sponsored by the National Science Foundation in the US and advances the use of "supercomputers" for large scale problems in science and engineering. NSF supports four supercomputer centers which do not just provide cycles to research groups, but play a major role in developing common software for different architectures and in educating the science community in using new architectures. These centers are evolving into a single nationwide "meta center" in which industry and academia collaborate regardless of distance.

Personal Computers and Intelligent Systems / F.H. Vogt (Editor)
Information Processing 92, Volume III
Elsevier Science Publishers B.V. (North-Holland)

Academic-Industry collaboration: A View of the European Scene from Industry

Brian Oakley

Logica UK Ltd, 67-87 Hampstead Road, London NW1, UK

Abstract

Unlike the picture in Japan, with a very few exceptions in Europe the high technology firms do not undertake basic research; they rely on their academic colleagues to carry out basic research, and to alert them if that work looks as if it is turning into something applicable. The problem lies in the gulf that can open up between research workers in the Universities and in industry, impeding the technology transfer. During the last 10 to 15 years there have been various schemes designed to bridge the gap.

The best firms, like ICI in the UK, go out of their way to know where the best academic research is going on, by putting grants, often quite small, to support research or research workers in all the best departments. This is not so much for the particular research undertaken under the grant, but for the window that it provides on all the work going on in those departments. In the UK this process has been institutionalised by the Science and Engineering Research Council awarding CASE grants to some post graduate PhD students. The topic is agreed between a particular firm and a particular academic department, and the student works partly in the university laboratory, partly in the industrial laboratory, jointly supervised. Over half the post graduate studentships awarded by SERC are now of this CASE type.

In recent years there has been a large growth of collaborative research projects involving academic and industrial workers. These have been stimulated by programmes such as the UK Alvey programme, and the European Community's Commission ESPRIT programme. Much of this work is in the Information Technology field, but there are Commission programmes in other fields, such as the BRITE programme. Of these programmes the ESPRIT programme is the most developed and extensive. Virtually every computing science department in the Community universities plays some part in the programme, and the same is true of the laboratories of all the major and many of the minor firms in the IT field in Europe.

As safety critical systems and secure systems become recognised as the leading edge of software technology, so will the part played by the academic world in generating the means to achieve these systems become recognised.

Personal Computers and Intelligent Systems / F.H. Vogt (Editor)
Information Processing 92, Volume III
Elsevier Science Publishers B.V. (North-Holland)

ENCOURAGING ACADEMIC/PRACTICTIONER COLLABORATION: DEVELOPMENT OF AN INTELLIGENT DECENTRALIZED SHOP-FLOOR CONTROL SYSTEM (LEITSTAND)

Prof. Dr. A.-W. SCHEER

Institut für Wirtschaftsinformatik, Universität des Saarlandes

D-6600 Saarbrücken 11, Im Stadtwald, Geb. 14.1

Recently, production control approaches in production planning and control systems (PPC systems) have shifted from centralized towards decentralized concepts [1] leading to the emergence of numerous shop-floor control systems (Leitstand). This decentralized approach is accompanied and supported by novel production organization concepts such as flexible manufacturing cells and -systems that provide higher production flexibility and responsiveness to varying market demands.

The basic ideas of the workstation-based shop-floor control system Intelligenter Leitstand FI-2* originated from a research project [2] conducted at the Institute for Wirtschaftsinformatik from 1985-87. The advent of powerful micro-computers with comprehensive graphical capabilities rendered possible the distribution and computer-supported conduct of control tasks at the shop-floor level. In the course of the project a prototype version of a decentralized system (DEPROS) was developed.

This prototype version served as the basis for the development of a commercial product, the FI-2. With an effort of about 10-15 man years the 'academic prototype' was - under consideration of requirements definitions from potential users - transformed into a marketable product. The major obstacle to overcome was the complexity of the integration with environment systems such as PPC- and data base systems as well as different hardware platforms.

The FI-2 is based on an interactive planning philosophy [3] that incorporates the production scheduler (and his highly specific knowledge) in the decision making process on the shop floor level. Further characteristics are a user-friendly, graphical interface (editable display of GANTT-diagrams) and the utilization of open standards such as X-Windows, SQL and Unix. The enhancement of its functionality is an evolutionary process, and further features such as expert system and simulation support are currently being developed.

REFERENCES:

[1] Scheer, A.-W.: "Neue Architekturen für PPS-Systeme", in: Scheer, A.W. (Ed.): Fertigungssteuerung - Expertenwissen für die Praxis. München/Wien 1991, p. 13-20.

[2] Loos, P.; Ruffing, T.: Verteilte Produktionsplanung und -steuerung unter Einsatz von Mikrocomputern, in: Scheer, A.-W. (Ed.): Veröffentlichungen des Instituts für Wirtschaftsinformatik, Heft 52. Saarbrücken 1986.

[3] Hars, A; Scheer, A.-W.: Entwicklungsstand von Leiständen, in: Scheer, A.-W. (Ed.): Veröffentlichungen des Instituts für Wirtschaftsinformatik, Heft 65. Saarbrücken 1989.

* Intelligenter Leitstand FI-2 is a trademark of the IDS, Prof. Dr. Scheer GmbH

AUTHOR INDEX

* Paper not submitted

IFIP

The INTERNATIONAL FEDERATION FOR INFORMATION PROCESSING is a multinational federation of professional and technical organisations (or national groupings of such organisations) concerned with information processing. From any one country, only one such organisation – which must be representative of the national activities in the field of information processing – can be admitted as a Full Member. In addition a regional group of developing countries can be admitted as a Full Member. On 1 October 1991, 46 organisations were Full Members of the Federation, representing 70 countries.

The aims of IFIP are to promote information science and technology by:

- fostering international co-operation in the field of information processing;
- stimulating research, development and the application of information processing in science and human activity;
- furthering the dissemination and exchange of information about the subject;
- encouraging education in information processing.

IFIP is dedicated to improving worldwide communication and increased understanding among practitioners of all nations about the role information processing can play in all walks of life.

Information technology is a potent instrument in today's world, affecting people in everything from their education and work to their leisure and in their homes. It is a powerful tool in science and engineering, in commerce and industry, in education and adminstration. It is truly international in its scope and offers a significant opportunity for developing countries. IFIP helps to bring together workers at the leading edge of the technology to share their knowledge and experience, and acts as a catalyst to advance the state of the art.

IFIP came into official existence in January, 1960. It was established to meet a need identified at the first International Conference on Information Processing which was held in Paris in June, 1959, under the sponsorship of UNESCO.

Organisational Structure
The Federation is governed by a GENERAL ASSEMBLY, which meets once every year and consists of one representative from each Member organisation. The General Assembly decides on all important matters, such as general policy, the programme of activities, admissions, elections and budget.

IFIP ORGANISATION CHART

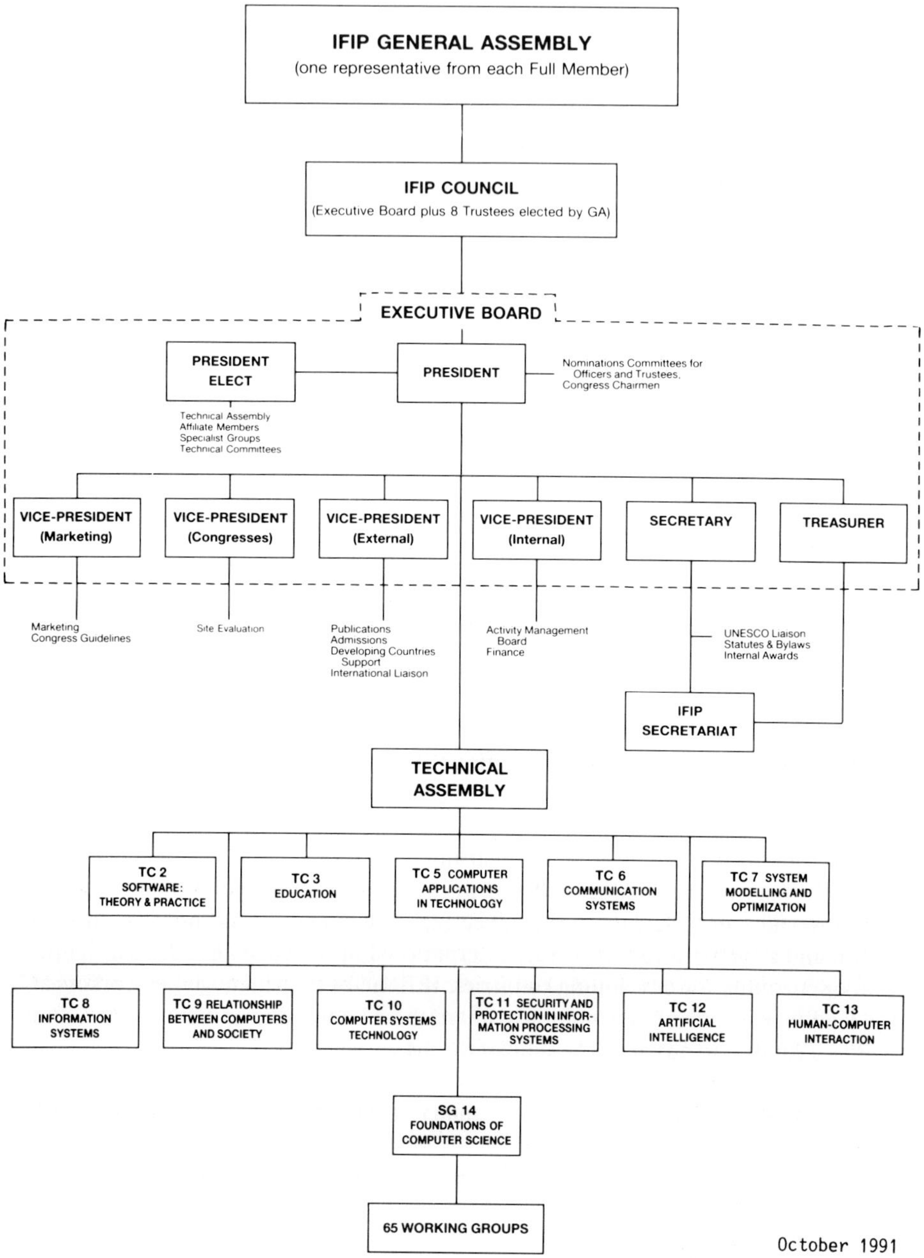

October 1991

The day-to-day work of IFIP is directed by its Officers: the President, Vice-Presidents, Secretary and Treasurer, who are elected by the General Assembly and together constitute the EXECUTIVE BOARD.

The COUNCIL, consisting of the Officers and up to eight Trustees elected from the General Assembly, meets twice a year and takes decisions which become necessary between General Assembly meetings.

The headquarters of the Federation are in Geneva, Switzerland where the IFIP Secretariat administers its affairs.

For further information please contact:

IFIP Secretariat
attn. Mme. GWYNETH ROBERTS
16 Place Longemalle
CH-1204 Geneva, Switzerland
telephone: 41 (22) 28 26 49
facsimile: 41 (22) 781 23 22
Bitnet: ifip@cgeuge51

IFIP's MISSION STATEMENT

IFIP's mission is to be the leading, truly international, apolitical organisation which encourages and assists in the development, exploitation and application of Information Technology for the benefit of all people.

Principal Elements

1. To stimulate, encourage and participate in research, development and application of Information Technology (IT) and to foster international co-operation in these activities.
2. To provide a meeting place where national IT Societies can discuss and plan courses of action on issues in our field which are of international significance and thereby to forge increasingly strong links between them and with IFIP.
3. To promote internation co-operation directly and through national IT Societies in a free environment between individuals, national and international governmental bodies and kindred scientific and professional organisations.
4. To pay special attention to the needs of developing countries and to assist them in appropriate ways to secure the optimum benefit from the application of IT.
5. To promote professionalism, incorporating high standards of ethics and conduct, among all IT practitioners.
6. To provide a forum for assessing the social consequences of IT applications; to campaign for the safe and beneficial development and use of IT and the protection of people from abuse through its improper application.

7. To foster and facilitate co-operation between academics, the IT industry and governmental bodies and to seek to represent the interest of users.
8. To provide a vehicle for work on the international aspects of IT development and application including the necessary preparatory work for the generation of international standards.
9. To contribute to the formulation of the education and training needed by IT practitioners, users and the public at large.

Note to Conference Organizers

Organizers of upcoming IFIP Working Conferences are urged to contact the Publisher. Please send full details of the Conference to:

Mrs. STEPHANIE SMIT
Administrative Editor – IFIP Publications
ELSEVIER SCIENCE PUBLISHERS
P.O. Box 103, 1000 AC Amsterdam
The Netherlands
telephone: 31 (20) 5862481
facsimile: 31 (20) 5862616
email: s.smit@elsevier.nl

IFIP TRANSACTIONS

IFIP TRANSACTIONS is a serial consisting of 15,000 pages of valuable scientific information from leading researchers, published in 35 volumes per year. The serial includes contributed volumes, proceedings of the IFIP World Conferences, and conferences at Technical Committee and Working Group level. Mainstream areas in the IFIP TRANSACTIONS can be found in Computer Science and Technology, Computer Applications in Technology, and Communication Systems.

Please find below a detailed list of topics covered.

IFIP TRANSACTIONS A:
Computer Science and Technology
1992: 19 Volumes, US $ 1181.00/Dfl. 2185.00
ISSN 0926-5473

IFIP Technical Committees
Software: Theory and Practice (TC2)
Education (TC3)
System Modelling and Optimization (TC7)
Information Systems (TC8)
Relationship Between Computers and Society (TC9)

Computer Systems Technology (TC10)
Security and Protection in Information Processing Systems (TC11)
Artificial Intelligence (TC12)
Human-Computer Interaction (TC13)
Foundations of Computer Science (SG14)

IFIP TRANSACTIONS B:
Applications in Technology
1992: 8 Volumes. US $ 497.00/Dfl. 920.00
ISSN 0926-5481

IFIP Technical Committee
Computer Applications in Technology (TC5)

IFIP TRANSACTIONS C:
Communication Systems
1992: 8 Volumes. US 497.00/Dfl. 920.00
ISSN 0926-549X

IFIP Technical Committee
Communication Systems (TC6)

IFIP TRANSACTIONS FULL SET: A, B & C
1992: 35 Volumes. US $ 1892.00/Dfl. 3500.00

The Dutch Guilder prices (Dfl.) are definitive. The US $ prices mentioned above are for your guidance only and are subject to exchange rate fluctuations. Prices include postage and handling charges.

The volumes are also available separately in book form.

Please address all orders and correspondence to:

ELSEVIER SCIENCE PUBLISHERS
attn. PETRA VAN DER MEER
P.O. Box 103, 1000 AC Amsterdam
The Netherlands
telephone: 31 (20) 5862602
facsimile: 31 (20) 5862616
email: m.haccou@elsevier.nl